Andrey Mir

Digital Future in the Rearview Mirror

Jaspers' Axial Age and Logan's Alphabet Effect

ISBN 978-1-7773589-1-4

Toronto, Canada

**We look at the present through a rear-view mirror.
We march backwards into the future.**

Marshall McLuhan.

The Medium Is the Massage: An Inventory of Effects, 1967.

Major developments, and very likely even all major developments, in culture and consciousness, are related, often in unexpected intimacy, to the evolution of the word from primary orality to its present state. But the relationships are varied and complex, with cause and effect often difficult to distinguish.

Walter Ong.

Interfaces of the Word, 1977.

But, of course, we must reckon with the fact that in our civilization, writing is clearly an addition, not an alternative, to oral transmission <...> The relationship between the written and the oral traditions must be regarded as a major problem in Western cultures.

Jack Goody and Ian Watt.

The Consequences of Literacy, 1963.

Table of contents

Introduction: Replaying history backward

We expect that new media will do new tricks to cover our old needs. We always think they will improve something we already have. Sometimes they do, but on their own terms. Eventually, media always condition us to do completely new tricks instead.

A notable example is the phonograph. Thomas Edison expected that his invention would capture sounds for storage, not distribution. The initial attempts were aimed at using the phonograph as a dictating machine for offices. But the phonograph eventually unleashed its completely different "purpose" upon humanity. Long story short: Edison begat the phonograph, the phonograph begat listening freed from the time and space of performance, emancipated listening begat the recording industry, the recording industry begat popular music, popular music begat show business, show business begat fandom culture, fandom culture begat the cult of celebrity, and the cult of celebrity begat Trump.

Here we see the media "butterfly effect": from a certain point of view, the phonograph eventually made Trump. Edison wanted the phonograph to become a new device fulfilling an already known function – dictation. But the phonograph has dictated otherwise.

This is how the technological imperative works: every medium emerges for some old tasks, but it then dictates its own true use. The instrumental use of the phonograph turned into an environmental force: the phonograph detached entertainment from the time and space of live performance. This forever changed not office practices, as initially intended, but humans' leisure time and mass culture.

Our inclination to expect a new invention to make an improvement on the past was noticed by Marshall McLuhan. In *The Medium Is the Massage*, he wrote:

> When faced with a totally new situation, we tend to always attach ourselves to the objects, to the flavor of the most recent past. We

look at the present through a rear-view mirror. We march backwards into the future.[1]

This McLuhanism is rather sarcastic. But can we really see anything useful in the rearview mirror while moving into the future? Yes, looking at the past helps to understand those media effects that were gone with old media but are often retrieved by new media, according to another McLuhan concept, the law of retrieval.

McLuhan & McLuhan (Marshall and his son Eric) introduced this law in the so-called Tetrad, which described four universal media effects: enhancement, obsoleting, retrieval and reversal. Any human technology, medium, or artifact:

1. Enhances something.

2. Makes something obsolescent

3. Retrieves something from the past that was previously obsolesced.

4. Flips into something opposite or reverses its effect or characteristics when pushed to the limits of its potential.

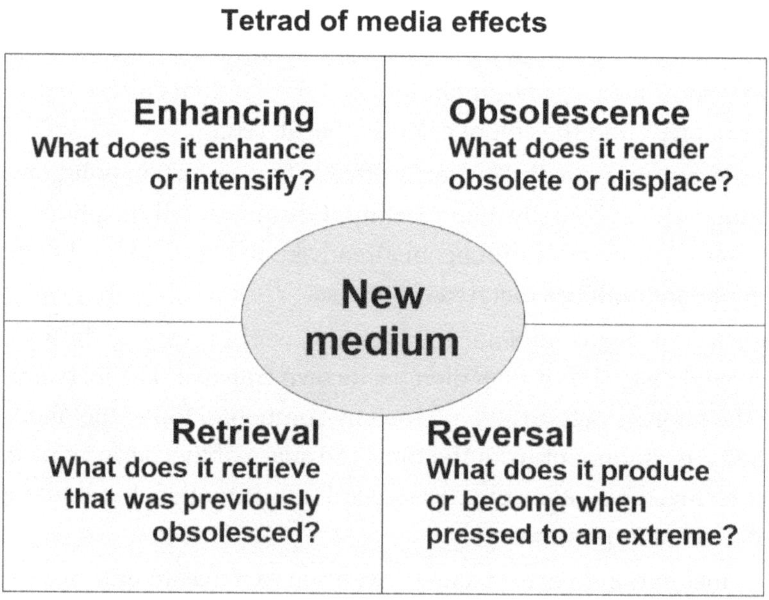

Figure 1. McLuhan's Laws of Media (the Tetrad), formulated as questions in: McLuhan, Marshall, and McLuhan, Eric. (1988). *Laws of Media*, p. 7.

---

[1] McLuhan, Marshall, and Fiore, Quentin. (1967). *The Medium Is the Massage*, p. 74-75.

Together, these four laws shape the Tetrad[1], a beloved intellectual toy of media ecologists for exploring the effects of any medium.[2] For example, when applied to cars, the Tetrad reveals the following media effects:

1. The car *enhances* mobility.

2. The car *obsolesces* horses and carriages.

3. The car *retrieves* traveling in an along-waterways fashion (roads like rivers) with the infrastructure developing along the roads and highways.

4. When pushed to extremes, the use of the car *reverses* its effect by creating traffic and gridlock, which restrain mobility.

(McLuhan & McLuhan themselves drafted the Tetrad for the car. According to them, the car: 1) *enhances* "privacy", "the ego trip", and "going outside to be alone"; 2) *obsolesces* "horse-and-buggy"; 3) *retrieves* "knight in shining armour", "the countryside", "river as a mode of traffic flow"; 4) *reverses* into "traffic jam" and "corporate privacy", "city (urb) into suburbs".[3])

Digital media have *enhanced* information exchange and storage and made *obsolete* offline life. But what do they *retrieve* and *reverse*?

In his time, Marshall McLuhan suggested that electronic media – TV and radio – retribalized society and turned it into a global village.[4] He wrote:

> Paradoxically, electronic man shares much of the outlook of preliterate man, because he lives in a world of simultaneous information, which is to say, a world of resonance in which all data influence other data. Electronic and simultaneous man has recovered the primordial attitudes of the preliterate world...[5]

---

[1] The Tetrad was first introduced by Marshall McLuhan in the 1970s in articles and at the Tetrad Conference organized by Paul Levinson in 1978 – see: Levinson, Paul. (2020). "More than a double-take: how I met Marshall McLuhan." *New Explorations Blog*. Later, the Tetrad made it in a book: McLuhan, Marshall, and McLuhan, Eric. (1988). *Laws of Media: The New Science*. Eric McLuhan finished the book using their collaborative notes with his father after Marshall passed away in 1980.

[2] See, for example, the Twitter account @McLuhanTetrad. Also, a board game "The MediuM", based on the Tetrad, was designed by Paolo Granata from University of Toronto in 2021. I had the honor and pleasure of participating in designing the game's rules.

[3] McLuhan, Marshall, and McLuhan, Eric. (1988). *Laws of Media*, p. 148.

[4] McLuhan, Marshall, and Fiore, Quentin. (1967). *The Medium Is the Massage: An Inventory of Effects*, p. 67.

[5] McLuhan, Marshall. (1974). "At the moment of Sputnik the planet became a global

This applies even more to digital media, as they have completed the submersion of people in a "world of simultaneous information." On one hand, digital media epitomize technological progress (so far). On the other hand, they revert society back to tribalism. To complete the Tetrad of media effects, digital media not only *enhance* information exchange and render offline life *obsolete* – they also *reverse* literacy and *retrieve* orality, as this book will endeavour to show.

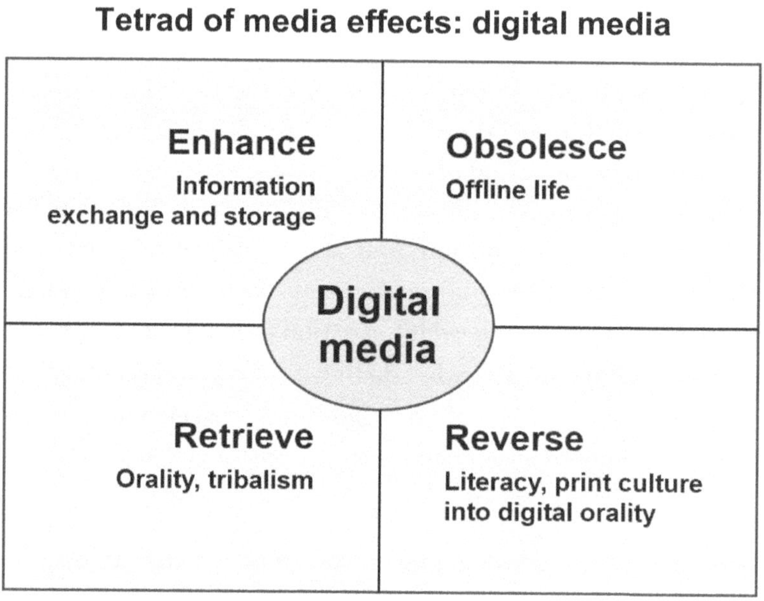

Figure 2.

The metaphor of the rearview mirror was used by McLuhan to describe the inherent retrospectivity of our media expectations; however, we can also use McLuhan's rearview mirror with a rational purpose – to see what media did to us in the past, in case those effects are now being retrieved.

If digital media retrieve the preliterate world, we can look back and see how things were before literacy, when orality determined minds and cultures. Moving forward into the future, it is worth checking the rearview mirror, as the contours of the digital future suspiciously resemble patterns from the tribal past.

This book is about orality, which once was obsolesced by writing, and about literacy, which is now becoming obsolesced by digital media.

---

theater in which there are no spectators but only actors," p. 49.

To manufacture a rearview mirror for such a futuristic retrospective, I employed the concept of the Axial Age advanced by German philosopher Karl Jaspers in his 1949 book *The Origin and Goal of History*. Jaspers suggested that in the 8th to the 3rd centuries BCE, simultaneously and independently in the East Mediterranean, China and India, powerful doctrines emerged through the teachings of Jewish prophets, Greek philosophers, Zarathustra, Buddha, Confucius, Laozi and some others. They introduced philosophical and moral categories that became universal for all humankind and through which humankind has been perceiving the world and itself ever since. Human consciousness, as we know it, emerged and outweighed, for some, the reflexes of everyday survival. Jaspers calls it the Axis of history and states that this was an event in which humans awakened to eventually become unified humankind. The local histories started gravitating to one world history, towards the unity of all humanity, a condition we approached in the 20th century, according to him.

To any media ecologist, a mysterious spiritual awakening of humankind dating from the 8th to the 3rd centuries BCE immediately brings to mind the introduction of the alphabet in Greece. Unfortunately (for this hypothesis), this coincidence does not cover the Axial events in China, as China has never had the alphabet, and it also does not explain the Indian contribution to the Axial Age, as India likely fully developed its alphabetic script later than Buddhism.

Nevertheless, the timeframe of the Axial Age and its main features obviously align with the changes brought by writing. Was the Axial Age a media effect caused by the transition from orality to literacy? If so, we can look there for parallels and patterns for understanding the reversal from literacy to orality that we are experiencing now because of digital media.

To adjust the rearview mirror to the right angle, I combined the framework of Jaspers' Axial Age with the concept of the alphabet effect developed by Robert Logan. For Logan, the alphabet contributed to such phenomena as monotheism, codified law, individualism, deductive logic, and abstract science. Not only does the emergence of these phenomena coincide with the time of Jaspers' Axial Age, but they also perfectly align with the logic and spirit of the Axial Age "awakening." I also used the ideas regarding the transition from orality to literacy proposed by Eric Havelock, Walter Ong, and other media ecologists. All the details may not be clearly seen in this rearview mirror, but the patterns seem to be recognizable.

In general, the development of writing and the transition from orality to literacy caused the tectonic cognitive and social shift. The shift from orality to literacy signified the move from magic to faith, from superstition to religion, from myth to logos, from polytheism to monotheism, from customs to laws, from moral relativism to moral absolute, from practical and negotiated truths to objective and absolute truth, from relation-centering to object-centering, from natural and supernatural "physics" to metaphysics, from the Dionysian to the Apollonian, from the "cycle of life" to personal destiny, from the agitation of tribal belonging to the individual tragedy of (not-)becoming.

At the roots of orality is the chanting shaman. At the roots of literacy is the writing priest (and their later iterations: philosopher, scholar, writer, journalist). The priests might continue to chant, but civilizations cannot help but emerge when the priests also write. They inevitably start recording the divine, dynastic, and celestial events as well as temples' works and offerings, thus becoming historians, scholars, and bureaucrats.

"At electric speed, all forms are pushed to the limits of their potential," wrote Marshall and Eric McLuhan.[1] As we already know from their Laws of Media, being pushed to the limits is a trigger for reversal. Electric and now digital media have created the ideal conditions for civilizational reversal. By reversing literacy and retrieving orality, digital media, essentially, are replaying the Axial Age backward.

Social media recreate orality in digital form by enabling a new linguistic phenomenon: digital speech. Digital speech encompasses the features of both oral and written speech. Like oral speech, digital speech permits the instant exchange of replies; like writing, it leaves behind a record and can be transmitted in time and space. On one hand, digital speech is an exchange between two or more people; on the other hand, it is fixed and observable to the audience. Exposure to the audience heats any conversation up. Digital speech is impulsive but not evanescent – it stays and involves others.

The ease of exchanging digital speech has shifted the focus of mass communication and the entire culture from reflections to reflexes and from substance to attitude. Historically and technologically, digital speech

---

[1] McLuhan, Marshall, and McLuhan, Eric. (1988). *Laws of Media: The New Science*, p. 109.

inherits from print literacy but retrieves orality. That is why it produces the state of mind and culture that can be called digital orality.

Robert Logan was the first to use the term "digital orality" in 2007. He introduced it to support and clarify the main term for this phenomenon, "tertiary orality", which was inspired by Walter Ong. Logan wrote:

> Walter Ong in his study of orality made a distinction between primary and secondary orality: "I style the orality of a culture totally untouched by any knowledge of writing or print, 'primary orality.' It is 'primary' by contrast with 'secondary orality' of present-day high-technology culture." Based on the conversational nature of the Internet and text-based communication I would like to suggest that there exists a third kind of orality, namely, tertiary or digital orality. Tertiary or digital orality is the orality of emails, blog posts, listservs, instant messages (IM) and SMS, which are mediated paradoxically by written text transmitted by the Internet. [1]

Logan used the term before the proliferation of social media, so he could not observe in detail the hybridization of oral and written speech into digital speech. His derivation of the "tertiary or digital orality" from Ong's succession of oralities was a pure and genuine insight, the farsighted introduction of a definition, the meaning of which still continues to be filled in by the subsequent development of media.

The ongoing shift from print literacy to digital orality underlies the entire set of reversals: from literacy to orality, from civilization to tribalism, from law to honour, from logic to magic, from individual morality to collective loyalty, from absolute truth to the relativism of justice, from writing scholar to chanting shaman, from book to meme, and so on. All of this started happening in the 2010s, after social media and other digital platforms began absorbing all human private and professional activities.

Historical time has accelerated. The awakening of humankind lasted, in Jaspersian chronology, from the 8th to the 3rd century BCE and comprised the entire Axial Age. The reversal Axis is rather an extended decade – the Axial Decade. What will awaken during it remains to be seen. The rapid development of AI gives a hint. Anyway, it is good timing to look at the

---

[1] Robert Logan first introduced the term "tertiary or digital orality" in the 2007 article "The Emergence of Artistic Expression and Secondary Perception" and then developed it in: Logan, Robert. (2010). *Understanding New Media: Extending Marshall McLuhan.* New York: Peter Lang. (Second edition: 2016.)

Axial Age in the rearview mirror and see what orality and literacy are and what the transition from orality to literacy did to people 25 centuries ago.

Will the reversal undo it? How much of it?

The study of orality and literacy is one of the specialties of media ecology. This book employs the views of Harold Innis, Eric Havelock, Marshall McLuhan, Walter Ong, Neil Postman, and many others who pioneered and advanced studies of orality and literacy. If one would like to get to know their ideas better but may not have enough time to read academic volumes, this book is a handy digest of the essentials of orality and literacy. But it is not a bookish summary. All the relevant ideas are selected to examine digital orality. Why do people on social media become so polarized and deaf to logic and reason? Why do people read less and demand more? How do social media change minds and society? What comes next? The answer to all of this is digital orality. What is digital orality? This book starts a series of projects answering this question.

The intellectual journey to the Axial Decade, in which we physically and virtually live, starts with the Axial Age 23–28 centuries ago. The reader will learn what is common between Sumerian clay tokens and Yellowstone wolves, between river control in the Nile valley and the Eurasian nomads who were the first to domesticate horses in the 4th millennium BCE, between the Aegean pirates and the alphabet, between Odysseus and Dostoevsky. It was interesting to write; my hope is that at least some of this amusement will survive reading, lingering with the reader.

I want to conclude the introduction by expressing my sincere gratitude to Robert Logan, whom I hope I can call my colleague and friend. Bob was very kind to welcome my first works in media ecology.[1] He introduced me to the Toronto McLuhanist circle and the wider media ecology community ten years ago. Besides personal gratitude, I want to highlight his invaluable scholarly contribution to media ecology. Logan's 1986 book *The Alphabet Effect* and his other works are among the most essential media ecological readings.

A. M.

November 2023, Toronto

---

[1] In 2014, Robert Logan wrote a review of my book: *Human as Media: The Emancipation of Authorship*. Later, we co-authored several articles and projects.

1. Media ecology of changes

Media appearance: the visibility of disturbance

Media change everything, and behind every change stands a medium. According to Marshall McLuhan,

> All media work us over completely. They are so pervasive in their personal, political, economic, aesthetic, psychological, moral, ethical, and social consequences that they leave no part of us untouched, unaffected, unaltered. The medium is the message. Any understanding of social and cultural change is impossible without a knowledge of the way media work as environments.[1]

Neil Postman adds:

> Technological change is neither additive nor subtractive. It is ecological. I mean "ecological" in the same sense as the word is used by environmental scientists. One significant change generates total change... This is how the ecology of media works as well. A new technology does not add or subtract something. It changes everything. In the year 1500, fifty years after the printing press was invented, we did not have old Europe plus the printing press. We had a different Europe. After television, the United States was not America plus television; television gave a new coloration to every political campaign, to every home, to every school, to every church, to every industry. [2]

If new media change everything, then the change is the way we know that both "media" and "everything" exist. How else would we recognize our being unless it changes? This brings to mind McLuhan's favourite "fish-water" metaphor: A fish is not aware of the water unless it is pulled out of it.[3] The changes reveal the Existing by turning it into the Being.

Media studies – and media ecology specifically – emerged because of changes in media in the 1950s and 60s. At that time, radio was still

---

[1] McLuhan, Marshall, and Fiore, Quentin. (1967). *The Medium Is the Massage: An Inventory of Effects*, p. 26.

[2] Postman, Neil. 1992. *Technopoly: The Surrender of Culture to Technology*, p. 18.

[3] See, for example: McLuhan, Marshall. (1969, March). "The Playboy Interview," p. 56.

perceived as a new medium; film and phonography, too, were in a stage of constant innovation. They all were modern things. All of a sudden, an even newer medium, television, emerged that could broadcast at once all kinds of news and entertainment that had before been delivered by the press, phonograph, movies, and radio. The changes brought by television reshaped mass culture, journalism, and the entertainment industries. It amused and disturbed the public. Such a profound cultural change, compressed in time, could not help but attract the attention of scholars.

The rapidly spreading and all-permeating effect of electronic media[1] prompted McLuhan, Postman and others to look for patterns and analogies. As electricity grew from an amenity to the technological platform changing all of humankind, McLuhan suggested to examine it environmentally and historically. For this, he had fertile soil prepared by his older colleague at the University of Toronto, Harold Innis.

In his 1950 *Empire and Communications* and 1951 *The Bias of Communication*, Innis revealed that the material form of communication favoured certain types of social order. For example, heavy and durable carved stones or clay tablets were time-biased media and emphasized religious power and rigid social hierarchy. Societies based on them, such as Ancient Egypt and Sumer, lasted millennia. Papyrus, on the other hand, was light but non-durable. It was a space-biased medium that emphasized political power and administrative control over ever-expanding territory, as exemplified by the Roman Empire.

Thus, media pushed civilizations towards extension in space or duration in time. Innis called this kind of media determinism "the significance of a basic medium to its civilization."[2] For Innis, history was a

---

[1] The question of what term, "electric" or "electronic" media, should be used remains open. McLuhan seemed to not distinguish between them. In earlier works, such as *Gutenberg Galaxy* (1962) and *Understanding Media* (1964), he used "electric media", as he often referred to the capacity of humankind to be connected at the speed of light. This sounded new and exhilarating at the time, and McLuhan loved poking virgin minds. "Electric media" sounds reasonable in the context of analyzing the effect of the telegraph, with which the victorious march of electric media started. However, in the 1969 interview to *Playboy*, which can serve as the best short compendium of his main ideas, "electronic media" emerged in his speech ("electric media" – 25 times, "electronic media" – 5 times). Perhaps the term "electric media" better suits highlighting their relation to electricity, while "electronic media" is a generic term for devices made of electronics. In media ecology, the later tradition inclines towards "electronic media".

[2] Innis, Harold. (1950). *Empire and communication*, p. 10.

sequence of epochs isolated by media: “Each epoch is distinguished by dominant forms of media that absorb, record, and transform information into systems of knowledge.”[1]

The transformation of information into knowledge created a mechanism of power: the “monopoly of knowledge” as Innis called it. This monopoly was in the hands of the caste maintaining communication and depended on the material properties of the dominant medium. If the dominant medium lost the competition to a new one, a civilization based on this medium would change or collapse. A civilization also collapsed when the dominant medium exhausted the civilization’s resources in space extension or time duration. Either way, the very materiality of the dominant media defined the nature and fate of civilizations.

Characteristics of Empire

(Alexander Watson, according to Harold Innis)

With durable media (stone, clay, parchment)	**With non-durable media** (papyrus, paper, electronic)
Heavy media	Light media
Biased towards time	Biased towards space
Duration	Expansion
Oral tradition	Written tradition
Continuity	Discontinuity
Poetry	News
Religious government	Secular/Military government
Language	Armed Forces
Spiritualism	Materialism
Communal man	Individualism
The ear	The eye
The land	The sea
Decentralization	Centralization
Hierarchy	Democracy

Figure 3. Source: Watson, Alexander. Introduction to: Innis, Harold. (2008 [1951]). *Bias of Communication*.

[1] Introduction by Paul Heyer and David Crowley to: Innis, Harold. (2008 [1951]). *Bias of Communication*, kl 422. (Here and further, “kl” stands for “kindle location” in those books that do not have a proper pagination in Kindle versions.)

In the introduction to the 2008 edition of Innis' *Bias of Communication*, Alexander Watson suggests a chart (Figure 3) that reflects Innis' understanding of how "the characteristics of media will influence the type of empire that employs them."[1]

Arriving in communications studies from political economy, Innis discovered that a communication perspective can reveal more about the nature and history of civilizations than studies of relations of production or belief systems because communications are integral to culture, economics, politics, education, arts, and all other aspects of social life.[2]

Thus, Marshall McLuhan had a well-detailed hypothesis connecting social changes with the changes in media. It was not without reason that McLuhan called his *The Gutenberg Galaxy* a footnote to Innis' observations:

> In short, Harold Innis was the first person to hit upon the *process* of change as implicit in the *forms* of media technology. The present book is a footnote of explanation to his work.[3]

The italic belongs to McLuhan – he highlighted the relations between the "process of change" and "forms of media". As James Carey wrote in 1969, McLuhan and Innis together advanced a theory of history in which "communication is central to social change and transformation".[4]

When McLuhan started looking for patterns and analogies of the effects of electric media, he revealed that electric media were changing the civilization that was shaped by printing. Thus appeared the metaphor of the Gutenberg Galaxy, a "place" in space-time where culture was determined and dominated by the printing press.

The printing press, in its turn, changed the previous culture based on handwriting. For this previous culture, the printing press itself was an agent of changes – hence the title of the 1980 book by Elizabeth Eisenstein,

---

[1] Introduction by Alexander Watson to: Innis, Harold. (2008 [1951]). *Bias of Communication*, kl 233.

[2] The idea expressed by Paul Heyer and David Crowley in their introduction to: Innis, Harold. (2008 [1951]). *Bias of Communication*, kl 426. "Communications have been integral to the functioning of all social institutions," as they write.

[3] McLuhan, Marshall. (1962). *The Gutenberg Galaxy*, p. 50. He repeated this acknowledgement in his introduction to the 1964 edition of Innis' 1951 *The Bias of Communication*.

[4] Carey, James W. (1969). "Harold Adams Innis and Marshall McLuhan", p. 271.

The Printing Press as an Agent of Change, another fundamental work in media ecology.

Combined with writing and the alphabet, the printing press continued and, perhaps, completed the cultural era of literacy. Literacy, in its turn, historically succeeded and offset orality – the preliterate, ritualistic, and mythological state of mind and culture.

Eric Havelock noticed that, in the span of just 12 months in 1962 and 1963, five fundamental works on literacy and orality were published.[1] He labeled this explosion of interest "the modern discovery of orality". Basically, this all was because of television and the shockwaves of cultural disturbances it produced.

Besides, television itself embodied orality. Havelock writes:

> Since, as literates, we have only very recently woken up to the presence of orality as a contemporary fact in our midst, revived in the electronic media, there need not be surprise if this provokes a new look at what may have been the role of orality in ancient Greece.[2]

Walter Ong sharpened this idea in his 1982 *Orality and Literacy*: "In this diachronic framework, past and present, Homer and television, can illuminate one another."[3] He writes:

> Our understanding of the differences between orality and literacy developed only in the electronic age, not earlier. Contrasts between electronic media and print have sensitized us to the earlier contrast between writing and orality. The electronic age is also an age of 'secondary orality', the orality of telephones, radio, and television, which depends on writing and print for its existence.[4]

So, as soon as communication scholars were attracted by the effect of television and started untangling a thread connecting TV and print, other

---

1 "The works in question were *La Pensee Sauvage* (Levi-Strauss), *The Consequences of Literacy* (Goody and Watt, an extended article), *The Gutenberg Galaxy* (McLuhan), *Animal Species and Evolution* (Mayr), and *Preface to Plato* (Havelock)," – Havelock, Eric. (1986). *The Muse Learns to Write*. p. 25.

2 Havelock, Eric. (1986). *The Muse Learns to Write. Reflections on Orality and Literacy from Antiquity to the Present*, p. 118.

3 Ong, Walter. 2002 [1982]. *Orality and Literacy*, p. 2.

4 Ong, Walter. 2002 [1982]. *Orality and Literacy*, p. 2.

media and the succession of their effects on society became noticeable. The large pattern of succession includes, in a reverse order, electric media, print, alphabet, writing, implements, and speech. (They all are media, according to the media ecological tradition, as they all mediate our perception of the world and operations within it.)

The scope of observation can be zoomed in. For example, within electric media we can distinguish telegraphy; radio transmission and radio broadcasting; phonograph; type recorder; telephone; silent, black-and-white, and color films; the monochrome and color television, and so on. All of them had different effects, but the principle stands: all media define certain modes of perception and operation and thus affect culture and society.

Yellowstone wolves and media-determinism

Explaining the incredible complexity of social, political, cultural, and economic life through the clay tablet or papyrus was sometimes labeled as a fallacy of techno-determinism. In its turn, techno-determinism was condemned for the alleged reductionism of complex social issues to a single factor.

In ecology, however, a single factor can legitimately have deterministic power. The leading global ecological discourse, global warming, is heavily "techno-deterministic" – its determining medium (the "agent of change") is carbon dioxide, which is exceedingly released to the atmosphere because of human activity.

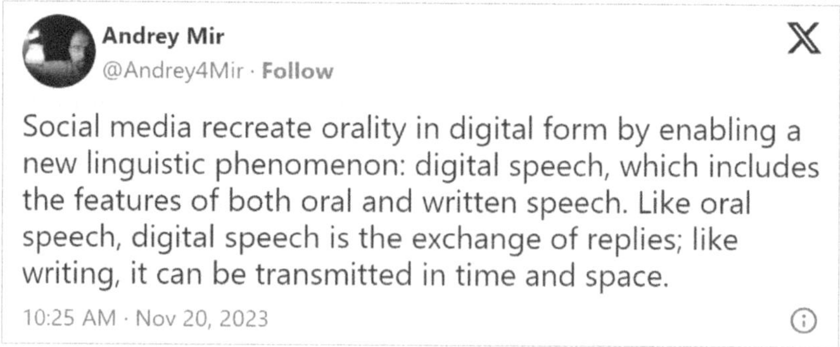
Andrey Mir
@Andrey4Mir · Follow

Social media recreate orality in digital form by enabling a new linguistic phenomenon: digital speech, which includes the features of both oral and written speech. Like oral speech, digital speech is the exchange of replies; like writing, it can be transmitted in time and space.

10:25 AM · Nov 20, 2023

The equilibrium in any ecosystem can be disrupted and re-established in a new way by a powerful enough single factor.

In the 1970s, Colombian drug lord Pablo Escobar ordered one male and four female hippos for his private zoo. By the 2020s, a herd of 140 animals had changed the regional ecosystem. They spoiled the lakes and rivers, changed flora and fauna, caused fish to die, ruined fishing, and interrupted the entire habitus of the locals.[1]

From 1995 to 1997, forty-one wolves were reintroduced in Yellowstone.[2] Wolves changed the number and behavior of elk and restored the balance of plants. Wolves affected other predators, which led to the restoration and increase of the diversity of birds and rodents. Without wolves, elks suppressed riverside plants, and this drove away beavers. After wolves were back, beavers returned, too, which altered the water system and even landscape and microclimate. The appearance of the wolves transformed the entire regional ecosystem.[3]

Can the Yellowstone ecosystem be "reduced" to wolves? Hardly so. But the wolves have certainly become the determinant of significant changes in the ecosystem. Scientists pointed out that a new equilibrium has been formed in the "phenomena called 'trophic cascades' or how species interact within a food web (i.e., how nature is organized, if one can characterize the near impossible complexity!)".[4] In other words, the wolves caused the cascade ecological effect.

The entire ecosystem can be affected not only by addition but also the removal of a single factor.

In India, farmers used to give their livestock diclofenac, an anti-inflammatory drug that was harmless to farm animals and humans. But the

---

1 See for example: Drost, Philip. (2022, October 25). "Why this doctor is castrating the offspring of Pablo Escobar's escaped hippos." *CBC*.

2 Smith, Douglas W., et al. (2019, April 25). "Wolf Restoration in Yellowstone: Reintroduction to Recovery." *Series: Yellowstone Science*.

3 The metaphor of wolves changing ecosystem was also used by Paolo Granata in his course on media ecology at the University of Toronto. Granata refers to Dennis Cali's 2017 book Mapping Media Ecology, and Cali in the book refers to an interview with T. David Gordon. The Yellowstone wolves are indeed a compelling example of ecological determinism and a strong response to accusations of "reductionism".

4 Smith, Douglas W., et al. (2019, May 16). "The Big Scientific Debate: Trophic Cascades." *Series: Yellowstone Science*. Volume 24, Issue 1: Celebrating 20 Years of Wolves.

presence of diclofenac in the corps of farm animals killed 99% of the population of vultures. Vultures were a crucial sanitary element in the ecosystem – they served as a natural animal disposal system. The vultures' metabolism trapped and killed pathogens thriving in carrion, thus preventing the spread of these pathogens. The vultures also suppressed other scavengers who spread diseases. This is particularly important in the conditions of the Hindu religion, in which 80% of population don't consume cow's meat and dead cows are left to nature.

After the vultures were almost gone, a huge number of animal carcasses were left to rot. They became a feeding ground for infectious germs and also for feral dogs and rats who spread other diseases, such as rabies. As the population of vultures plummeted from 40 million to just 19 thousand, India's feral dog population increased by at least 5 million, resulting in over 38 million additional dog bites and more than 47,000 extra deaths from rabies.[1] Studies showed that the loss of vultures in some regions raised all-cause human death rates by more than 4%.[2] This is now called the "Indian vulture crisis", and the country is struggling to restore the vulture population.

In 1958, the communist regime in China announced the Four Pests program aimed at the extermination of rats, flies, mosquitoes, and sparrows. The "Smash sparrows program" led to particularly dramatic consequences. Sparrows were guilty of eating grains, seeds and fruits, so the Communist Party sentenced them to death to increase agricultural productivity during the so-called Great Leap Forward. Millions of Chinese, especially school pupils and youth, were mobilized to kill birds and destroy their nests. In 1958, in just one day of national anti-sparrow action, 310,000 sparrows were killed in Peking and an estimated 4 million across China, according to the victorious reports of Radio Peking. 16-year-old Yang Seh-mun became a national hero for killing 20,000 sparrows.[3]

The extermination of sparrows disturbed the ecological balance and resulted in surging locust and insect populations that destroyed crops.

---

[1] Burfield, Ian, and Bowden, Chris. (2022, September 28). "South Asian vultures and diclofenac". *Cambridge Core Blog*.

[2] Frank, Eyal, and Sudarshan, Anant. (2023, January 21). "How human and ecosystem health are intertwined: Evidence from vulture population collapse in India." *VoxDev*.

[3] *Time*. (1958, May 5). "Red China: Death to Sparrows."

Along with other governmental policies within the Great Leap Forward, including massive deforestation, the reorganization of farming, and inefficient food redistribution within the planned economy, this led to the Great Chinese Famine, one of the deadliest famines and the largest man-made disaster in human history. The estimated death toll was 15 to 50 million.[1] In some provinces, up to 18% of the population died.

Escobar's hippos, Yellowstone's wolves, veterinary diclofenac, and the killing of sparrows were "single factors" that disrupted the ecological equilibrium and altered the ecosystem through the cascade effect. Similar to the domino effect, even a slight disturbance of the balance can release significant forces. These forces belong not to this initial factor or agent but to the masses that come into movement after the triggering factor disturbs the equilibrium in an ecosystem. A small domino piece, when pushed in the right place of the system's equilibrium, eventually can move incomparably larger masses.

The domino effect is mounting but linear. The cascade ecological reaction can also be overlapping (and enlarging because it is overlapping). The next events are affected not just by the previous events but also by the cumulative or reverberating impacts of the pre-previous events. This is called the "ripple effect". Ripples of different speed and potency can cross, overlap, and turn into rogue waves that reshape ecosystems and civilizations. So, yes, behind a simple media deterministic statement, such as "The wolves changed Yellowstone", there are complex ecological mechanisms, some hard science, and even some sophisticated math.

In this light, Lance Strate in his 2017 *Media Ecology*, a must-read textbook in the field, suggests considering "For Want of a Nail," a rhyme that has been a longstanding part of English folk tradition:

> For want of a Nail the Shoe was lost;
> For want of a Shoe the Horse was lost;
> And for want of a Horse the Rider was lost,
> Being overtaken and slain by the Enemy,
> All for the want of Care about a Horseshoe-Nail.

Strate also mentions another variation that includes a message as a part of events: "for want of a rider the message was lost, for want of a

[1] According to various sources listed in Wikipedia: "Great Chinese Famine".

message the battle was lost, for want of a battle the kingdom was lost, and all for the want of a horseshoe-nail." He writes:

> "For Want of a Nail" tells the story of a series of causal events, each one escalating in importance, in a manner that we might refer to as a snowball effect, or butterfly effect, the idea that small changes can reverberate and grow into much larger ones, especially if they become part of a positive feedback loop.[1]

Further, Strate comes up with a possible explanation of the "reductionist" accusations against media deterministic concepts:

> But what happens when we collapse the chain, and express the same idea in a more economical, less poetic, summary fashion, that the loss of a nail caused the loss of a kingdom? This sort of abbreviation results in a statement that strains credulity, that most would consider an exaggeration at best. The same might be said of a statement such as, the stirrup caused feudalism.[2]

Strate quotes Neil Postman (his professor in the 1980s), who repeated after Huxley that we all are "Great Abbreviators". Strate offers samples of such abbreviations:

> We might say that evolution *caused* humans to stand erect, that gravity *causes* objects to fall to the ground, and that entropy *causes* systems to seek equilibrium, statements that are properly understood as a kind of shorthand for more nuanced scientific theory.[3]

McLuhan was, of course, among the greatest abbreviators. He did not hesitate to make statements that cut out boring nuances and jumped right to the key points. Strate quotes some McLuhanisms from *The Gutenberg Galaxy* (1962):

> "The interiorization of the technology of the phonetic alphabet translates man from the magical world of the ear to the neutral visual world."
>
> "Schizophrenia may be a necessary consequence of literacy."

---

[1] Strate, Lance. (2017). *Media Ecology*, p. 155.

[2] Strate, Lance. (2017). *Media Ecology*, p. 155.

[3] Strate, Lance. (2017). *Media Ecology*, p. 154.

> "The alphabet is an aggressive and militant absorber and transformer of cultures, as Harold Innis was the first to show."
>
> "Print created national uniformity and government centralism, but also individualism, and opposition to government as such."[1]

From this angle, Strate analyzes the role of the stirrup in forming the socio-economic conditions of feudalism in Medieval Europe, as suggested by Lynn White in his 1964 book *Medieval Technology and Social Change*.[2] In McLuhan's interpretation, White "explains how the feudal system was a social extension of the stirrup."[3] To pinpoint the issue, Strate suggests that if he were to make the claim that the "stirrup *caused* feudalism," it would come across as incongruous and perhaps even absurd, despite (or because of) its likeness to scientific formulation. But it might also "perform a heuristic function, leading to further discussion and investigation."[4]

Of course, there is a chain of more nuanced and overlapping occurrences connecting the stirrup and feudalism. The stirrup allowed a mounted warrior to use heavy weaponry and the power of a galloping horse for attacks. This created a superior battle technique and allowed extended conquest and expanded military gains. But this military technique also required the production of expensive heavy weaponry and armor. The assistance of servants and foot soldiers was also required. They would help the horseman to mount the horse, but they also would fight on his flanks, precisely in the manner of the modern infantry accompanying a tank in the battlefield. So, mounted warriors simultaneously became the captains of these military units.

Therefore, it well can be said that the new combat technique led to new socio-economic relations. Mounted warriors received a well-deserved share in the war gains and, in return, were obliged to maintain their military units. This entailed knighthood with respective economic, military, and political relations between the vassals and the sovereign. Knighthood also created the ethics and aesthetics of chivalry with its poetry, rituals, and

---

1 Strate, Lance. (2017). *Media Ecology*, p. 156-157.

2 In his 1964 book *Medieval Technology and Social Change*, Lynn White advanced the theory that feudalism in Europe developed as a result of the introduction of the stirrup to cavalry. The theory spurred the so-called "Great Stirrup Controversy" and many accusations in techno-determinism and reductionism.

3 Strate, Lance. (2017). *Media Ecology*, p. 156.

4 Strate, Lance. (2017). *Media Ecology*, p. 157.

even gender roles: chivalry, in French, meant cavalry or horsemanship. And here we have, finally, the complete picture of feudalism.

This is what Postman meant when he said that technological changes are ecological: "I mean 'ecological' in the same sense as the word is used by environmental scientists. One significant change generates total change."[1]

Within the ecological framework, media determinism is not reductionism. Media determinism is "inductionism". It represents the inducing – formative, terraforming – power of media. Media determinism is not the order of things but an optic for looking at this order. Rejecting media determinism means declining a goldmine of insights. And vice versa: as soon as you accept the optic of media determinism, your life becomes a captivating ethnographic expedition.

Karl Marx was a latent media determinist. According to him, "The hand-mill gives you society with the feudal lord; the steam-mill society with the industrial capitalist."[2] On another occasion, in a passage written a century before McLuhan, Marx asked:

> Is Achilles possible when powder and shot have been invented? And is the *Iliad* possible at all when the printing press and even printing machines exist? Is it not inevitable that with the emergence of the press bar the singing and the telling and the muse cease; that is, the conditions necessary for epic poetry disappear?[3]

Vladimir Lenin reworked the media determinism of Marx into media ecological *engineering*. His famous formula of communism stated: "Communism is the power of the Soviets plus the electrification of the whole country".[4] As steam engines, according to Marx, brought capitalism, electricity, according to Lenin, should have brought communism. It was not, of course, some "linear" naivety of reductionism. Lenin understood that electricity would favour large industrial enterprises, the cradle of the proletariat, and thus would disturb the small-holding economic structure that suited the agricultural economy based on the peasantry with its small-

---

[1] Postman, Neil. (1992). *Technopoly: The Surrender of Culture to Technology*, p. 18.

[2] Marx, Karl. (1847). *The Poverty of Philosophy*. Chapter 2.1, Second Observation, Para 2.

[3] Marx, Karl. (1859). *A Contribution to the Critique of Political Economy*. Introduction, Appendix 1, Section 4.

[4] Lenin, Vladimir. (1920, December 22). "Report on the work of the Council of People's Commissars." in V. I. Lenin, *Collected Works* (Moscow: Progress Publishers, 1964), Vol. XXXI, pp. 513-518.

proprietor consciousness, then the predominant demographic of Russia. The peasantry was receptive to the bourgeois mentality and therefore posed a threat to communism.[1] So, electrification was tasked with reshaping the peasant country, much like the wolves in Yellowstone. The ecologists in Yellowstone were ecological engineers, too. For them, wolves were the medium of ecosystem engineering – terraforming. (Whereas hippos were a medium of entertainment for Escobar and their reshaping of the ecosystem was an unintended consequence).

Terraforming is the ultimate environmental power of media, whether applied by an ingenious mind or unleashed by itself, naturally. New media, when spread enough and massively used, transform from an instrument to an environmental force.[2] As soon as people start using a medium, they become a part of the environment created by this medium. The terraforming power of media is not a figure of speech. Humans with their media have physically reshaped the planet and even near space, with both intended and unintended outcomes.

Affordances we can't refuse

You cannot walk on the water unless you're Jesus or a Jesus lizard. The water affords you only to swim, glide, dive, or sink. The materiality of the environment dictates the ways of interacting with it. Based on the verb "afford," in the late 1960s, psychologist James Gibson coined a new word, *affordance,* which became a term signifying the types of interactions the environment allows its inhabitants to engage in.

Different affordances are offered by different elements of the "terrestrial environments". Affordances, however, describe not the innate physical characteristics of these elements but rather the compatibility of users with those physical characteristics. For example, the affordances of water are not the same for humans, swans and fish. Each of these "users" has their own "compatibility" with water.

---

[1] Mir, Andrey. (2022). "Media-ecological engineering of the Soviets." Explorations in Media Ecology, Volume 21, Issue 2-3, Oct 2022, p. 143 - 155.

[2] Miroshnichenko, Andrey. (2021). "Media and Responsibility for Their Effects: Instrumental vs. Environmental Views". *Laws*, 10, no. 2: 48.

Affordances are not just possibilities of use: they invite to act in a certain way. In the 1980s and later, Donald Norman extended Gibson's theory of affordances to technological design and human-computer interactions. He wrote:

> Affordances provide strong clues to the operations of things. Plates are for pushing. Knobs are for turning. Slots are for inserting things into. Balls are for throwing or bouncing. When affordances are taken advantage of, the user knows what to do just by looking: no picture, label, or instruction needed.[1]

Unlike animals, living in the natural environment with its natural affordances, humans live in the man-made environment, which is shaped by our interfaces and products of our technologies – by our media. Human environmental affordances are media affordances.

Things around us tell us what we can or cannot do with them. Among predecessors who helped form his concept, Gibson quoted Kurt Koffka, who in his 1935 *Principles of Gestalt Psychology* wrote that, "Each thing says what it is. ... a fruit says 'Eat me'; water says 'Drink me'; thunder says 'Fear me'."[2]

Just like Vito Corleone, the environments make us offers we can't refuse. Affordance illustrates the "compelling" power of media. As long as a medium offers some convenience (extension in time and space), we can't help but use it in a way that the affordance of this medium dictates. Affordance is a manifestation of environmental passive aggression. A metaphorical illustration for this is a stranger politely holding a door for you well in advance before you reach it, thus making you hurry up.

Some affordances could be called *hard affordances* – they offer only certain ways of interacting with objects, such as a door with a metal plate or stairs. You can only push that door or only walk up and down on those stairs. Other environments offer *soft affordances*: they can be interacted with in a variety of ways but still invite to choose a "preferable" use.

For example, social media seemingly provide a variety of applications. Users can chat, look for friends and useful information, promote themselves and their businesses, create communities or organize political actions. You'd think you could use social media to simply do what you

[1] Norman, Donald. (1988). *The Psychology of Everyday Things*, p. 9.

[2] Gibson, James. (1986 [1979]). *The Ecological Approach to Visual Perception*, p. 138.

want, but the design of social media is aimed at greater engagement for better ad targeting. This design favours behaviours that cause a better response, and such behaviours most likely consist of rather salient than modest manifestations. In other words, whatever opportunities social media provide, their ultimate environmental affordance leads to the amplification of extremes and, eventually, to polarisation. Individually, we can withdraw or abstain, but, as a society, we've been given an offer we can't refuse. Society can't help but engage more and more on social media and get more polarized. Affordance – even a seemingly soft, inviting affordance – in fact, compels.

In any ecosystem, affordances are more powerful than restrictions. Restrictions can be resisted; mass resistance to restriction can even create enough force to overturn the ecosystem. Unlike restrictions, affordances are not tangible, as they shape behaviour unnoticeably. It is hard to resist something you do not sense. Mass resistance to affordances is impossible.

Another approach to the theory of affordances can be made within the framework of the system theory. In his *Media Ecology*, Lance Strate refers to the "relationship of downward causation". Any part of the system has a set of functions predefined by its role in the system. Strate writes:

> Downward causality is the causality of the environment in relation to that which it contains, or the system to its parts, and it is a causality based on constraints, rather than the positive impetus of efficient cause.[1]

The system "obliges" its parts through downward causality. A piece of a puzzle must fit the picture. A wolf occupies its place in the food chain. An actor must perform their role in the play. A footballer must play at a certain position for the team. The game invites them to do certain things, and they are constrained by their role on the team. Downward causality can be seen as a type of environmental affordance. If you are a part of a system, the system is your environment, and the affordance it suggests will be rather hard – not just inviting, but more likely dictating.

Keeping the concept of environmental affordances in mind, it is quite justifiable to state that, yes, the stirrup caused feudalism. And, yes, the wolves changed the Yellowstone ecosystem. And, yes, electricity created the

---

[1] Strate, Lance. (2017). *Media Ecology*, p. 178.

global village. Put the idea of environmental affordances behind such "techno-deterministic" statements, and you will see that this is the ecological, not technological, kind of determinism: media determinism.

Robert Logan, who endeavoured, with a pass from the late McLuhan, to establish the connection between the alphabet and monotheism, does not insist on direct causality. "It is not possible to establish any causal relations or direct impacts," he states. But his wording implies the role of environmental affordances, too:

> We shall find, however, that the alphabet provided a climate in which abstract notions such as monotheism, codified law, science, and logic could flourish.[1]

I'd go further and say that his concept implies that, yes, monotheism, codified law, abstract science and deductive logic were, indeed, the effects of the alphabet, as the title of his book, *The Alphabet Effect*, directly suggests. Phonetic writing introduced symbols that had no semblance with what they signified. This put the mind of the user at a level of abstraction that was earlier unaffordable: mental constructions became completely detached from the sensory experience.

In its turn, abstracting that had no tethering in sensed reality afforded the concept of the spiritual absolute, which happened to be beneficial for the Hebrews, the inventors of the proto alphabet, in their struggle for national identity against the surrounding powers based on polytheism. The spiritual absolute, one God above all, turned out to be superior to the cohorts of Egyptian or Babylonian gods-specialists with their ancient craft-magic. Monotheism is the ultimate development – and the ultimate affordance – of the symbolic abstraction brought about by phonetic writing.

The compelling affordance of media does not mean that a medium, wherever and whenever it is introduced, automatically leads to a predicated and identical response in any ecosystem. The affordances of a medium interact with other environmental affordances and shape unique equilibriums in different conditions. Nevertheless, the affordance of a certain medium forms recognizable patterns of environmental response. The ecological determinism of media gives us an optic to see the logic of

[1] Logan, Robert. (2004 [1986]). *The Alphabet Effect*, p. 143.

historical processes. Moreover, history itself is linear and progressive precisely because of the logic of media evolution.

Interestingly, we tend to believe more in the transformative power of the wheel than in that of papyrus. Postman writes in this regard:

> We have seen enough by now to know that technological changes in our modes of communication are even more ideology-laden than changes in our modes of transportation. Introduce the alphabet to a culture and you change its cognitive habits, its social relations, its notions of community, history and religion. Introduce the printing press with movable type, and you do the same. Introduce speed-of-light transmission of images and you make a cultural revolution. Without a vote. Without polemics. Without guerrilla resistance.[1]

The notion of clay tablets causing Sumerian urbanization, papyrus causing the Roman Empire, or the alphabet causing monotheism may sound reductionist, indeed; however, the statement "The Internet has changed everything" is entirely acceptable. This is either because the terraforming power of media has grown with the passage of time or because we did not fully understand the effects of past media.

The linearity of media evolution – and history

Media are not just a terraforming device but also a time-binding device. Media make history while also periodizing it into ages. This "ageism" of media-ecological study is inevitable: every good media ecologist must engage in epoch-making. Many media ecologists were involved in charting historic periodization through media.

Harold Innis focused on empires and other forms of social organizations tied to forms of communication. Roughly, his historical periodization could be determined through clay tablets and hieroglyphs, papyrus, parchments codex, and paper. In his 1948 essay *Minerva's Owl*, Innis suggests a page-long list of media that defined their epochs, from clay and the stylus, to "celluloid in the growth of the cinema; and finally the radio."[2] His *Bias of Communication*, containing *Minerva's Owl*, is a hymn to historical media determinism.

---

1 Postman, Neil. (2006 [1985]). *Amusing Ourselves to Death*, p. 157.

2 Innis Harold, (2008 [1951]). *Bias of Communication*, p. 3-5

Marshall McLuhan in his works talked about the oral age, the literate age (writing, the alphabet, printing) and the electric age (starting with the telegraph and leading to retribalization/the global village).

Walter Ong wrote about the states of mind as defined by the state of media/communication. These states of mind constituted a linear historical succession. He singled out primary orality – literacy – secondary orality.

Neil Postman described the forms of cultural and social organization as determined by the effects of respective media in historical succession. In his 1992 *Technopoly*, he singled out tool using – technocracy – technopoly.[1] Postman also offered, perhaps, the best description of historic media determinism:

> For although culture is a creation of speech, it is recreated anew by every medium of communication—from painting to hieroglyphs to the alphabet to television. Each medium, like language itself, makes possible a unique mode of discourse by providing a new orientation for thought, for expression, for sensibility. Which, of course, is what McLuhan meant in saying the medium is the message.[2]

Paul Levinson, in his 1978 doctoral thesis, supervised by Neil Postman, introduced the "anthropotropic model" of media evolution, published later as a monograph.[3] This was the first academically developed concept of media evolution. Levinson singled out three stages of media evolution: Stage A: non-technological, based on immediate sensory perception; Stage B: the senses are extended by technologies at the cost of the sensorium's integrity; and Stage C: the integrity of sensorium perception is regained while extending the senses across time and space.[4]

Joshua Meyrowitz, through his "medium theory", singled out cultural phases: traditional oral cultures – the transitional scribal phase – modern print culture – postmodern global electronic culture.[5]

---

[1] Postman, Neil. (1992). *Technopoly: The Surrender of Culture to Technology.*

[2] Postman, Neil. (2006 [1985]). *Amusing Ourselves to Death*, p. 10.

[3] Levinson, Paul. (2017 [1978]). *Human Replay: A Theory of the Evolution of Media.* Connected Editions.

[4] Levinson, Paul. (2017 [1978]). *Human Replay: A Theory of the Evolution of Media.* See also my review of Levinson's book: Mir, Andrey. (2022). "Media evolution – the evolution of what? Thoughts on the margins of Paul Levinson's *Human Replay.*" *ETC: A Review of General Semantics,* 79:1-2 (2022).

[5] Meyrowitz, Joshua. (2010). "Media evolution and cultural change", pp. 52-63.

Robert Logan, besides developing the concept of the alphabet effect, advances the theory of six languages: speech – writing – mathematics – science – computing – the Internet.[1]

Pierre Lévy suggested the following stages of "Media and Culture Evolution: oral – scribal – literate – typographic – algorithmic. "At each stage," writes Lévy, "new political forms have emerged: palaces-temples and first states with writing, empires and cities with the alphabet or paper, nation states with printing and electronic media."[2] (Figure 4.)

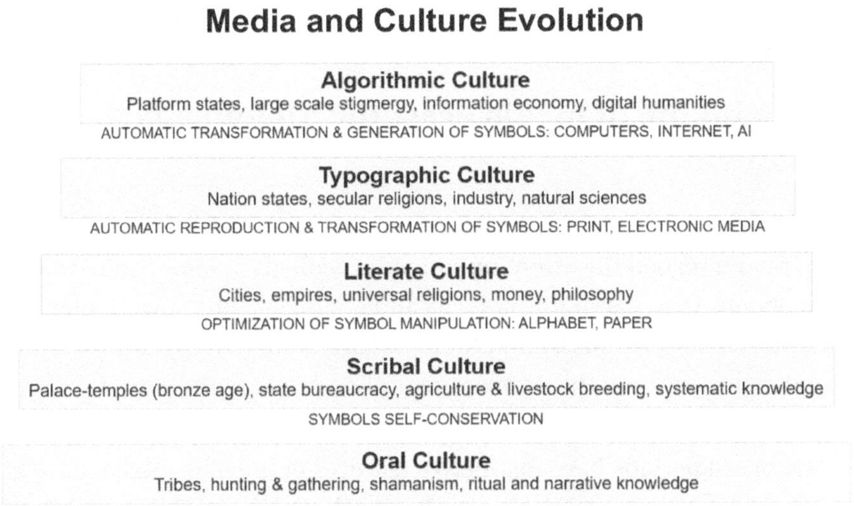

Figure 4. Source: Lévy, Pierre (2023). "The digital public sphere." *Intellect Metadata Blog*.

To that cohort of authors with historical media periodization, many others can be added whose periodization did not involve media directly but clearly referred to the process of media and technological development. One of the most prominent among them was, of course, Karl Marx, who tied historical development to the development of means of production, productive forces, and relations of productions. In the Marxist tradition, this gave the sequence of socio-economic formations: the "primitive communism" of the tribal society, slave society, feudalism, capitalism, socialism and, finally, global, stateless communism. Another classical

[1] Logan, Robert K. (2004 [2000]). *The Sixth Language: Learning a Living in the Internet Age*, Second Edition. Blackburn Press.

[2] Lévy, Pierre (2023, May 20). "The digital public sphere." *Intellect Metadata Blog*.

model was supported by Alvin Toffler in his concept of the Three Waves of history: agricultural society, industrial society, and post-industrial society.[1]

Karl Jaspers in his 1949 *The Origin and Goal of History* suggested his own "Schema of world history". According to Jaspers, humans came from a single source, some biological state lost in the darkness of our primordial past, and are moving toward one single goal – to be united as humankind. In its movement toward unity, humankind has passed through several stages, the most crucial of which was what Jaspers calls Axis, or the Axial Period – I prefer the translation "Axial Age"[2] – which occurred from the 8th to 3rd centuries BCE.

The shrinking of media eras: the Singularity countdown

As was the case with television in the time of McLuhan and Postman, digital media turned the attention of media ecologists, once again, to past media epochs in a search for patterns and analogies. But now, thanks to Innis, McLuhan, Postman, and others, we are better equipped to see the dependencies between the development of society and the evolution of media.

Historical periods have distinctive features defined by media. Give a media ecologist information about what medium is used by the Martians – carved stones, inks on animal skin, or neurotransmitters – and we will describe some fundamental principles of the current Martian civilization. But historical periods also have a distinctive temporal characteristic in their progression: each following historical period was shorter than the previous one. History accelerated because the change of media forced it.

Rough but simple and obvious calculations make apparent the pace of this acceleration. The sensory/cultural mode of orality, maintained by respective media devices (speech, implements), lasted about three to five

---

[1] Toffler, Alvin. (1980). *The Third Wave*. Toffler implies that agricultural society replaced the society of hunter-gatherers, but he does not recognize hunter-gatherers as a "wave" of history; essentially, they did not form a society. Interestingly, Karl Jaspers held to the same tradition: he recognizes the hunter-gatherer stage of human evolution as prehistory, claiming that history started with the first agricultural irrigation civilizations. Regardless, the arrival of each of Toffler's next waves clearly followed changes in "basic media" (Innis).

[2] German *Achsenzeit*, "axial time", inclines more towards "times/epoch/era/age" than just "period".

thousand generations of humans[1]. Writing enclosed 170 generations. Print dominated for about 15 generations. Electric media, starting with the telegraph, then radio and TV, has been affecting the sensorium and society for 5 generations.

This progression gives us a numerical sequence "5000 – 170 – 15 – 5". It resembles a countdown. On the count of "one", the length of the era will align with the lifespan of the generation.

In "Human as media"[2], I suggested the notion of the "pivotal generation" – the generation whose lifespan, for the first time in history, became longer than a technological era. The "pivotal generation" consisted of people born in the middle of the 20th century. Their life encompassed two or even three eras – agricultural, industrial, and post-industrial. A typical feature of this generational shift in most countries has been grandparents starting their lives in agricultural or industrial settings and their grandchildren belonging to digital migrants or digital natives.

After the pivotal generation, historical periods measured by dominant technology have started offsetting each other within the lifespan of a generation. It means that every one of us experiences the arrival of a medium that would have made its own epoch in the good old times: the internet, cellphones, tablets, smartphones, social media, VR, generative AI, and brain-machine interfaces... The historical explosions of new media, once quite rare and distinctive, have now merged into the rumble of a rocket launch. Its thrust stuns the human sensorium and disturbs the social ecosystem, which no longer has enough time to achieve a new equilibrium after being disturbed by the previous new medium.

The acceleration of historical time means that increasingly more "media events" (and events in general) happen in a time period. This gives us another description of the shortening of the historical era down to the size of a lifespan and below. The accelerating increase of events per a period is graphically represented by the exponential growth curve. Such exponential growth of events is, essentially, a portrait of the Singularity: the Singularity happens on the "vertical end" of this curve.

---

1 If we agree that speech and implements emerged 100–150 thousand years ago, the latest time-mark in the consensus of paleoanthropologists. Other estimates move the emergence of speech and tools as far in human history as 2 million years ago. This makes the acceleration of historical time even faster.

2 Miroshnichenko, Andrey. (2014). *Human as media. The emancipation of authorship*.

If the count "one" in our countdown of shrinking media eras gives us the pivotal generation (for whom the era shorter than a lifespan), then what will happen on the count "zero"?

The Singularity, of course. The fact that eras have already shrunk below the length of a generation lifespan means that the "Singularity is near"[1] indeed.

It is even possible to calculate the point "zero" on the historical timeline for the countdown "5000 – 170 – 15 – 5" that represented the lengths of the eras dominating by speech, writing, printing, and electricity, respectively. The progression indicates that the length of the digital era will be 1–1.5 generations, which sets up the "point zero" sometime in the 2040–2050s (assuming that the digital era started, roughly, in 2000).

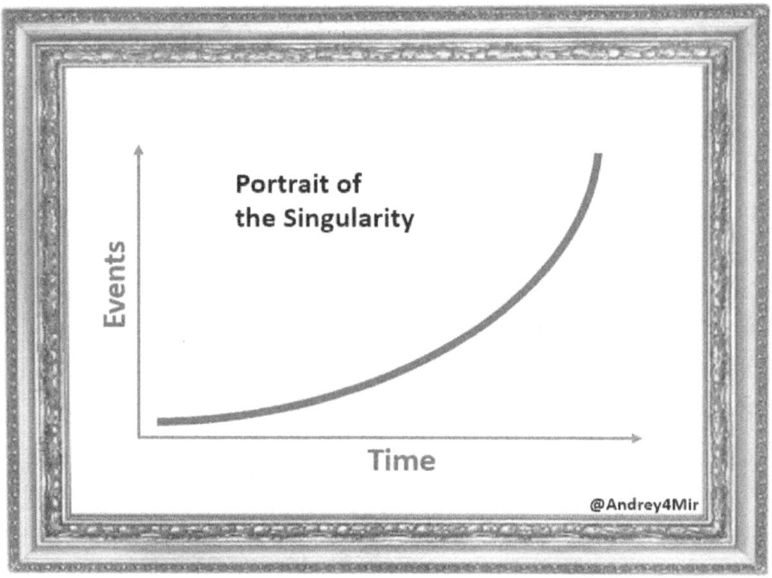

Figure 5.

This is pure speculation and the epitome of media conspiracy, so to speak. However, the logic of the shrinking of historical eras (or the accelerating of historical time) is implacable. One can consider other milestone media inventions that have defined the pace of media evolution, including various means of transportation such as walking, horses, sailing,

[1] *The Singularity Is Near: When Humans Transcend Biology* is a 2005 book by Ray Kurzweil. He predicted the advent of the Singularity in 2045.

steam engines, internal combustion engines, and jets. The lengths of eras dominated by those transportation media will give the same progression of shrinking the eras (or accelerating the historical time). The math behind this progression might not be solid, but media ecology as a "field of inquiry" (Strate) works with pattern recognition, not with exact calculations. This countdown will also point at the same mid-21st-century mark as "point zero" of the Singularity countdown. This is within the reach of one generation, i.e., us or our children. Watching the development of AI and cognitive interfaces will help to specify the exact date.

Looking at the historical Axial Age from today's Axial Decade

We are already living through the first stage of digitality – digital orality, the communion of humans by means of digital communication. Digital orality is the instant exchange by clicks.[1] It's a completely new mode of humans' interaction with the environment and each other.

Digital orality is simultaneous and impulsive like instant oral exchange but recordable, shareable, and transportable like writing and print. The evanescent exchange, typical for oral conversation between immediate interlocutors, becomes recorded, stored and accessed by distant others. What happens "just now" between two is not going to stay "just now" and between them. A user observes a tremendous number of conversations and the self-exposures of others, to which this user is supposed to react. The implosion of the world into the user's brain is causing an unprecedented overload of demands for responses from others. Dunbar's number of 150 meaningful connections with others, for which the brain of primates was originally designed, has been overruled by the design of social media.

This new form of simultaneous and immediate, yet lasting and shareable interaction with each other and the environment creates, at the very least, preconditions for a tectonic cultural shift. Some aspects of this shift are acknowledged and reflected upon. Much opaquer is the fact that digital orality creates an environment that is an alternative to the physical world, enabling humans to resettle within it, with new capacities to colonize time instead of space.

---

[1] Mir, Andrey. (2022, Winter). "The Medium Is the Menace. Ubiquitous digital media offer potent rewards – but at the price of eroding our sensory and social capacities." *City Journal.*

Since we live inside the process, it is hard for us to notice it, let alone to assess its scale. We experience its routine without recognizing its formative effect. In the meantime, the game-changing effect of digital orality will exceed the media effect of printing or electricity and can be compared to that of writing or even speech. We are certainly dealing with a historical axis in a Jaspersian sense.

Are we living through a new Axial Age? I believe we are. Though, due to the acceleration of historical time, this is rather the Axial Decade, the "long decade" of the 2010s, in which some formative events of the digital era started happening and will continue to happen for some time.

According to Jaspers, the Axial Age was the period (from the 8th to 3rd centuries BCE) when "man, as we know him today, came into being"[1]. In the most general sense, the Axial Age reflected the emergence of humans' capacity for self-reflection, something that Walter Ong called the "inward turn". Ong saw the inward turn as the effect of writing: people were naturally born to orality, but when they acquired literacy, an artificial skill not directly required for physical survival, it led to the shock of self-awareness.

"Writing is consciousness-raising," writes Ong.[2] With an ability to think not just of food and survival but also of self – this is the inward turn – humankind as such awakened. Humans became aware that they are what they are and that they have history. Interestingly, Jaspers described that the same effect emerged in the Axial Age but did not attribute it to writing, leaving some mysterious historical force as the cause.[3]

Today's Axial Decade is a McLuhanist reversal of Jaspers' Axial Age. The implosion of the world into the user modifies the "inward turn" into the "outward turn" or better to say into the "inward-out turn". Unlike Jaspers' Axial Age that separated humans from the natural environment, the current Axial Decade immerses humans into the induced digital environment.

---

[1] Jaspers, Karl. (2021 [1949]). *The Origin and Goal of History*, p. 9.

[2] Ong, Walter. 2002 [1982]. *Orality and Literacy*, p. 174. Walter Ong borrowed the term "inward turn" from Erich Kahler's *The Inward Turn of Narrative* (1973) and developed it in application to literacy.

[3] Although Jaspers did demonstrate some aptitudes of a media-determinist, he was not ready, at the time, to walk this path to the end.

If the essence of today's Axial Decade is the reversal of Jaspers' Axial Age, then we can learn more about the current Digital Axis by looking at what happened in the original Axial Age as described by Karl Jaspers and also through a media interpretation of the Axial Age, particularly through Robert Logan's alphabet effect.

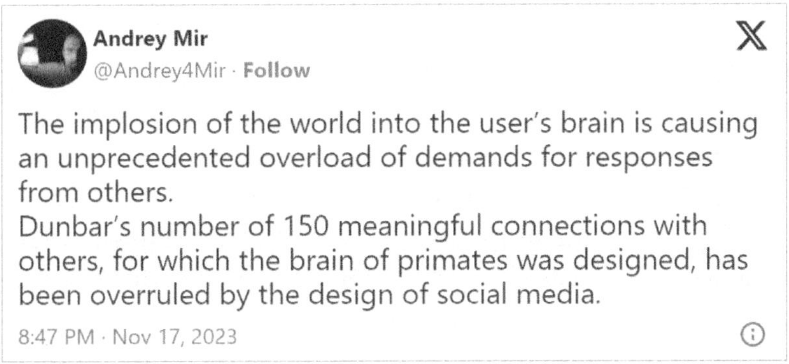
Andrey Mir
@Andrey4Mir · **Follow**

The implosion of the world into the user's brain is causing an unprecedented overload of demands for responses from others.
Dunbar's number of 150 meaningful connections with others, for which the brain of primates was designed, has been overruled by the design of social media.

8:47 PM · Nov 17, 2023

2. Karl Jaspers and his "Schema of world history"

Prehistory and the Promethean Age

Jaspers divided "the whole of history" into three successive phases: prehistory, history and world history.

Prehistory was the lengthiest period of human evolution. It started with the formation of races, languages, and myths and continued with the "silent spread of technical inventions and the migrations."[1] In the prehistoric period, humans formed all their "elemental impulses and characteristics."[2] Prehistory lasted until the inception of the first ancient civilizations in Egypt and Mesopotamia.

What made us humans so special among other biological species? Why did it happen to us? Why did it happen at all? Jaspers calls it the "enigma of humanity"[3] represented in the unique quality of the human species: a predisposition to historical evolution despite our biological nature.

For some reason, as Jaspers points out, our biological evolution did not give us strong specialized organs, such as big fangs, sharp horns, strong muscles, or armor. In some ways, this deficiency of specialized organs made humans inferior to many other animals, but it was precisely this lack of organ specialization that turned into a strength. Adaptability without powers required intellectual flexibility and ingenuity, which are unnecessary for species with greater physical gifts. Though physically inferior to animals, man became superior "through the medium of his consciousness, to follow paths quite different from those taken by animals in bringing his existence to realization," according to Jaspers.[4] Thanks to the absence of organ specialization, humans were compelled to fashion their environment, in which their "organs were replaced by implements."[5]

---

[1] Jaspers, Karl. (2021 [1949]). *The Origin and Goal of History*, p. 50.
[2] Jaspers, Karl. (2021 [1949]). *The Origin and Goal of History*, p. 83.
[3] Jaspers, Karl. (2021 [1949]). *The Origin and Goal of History*, p. 83.
[4] Jaspers, Karl. (2021 [1949]). *The Origin and Goal of History*, p. 45.
[5] Jaspers, Karl. (2021 [1949]). *The Origin and Goal of History*, p. 46.

Here, Jaspers implies the idea of media as "the extensions of man" (McLuhan).

The logic of his reasoning also aligns with the myth of Prometheus. According to the classical reading of the myth by Plato in *Protagoras*, the gods created mortal creatures from earth and fire and ordered the Titan brothers, Prometheus and Epimetheus, to equip them with different powers so they could survive in the harsh conditions of Nature. Epimetheus, whose name means "he-who-thinks-after," took the job and assigned strength, teeth, swiftness, wings, claws, hoofs, and so on to different creatures. For some reason, humans stood last in the queue. So, when they came to the dispensation, nothing was left for them.

Prometheus, whose name means "he-who-thinks-ahead," obviously was not thinking ahead when he agreed to give the job to his dumb brother. When Prometheus came to inspect the distribution of powers, "he found that the other animals were suitably furnished, but that man alone was naked and shoeless, and had neither bed nor arms of defense." To provide humans with at least some abilities to survive, Prometheus "stole the mechanical arts of Hephaestus and Athene, and fire with them (they could neither have been acquired nor used without fire), and gave them to man."[1]

This myth has no historical plausibility and yet manifests the essence of humans becoming so different from other species. The difference was made by media: the acquisition of the earliest media was the factor that separated humans from the animal kingdom. The acquisition of Promethean media signified the beginning of the divorce of humans from Nature.

Jaspers does not use the concept of media, nor does he refer to the myth of Prometheus directly. But he uses the term "Promethean Age" when referring to prehistory, so he certainly implies the allusion to the myth. Interestingly, Jaspers stands in as a true media ecologist when he writes:

> There would be no technology in Paradise. Technology serves the purpose of ridding man of the burden of want; this first compels him to maintain his physical existence by work and then enables him, without the compulsion of want, to extend his existence into the incalculable structure of an environment which he himself has shaped.[2]

---

[1] Plato, *Protagoras*, [321].

[2] Jaspers, Karl. (2021 [1949]). *The Origin and Goal of History*, p. 132.

Jaspers describes humans' first "historical acquisitions" in quite a McLuhanesque way when he writes that, in the Promethean Age, "man first came into possession of his world through tools, fire and speech."[1]

Thus, biological evolution prepared humans for historical evolution. In prehistory, humans became increasingly suitable biological material for recording cultural heritage. This dual biological-precultural legacy of prehistory has remained in the core of human nature until today. Perhaps, remembering the atrocities of the recent Nazi regime[2], Jaspers mentions that what was shaped in prehistory, all those primeval desires and impulses, have always remained in the core of human nature, while the later cultural wrapping can be easily shed under certain circumstances.[3]

Prehistory lasted an enormously long time, during which the human race made its appearance. But we know little about this period, especially compared to its length. Humans remained very close to Nature and very dependent on its caprices. Humans' way of life might have differed from that of animals, but the "meaning" of life did not differ much from that of other living beings. As Jaspers put it,

> Before history, all that happened in the isolation of human groups unaware of their interrelatedness was an entirely repetitive continuance of living, still closely allied to the processes of nature.[4]

Most importantly, humans were not aware of their own existence until history commenced. And then this happened:

> Instead of endlessly repeating the natural and constant cycle of life, as do the animals, he became capable of creating history... Man achieves history, on the foundation of the purely repetitive function of natural life, which he shares with everything living.[5]

---

[1] Jaspers, Karl. (2021 [1949]). *The Origin and Goal of History,* p. 157.

[2] Jaspers lived in Germany under the Nazis. Because of his "connection with the Jew" (Jewish wife), he was forced to retire from teaching, remain under a publication ban and live under the fear of being sent to a concentration camp. Another of his great contributions to world philosophy is his famous *The Question of German Guilt* published in 1947, two years before *The Origin and Goal of History.*

[3] For example: "That which is biologically inheritable is permanent; the cultural heritage can be destroyed and forgotten in a very short space of time." Jaspers, Karl. (2021 [1949]). *The Origin and Goal of History,* p. 44.

[4] Jaspers, Karl. (2021 [1949]). *The Origin and Goal of History,* p. 32.

[5] Jaspers, Karl. (2021 [1949]). *The Origin and Goal of History,* p. 46.

The beginning of history: the Ancient Civilizations

According to Jaspers, at approximately the same time, though stretched across two millennia, the three earliest civilizations arose in three regions of the Earth:

1) The Sumero-Babylonian, Egyptian, Aegean world from 4000 BCE

2) The pre-Aryan Indus culture of the third millennium, circa 3300 BCE

3) the ancient Chinese world of the 2nd millennium BCE (perhaps even earlier).

As Jaspers writes:

> In Egypt, Mesopotamia, the Indus valley and in China along the banks of the Hwang-ho, analogous civilisations sprung up in the river valleys characterised by the central administration of a highly evolved mechanism for satisfying the needs of the community.[1]

All of a sudden (historically, of course), the cultural atmosphere in these regions became drastically different from that of prehistory. People organized in large, centralized states and started speaking to each another in written documents and constructing large buildings.[2]

Water control played a crucial role in the emergence of these civilizations. First, the technology of river control required sophisticated engineering, agricultural and astronomical knowledge, along with an unprecedented scale of social and labour cooperation. Second, irrigation provided an unprecedented surplus of provisions. Third, the monopoly over water supplies was seized by those who knew the river cycles – the priests who represented the divine authority of natural cycles (the kings, pharaohs). They maintained their power with religious cults and military forces and thus ruled the land: they protected the farmers and collected taxes/offerings. They secured their wellbeing from inner and outer threats while subduing neighboring tribes.

[1] Jaspers, Karl. (2021 [1949]). *The Origin and Goal of History*, p. 20.

[2] Jaspers does not focus on it, but the construction of buildings larger than shelters signifies, first, some collective need for such buildings, obviously religious and bureaucratic, and, second, the ability to build such buildings. Both aspects can certainly be seen as the additional signs of the shift from prehistory to history.

With the growth of centralized bureaucratic and military power, the first ancient civilizations also became the first "world empires," starting with Mesopotamia, as Jaspers sees it.

The shift from riverbank villages to river valley civilizations signified the development of a complex social and religious hierarchy. As coordination of the masses was based on the cults of the gods of the river, sun, and fertility, large and powerful temples were built that accumulated and applied the needed knowledge in exchange for political and economic power. The monopoly over water supplies meant also the "monopoly of knowledge," as Harold Innis called it to characterize the role of scribes-priests.

Summarizing, Jaspers suggests that the beginning of history was marked by certain "tangible events," such as:

1) The centralization of civil services and power needed for organizing river-control and irrigation.

2) The discovery of writing – a necessary precondition for such organization.

3) "The genesis of *peoples* who feel themselves a unity with a common *language*, a common culture and a common body of *myths*"[1] and the emergence of the first states and empires out of it, beginning with Mesopotamia.

4) The introduction of horse and war-chariots with the subsequent development of a new kind of heroic epos and individualistic consciousness centred around the courage of the rider and conqueror.

Prior to history, humans adjusted their living to what Nature would afford. The "leap from this mere happening into history"[2] meant the emergence of humans' agency over natural forces and affordances. Since irrigation required complex organization, knowledge, and control, human interaction with the environment switched from survival to mastery, from adaptation to terraforming.

The movement from Nature to culture reshaped the collective and individual mentality of humans.

First, according to Jaspers, "consciousness and recollection, by the handing on of spiritual acquisitions... set man free from the mere present."

---

[1] Jaspers, Karl. (2021 [1949]). *The Origin and Goal of History*, p. 55, italicized by Jaspers.

[2] Jaspers, Karl. (2021 [1949]). *The Origin and Goal of History*, p. 56.

Second, rationalisation and technologies "set man free from dependence on his immediate environment for the satisfaction and safeguarding of his vital needs."

Third, types of individuals emerged, such as rulers and sages, "whose deeds, achievements and destinies were in full view of the masses – this was the first step toward setting men free from the apathy of self-awareness and the fear of demons."[1]

"Only with the beginning of history did man become truly human," states Jaspers. "Through history man has become the being that strives to rise above itself."[2]

Humans started recognizing their potentialities as part of their essence. "With the leap to history *transitoriness becomes conscious*. Everything in the world has its appointed time and must pass away. Man alone knows of his own death."[3]

The value of individual life revealed the value of the individual. The tensions between outstanding individuals and the masses became a recognizable historical force. As Jaspers put it,

> History is a continual thrusting forward on the part of single individuals. They call to the rest to follow them. Whoever hears and understands them joins them in the forward movement.[4]

The growth of social complexity divorced humans further from Nature but did not yet become pivotal for human self-consciousness. Describing the similarities between the first civilizations, Jaspers writes:

> The analogous basic features – large-scale organisations, writing, the dominant social position of the scribe class – gave rise to a type of human who, despite his more refined civilisation, has something unawakened about him.[5]

The awakening of humans happened in the Axial Age; it constituted the Axial Age.

---

[1] Jaspers, Karl. (2021 [1949]). *The Origin and Goal of History*, p. 56.

[2] Jaspers, Karl. (2021 [1949]). *The Origin and Goal of History*, p. 57.

[3] Jaspers, Karl. (2021 [1949]). *The Origin and Goal of History*, p. 57, italicized by Jaspers.

[4] Jaspers, Karl. (2021 [1949]). *The Origin and Goal of History*, p. 57.

[5] Jaspers, Karl. (2021 [1949]). *The Origin and Goal of History*, p. 58.

The Axial Age

Jaspers approaches the idea of historical pivots from the point of view of the Western culture based on Christianity. The Christian view of history has its pivot – the appearance of the Son of God among men. It divides history into "before" and "after." But the Christian faith, says Jaspers, is only one faith, not the faith of all humankind. Using the "axial pattern" of history employed in Christianity, Jaspers looks for a common axis for all of humankind outside the cultural domain of Christianity.

Is it possible to find such a pivotal event, whose formative effect would divide history into "before" and "after" and be sensed and recognized by all of humankind? Jaspers suggests he has found such an event, or series of formative events, which he unites under the label of the Axial Age. He writes:

> This axis would be situated at the point in history which gave birth to everything which, since then, man has been able to be, the point most overwhelmingly fruitful in fashioning humanity to give rise to a common frame of historical self-comprehension for all peoples – for the West, for Asia, and for all men on earth, without regard to particular articles of faith. It would seem that this axis of history is to be found in the period around 500 B.C., in the spiritual process that occurred between 800 and 200 B.C. It is there that we meet with the most deepcut dividing line in history. Man, as we know him today, came into being. For short we may style this the 'Axial Period'.[1]

The key characteristic of the Axial Age is the pivotal shift of human thinking from everyday concerns to the enquiry into the meaning of life. The recognition of the isolated fact of life called for explanation beyond mere survival. People realized there should be something bigger than everyday, repetitive living. They started enquiring into their existence, and thus their existence turned into being. Humankind became aware of itself and the Universe around (and the Universe inside). Immediately, "the Ultimate Question of Life, the Universe, and Everything" emerged and, most importantly, different approaches to address this question appeared that still exist and trouble acquisitive minds. The awareness of one's own

---

[1] Jaspers, Karl. (2021 [1949]). *The Origin and Goal of History*, p. 8.

existence that struck human consciousness in this period triggered an unprecedented intellectual, spiritual, and ethical revolution that has never been seen in history either before or after, neither in content nor in scale.

The Axial Age is also remarkable in terms of its time-space characteristics. It happened simultaneously in three narrow and separated areas: the Near East (and Greece), China, and India. In all three areas, there were the potent cultural and spiritual legacies of the pre-Axial cultures: Egypt and Mesopotamia in the Near East, the Indus and then the Ganges valleys in India, and the Hwang Ho Valley in China. All these pre-Axial civilizations were based on river control.

Here is a description of the Axial Age's essence in Jaspers' own words:

> What is new about this age, in all three areas of the world, is that man becomes conscious of Being as a whole, of himself and his limitations. He experiences the terror of the world and his own powerlessness. He asks radical questions. Face to face with the void he strives for liberation and redemption. By consciously recognising his limits he sets himself the highest goals. He experiences absoluteness in the depths of selfhood and in the lucidity of transcendence...
>
> All this took place in reflection. Consciousness became once more conscious of itself, thinking became its own object. Spiritual conflicts arose, accompanied by attempts to convince others through the communication of thoughts, reasons and experiences...
>
> In this age were born the fundamental categories within which we still think today, and the beginnings of the world religions, by which human beings still live, were created. The step into universality was taken in every sense.[1]

In China, India and the Near East, the foundations of universal history were set up. "Human existence becomes the object of meditation, as history. Men feel and know that something extraordinary is beginning in their own present."[2] Jaspers calls this the "awakening of the specifically human spirit." Humans recognized that they were "faced by catastrophe and feel the desire to help through insight, education and reform." This specifically human ethos of overcoming, salvation, and progress has driven history and humankind until the present: "Until today mankind has lived

---

1 Jaspers, Karl. (2021 [1949]). *The Origin and Goal of History*, p. 9-10.

2 Jaspers, Karl. (2021 [1949]). *The Origin and Goal of History*, p. 12.

by what happened during the Axial Period, by what was thought and created during that period."[1]

One of the main characteristics of the Axial Age, according to Jaspers, was the emergence of the major world religions. Out of magical rituals, human thought transformed into faith, a complex and abstract vision of the human past, present, and future. "The prophetic religion of the Jews set the minds of men free from magic,"[2] writes Jaspers. He sees a similar metamorphosis in the East, marked as "the transmutation of the magico-metaphysical into ethicism by Jainism and by Buddha."[3]

The rise of the world religions was accompanied by the emergence of major moral teachings and philosophical doctrines. In China, Confucius and Lao-tse set up the fundamentals of their philosophies as Confucianism and Taoism emerged. In ancient Iran, the teachings of Zarathustra became one of the first organized faiths with a monotheistic framework, advancing the notions that influenced many religions and philosophical schools, such as the dichotomy of good and evil, free will, and others. In India, Gautama Buddha and Mahavira developed their teachings of Buddhism and Jainism. The Hebrew prophets professed monotheism and laid the foundations for Abrahamic religions. In Greece, Homer created his poems in the dawn of the Axial Age. Hellenic and thereafter Western philosophy commenced with Parmenides, Heraclitus, Socrates, Plato, Aristotle, and other great Greeks, who emphasized reason as the method of knowing true things and distinguishing them from their appearances. The tragic spirit, one of the fundamental prerequisites of the Axial Age according to Jaspers, took its classical shape in the tragedies of Aeschylus, Sophocles, and Euripides.

These wisemen, prophets, and thinkers drove the unprecedented shift in human consciousness towards rational inquiry about the spiritual foundations of life. In the words of Jaspers,

> The Mythical Age, with its tranquility and self-evidence, was at an end. The Greek, Indian and Chinese philosophers were unmythical in their decisive insights, as were the prophets in their ideas of God. Rationality and rationally clarified experience launched a struggle against the myth (*logos* against *mythos*); a further struggle developed for the transcendence of the One God against non-

[1] Jaspers, Karl. (2021 [1949]). *The Origin and Goal of History*, p. 14.

[2] Jaspers, Karl. (2021 [1949]). *The Origin and Goal of History*, p. 87.

[3] Jaspers, Karl. (2021 [1949]). *The Origin and Goal of History*, p. 71.

> existent demons, and finally an ethical rebellion took place against the unreal figures of the gods. Religion was rendered ethical, and the majesty of the deity thereby increased.[1]

Through recognizing themselves in historical time, humans also became aware of their fate as something separate from "repetitive living," as Jaspers described the prehistoric human condition. He writes:

> For the first time *philosophers* appeared. Human beings dared to rely on themselves as individuals. Hermits and wandering thinkers in China, ascetics in India, philosophers in Greece and prophets in Israel all belong together, however much they may differ from each other in their beliefs, the contents of their thought and their inner dispositions. Man proved capable of contrasting himself inwardly with the entire universe. He discovered within himself the origin from which to raise himself above his own self and the world.[2]

During the Axial Age, humans completed their divorce from Nature and found what is human in being humans. The human species established humankind.

What caused the transition from magic to religion, from myth to logos, and from polytheism to monotheism, Jaspers does not ask. He just postulates these outcomes as central and universal for all three regions that contributed to the Axial Age.

As will be demonstrated in later chapters, all the key features of the Axial Age, as described by Jaspers, align with the effects of the transition from orality to literacy.

After the Axial Age

"The Axial peoples are the Chinese, Indians, Iranians, Jews and Greeks," states Jaspers[3]. However, while commencing in certain small regions, the spirit of the Axial Age has become historically all-embracing and eventually permeated across the globe. All tribes, nations and cultures were offered, or rather forced, to join this historical mainstream that sucked in everything it came across.

---

1 Jaspers, Karl. (2021 [1949]). *The Origin and Goal of History*, p. 9-10.

2 Jaspers, Karl. (2021 [1949]). *The Origin and Goal of History*, p. 10.

3 Jaspers, Karl. (2021 [1949]). *The Origin and Goal of History*, p. 61.

The spiritual and intellectual power of the Axial Age created the unifying force that led humankind to unity, showing no mercy to those not fitting in along the way. As Jaspers put it, after the Axial Age all people either "remained in a primitive state or took part in the new course of events."[1] Those who were not assimilated kept living in "the residue of prehistory." But the space they occupied has been shrinking ever since then. "The prehistoric peoples remain prehistoric until they merge into the historical movement that proceeds from the Axial Period, or die out. The Axial Period assimilates everything that remains," writes Jaspers.[2] The process of the vanishing of "the residue of prehistory," according to Jaspers, reached its final stage in Jaspers' "now," meaning the mid-20th century.

Universalization did not happen fast. In each historical period, various centers of power exercised, to their benefit, their growing (and sometimes declining) cultural, political, and military control over less potent neighbours and the "prehistoric and unhistoric peoples" they were technologically capable of putting their hands on. For example, as Jaspers writes,

> A visitor from some other planet who had travelled around the earth in about a.d. 700 would perhaps have found in Tshangan, then the capital of China, the highest seat of the spiritual life of the earth, and in Constantinople a remarkable residue; the northern districts of Europe would have appeared to him mere realms of barbarism.[3]

Jaspers thinks that Europe, India and China had reached a "uniform level of civilisation" by the 1400s. In the 1500s, Europe began shaping the modern West, and "Europe's character" became "the moulder of the earth."[4]

After the 1500s, according to Jaspers, a European and Westerner, the "West has played a paramount role in shaping the world... During the last few centuries the West has given its imprint to the whole world."[5] Jaspers, however, is not blind to the price, admitting that, "To the European

---

[1] Jaspers, Karl. (2021 [1949]). *The Origin and Goal of History,* p. 15.
[2] Jaspers, Karl. (2021 [1949]). *The Origin and Goal of History,* p. 15.
[3] Jaspers, Karl. (2021 [1949]). *The Origin and Goal of History, p.* 87.
[4] Jaspers, Karl. (2021 [1949]). *The Origin and Goal of History, p.* 88.
[5] Jaspers, Karl. (2021 [1949]). *The Origin and Goal of History, p.* 79-80.

consciousness of that time, the rest of the world was colonial territory, of secondary importance, destined as a source of booty for Europe."[1]

To explain the European breakaway from other Axial civilizations, Jaspers highlights three factors. First, the prophetic religion of the Hebrew "set the minds of men free from magic and the transcendence of objects with a radicality such as had not occurred anywhere else on earth." Although it did so "only for a historically limited moment and for a small number of people, it left its message in the Book for all who came after and who were capable of hearing it."[2]

Second, the Greeks "created a clarity of distinctions, a plasticity of spiritual forms and a consistency in the operations of reason never before attained anywhere in the world."[3] Finally,

> Christianity realised awareness of the most extreme transcendence – as India and China also succeeded in doing – but with the difference that Christianity fettered this realisation to the world of immanence, and thereby brought about the perpetual unrest involved in the task of giving a Christian conformation to the world.[4]

In other words, the Judaic transformation of magic into ethic with the message written in the Book, the clarity of Hellenic reasoning, and the Christian thirst for salvation coupled with messianism (out of "perpetual unrest") enabled Judeo-Christian tradition to succeed the most among the initial Axial civilizations in spreading the Axial virus of uniformity.

Jaspers, however, does not explain why these three factors remained dormant for a millennium until the 1500s, causing Europe to lag behind technologically and culturally compared to the more advanced civilizations of the East. He mentions printing but does not give it significant consideration. Jaspers often notices the outcomes of media effects but does not see media effects themselves.

The European pivot in the 15th and 16th centuries was so significant that Jaspers even asks himself, if "Europe's exceptional spiritual achievements from 1500 to 1800, that outshine science and technology – Michelangelo,

---

[1] Jaspers, Karl. (2021 [1949]). *The Origin and Goal of History*, p. 144.
[2] Jaspers, Karl. (2021 [1949]). *The Origin and Goal of History*, p. 87.
[3] Jaspers, Karl. (2021 [1949]). *The Origin and Goal of History*, p. 88.
[4] Jaspers, Karl. (2021 [1949]). *The Origin and Goal of History*, p. 88.

Raphael, Leonardo, Shakespeare, Rembrandt, Goethe, Spinoza, Kant, Bach, Mozart" can be recognized as the second Axial Age. But no, he concludes that the rise of Europe after the 1500s did not comprise the second Axial Age: "The purity and clarity, the ingenuousness and freshness of the worlds of the first axis are not repeated."[1]

World history, at last

The latest pivot in history, which was almost as significant as the Axial Age itself, was the Technological Age. It started in Europe in the 1500s and then spread around the world. The uniformity of cultural values founded in the Axial Age and the uniformity of technological advancements established in the Technological Age led humankind to the third, latest, stage in the historical development of humankind, which we are entering now, writes Jaspers in 1949. This phase is the actual "world history." According to Jaspers, "there has been no world history until now, but only an aggregate of local histories."[2] Eventually, the various local histories started merging into one history for all of humankind.

This is how three successive phases, *prehistory*, *history* (of civilizations), and *world history*, in Jaspers' view, constitute the "whole of history."

The historical tendency towards the uniformity of humankind was initially shaped in the Axial Age and ultimately enforced by the European powers that not only wanted to expand but also were technologically capable of expanding to other continents. The turn from local histories to world history meant that different countries started using same technologies within the same agenda.

The most obvious confirmation of this global unity was... the world wars. As Jaspers put it,

> In the First World War these spaces were already brought into play. It was still a European war, however... It was only in the Second World War that all of them, the whole globe, were committed to the full... In fact it was the first real World War. World history, as one single history of the whole world, had begun.[3]

---

[1] Jaspers, Karl. (2021 [1949]). *The Origin and Goal of History*, p. 88.

[2] Jaspers, Karl. (2021 [1949]). *The Origin and Goal of History*, p. 32.

[3] Jaspers, Karl. (2021 [1949]). *The Origin and Goal of History*, p. 144.

Through the global wars and their resolutions, humankind came to be one for the first time. The treaties after the world wars decided the fates of the continents[1] and, eventually, the entire world. Even though many nations remained uninvolved in making decisions, they were affected by the global political-economic, cultural, or technological development anyway. Jaspers does not mention it, but the commencement of world history was marked not only by the world wars but also by the emergence of new international entities. The League of Nations was organized in 1920 and represented 58 countries in its peak in 1934. The United Nations was organized in 1945 and eventually incorporated all the countries in the world (193 countries in 2022).

The principal novelty of these organizations was that they were not alliances of allies. They united not only nations that maintained friendly or trade relations but also nations that were enemies and did not want to maintain any relations whatsoever. But, in the spirit of Jaspers' "world history," they joined the worldwide political and cultural movement, thus literally representing all of humankind in an institutionalized form.

The local histories of nations continue in parallels – in the same manner as we still can observe some rare cases of people living in prehistory. But world history is also evident: it is structured and even institutionalized. The differences remain, but at a certain level of generalization, all humans have acquired and embraced the shared values of humanism, living standards, the standards of human rights, business standards, the standards of communication, and so on. In the 20th century, for the first time in history, the globally shared agenda emerged. Religious or political regimes that oppose the globally shared agenda and values are universally condemned; therefore, they are a part of the global world anyway. Any significant divide – say, between progressives and conservatives – is global and, actually, unifying. Lately, a trend has emerged that rejects universality as a colonialist principle, thus establishing a colonialist universality of the next level. Even antiglobalism is, in fact, the best proof that globalization has happened.

As Jaspers writes:

---

[1] Jaspers was right: WWI was not an actual *world* war. The Treaty of Versailles in 1919 regulated inner European affairs. But WWII ended with a series of decisions that not only remapped Europe but also established a new political and economic order in the entire world, to which the foundation of the United Nations in 1945 was the best proof.

> The essential fact is: There is no longer anything outside. The world is closed. The unity of the earth has arrived. New perils and new opportunities are revealed. All the crucial problems have become world problems, the situation a situation of mankind.[1]

The coming of humans into the unity of humankind is, according to Jaspers, the "goal of history," the completion of the long history with its pivotal moment, the Axial Age, when the main principles of this unity, in however simple forms, were revealed and established.

In the concluding chapters of his treatise, Jaspers speculates about the nature of this newly forming worldwide human unity. He suggests that it could lead to either a "world empire" or a "world order." He implies that this outcome will be determined by the civic and cultural choices of humankind, which are rooted in our understanding of history.

Communication media do not slip past Jaspers' attention. Describing the upcoming unity of the world, Jaspers writes:

> What is historically new and, for the first time in history, decisive about our situation is the real unity of mankind on the earth. The planet has become for man a single whole dominated by the technology of communications; it is 'smaller' than the Roman Empire was formerly.[2]

The last sentence sounds like Jaspers stopped just short of saying "global village." The context and metaphor are indeed strikingly similar to those Marshal McLuhan used when describing the effects of electronic communications: "The Global Village is at once as wide as the planet and as small as a little town."[3] Ten to fifteen years before McLuhan, Jaspers comes to the same idea: communications made the world small ("smaller than the Roman Empire"). Because of communication, everything is within arm's reach for everyone. This global proximity, induced by communication technologies, has made the world become one.

---

[1] Jaspers, Karl. (2021 [1949]). The Origin and Goal of History, p. 144.

[2] Jaspers, Karl. (2021 [1949]). The Origin and Goal of History, p. 143.

[3] Film *This Is Marshall McLuhan: The Medium Is the Massage.* (1967). Directed by Guy Fraumeni and Ernest Pintoff. 17:00.

3. What caused the Axial Age?

The legacy of the first civilizations: necessary but not sufficient

As a meaningful feature of the Axial Age, Jaspers emphasizes not only the emergence of reflexiveness but also the "total universal parallelism" of reflexiveness in three independent regions. The key thinkers and ideas appeared "during these few centuries almost simultaneously in China, India, and the West, without any one of these regions knowing of the others."[1] He sees this mysterious coincidence as "the manifestation of some profound common element, the one primal source of humanity."[2]

This common element did not emerge wherever humans settled across the globe; it appeared in these three specific areas in this specific time. So, the mystery of the Axial Age has a temporal and spatial dimension.

The time and space specificity of the Axial Age dismisses the assumption that the awakening of human reflexiveness occurred simply in an inevitable time when the human race developed enough and reached the needed conditions. Human neurophysiology might have been innately "designed" for reflexiveness, but the Axial Age was not experienced by every local culture. On the contrary, it took root only in very specific and incredibly small areas as compared to the general proliferation of humans across the planet. Other cultures did not experience the Axial Age but rather integrated, sooner or later, those fundamental "common elements" of spirituality first revealed in the Axial Age by the Axial civilizations.

Even the three regions that hosted the Axial Age remained isolated. They developed separately with very little awareness of each other until only a few centuries ago. And it was not until the present, as Jaspers writes, when local cultures finally started becoming united in all possible political, economic, and cultural ways, with shared values, standards, hopes, crises, and wars.

The spatial riddle of the Axial Age mystery is perhaps the easiest to solve. The Axial Age happened in the cultural footsteps of ancient civilizations that grew in complexity due to a need for river control.

---

[1] Jaspers, Karl. (2021 [1949]). *The Origin and Goal of History*, p. 9.

[2] Jaspers, Karl. (2021 [1949]). *The Origin and Goal of History*, p. 20.

Nevertheless, not all early agrarian civilizations contributed directly to the Axial Age. The Egyptian and Mesopotamian cultures had existed for more than 2000 years before the Axial Age and "did not give birth to any Axial Period," according to Jaspers.[1] Their legacy was in part carried into the Axial Age by the Hebrews and the Greeks. Something that did not happen to the Egyptians and Sumerians/Akkadians happened to the Hebrews and Greeks. The same historical and cultural gap divided the first civilizations and the Axial Age in India and China.

So, the simple presence of an ancient civilization did not automatically lead to the Axial Age. The precedency of the first civilizations might have been necessary but not the only factor needed for the Axial Age to begin.

Media effects of horses

The most plausible hypothesis Jaspers observes as a possible cause for the Axial Age is Alfred Weber's theory about the invasion of equestrian people from the Eurasian Steppe.

The people of the Great Steppe domesticated horses, which lived there in plenty, sometime in the 4th millennium BCE. Horse riding and transportation, along with using chariots, made the people of the Steppe unrivalled migrants, raiders, and conquerors of the time. Little material evidence of their conquests survived through time except for that of the greatest importance – language.

The language the equestrian people spread across Eurasia is considered the Proto-Indo-European language. It contributed to the languages spoken now by most of humankind. The media-deterministic connection between the domestication of horses in the Steppe in the 4th millennium BCE, the migration of the horsemen in the 3rd to 1st millennia BCE, and the contemporary world map of languages is fascinating.

People of the Eurasian Steppe had very specific conditions that predefined their way of life and social structure. Unlike "cereal" – agrarian – civilizations that were tied to sources of water and led a sedentary lifestyle, people of the Steppe had to be pastoral nomads or semi-nomads. They were tied to the cycles of their herds and therefore to the Steppe seasons, not to the cycles of crops and rivers. Travelling with herds and

---

[1] Jaspers, Karl. (2021 [1949]). *The Origin and Goal of History*, p. 71.

carrying belongings meant settling down temporarily at new places all the time. Appropriating and re-appropriating lands for pastures and settlements along certain routes of migration was at the core of their provision strategy and cultural code.

Such a lifestyle favoured opportunism and a rather high level of aggressiveness (as compared to cereal farmers). Kinship was maintained not through land but through the lineage of cattle owners and warriors. Unlike the agrarian cultures with their significant matriarchal element reflecting the fertility of the land, nomads were more predisposed to patrilineal and patriarchal social regulation, with an emphasis on masculinity and aggression due to the practices of pathfinding, appropriation, and conquest.

Affordance dictates. Once you acquire a means of transportation, you can no longer remain a homebody. The capacity of the horse to cover large distances dictated the movement of the Steppe people across the continent in all directions. The media revolution of harnessing horsepower was one of the most fundamental in history. A band of horse riders in a month could travel the distance that cereal people would not have traveled in their lives or in the combined lives of several generations. The historically instantaneous mixture of different cultures, including two completely opposite types of culture, nomadic and sedentary, occurred for the first time in history and led to the decline or reshaping of those first agrarian civilizations.

Before horses, the opportunism and aggressiveness of the nomads had been an internal problem of the Great Steppe. With horses, it became the problem of the entire continent.[1]

The genetic data show that, at some points in the history of different local cultures in Europe and Asia, there was a sudden arrival of the external paternal lineage specific to the people of the Steppe. The Eurasian nations of horsemen and charioteers penetrated Europe and the Mediterranean by the end of the third millennium. Another wave reached Iran and India in about 2000-1000 BCE. The spread of horse-riding technology also reached China by the end of the second millennium. Thus, by the beginning of the first millennia BCE, sometime 200–300 years before Jaspers' Axial Age, all

[1] Considering the later importance of the stirrup for the Mongolian Empire and feudalism in Europe, it can be said that horses were one of the most important mediums in the history of humankind on par with fire, the wheel, writing, printing, and electricity.

three Axial regions had experienced the invasion of the horse-riding nomadic spirit, a complete opposite to the sedentary lifestyle.

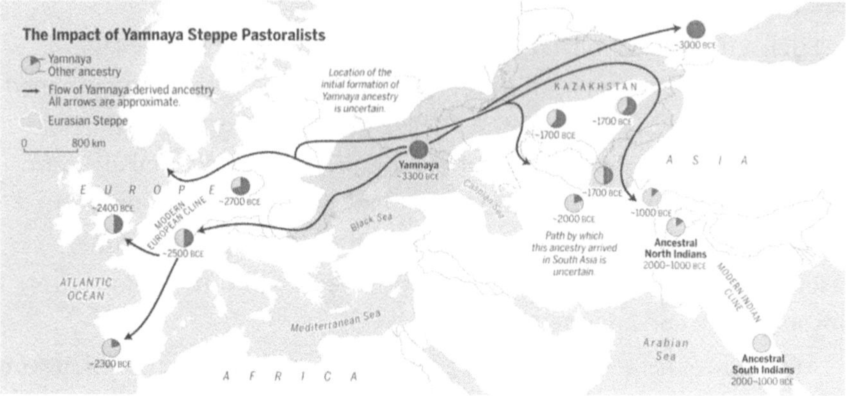

Figure 6. The Bronze Age spread of Yamnaya Steppe pastoralist ancestry into two subcontinents – Europe and South Asia. Pie charts reflect the proportion of Yamnaya ancestry, and dates reflect the earliest available ancient DNA with Yamnaya ancestry in each region. Source: Narasimhan, Vagheesh M., et al. (2019). "The formation of human populations in South and Central Asia."

Whether through military conquest due to superior forms of warfare or just fast migration, the Eurasian tribes of horse riders arrived at all surrounding regions and introduced horses to cultures that had previously not known them. This had to make a huge impact. The armed farmers or even professional foot soldiers of the pre-equestrian cultures must have been shocked upon seeing approaching cavalry. We can find a demonstration of this impact in comparatively recent history. For the indigenous peoples of the Americas, seeing a mounted Spaniard would signify the end of the world they had known, both metaphorically and literally. Riding a mighty animal three to four times the size of human had to appear as a god-like ability, especially for sedentary people that had not seen many new things in their lives.

But the military superiority of the horse riders was not the only or the decisive factor of the cultural shock. In two or three generations, the indigenous people of the river valley civilizations would learn to ride horses, as the indigenous people of the Americas learned in their time. But the mastery of riding would change the perception of the world and the world itself.

What was so special about the people who rode horses, wagons, and chariots? The difference between them and the previous cultures of cattle breeders and plant growers was tremendous. Referring to Weber, Jaspers writes:

> The men of these equestrian peoples came to experience, thanks to the horse, the limitless vastness of the world. They took over the ancient civilisations by conquest. In hazards and disasters they experienced the problematic character of existence, as master-peoples they developed an heroico-tragic consciousness that found expression in the epic. <...> History became a conflict between these two forces: the old, stable, unawakened matriarchal powers against the new, mobile, liberating tendencies of the equestrian peoples which were rising into consciousness.[1]

Unlike ancient infantry or farmer militias, for which numbers mattered the most, horseback riding and riding war chariots emphasized individual mastery over complex battle "equipment." The use of a new and superior battle technique "brought with it a spirit of mastery that is bound up with the taming and curbing of the horse, the courage of the rider and conqueror and the feeling for the beauty of the animal," according to Jaspers.[2]

Due to the ability to cover large distances, the horseman is not immersed in a familiar environment. This cultivated a distinct ethos of solitude in individuals who confronted an unknown destiny/environment that required taming/colonization. The environment is always strange to the horsemen, so they must rely on themselves, their medium (their tamed but powerful animals), and the comradery of the fellow raiders, who are always looking for a good Wild Hunt.

The clash between sedentary and nomadic mentalities

Jaspers mentions the invasion of the equestrian people in the future Axial regions as a possible precursor for the Axial Age to emerge but does

---

[1] Jaspers, Karl. (2021 [1949]). *The Origin and Goal of History*, p. 24.

[2] Jaspers, Karl. (2021 [1949]). *The Origin and Goal of History, p*. 55.

not accept it as a sufficient cause. We could ponder this topic a little more and see what the nomadic mentality could contribute.

Some findings in genetics, archaeology and mythology allow speculation that young males of these tribes would gather into sorts of training camps somewhere outside of main settlements. These bachelor warbands are known in ethnography as "koryos," the groups of unmarried warriors who were temporarily exiled from their tribe to protect the community from their aggression and direct their violence toward outsiders. In Europe, the latest Great Steppe iteration of the koryos might be seen in the Cossacks, whose culture has survived until modern times. Another ethnographic footprint of the koryos that survived through at least five millennia can be the folklore motif of the Wild Hunt and also the story of Snow White and the Seven Dwarfs, though generously romanticized.

In such bachelor warbands, adolescents and young men would go through cruel rites of passage, acquire the skills of fighting and robbery, protect their communities from others, rob others and take their wealth and females. While in bands of koryos, they would establish their military brotherhood and also military alliances with the bachelor warbands of other tribes. Eventually, the koryos would either become the conquerors of strangers' lands or return to their native community. In both cases, they would get married, settle down and form military aristocracies in the respective communities.

The painful rites of passage;[1] the individual bonds with the powerful animal; the nobility earned in raiding, looting, enslaving, and murdering; the spirit of an explorer and warrior – all of this shaped not only a more opportunistic and aggressive but also a more individualistic mentality with a hyper-emphasized role of honour in social regulation. This was a completely different type of mentality, unknown to agrarian civilizations.

The assault of horse rider culture on the old farmer settlements happened historically instantly. As geneticist and anthropologist Razib Khan writes,

> Additionally, while the earliest farmers seem to have incrementally opened the land for cultivation in small clusters of families that

---

[1] Ritualistic trial by pain for acceptance is perhaps the first glimpse of individualism in human history. In showing skills, apprentices repeat and eventually replicate their masters. As for pain, it's only yours. By overcoming physical suffering, a young koryos would prove himself.

> diffused outward as a gradual wavefront, colonizing new territories over thousands of years, the herders from the steppe hit Europe like a thunderclap. It took just a few centuries after 3000 BC for masses of young men on the hunt for new pasturelands, wives and slaves to remake most of the continent in their patriarchal, pastoral image.[1]

But horse riding itself could not and did not cause the Axial Age. The proof is simple: the Eurasian Steppe, the cradle of horse riding, is not known either for hosting ancient civilizations or for participation in the Axial Age. Whatever spiritual traits the horsemen possessed, the historically decisive effect of these traits was unveiled only after their interaction with the ancient sedentary civilizations of river valleys. The arrival of horsemen initiated the transformation of these civilizations.

The mythology of sedentary cultures has to be mostly about survival through adaptation to the cycles of life, specifically the cycles of the river. The world of a river-valley dweller has to be heavily rigid and ritualistic. Following seasonal protocols is the foundation of well-being and survival. There is neither demand nor even room for innovation. The way of acquiring knowledge is accumulation and compliance, not exploring and probing. A farmer family succeeds when it merges with the environment at least for several seasons, while a nomad is always an invasive species and destined to behave accordingly. A farmer invests and produces, whereas a nomad searches and takes.

To use McLuhan's language, the river-valley culture has to be environmental, while the equestrian culture has to be anti-environmental. Nomads always come to take. Their environmental "awareness" is close to zero. Their environmental "accountability" is embedded not in their arrangements with the divine patrons of local resources but in the migratory pattern of nomads themselves. They exhaust local resources and go, letting the local ecosystem replenish – if it still can. If it cannot, the migratory route will change. This way of consuming Nature is completely opposite to the farmers' lifestyle and ethos. "They came, they took, they surely slaughtered, and they clearly fathered," writes geneticist Razib Khan about the Steppe nomads.[2]

---

[1] Khan, Razib. (2022, April 25). "Euro Vision (part 2). Eurasia's End." *Razib Khan's Unsupervised Learning Blog*.

[2] Khan, Razib. (2021, May 7). "Steppe 1.0, Going Nomad. The early Indo-Europeans' great leap forward." *Razib Khan's Unsupervised Learning Blog*.

The mythology of river-valley cultures also must be filled with a sense of commonality (river control is a collective enterprise), with a significant matriarchal element, hence the powerful cults of the goddesses of fertility in the Egyptian and Sumerian cultures. Such mythology has to be about preserving, keeping, rebirthing, and restoring. On the contrary, the mythology of a horse-riding culture has to be about conquest, looting, fighting, and becoming. It has to give significant consideration to the individualistic spirit of heroes – the "heroico-tragic consciousness" mentioned by Jaspers.

In sedentary cultures, changes are divine. Within the divine order of things, decisions belong to gods. People can only ask, negotiate, or guess. Their agency over their own life is almost indistinguishable. Rulers are also considered to be gods. If there are outstanding individuals, such as kings, magicians, or warriors, they are demigods as well or bound with gods in some other ways.

There are no natural cycles or divine will in riding a horse. A horse awaits a rider to command where to go – a rider makes choices. Since significant distances can be covered, the probability of the unknown in tomorrow's settings grows. Where will the riders and horses sleep and drink the next day? What will they eat? What gains and troubles await them? The repetition of yesterday's experience might not meet the demands of tomorrow.

Travelling entails adaptive and innovative behaviour. Human decision-making is embedded in the affordances of horse-riding. Divine forces interfere, of course, but a rider contributes with his decisions and shares responsibility for the outcome. By owning their decisions, humans grew into the masters of their fate.

The very settings of these two cultures create two different types of individuals. A river-valley individual is innately endowed with a static property of *belonging*. A horse-riding individual is innately tasked with the dynamic challenge of *becoming*.

In the clash of the horse riders with the river-valley civilizations, the two cultures merged. The oxen were disturbed by the horses. If Troy had been captured by the "earliest Greeks" – the non-Indo-European Minoans of Crete – and not by the Indo-European Mycenaeans, the computer virus malware today would have been called a "Trojan Ox," not a "Trojan Horse."

The heavy *ritualism* of the river-valley civilizations was disrupted by the innate *opportunism* of the equestrian invaders. The natural and supernatural knowledge accumulated by the greatest ancient civilizations over millennia of observations of natural cycles was injected with human agency trained to manage tomorrow and fate in unknown conditions.

This is a prerequisite of the Axial Age that Jaspers looked for. In such an amalgamation, the individual appears – the first true human individual, not some analog embodiment of supernatural forces. Listing the processes that characterized the "leap from mere happening into history," Jaspers marks out, among other factors, this "emergence of men" – "in the shape of rulers and sages, whose deeds, achievements and destinies were in full view of the masses – this was the first step toward setting men free from the apathy of self-awareness and the fear of demons."[1]

This started happening in the ancient civilizations affected by the mentality of the horse riders. Heroes and kings might claim that their origins descended from gods, but they steadily grew more and more human. The Axial Age signified the shaping of human individuality. This Jaspers' observation is worth repeating:

> For the first time philosophers appeared. Human beings dared to rely on themselves as individuals... Man proved capable of contrasting himself inwardly with the entire universe. He discovered within himself the origin from which to raise himself above his own self and the world.[2]

Heroes, kings and queens, prophets, sages, and the like were the first discernible human *identities*. They not only represented the divine before humans but also began representing humans before the divine.

The emergence of outstanding human actors and their juxtaposition to the masses simultaneously signified also the emergence of politics, because heroes, king, and prophets needed the masses of admirers and followers and, in one way or another, competed for their attention/loyalty. With magic turning into religion and the emergence of noble individuals within sedentary civilizations, politics separated from cults.

So, the equestrian theory might explain the uniformity between different Axial cultures in three independent Axial regions invaded by

[1] Jaspers, Karl. (2021 [1949]). *The Origin and Goal of History*, p. 56.

[2] Jaspers, Karl. (2021 [1949]). *The Origin and Goal of History*, p. 10.

horse riders in the course of the second millennium BCE, as well as the absence of Axial events in Egypt and Babylonia, which were less affected by the equestrian invasion and better preserved their ritualism.

Nevertheless, Jaspers points out some aspects that reject the equestrian theory as a satisfactory explanation for the Axial Age's origin. Particularly, as Jaspers notes, heroic sagas and the epic were of paramount importance for the "Indo-German people" – Indians, Greeks, Teutons, as well as Celts, Slavs and the later Persians, who "discovered, shaped and evolved the tragic spirit." But "the Jews and Chinese, who were so essential to the Axial Period, are not Indo-Germanic at all."[1]

Moreover, the Semitic people "experienced no mingling with equestrian peoples and yet, through the prophets, produced an essential factor in the spiritual creation of the Axial Period."[2] The same goes for China, "which produced the rich contents of the Axial Period, but neither the tragic consciousness nor the epic."[3]

Most importantly, the invasion of Eurasian nomads into surrounding lands in the West, South and East lasted for more than a thousand years. It did not trigger the local Axial events in the affected lands immediately. This millennium could be seen as the "incubation" period for the Axial Age, according to Jaspers. He highlights that the spiritual development of the Axial Age was a long process, but the Axial Age itself happened with "astonishingly exact simultaneity." He writes: "Geographical situations and historical constellations may have given rise to the preconditions; but what set the work of creation in motion remains the great enigma."[4]

The enigma of the Axial Age through the lens of media ecology

Horses with wagons and chariots, which enabled the great migration of nations in the 3rd to 1st millennia BCE and the following clash between sedentary and nomadic mentalities, were the first medium that likely contributed to the Axial Age. Another medium was writing, which emerged and developed into its phonetic forms in the same time period.

---

1 Jaspers, Karl. (2021 [1949]). *The Origin and Goal of History*, p. 65-66.

2 Jaspers, Karl. (2021 [1949]). *The Origin and Goal of History*, p. 25.

3 Jaspers, Karl. (2021 [1949]). *The Origin and Goal of History*, p. 24.

4 Jaspers, Karl. (2021 [1949]). *The Origin and Goal of History*, p. 24.

Jaspers tied writing to the tasks of organizing river control. This involved the temple bureaucracy that, on the one hand, accumulated the "divine" knowledge of high waters and droughts and, on the other hand, directed irrigation works while taking offerings in return. All these tasks required recording certain events and transactions – calendar/celestial, meteorological, engineering, commercial, etc.

Writing also signified the beginning of history, according to Jaspers. He writes:

> History extends as far back as linguistic evidence. ...All non-verbal artifacts from prehistoric excavations seem to us lifeless in their dumb silence. ...Nowhere does linguistic evidence extend further back than 3000 B.C. History has therefore lasted about 5,000 years.[1]

According to Jaspers, the material artifacts of the earlier periods might indicate the complexity of cultural life, but they remained prehistoric – until something was written. To simplify, irrigation pushed history to begin, but history started with writing. The first civilizations left written records – this is how we know they were civilizations.

Similar ideas were expressed, but from the angle of linguistics, by Ignace Gelb, a historian linguist who studied the origins of writing systems. According to him,

> All the factors - geographic, social, economic - leading towards a full civilization simultaneously created a complex of conditions which could not function without writing. ... *Writing exists only in a civilization and a civilization cannot exist without writing.*[2]

Assessing the role of writing in the beginning of history, Jaspers points at its socio-forming power, totally in a media ecological sense. He notices that "The indispensability of writing to administration led to the acquisition of a dominant social position by the scribes, who formed an intellectual aristocracy."[3] This resonates with one of Harold Innis' main concepts, the "monopoly of knowledge." As this monopoly belonged to the class of priests, they were the managerial class that exercised power on behalf of a divine ruler (king, pharaoh).

---

1 Jaspers, Karl. (2021 [1949]). *The Origin and Goal of History*, p. 36.

2 Gelb, Ignace. (1963 [1952]). *A study of writing*. pp. 221-222, italicized by Gelb.

3 Jaspers, Karl. (2021 [1949]). *The Origin and Goal of History*, p. 55.

Writing, however, itself had a long history of evolution. It started sometime in 3300–3100 BCE in Mesopotamia and Egypt, 25 centuries before the Axial Age. At the same time, thinking of Jaspers' periodization of the Axial Age – 800–200 BCE – any media ecologist immediately recognizes the very specific time of writing's development: the invention and initial proliferation of the alphabet.

The concept of the alphabet effect was developed by Robert Logan at the suggestion of Marshall McLuhan. Here's how the idea of the alphabet effect began to take shape. In the 1970s, Robert Logan, now professor emeritus at the University of Toronto, taught his seminar, "The Poetry of Physics and the Physics of Poetry." After working for three months in Mexico with futurist Ivan Illich in 1974, Logan decided to organize similar futurist studies in Toronto and started recruiting professors.

One professor, who happened to be the associate director of McLuhan's Centre for Culture and Technology, suggested to invite McLuhan and called him. When he mentioned Logan's name, McLuhan asked: "is that the Bob Logan who teaches the 'Poetry of Physics' course?" After receiving an affirmative answer, McLuhan said to send Logan over for a luncheon.

At the lunch, McLuhan asked what Logan had learned while teaching the course "The Poetry of Physics." Logan explained that he was fascinated by the problem posed by Joseph Needham, a British biochemist, historian of science and sinologist, of why abstract science began in the West despite the fact that so many technologies had originated in China. Logan proposed that since monotheism and codified law were unique to the West and that together they gave rise to a notion of universal law, this might explain the Needham paradox. McLuhan nodded approvingly and then asked: "Bob, what else do we have in the West that is not present in China?" As Logan recollected, he was totally intimidated by McLuhan, who seemed to be "talking at 100 miles per hour." When Logan admitted he gave up, McLuhan smiled and said, "The alphabet, of course."[1]

McLuhan and Logan then co-authored an article, "Alphabet, mother of invention," published by Neil Postman in *Et Cetera* in 1977.[2] Interestingly,

---

1 Robert Logan recollects the details of the conversations with McLuhan in his memoir: Logan, Robert K. (2020) "'The alphabet, of course': How I met Marshall McLuhan." *The New Explorations Blog*. Also see: Logan, Robert. (2004 [1986]). *The Alphabet Effect*, p. 6.

2 McLuhan, Marshall, and Logan, Robert. (1977). "Alphabet, mother of invention". *Et Cetera*, pp. 373-383.

in response to the article, Neil Postman wrote to Marshall McLuhan that this was "the best paper McLuhan had written from a left-brain point of view." This was, of course, due to the contribution of Logan, a physicist. McLuhan usually "wrote" by dictating his texts to his secretary or co-authors using numerous metaphors and provocative "probes," as he called them. But this time, it was Logan who recorded and refined their collaborative work. This is why Postman recognized it as a "left-brain" writing (more logical, analytical, and sequential as opposed to "right-hemisphere" thinking, which is more imaginative, intuitive, and holistic).

Later, Logan developed these ideas in his 1986 book *The Alphabet Effect.* To my knowledge, neither McLuhan nor Logan saw the parallels between the alphabet effect and Jaspers' idea of the Axial Age. Robert Logan started thinking about this parallelism after I told him about my work on this project sometime in 2022. Nevertheless, Logan and McLuhan identified, basically, the same processes that culminated in Jaspers' Axial Age, but from a different perspective. As Logan recollects,

> We concluded that all of these innovations, including codified law in Mesopotamia, the alphabet in the Sinai, monotheism in Israel, science and logic in Greece, arose within the very narrow geographic zone between the Tigris-Euphrates river system and the Aegean Sea, and within the very narrow time frame between 2000 B.C. and 500 B.C.[1]

They suggested that codified law, the alphabet, monotheism, abstract science and deductive logic created an environment for their mutual development. All these key factors of civilizational development can be represented through the history of writing, with its culmination in the alphabet sometime in the 8th–5th centuries BCE, precisely at the beginning of Jaspers' Axial Age.

Jaspers mentions the alphabet only once, very tangentially, just as a form of later writing development. He sees neither specific effects, no role of the alphabet in the Axial Age nor in any historical processes he describes. In the meantime, even the brief description of the social and cognitive transformations tied to the alphabet effects immediately indicates an overlap with the main effects of the Axial Age.

---

[1] Logan, Robert K. (2020) "'The alphabet, of course': How I met Marshall McLuhan." *The New Explorations Blog*.

The hypothesis about the parallelism between the alphabet effect and the Axial Age would have been a perfect solution to the enigma of the Axial Age's origins had it not created yet another mystery instead: the mystery of China. China has never had an alphabet but still heavily contributed to the Axial Age, according to Jaspers.

Nevertheless, the synchronicity of the Axial Age with the alphabet is so seductive and the similarity of the alphabet effects to the effects of the Axial Age is so inviting that the connection between the alphabet and the Axial Age will be explored. As for the inconvenient mystery of China, it will be dealt with separately in a later chapter.

Additionally, Walter Ong and Eric Havelock in their explorations of the cultural transition from orality to literacy, essentially reiterated the main characteristics of Jaspers' Axial Age. This parallelism particularly transpires in Havelock's analysis of Plato's rebellion against Homeric poetry (read: against the mindset of orality) and in Ong's concept of the "inward turn" that literacy caused in human consciousness.

As far as I know, Jaspers' concept of Axial Age has never been examined from the perspective of media ecology and media effects. Filling this gap might hold some academic interest. Most importantly, however, it will shed light on the digital future, as digital media of our times started a reversal replay of Jaspers' Axial Age, bringing us from Axial "self-reflexiveness" back to the pre-Axial hypnotic and selfless state of environmental immersion. The difference is that the environment in which we are now getting immersed is new – it is the digitally induced environment. McLuhan, once again, foresaw this: "The new media are not bridges between man and nature; they are nature."[1]

[1] McLuhan, Eric, and Zingrone, Frank, editors. (2005). *Essential McLuhan*, p. 201.

Today's reversal replay of the Axial Age can be understood by examining the media effects of orality and literacy and their mutual transformations, which occurred during the development of writing.

4. The history of writing

Binding time: from cave paintings to writing

According to the latest scholarly consensus, writing was invented independently in the Near East, China, and Mesoamerica.[1] Concerning the regions of the Axial Age, writing appeared around 3300 BCE in Mesopotamia, around 3200 BCE in Egypt, in the early 2nd millennium BCE in the Indus valley,[2] and in the mid-2nd millennium BCE in China.

Cave paintings, of course, were known to humans long before writing. Some pictures on cave walls and ceilings are reported to be 35–40 thousand years old. But the very nature of cave paintings was artistic and mystic rather than aimed at preserving memory.

Cave paintings reflected emotions and, as a medium, extended feelings. Notations dealt with time and, as a medium, extended memory. Of course, the boundary can be blurred, as cave paintings de facto also served for memorization or instruction. But this was not the primary impulse for their creation; rather, it was a side-effect. Any notations, on the contrary, even the most primitive ones, expressed neither a mystical admiration of the world nor emotional impressions of events. They stored raw data for later retrieval. There is no other purpose in scratching marks other than conveying their count as a record of an event through time. The consensus among scholars leans toward the hypothesis that writing originated from the notations of counting.[3]

Hunters and gatherers could leave marks to return to valuable findings; they could leave signs marking a path or territory. However, these would be just markings of a spot or territory, not much different from those made by

---

[1] See, for example: Schmandt-Besserat, Denise. (2014). "The Evolution of Writing" In: James Wright, editor, *International Encyclopedia of Social and Behavioral Sciences*, Elsevier.

[2] Dating back to the 3rd millennium BCE, the inscriptions of the first major civilization in India, the Indus (or Harappan) civilization, were very short. So, it is not clear whether they represented a fully fledged writing system or just a set of symbols for pottery marking or seals. The inscriptions have not been deciphered yet. The fully developed writing system in India appeared by the 3rd century BCE – the Brahmi script and some others.

[3] The hypothesis of writing's origin out of counting belongs to Denise Schmandt-Besserat and is largely accepted by archeologists.

animals. Interestingly, the content of the most ancient cave paintings often consisted of hand stencils. The oldest ones, found in the Cave of Maltravieso, Spain, were dated to 64,000 years ago. This was a time when mostly Neanderthals, not Homo sapiens, inhabited Europe. A hand stencil basically meant "John was here." It was a "physiological" signal of presence sent not to other animals but to fellow humans, because only humans could recognize the iconic sign (in Pierce's terminology) already carrying some symbolic meaning of presence.

Of course, spatial markings had a temporal dimension, as a mark would be "read" sometime later. But the meaning of territorial marks was bound to space, not time.

It took millennia for humans to develop the temporal significance of marking over the spatial significance. The notches symbolizing the number of passed goods or passed moons signified, perhaps, the first human experience of abstraction – the abstraction from the immediate "here and now." The significance of such notations was not tied to locating space but exclusively to extending meaning in time. It signified the withdrawal from being immersed in the immediate environment, the withdrawal from "living-now" – a cognitive operation that animals are incapable of.

This recalls the taxonomy of three classes of life proposed by Alfred Korzybski, the founder of general semantics. In his 1921 book *Manhood of Humanity*, he set out to define what is uniquely human in humans. He posited that plants are energy-binding, animals are space-binding, and humans are time-binding[1] (to which Douglas Rushkoff added 98 years later: "... and computers are human-binding."[2])

Promethean media helped people better bind space. They helped people become better animals in resisting the harsh forces of Nature and prevailing over other animals. This is essentially what the myth of Prometheus is about – the Promethean gifts compensated humans for the lack of powers given to other animals. But on top of this, humans also developed the ability to bind time. Binding time made humans capable of using a resource that is not available to either plants or animals – the lessons of life learned by previous generations.

---

[1] Korzybski, Alfred. (2022 [1921]). *Manhood of Humanity*, pp. 140-141.

[2] "If plants bind energy, animals bind space, and humans bind time, then what do networked algorithms bind? They bind *us*. On the internet of things, we the *people* are the things." – Rushkoff, Douglas. (2019). *Team Human*, p. 74-75.

Before writing, the human ability of time binding was limited to collective memory, language, mythology, and tribal cultural heritage. All these abilities were tied to their carriers, humans themselves. Writing became the first post-Promethean medium. It detached the time-binding function from its carriers, humans, and assumed this function itself. Yes, writing can also bind space, as it is capable of conveying messages across distances. However, its function of binding space is more of a derivative – a useful side effect of its primary time-binding function.

Since the time-binding capacity of humans was greatly enhanced by writing, it becomes clear why writing marked the onset of both history and civilization. Before the advent of writing, humans were the foremost space-binding species, with some capacity for time-binding. With writing, time-binding irrevocably withdrew humans from competition with animals and put them into a league of their own, the league of historical beings, humankind.

The paradoxical and worrying reversal occurred with the advent of electronic media. Unlike writing and printing, electronic media are space-biased according to Innis and therefore space-binding according to Korzybski. But since the capacity of electronic and now digital media to bind space has no spatial limitation, they can also be called space-ignorant. Space of any magnitude does not matter for digital media; they connect the ends of any distance instantly. As there is no spatial delay in content transportation, electric and now digital media flatten time back into "now" and return the temporal frame of perception to a tribal state (McLuhan's "retribalization").

From counting to notations: tallies

Notches, knots, pebbles, or shells were initially used to memorize a count or an event, with a very vague reference to what exactly was counted. Funny thing: I am personally familiar with the use of such ancient forms of tallying in everyday routines. My grandma, Babushka Fesha, an illiterate Ukrainian countrywoman born at the very beginning of the 20th century, employed such a mnemonic technique of notation. Her external memory, her solid-state drive, was her... headscarf. If she needed to memorize something, she would tie knots on the ends of her headscarf. The knots represented things she needed to remember or to do – it was her "to-do list." When she fiddled with the ends of the headscarf, she would sense a knot and recall exactly what she needed to do. The constant presence (or rare absence) of the knots organized her day. It was a means of time management for her. The knots on the left and right ends of the headscarf had different meanings, but I do not remember what exactly, unfortunately. The meaningful use of the left or right sides made it more complex than just a binary code.

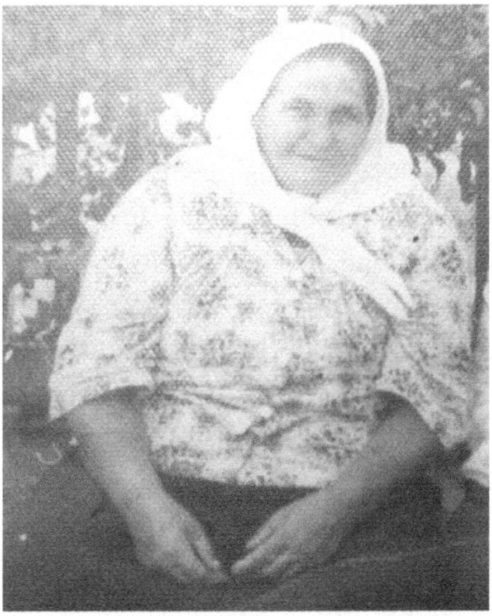

Figure 7. My grandma, Babushka Fesha, Feodosia Kirsantievna Miroshnichenko (1905–1980), photographed sometime in the mid-1970s. Her headscarf has no knots here, nothing to worry about, so she looks relaxed.

This mnemonic technique persisted for tens of thousands of years among people who did not know writing. It's far more ancient than the wheel. The recording of data with knots that my grandma used is a distant cousin to the Quipu, a knot-record system used by the Incas and other ancient Andean cultures in South America to keep records and communicate information through string and knots.

All cultures have or had such or similar tallying systems of "to-do" notes and reminders. In Chinese, it would be 结绳记事 (jiéshéngjì shì) – "to knot a rope to record an event." In English, we can see a footprint of it in the idioms "a notch on (someone's) belt" or "notch up" as a mark of achievement. In Russian, the use of such a tally system is reflected in a set of proverbs, such as "Make yourself a knot for memory!" or "Notch it on your nose!"[1]

[1] "Nose" in the last example sounds and means "nose", but there was also a now-lost

The tallies of achievements and victories were used not just as reminders but also as rank identifiers. The notches on clubs or other weapons were tallies of animals or enemies taken down. When someone saw a warrior with a richly notched club, they would immediately know he was a merciless and high-ranked fighter. This form of tallying still lives in military practice: snipers make notches on the butt of the rifle and aces paint stars on the fuselage after each shot enemy.[1] Another name for an ace or any high-class specialist is "topnotcher." A four-star general is a powerful warrior. Richly notched clubs are still used by the most dreadful warriors, though mostly at parades – in the form of marshal batons.

As soon as someone starts marking events or "recording" reminders with pebbles, knots, notches, or scratches, the notations inevitably develop into an increasingly more complex system of recording. In the 2000 movie *Cast Away*, Tom Hanks' character, a FedEx manager, is stranded on a small island after a plane crash. Sometime later, he starts drawing on the wall of his cave. In the beginning, he displays "residual literacy" – using a piece of charcoal, he tries to calculate the areas where he could have been searched for and where he is lost. The cave wall is a whiteboard to him. Soon enough, though, he downshifts to "true" cave paintings – we see hand stencils on the wall. Four years later, however, there is an 8-shaped line with notches representing the movement of the sun beam's spotlight on the wall. It's a calendar, with days, months, and monsoon seasons.

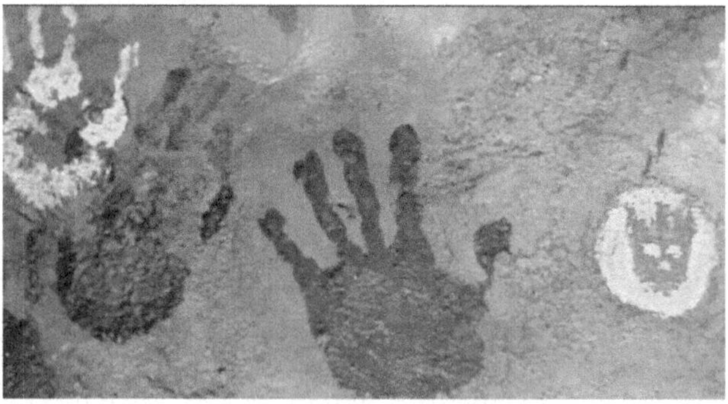

meaning of "nose" in old Slavic – a small wooden tablet on which one could scratch some personal reminders. The lost homophony of "nose" as "wooden tablet" and "nose" has made this proverb a funny and kind of mocking suggestion to better memorize things.

[1] Interestingly, an ace pilot exposes the stars to others and thus conveys the ceremonial message, while the notches on the sniper's rifle are not visible to anyone except the snipers themselves. They do not convey the message of rank; they are purely ritual tallying, an intimate ritualistic marking for self.

Picture 8. The "evolution" of cave paintings and notations in the movie *Cast Away*.

His notation system is not just a binary code to mark his mere presence or count the days passed; it contains complex astronomical and meteorological knowledge allowing him to plan his escape from the island with the help of the right wind. Interestingly, the meaning of his wall calendar is more or less recognizable to anyone – it's archetypical.

It's only logical that, with the passing of historical time, tallying develops complexity in not just quantitative but also qualitative notations. If the pebbles, notches, or knots stand for certain types of events or items, they have to acquire the symbolic quality of the events or units they signify. Certain shapes or colors of pebbles, notches, or knots have to obtain certain qualitative values. For example, three pebbles with curvy scratches could represent three borrowed sheep, and five pebbles with punched dots could signify five jars of oil. The pebbles become tokens.[1] A sealed pot with such tokens would constitute a contract, a record of a transaction. After some development, such tallies would evolve into a recognizable system of notations accepted within a tribe or between neighboring tribes.

From tokens to cuneiform

The evolution from tallies to tokens and further to the full-fledged writing system of Mesopotamian cuneiforms was explored and explained by Denise Schmandt-Besserat, the author of the most compelling and widely acknowledged theory of writing's origin. One of the most important

[1] It can be said that money, writing, and calendars originated from one source – from the ancient tallying system developed in different but archetypically similar material forms in any preliterate culture.

conclusions Schmandt-Besserat supported was the thesis that writing emerged out of economic records. The vast amount of archaeological data from other regions that had early inscriptions confirmed that those inscriptions primarily signified economic transactions or rights of property. But these were Sumerian cuneiforms that allowed Schmandt-Besserat to trace, with a precision unimaginable for prehistory, the logic and exact stages of writing's origin. She writes:

> Writing may have been invented independently three times in different parts of the world: in the Near East, China and Mesoamerica. ...Of these three writing systems... only the earliest, the Mesopotamian cuneiform script, invented in Sumer, present-day Iraq, c. 3200 BC, can be traced without any discontinuity over a period of 10,000 years, from a prehistoric antecedent to the present-day alphabet.[1]

We owe this phenomenon to clay, the unique plasticity and durability of which played a crucial role not only in the transformation of tallies to tokens and tokens to cuneiforms but also in preserving these stages until the present. In other regions, material carriers for tallies and their "smart" heirs, tokens, were pebbles, knots, shells, wooden sticks, bones, and whatever else was countable, storable, recognizable, and transportable. In the valley of the Tigris and Euphrates, it was river clay that was amply used for pottery and other handcrafts. Clay naturally became the best technological solution for tallies to acquire a three-dimensional material form of tokens. The very materiality of clay called for giving tokens different shapes. It was the affordance of the material that predestined a full sway from the dumb quantity of tallies to the symbolic quality of tokens. Easy to sculpt, clay tokens were hard to break after being dried or burned. This made them the perfect material for the job.

In 7500–3500 BCE, Mesopotamian clay tokens had already been made in different shapes and sizes, representing different commodities and measures. The next generation of tokens appeared with the first cities, in 3500–3100 BCE. They had new and more complex geometrical forms, but some were also shaped in naturalistic forms of vessels, tools, and animals. Unlike the plain tokens of the early period, later tokens were often covered with lines and dots that carried additional qualitative meanings.

---

[1] Schmandt-Besserat, Denise. (2014). "The Evolution of Writing."

Dozens of token types and incisions on them represented a sort of commercial vocabulary signifying a complex economic life in the emerging civilization. Some tokens had holes and could be strung for storing. Others were stored in bullae, clay-made round-shape jars, or envelops.

Figure 9. A bulla with tokens from Susa, Iran, circa. 3300 BCE. The lenticular disks stand for "a flock" (~10 animals?). The large cone is a very large measure of grain, and the small cones are small measures of grain. Source: "Tokens: their significance for the origin of counting and writing." Denise Schmandt-Besserat's website at the University of Texas at Austin.

The sealed clay bullae and envelopes were practical for storing tokens but impractical for "reading" the records. A clay bulla would need to be broken each time when its content needed to be read. Eventually, somebody came up with the idea of putting imprints of the tokens on the bulla while the clay was still wet. Three-dimensional complex tokens turned into two-dimensional imprinted signs; thus, the crucial pivot to pictographic writing had commenced.

From then on, people could see exactly which tokens and how many of them were in the clay envelope. At this point, the information on the surface of the envelope became sufficient – it would communicate the same data as the tokens inside. Soon after, it became clear that having tokens and putting them into bullae involved redundant effort. Media evolution followed the economy of efforts. The container became the medium: the clay envelope evolved into the clay tablet.

Initially, clay tablets were oval shaped in the semblance of bullae. Then they acquired a rectangular form more suitable for stockpiling. Next, instead of tokens, whose impressions would not always give the desired quality, people started drawing the same signs with sharpened sticks. Drawing allowed the repertoire of signs to be increased: scribes now could not only imitate the imprints of former tokens but also draw something else, such as simple animalistic images or additional tallies. Instead of several dozen tokens (or their imprints) representing basic commodities and their quantities, several hundred signs appeared, commonly called proto-cuneiform.

Figure 10. Pictographic tablet from Godin Tepe, Iran, c. 3100 BC. The tablet combines both incisions and token impressions. The incised sign stands for a jar of oil, the circular signs stand for 10, and the wedges for 1 = 33 jars of oil. Source: Schmandt-Besserat, Denise. (2013). "Tokens and writing: the cognitive development."

Perhaps dragging the tip of the stick through the wet clay was not an optimal technique because the blobs of clay would often spoil the lines. At some point, the scribes returned to the technique of impression, but now it was impressions made by a reed's edge. The reed's edge allowed them to make clean and clear wedge-shaped imprints. Combinations of these imprints in different patterns roughly imitated the forms of earlier tokens and pictograms.

The evolution of cuneiforms

Proto-cuneiform tablet, Jemdet Nasr period, c. 3100–2900 BC.

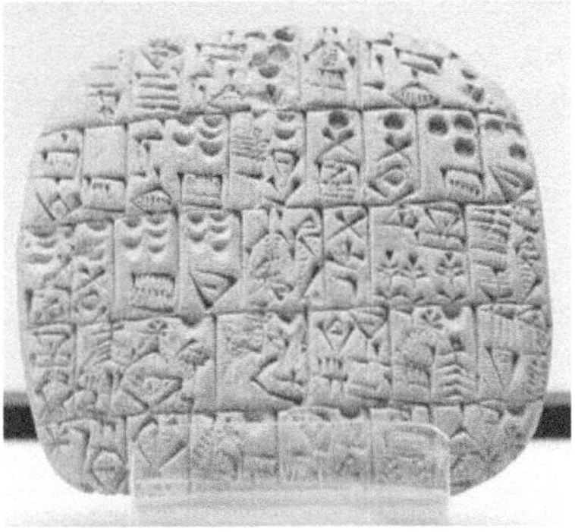

Contract for the sale of a field and a house in the wedge-shaped cuneiform adapted for clay tablets, Shuruppak, circa 2600 BC.

Babylonian tablets of the time of Hammurabi (circa 1750 BC).

Figure 11. Source: Wikipedia, "Cuneiform".

Scribing and pressing signs with reeds simplified the pictograms. They started losing their semblance with naturalistic objects and the original tokens. This way, circa 3300 BCE in Mesopotamia, the cuneiform script emerged. From pictorial images representing the basic items and commodities for purposes of bookkeeping, data records evolved into pictograms representing things and further to ideographic signs representing ideas. The system fitted bookkeeping very well but was not yet effective enough for recording speech.

Clay tokens represented an important stage of the Mesopotamian transition from notation to writing. Thanks to clay tokens, we can trace the logic of this process. Many other regions with an extensive exchange of commodities employed tokens, too, for recording transactions and wealth, but tokens were made of other materials. They could evolve into a monetary semantic system but did not become a link between tallying and writing.

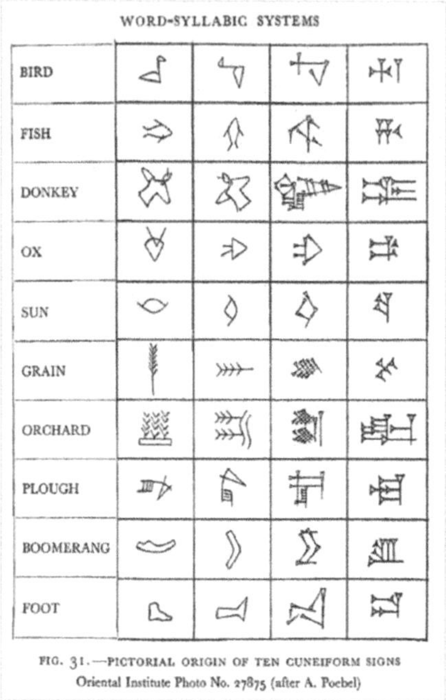

Source: Gelb, Ignace. (1963 [1952]). *A study of writing*, p. 70.

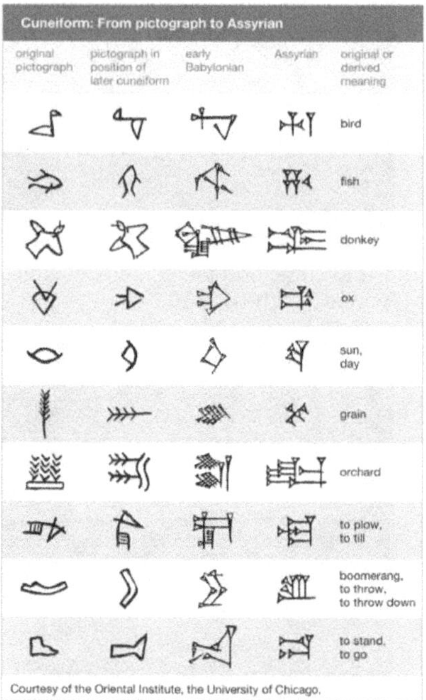

Source: Britannica, "Sumerian writing."

Figure 12.

The Egyptians might have seen Sumerian writing and got the idea, so likely did the Minoans of Crete who traded with the Egyptians. Both the Egyptians and the Minoans developed, however, completely different scripts. In ancient China, Mesoamerica and, perhaps, a couple more regions, where protowriting emerged independently, people managed to find their own ways to transition from notation to writing. Scratching notations to record economic transactions and celestial or other events was accompanied by pictures, which evolved into sustainable symbolic signs. All systems of writing, including the alphabet, have been derived from these sources of writing, with Sumerian, Egyptian and Chinese protowriting having the most profound historical significance.

From pictograms to phonograms

Pictograms developed according to common principles: their shapes became more abstract and their meaning more universal. They transformed into ideograms, signs for ideas and notions, and logograms, signs for words. For example, a schematic picture of a foot could signify not just a foot, but also the idea of "walking," while a schematic picture of a boat could represent the idea of traveling by lake or river, and so on.

There was, however, a class of words that could not be represented in pictograms, logograms, or ideograms. Such were the names of individuals – proper nouns. Since writing began as the recording of economic transactions, recording names was a challenge from the very beginning. In early pictographic protowriting, individuals could be represented by the pictures of their totemic animals. This would work, however, only within a small tribe. Within an urbanized community with a vivid commercial life, totemic affiliation would not provide the reliable identification of individuals.

So, the first scribes were tasked with inventing a method for writing down individual names. For gods or the royalty, special signs could be and were introduced. But all others needed to be named in writing as precisely as they were named in spoken speech. Written signs, initially designed to reflect a visual semblance or a metaphorical affiliation with objects, needed to somehow represent the sounds of names.

A solution was found – the scribes started using logograms of words, preferably monosyllabic, that sound exactly like the name of the person. This method is still used in rebuses. For example, to write the name "Neilson" in pictograms, you can draw a picture of a knee and a picture of the sun.

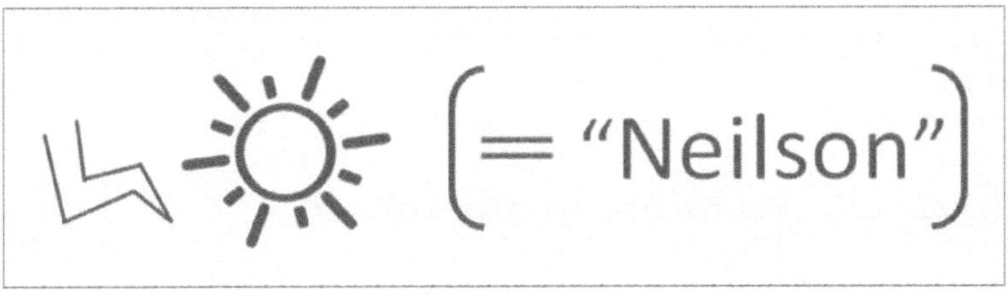

Figure 13.

It was necessary also to simultaneously let the reader know that these two pictograms need to be read together and through their phonetic value.

For this, special additional signs, determinatives, were usually put before pictograms that needed to be read phonetically.

Today, such rebuses are used as puzzles. But when you use this principle frequently, you eventually isolate a set of signs (pictograms or logograms) that are particularly good at representing sounds. Eventually, the signs that were most suitable for recording sounds transformed into stable phonetic elements both in Mesopotamian cuneiforms and Egyptian hieroglyphs, as well as in other logographic writing systems, as they encountered the same issues with proper names and found the same solution.

Fascinatingly, we can still trace the footprints of this transformation from pictograms to phonograms in the modern-day alphabet. For example, the Egyptian hieroglyph depicting an ox's head developed into the Semitic letter *Aleph*, Greek letter *Alpha*, and English letter *A*, which still resembles an ox's head turned upside down, but only if you know its history.

Along with the transformation of writing to accommodate more phonetic elements, signs became less pictorial and more abstract – less iconic and more symbolic (in Pierce's classification of signs).

Sumer writing mimicked reality even less after the Akkadians, a northern Semitic people, conquered Sumer in 2340 BC and established the bilingual Akkadian Empire, whose population spoke Sumerian and Akkadian but kept using Sumerian cuneiform. The writing system had been slowly changing to accommodate the Akkadians, who could not understand Sumerian words. Thus, the role of determinatives and phonetic elements grew as did the abstract meanings of pictograms, logograms, and ideograms, while their number became smaller. The later Akkadian-Babylonian syllabic system developed some distinctive features of phonetic writing. And yet it could represent not spoken speech but only its rough "outline." Reading such script was not exactly "reading" but rather interpreting.

From hieroglyphs to the proto alphabet

Scholars have differing opinions regarding the origin of Egyptian writing. Similar to Sumerian cuneiforms, Egyptian hieroglyphs originated from pictograms; however, their style and material techniques differed significantly. The earliest known examples of Egyptian writing were carved on slate palettes. Carving on soft stones was perhaps the main form of Egyptian writing and gave it its name: "hieroglyph," which means "sacred carving <on stone>" in Greek. The material and technique predefined the shapes of symbols, which were very different from those pressed with reed on clay. Nonetheless, the Egyptians also wrote on clay tags, other clay items, and papyrus, which enabled the faster and simpler versions of hieroglyphic writing known as hieratic and demotic.

Harold Innis proposed an interesting hypothesis concerning the contribution of burial rituals to the emergence of writing that reflects the Egyptians' inclination for controlling time. As he puts it:

> Success of the monarchy in acquiring control over Egypt in terms of space necessitated a concern with problems of continuity or time. The idea of immortality strengthened the position of the monarch. Mummification and construction of the pyramids as devices for emphasizing control over time were accompanied by the development of the art of pictorial representation as part of the funerary ritual and by the emergence of writing.[1]

Innis, therefore, highlights the very essence of writing, its time-binding capacity, as a practical reason for writing to emerge in Ancient Egypt.

Mesmerized by the majesty of the Nile, the Egyptians might have indeed had a stronger religious piety for the river and its cycles than the Mesopotamians, who witnessed the divine grace of two rivers. Perhaps, the rivers' behaviour there was not so much regular and depended also on the winds and sea tides (hence frequent and often unpredictable floods). In Mesopotamia, religious sentiment might have been split between the Tigris, the Euphrates, and the valley between them, leading to the strong presence of fertile-matriarchal elements in Sumerian and Accadian beliefs.

For the Egyptians, the Nile stood alone, and it might have fostered a stronger sense of piety towards the supreme god, almost at the level of monotheism. The divine majesty of the Nile and the cycles of the great river may have also fostered a stronger sense of cyclical time that influenced the religious beliefs of the Egyptians. The cycles of the river were matched with celestial events, and the priests revealed the divine order of things. The divine order of things allowed the establishment of a similarly cyclical human order. By following proper cycles and reverence for the divine,

---

[1] Innis, Harold. (2008 [1951]). *The Bias of Communication*, p. 34.

humans could thrive using the grace of the Nile. To maintain order, the authority of the god-pharaoh was established supported by the central administration with the learned priests in charge.

To maintain proper cycles and meet the demand of cyclical order, a precise time measurement was required. This led the Egyptians to the invention of the calendar. Egyptian time measurement relied on the Sun and Sirius. Since astronomical events could be traced back in history, it is assumed, following the cycles of Sirius' rise in a certain position in the sky, that the beginning of Egyptian time measurement could be dated to 4241 BCE. This year is seen by some as the first exactly established date in history. Harold Innis mentions it, too, when he writes that the power of the king "was possibly strengthened with the beginnings of the measurement of time on July 19, 4241 B.C. when Sirius arose at sunrise and prediction of time became more certain with recognition of a year of 365 days."[1]

One way or another, the Egyptian calendar highly likely predated Egyptian writing.

Finally, the time-cyclical religious sense made the Egyptians also particularly sensitive to the time of life, death, and eternal afterlife. Burial rituals should defy time, and thus rich symbolic ornaments telling the stories of gods, of life and death, and the like became a time-defying device, too (along with the pyramids, which have indeed defeated time). This could have become a spiritual source of writing. The Egyptian priests were well equipped in the technique of pictographic storytelling, which could have helped them develop hieroglyphic writing for economic purposes.

Egyptian writing emerged around 3100 BCE, shortly after Sumerian cuneiforms. Considering the geographic proximity and cultural influence of Mesopotamia on Egypt, scholars believe that Sumerian writing might have inspired the development of Egyptian hieroglyphs, though no direct connections have been detected.

According to the principles of writing evolution, Egyptian hieroglyphs developed from pictograms to a logographic-syllabic system similarly to Sumerian writing. Just like Sumerian cuneiform, Egyptian hieroglyphs faced challenges with names and foreign words, leading to the development of phonetic elements. Some word signs became the signs for syllables that sounded similar to those words.

[1] Innis, Harold. (2008 [1951]). *The Bias of Communication*, p. 93.

The evolution of hieroglyphs

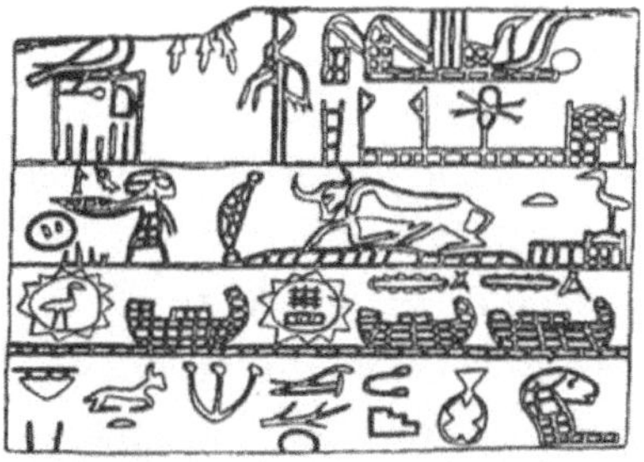

The early Egyptian pictographic. The Ivory plaque of Menes (3200–3000 BCE).

Hieroglyphs on stela in the Louvre, circa 1321 BCE.

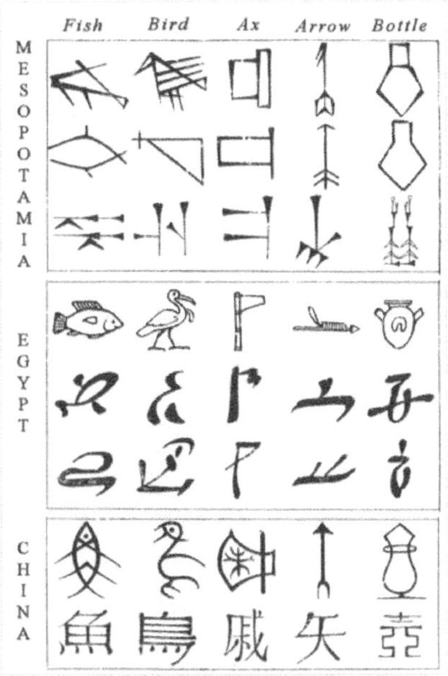

Comparative evolution from pictograms to abstract shapes, in cuneiform, Egyptian and Chinese characters.

Figure 14. Source: Wikipedia, “Egyptian hieroglyphs”.

In Sumer, the phonetic potential of cuneiform was amplified when the Akkadians conquered Mesopotamia and adapted the Sumerian script for their language. A similar phonetic leap of borrowing happened to the Egyptian hieratic script when the Seirites, one of the West Semitic peoples, adopted phonetic elements of Egyptian writing for their language.

Egyptian writing represented a level of complexity that the Semitic semi-nomads and workers could not handle. As Robert Logan observes, they were not educated in the Egyptian scribal tradition, which was purposefully kept complex by the priestly class to maintain their “monopoly of knowledge” and the privileges it accompanied.[1] As a result, the Seirites, who worked as miners for the Egyptians around Mount Seir, adopted only those phonetic elements of hieroglyphics they could understand. The Seirites began using them to record the main syllables of their own language.

[1] Logan, Robert. (2004 [1986]). *The Alphabet Effect*, p. 37.

Eventually, around 1800–1500 BCE, the Seirites developed a form of phonetic writing known as the Proto-Sinaitic script. Later, other Semitic people, the Phoenicians (circa 1100 BC), further developed it into a syllabic proto alphabet with only consonants. Subsequently, this proto alphabet was refined into a full alphabet by the Greeks around 800 BC. It is believed that writing emerged independently in several geographical areas, but the alphabet was invented only once in this specific location. All the existing alphabets or alphabetical principles were derived from this accidental borrowing of the twenty-two uniconsonantal hieroglyphic signs by the Semitic tribe of the Sinai Peninsula.

Interestingly, the evolution of writing often occurred through cultural borrowings and appropriations. In the history of writing, appropriations always created the affordance of reformation, modernization, and enhancement. In the case of the Semites borrowing phonetic signs from the Egyptians, the cultural appropriation by the new users freed the writing system from the rigid caste control of the priestly elites. As Ignace Gelb put it in 1952,

> The reason for this does not lie solely in the conservative attachment of a people for their own writing. It is rather the protection of vested interests of a special cast, religious (Egypt, Babylonia), or political (China), that frequently may have been responsible for maintaining a difficult and obsolete form of writing, making thus its general use by the people impossible. It is therefore foreign people, not bound by local traditions and religious or political interests of an alien group, that are frequently responsible for introducing new and important developments in the history of writing.[1]

Harold Innis also emphasized both the role of a complex writing system in preserving political power and the role of borrowings. As he describes it,

> Monopolies of knowledge to an important extent dominated by priestly organization and protected by complex types of script such as the cuneiform and the hieroglyphic checked the growth of political organization. Escape from these monopolies came from the fringes of Babylonian and Egyptian civilizations in which new languages among primitive peoples demanded simplicity. Semitic peoples in contact

[1] Gelb, Ignace. (1963 [1952]). *A Study of Writing*, p. 165.

> with Egypt before 1500 B.C. apparently invented an alphabet in Palestine and perfected it on the Phoenician coast.[1]

The Acadians did not speak Sumerian and borrowed – and thereby refined – the syllabic principle. The Semites were not proficient in the sacred complexity of the Egyptian hieroglyphs and borrowed the phonetic elements, having refined them for further, purely phonetic, use. The Greeks were not bound by the consonant tradition of the Phoenician script and added vowels, thus completing the invention of the alphabet.

This is why the borrowed or adopted codes generally tend to be more logical and refined than inherited ones. As Gelb put it,

> In all cases it was the foreigners who were not afraid to break away from sacred traditions and were thus able to introduce reforms which led to new and revolutionary developments.[2]

Thus, major advances in writing were made through borrowing and appropriation. Borrowing allowed for revision and selection based on pure functionality while disregarding the burden of cultural traditions. The alphabet was invented through a series of counter-cultural appropriations.

Alphabet: the meaning through the meaningless

Sometime in the 9th or early 8th century BCE, the Greeks became those foreigners who introduced "reforms which led to new and revolutionary developments." Gelb suggests that the Greeks did not come to the Asiatic coast to borrow the Semitic script. It was the Phoenicians, mainly merchants and seafarers, whose trading posts were scattered throughout the Greek lands, who brought their writing to the Greeks.[3]

Eric Havelock refers to a hypothesis that the Greeks were "envious" of the practice of the denotation of property by the Phoenicians, their neighbours in the bilingual communities in Cyprus, Crete, or Al Mina.[4] The act of dedication was important in an oral society. The giver would proclaim who gives what to whom, and this would signify a contract or a

1 Innis, Harold. (2008 [1951]). Bias of Communication, p. 38.

2 Gelb. (1963 [1952]). *A Study of Writing*, p. 196.

3 Gelb, Ignace. (1963 [1952]). *A Study of Writing*, p. 178.

4 Havelock, Eric. (1986). *The Muse Learns to Write*, p. 85.

"legal" passage of a gift or a purchase. The Phoenicians would do this by inscribing the names of the giver and receiver on the object or the accompanying tags. The Greeks saw their Phoenician neighbors doing this and were seduced by the magical meaning of such a practice: the inscriptions made objects speak for themselves and much more reliably than the words said by someone to someone somewhere somewhen.

According to this hypothesis, the Greeks borrowed not writing per se, but the written act of dedication, both commercial and religious. From this "entry point," they started using and developing the means of dedication – the proto alphabet. This hypothesis is supported by archaeological data: the earliest found Greek inscriptions on objects often signify the owners and the circumstances of passing the rights of property.

After borrowing the alphabetic inscriptions, the Greeks made the final tweak that completed the invention of the alphabet – they assigned some letters to represent vowels. It is believed that the role of vowels in Greek, an Indo-European and more vocal language, was more crucial for differentiating lexical meanings than in Semitic languages, which belonged to the Afro-Asiatic language family. The hypothesis remains debatable: lexical meanings can depend on vowels in Semitic languages, too. The invention of letters for vowels by the Greeks can rather represent another case of transcultural borrowing: the new user grasped the idea of a code but felt free to reassign some signs, while the old user remained bound by the tradition.

However, the hypothesis of adjusting the alphabet according to the vocal nature of a language highlights the fact that national languages can have different "requirements" for writing systems. For Chinese, for example, the alphabet would not work because Chinese is a tonal and predominantly monosyllabic language. In Chinese, most words consist of only one syllable, and many syllables have similar sounds but carry different lexical meanings depending on the flat, rising, or falling tone of pronunciation. For instance, the word *ma* can mean "mother," "hemp," "horse," "to scold," or a question particle, depending on the pitch of pronunciation. Representing such tonal distinctions by special diacritic signs in an alphabetic script is theoretically possible,[1] but it creates a

[1] Several attempts at alphabetization of the Chinese script were made. One of them, Pinyin, is even now used to input Chinese characters on Latin keyboards. However, all these alphabets are approximations of Chinese writing and cannot fully capture its richness. They

complexity that simply kills the main value of the alphabet – its graphic simplicity and phonetic universalism.

However, for Indo-European languages, the evolution of the alphabet was of great importance. Besides, the Greeks fulfilled the very basic principle of the alphabet: one letter per sound, with no additional guiding signs or prompts. No longer was the reader required to guess. Before the alphabet, even having elaborate phonetic syllabaries with vowels, readers were interpreters. With the alphabet, reading became *reading* in the most *literal* sense of the word. A small set of letters could now record any spoken word. Respectively, any written word, even an unfamiliar one, could be read exactly as it sounds (except for tonal languages, of course).

In reality, the practical applications of the "letter-per-sound" alphabetic capacity are not ideal even for Indo-European languages. Some sounds are written with several letters (like "th"), and some letters or combinations of letters might be vocalized differently in different positions. So, you still need to "know in advance" how to read differently the same combinations of letters in some particular words. However, these deviations from the alphabetical principle reflect rather cultural deposits of certain languages and epochs, such as the French influence in English, for example. Nevertheless, despite these cultural-legacy peculiarities, the principle of the alphabet is incredibly simple and clear: a letter stands for a sound. By combining letters, you can form sounding words. Regardless of how many words are in a language, you can represent all of them with just two to three dozen letters.[1]

Before the emergence of the alphabet, the pictographic, logographic, and even some syllabic signs of writing retained some direct or residual semblance to the objects or meanings they represented. The meaning of signs needed to be matched to something and guessed. This intellectual operation ("something stands for something else") reflected analog thinking, a feature of the magic and immersive – environmental – consciousness in which everything is connected with something else.

The letter represented a meaningless sound, which, in reality, did not exist by itself. The coding of meanings through fully meaningless signs irrevocably broke the magic spell of orality that held the human mind

---

are primarily used for transcultural purposes such as Latin keyboard input and teaching foreigners.

[1] The largest alphabet is Khmer/Cambodian – 74 letters.

hostage even under the early systems of writing. Being seemingly just a recording device for speech, the alphabet created a new form of speech – written speech. And since language was always a thought shaper, the new form of speech *afforded* a new form of thinking. A new medium, the alphabet, unleashed its own affordances and reshaped the human sensorium, cognitive abilities, culture, and society. According to McLuhan, "By the meaningless sign linked to the meaningless sound we have built the shape and meaning of Western man."[1]

Robert Logan offered the most comprehensive description of the main effects of the alphabet. He wrote:

> The magic of the phonetic alphabet is that it is more than a writing system; it is also a system for organizing information. Of all mankind's inventions, with the possible exception of writing itself, nothing has proved more useful or led to more innovations than the alphabet. <...> It has influenced the development of our thought patterns, our social institutions, and our very sense of ourselves. The alphabet, as we shall discover, has contributed to the development of codified law, monotheism, abstract science, deductive logic, and individualism, each a unique contribution of Western thought.[2]

Logan highlights that the five or six hundred years after the adoption of the alphabet in Greece was one of the most creative periods in human existence. Within this short period, many fundamental elements of Western civilization emerged that had a significant impact on all of humanity, such as abstract science, formal logic, axiomatic geometry, rational philosophy, and representational art. Once again, the parallel with Jaspers' Axial Age is more than evident.

From recording events to recording speech

The evolution of writing was not just the evolution of the semantic and syntactic means of recording; it was also the evolution of affordances. The evolution of writing followed a certain inner logic and enabled the mind and society to progressively develop different modes of operation with the world.

---

[1] McLuhan, Marshall. (1962). *The Guttenberg Galaxy*, p. 50.

[2] Logan, Robert. (2004 [1986]). *The Alphabet Effect*, pp. 1-2.

In 1952, Ignace Gelb, a Polish-American historian and Assyriologist, introduced a unified theory of writing, which he suggested calling *grammatology*. Like any general theory, it faced accusations of oversimplification and forcibly fitting details into the model. Nevertheless, the value of Gelb's approach lies in his global framing and persistence in seeing the bigger picture. This aligns him with Jaspers, who published *The Origin and Goal of History* just three years before.

The theory Gelb advanced suggests a general pattern in the development of writing. While local writings may have their specific characteristics, the writing of humankind developed from being purely pictographic to becoming more phonetic and from reporting events to recording speech. This development could occur within a national culture or, more likely and more profoundly, through transcultural borrowings and appropriations. Not all writing systems went through all stages of this development. But all of them developed from being purely pictorial to becoming more or less phonetic. Gelb recognizes this as a common pattern, the essential principle of grammatology, and not merely a historical coincidence.

In its historical development from pictorial to phonetic, writing went through three main stages, according to Gelb. The first stage is represented by "primitive drawings" – pictures that syncretically express emotions, magical or aesthetic feelings, impressions of events, and, occasionally, messages.

The second stage is represented by the "forerunners of writing." Gelb calls this stage "semasiography" – from the Greek *semasia*, "meaning, signification," and *graphe*, "writing." The pictures of this stage "convey the general meaning intended by the writer."[1] Gelb implies that the authors of semasiographic pictures wanted to send a message, so the significance of the drawings goes beyond artistic-aesthetic or magical purposes. However, they were not yet considered writing, as none of the linguistic forms were recorded.

Semasiographic pictures recorded the events and served as a means of memorization or communication, according to Gelb. In pictograms, typical objects such as figures of humans or animals became less similar to their referents and more abstract and geometrical. Thus, even prior to the

[1] Gelb, Ignace. (1963 [1952]). *A Study of Writing*, p. 191.

emergence of writing, pictograms had already demonstrated an increase in abstraction in "recording" reality.

Gelb states that,

> The signs in all the original systems of writing are pictorial in character and are employed to represent objects of the surrounding world. As human beings all over the world and the objects by which they are surrounded, have much in common, we should naturally anticipate that the pictures they devised for their writings would also have many points of resemblance. Thus, men and parts of the body, animals and plants, tools and weapons, buildings and structures, sky, earth, water and fire are everywhere represented by pictures characterized by great similarity in form, because all of these things actually exist in similar forms.[1]

The principles that influenced the further development of pictograms were also universal. The schematization of initial pictograms resulted in a relatively limited repertoire of geometric signs that could represent meanings or sounds in the most economical ways. Gelb refers to an experiment in which a 9-year-old girl was tasked with composing an original alphabet. She came up with 26 signs, seven of which closely resembled the signs of Phoenician script, while others resembled Sinaitic, Cretan, and Cypriote symbols.[2]

The third stage in the development of writing is "full writing," which is characterized by the increasing role of phonography. Writing begins to represent not just objects and events but also linguistic phenomena – words, syllables, and sounds.

According to Gelb, the development of writing was "unidirectional." This means that writing tends to reach its ultimate development by passing through the stages from pictography towards logography, syllabography, and, possibly, the alphabet – "in this and no other order." Describing the "unidirectional development of writing," Gelb states:

> No writing can start with a syllabic or alphabetic stage unless it is borrowed, directly or indirectly, from a system which has gone through all the previous stages. A system of writing can naturally stop at one stage without developing farther. Thus, a number of

[1] Gelb, Ignace. (1963 [1952]). *A Study of Writing*, p. 218.

[2] Gelb, Ignace. (1963 [1952]). *A Study of Writing*, p. 146.

> writings stopped at the logographic or syllabic stage. <....> There is no reverse development: an alphabet cannot develop into a syllabary, just as a syllabary cannot lead to the creation of logography.[1]

The development of writing tends to be accelerated by borrowings and inhibited by the control of the ruling caste. In striving to explain why some writings "naturally" stopped at the logographic or syllabic stage and did not evolve into an alphabet, Gelb suggests that political or religious bureaucracy might negatively affect the development of writing. Gelb calls the ritualistic burdening and slowing down of writing development "retrograde evolution":

> The retrograde evolution of individual writings was frequently facilitated whenever they fell under the control of a priestly or political caste. In such cases the system gradually became so overburdened with various artificial and baroque deflections that they grew too difficult for large masses of people to master.[2]

As an example of such a (counter-) development of writing, Gelb mentions Egyptian hieroglyphics. They existed for more than three thousand years and branched out into the demotic and hieratic scripts, which, in turn, gave birth to the Semitic proto alphabets and eventually the Greek alphabet. However, hieroglyphics remained highly resistant to change due to the control of the temple bureaucracy.

By the time of the Ptolemaic dynasty (305–30 BCE), Egyptian hieroglyphics had accumulated such a level of complexity that they became exceedingly cumbersome for everyday use beyond religious purposes. As a result, after the decline of the religious caste, the Egyptian and descendant cultures abandoned hieroglyphics and switched to the Coptic, Semitic, and Greek systems of writing. Interestingly, all these writing systems, in one way or another, derived from Egyptian hieroglyphics centuries before that and succeeded in their development precisely because they were borrowed by other cultures that were not overwhelmingly constrained by the priestly caste. Egyptian hieroglyphics ceased to be used and understood sometime in the 4th century CE after enduring for 3500 years – longer than any other writing system on Earth.

---

[1] Gelb, Ignace. (1963 [1952]). *A Study of Writing*, p. 201.

[2] Gelb, Ignace. (1963 [1952]). *A Study of Writing*, p. 202.

While the “universal” and “unidirectional” development of writing systems can be halted at the logographic or syllabic stage due to the rigidity of political or religious bureaucracies, according to Gelb’s view, or due to the structural and phonetic nature of language itself, which may be a more accurate explanation for certain writing systems, the complete possible development of phonetization in writing is represented by the alphabet. Gelb writes:

> The development of a full Greek alphabet, expressing single sounds of language by means of consonant and vowel signs, is the last important step in the history of writing. From the Greek period up to the present, nothing new has happened in the inner structural development of writing. Generally speaking, we write consonants and vowels in the same way as the ancient Greeks did.[1]

Gelb’s grammatology – the theory of writing’s origin, can be presented in a chart. (Figure 15.)

Digital media reverse Gelb’s universal principle of the unidirectional development of writing and retrieve Gelb’s semasiography – non-verbal visual communication. This started earlier: as McLuhan famously said, “Ads are the cave art of the twentieth century.”[2] Print and TV ads turned literate humans into new hunters and gatherers – consumers. Digital orality has furthered this reversal, enabling users to create their own cave paintings as they now communicate their impressions of the world through smileys, emojis, gifs, memes, and reels that may not employ written inscriptions and still convey meanings by the means of semasiography.

---

[1] Gelb, Ignace. (1963 [1952]). *A Study of Writing*, p. 184.

[2] McLuhan, Marshall. (1970). *Culture is Our Business*. “Author’s Note,” p. 7.

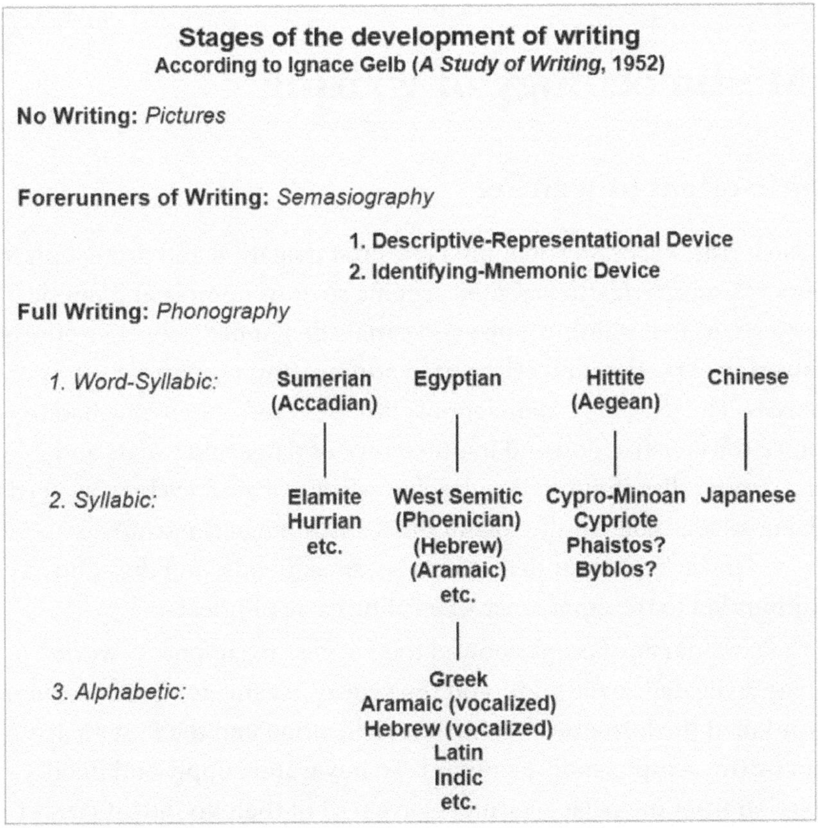

Figure 15. The stages of the development of writing, a chart from: Gelb, Ignace. (1963 [1952]). *A Study of Writing*, p. 191.

5. Media ecology of writing

Ripple effect of writing

The fertile soil of Mesopotamia required irrigation and protection from frequent floods. Irrigation created specific socio-economic and political conditions, as maintaining dams and canals demanded collective efforts, engineering expertise, and centralized administrative control over resources. The need for a managerial class emerged – someone had to organize the construction and maintenance of dams and canals and manage water distribution. Besides, knowledge of river cycles was needed. Such knowledge could only exist in the form of magical narratives about the gods whose behaviour defined the seasons, floods, and droughts. These conditions led to the emergence of a ruling caste of priests.

The abundance of crops allowed the farmers to support powerful temples dedicated to the gods, and the priests became temple bureaucrats. This entailed the formation of the first civilization and the first palace economy (or, temple-state economy). To buy water supply and flood protection from the palace, farmers gave part of their abundant crops to the priests as a water fee. This fee also served as a religious offering, an infrastructure levy, and, in a sense, a science tax.

The functioning of such an administrative and economic system couldn't help but enable bookkeeping. To allow water into certain canals, the priests-administrators needed to know if the farmer or village had paid their water dues. Celestial and river events were also recorded, forming a proto calendar, the foundation of the priests' knowledge. Economic records accompanied all other business relations. Contracts and bills of debt registered the exchange of products between farmers and craftsmen or between merchants.

In short, the palace economy created the affordance for writing. Writing appeared wherever the palace economy took shape – from Mesopotamia and Egypt to the Indus Valley and Mesoamerica. It perhaps can be concluded that writing emerged only in the conditions of the palace economy with its ruling caste of priests-bureaucrats. Many prehistoric cultures developed systems of proto-writing and pictography, but writing emerged out of economic records and only because they were maintained by a special caste of scribes, who belonged to the priestly bureaucracy.

From a slightly different perspective, these were economic records that, once discovered, evolved in writing and created the class of scribes-priests-bureaucrats and the entire palace economy, the first form of human civilization.

In any case, irrigation, the temple-palace economy, writing, and the special caste of temple administrators who controlled society through the means of writing, emerged together and conditioned each other's development. Irrigation was the first truly terraforming media project of humans in the most literal sense. Irrigation also terraformed the planet in a figurative sense, as it enabled both the first civilizations and, most importantly, writing, the foundation of all civilizations and of *the* civilization of humankind. In the spirit of Logan & McLuhan's article "The alphabet, mother of invention," it can be said that irrigation was the mother of writing.

By keeping their records, the caste of priests maintained their privileged position in society. This forced them to protect and develop writing as their unique prerogative. From this point on, the ripple effect of media started affecting humans' mental capacities and social organization. Writing changed thing after thing, creating new human conditions.

First, writing radically transformed the epistemology of sacred knowledge. Prior to it, the shamans of magical cultures transmitted knowledge to their apprentices through oral tradition and magic items. In such an order of things, nothing encouraged the multiplication of knowledge. New knowledge would most likely have been rejected.

Writing, on the contrary, not only preserved all previous experiences but encouraged new records. Once you have a means of recording, you must record something, and this something must be worthwhile, which means selection. On top of this, writing recorded new data and events in an already-sacred form – in the form of sacred signs, thus legitimizing the acquisition of new knowledge. Being recorded, any new experience or event was introduced into the "legitimate" sacred practice for those who read it afterward.

Shamanic teaching became impossible after the introduction of writing. Writing transformed former shamans into priests and temple bureaucrats.

Being able to write and read, the priests were encouraged to preserve, produce, and collect records. Thus, for the first time, a scientific ethos emerged aimed at the deliberate augmentation of knowledge.

Writing is not just the recording of data. It requires an infrastructure for collecting and studying what has been already written. In Mesopotamia, the first libraries emerged. The priests and kings hunted for ancient tablets and then studied and rewrote them. By the time of the first famous ancient library, the royal library of King Ashurbanipal (the 7th century BCE), thousands of learned men were involved in library science. Libraries became one of the fundamental imperial institutions that maintained the "monopoly of knowledge." Ashurbanipal was a brutal despot, but he recognized the importance of not just written tablets but also the extensive and diverse collection of knowledge. His library was reported to contain 30,000 clay tablets.

When librarians were to decide how to stockpile the tablets, they needed to classify them somehow. They started inventing the grounds for the classification of writings, which became the grounds for the classification of knowledge. Knowledge was rationally divided into the disciplines.

The shamans and sorcerers of the preliterate magical cultures simply did not have the need for abstract classification. All things belonged to natural clusters, such as earth or heaven, land or water, etc. All knowledge was syncretic in magical consciousness. All things were in relationships, and proximity or similarity between things defined their nature and their place in the world.

Writing changed the logic of grouping things. The preservation of written data compelled a knowledge-seeker to categorize subjects according to their applicability, origin, or other inherent features. Thus, the very concept of classification emerged along with fragmentation, unification, and standardization. Instead of being defined through their relationship with other things, objects and subjects acquired their own inner ideas. In Mesopotamian and Egyptian libraries, a long journey towards Platonic idealism began.

Writing also required a complex process of learning. For that purpose, schools were organized. "The major aim of the scribal school quite naturally was professional training to satisfy the economic and administrative needs of temple and palace bureaucracies," writes Logan.[1] So, irrigation was the mother of writing and the grandmother of libraries and schools.

However, teaching writing required an understanding of what it is. How do certain signs represent certain things? What mysterious force ties them together? How do certain words go along with certain words, each time in different conjunctions but somehow consistently? What mysterious force binds them together?

Through the teaching of writing, semiotics and grammar were summoned into being. Writing made people aware of the properties of speech and thinking. As soon as the need to teach and comprehend writing emerged, Babylonian scholars inevitably faced the same questions that de Saussure, Vygotsky, and Chomsky dealt with five thousand years later. As Neil Postman puts it,

> Writing freezes speech and in so doing gives birth to the grammarian, the logician, the rhetorician, the historian, the scientist – all those who must hold language before them so that they can see what it means, where it errs, and where it is leading.[2]

Thus, the need of the priestly caste to secure its privileged status brought about the creation of an entire complex of institutions and disciplines to maintain writing itself. Along with libraries, schools, and scribes' shops, new cognitive activities emerged, such as unification and standardization, the classification of knowledge, the specialization of disciplines, and reflection upon the nature of writing and knowledge in general. Writing transformed the priests into scholars. In discussing the role of writing in Mesopotamia, Logan titles the respective chapter "Introduction to science."[3] Writing encouraged the specialization and fragmentation of subjects, which eventually contributed to tunnel vision – the ability to focus on subjects isolated from the environment.

With the passage of time, the writing systems of the Sumerians and Egyptians developed phonetic elements that represented syllables rather than words or ideas. The development of phonetic elements was an incredible next leap of abstraction. Humans learned to record something

---

1 Logan, Robert. (2004 [1986]). *The Alphabet Effect*, p. 82.

2 Postman, Neil. (2006 [1985]). *Amusing Ourselves to Death*, kl 402.

3 Logan, Robert. (2004 [1986]). *The Alphabet Effect*, p. 81.

that was not tangible – sounds. In oral and magical thinking, if there is a sound, then there should be someone who makes it. For the oral mind, there is no way to isolate a sound from its source. Early writing consisted of pictograms and logograms that reflected visible and tangible things or their moves and changes, which were also visible and tangible. But sounds, especially those comprised of only a part of a word (such as syllables and phonemes), could not be "isolated" by any sense, including hearing. Recording phonetic elements required exclusively cognitive, not sensorial, operation.

The phonetic elements of Sumerian writing, the first syllables and phonograms, proved that sounds can be "caught" and detached from the speaker. The power of such a revelation might have been truly magical. But the way of realizing it was utterly rational and intelligible. It was discovered that things could be captured not only in pictures but also by the signs recording sounds. Such complexity of intellectual fragmentation and abstraction was certainly impossible for the preliterate mind to comprehend. There had simply been no need for it.

The elements of abstraction, universality, and classification started growing as features of Babylonian thinking under the influence of phonetic writing, as argued by Logan. This not only promoted a spirit of scientific inquiry but also resulted in the Hammurabi code (1792–1750 BCE), a set of 282 rules that established principles for commercial interactions and punishments for misdeeds. The previous oral tradition of legal judgment, mostly confined to the action of authority or collective, was for the first time in history objectivized, structured, conceptualized, and codified.

Following the Hammurabi code, other forms of abstract and codified knowledge appeared, such as mathematical tables aimed at simplifying calculations and tables of weights and measures used in commerce. From the social practices of the priestly class, who maintained writing to secure their privileges, an entirely new environment emerged in which reality was rationalized and brought into order.

However, as Logan states, the lack of fully alphabetic writing prevented the Mesopotamians from achieving the level of pure abstraction typical for the moralistic laws of the Hebrews or the logical laws of the Greeks. For example, the Mesopotamians understood the grammatical classification of words, but they never formulated explicit rules of grammar.[1] The newly invented classification of things and deeds remained connected to practical tasks.

A question may arise: How could writing so powerfully affect society and thought if barely hundreds or thousands of people were literate in the irrigation civilizations? The literacy of the Sumerians and then the Akkadians was a form of craft literacy, as Havelock would describe it, or better to say "sacred literacy": it was used mainly by the caste of priests for their professional needs. However, the monopoly on knowledge granted political control, and thus the use of the medium became political power, even though only a relatively small portion of the population used this medium.

In his historical study, Jaspers also acknowledged that the influence of writing originated from its use by the bureaucratic elite, and, conversely, the influence of writing gave rise to this bureaucratic elite. "The indispensability of writing to administration led to the acquisition of a dominant social position by the scribes, who formed an intellectual aristocracy," he writes.[2]

Those who maintained records and had access to them wielded religious and political power. This explains the ripple effect of early writing, even though most of the population was not literate and therefore could not experience the direct effects of writing. Writing influenced society through the elites who used it. Innis noticed this symbiosis of power and writing in his *Empire and Communication*:

> The old magic was transformed into a new and more potent record of the written word. Priests and scribes interpreted a slowly changing tradition and provided a justification for established authority. An extended social structure strengthened the position of an individual leader with military power who gave orders to agents who received and executed them. The sword and pen worked together.[3]

---

[1] Logan, Robert. (2004 [1986]). *The Alphabet Effect*, p. 85.

[2] Jaspers, Karl. (2021 [1949]). *The Origin and Goal of History*, p. 55.

[3] Innis, Harold. (1950). *Empire and Communications*, p. 11. Interestingly, Innis published his main communication treatises, *Empire and Communications* and *The Bias of Communications*, in 1950 and 1951, respectively, which coincided with the publication of Jaspers' *The Origin and Goal of History* in 1949. While Innis focused on the social and cognitive effects of writing, the consequences he described aligned with Jaspers' idea of the

In the cascades of media effects, writing altered cognitive abilities and social structures. Moreover, the changes triggered by writing themselves caused further changes.

Service and disservice of writing

Media studies in general explore what we do with media. Media ecology looks at what media do to us. When we see media as tools for completing some tasks or achieving some goals, we think of how well or not so much well they serve us. However, since media create our environment, their environmental impact can also be detrimental to us.

People have always complained about new media because new media always disturb the previous order of things. Therefore, both the perceived effect of media and their real impact can be evaluated in terms of not only service but also disservice, to use McLuhan terminology.[1]

The first to recognize media's capacity of disservice was Egyptian King Thamus, as recounted by Socrates in Plato's *Phaedrus* (c. 370 BCE). Some accounts hold that another name of Thamus was Ammon, which means he was the supreme god who ruled Egypt and the entire world. The god Theuth was his court scientist. Among many other arts, including arithmetic, geometry, and astronomy, Theuth also invented writing.[2] He brought these inventions to King Thamus for approval.

King Thamus assessed Theuth's innovations, praising some of them and rejecting others. When it came to letters, Theuth the Inventor proudly

---

Axial Age. Thus, the foundations of media ecology (Innis) and Jaspers' concept of history overlapped from the very beginning, despite Jaspers and Innis being most likely unaware of each other's works at the time.

[1] For example: "All I am saying is that any product or innovation creates both service and disservice environments which reshape human attitudes." McLuhan in a letter to Jonathan Miller on 22 April 1970; in: Molinaro, McLuhan & Toye 1987, p. 404.

[2] The archetypal role of a deity who favored humans and provided them with knowledge and technology was later embodied by Prometheus. According to some accounts, Prometheus not only gifted humans with fire and crafts but also the arts of numbers and, by association with numbers, letters. It's worth noting that in the early Greek antiquity, numbers (math, accounting, and geometry) were still of higher divine significance than letters (writing), which might support Schmandt-Besserat's theory regarding the origin of writing from tokens and counting.

presented them: "I have discovered a potion for memory and for wisdom,"[1] as recounted by Socrates. Thamus the Inspector, however, saw the danger. This is how Thamus responded:

> O most expert Theuth, <...> since you are the father of writing, your affection for it has made you describe its effects as the opposite of what they really are. In fact, it will introduce forgetfulness into the soul of those who learn it: they will not practice using their memory because they will put their trust in writing, which is external and depends on signs that belong to others, instead of trying to remember from the inside, completely on their own. You have not discovered a potion for remembering but for reminding; you provide your students with the appearance of wisdom, not with its reality. Your invention will enable them to hear many things without being properly taught, and they will imagine that they have come to know much while for the most part they will know nothing. And they will be difficult to get along with, since they will merely appear to be wise instead of really being so.[2]

Neither Theuth nor Thamus discussed what exactly humans would write down with Theuth's invention. It did not matter. Writing itself, regardless of the content of what was written, would affect humans. Both ancient Egyptian deities agreed that the medium is the message. Five millennia before McLuhan, they naturally established that is the medium itself, not the message, that "reshapes human attitudes" (McLuhan).

In their debate over writing, the Egyptian gods also touched upon some other of McLuhan's ideas. They both held that writing was an "extension of men" – the extension of the human mental capacity of memorizing and data processing. Theuth believed that this extension would be a beneficial service to the wisdom and memory of the Egyptians. King Thamus, on the contrary, knew that if people were to extend their memory from the inside of the body to the outside, into a media device of letters, they would have their natural wisdom and memory "numbed" or "amputated" (McLuhan's terms). Thamus essentially described how the natural equilibrium of the senses and cognitive faculties would be disturbed by the new medium. And this is precisely what happened in history, despite his divine objection and direct prohibition.

---

[1] Plato. *Phaedrus*, [275-275b]. Translated by Harold N. Fowler (1925).

[2] Plato. *Phaedrus*, [275-275b]. Translated by Harold N. Fowler (1925).

The service of any media is the extension of cognitive or physical human faculties. However, as McLuhan highlights, by reaching farther, any new media extension supplies 1) more data and 2) more intense data for sensory and cognitive processing, thus causing sensory and cognitive overload in people, leading to frustration and anxiety. McLuhan writes:

> In the physical stress of superstimulation of various kinds, the central nervous system acts to protect itself by a strategy of amputation or isolation of the offending organ, sense, or function.[1]

There could also be another explanation for this "self-amputation": if capacities are not used and trained, they deteriorate. If neurons are not fired together, they are not wired together.

So, the disservice of media comes through numbing and amputating capacities or organs that had been responsible for those functions that are now extended outside the body and into a media device. This can be stated in the form of a paradox: a new medium debilitates certain human faculties while enhancing general human performance.

The services and disservices of media manifest at both individual and social levels.

When used as an instrument, writing (like any other medium) affected the sensory-cognitive capacities of the user. Writing has improved the memory function of humans as social beings but diminished the memory capacity of humans as physical beings. Writing has increased the capacity of abstraction, and humans have acquired confidence in judging things they have never encountered; but in return, they have lost proficiency in encountering things and operating with them in a natural environment.

When the individual use of writing reaches sufficient statistical scale, the instrumental effect of writing turned into an environmental force. The individual memory capacities of humans deteriorate but the collective memory capacities are tremendously enhanced, which leads to increased social complexity. To deal with the new levels of data complexity, new social institutions need to be introduced: scribes, scholars, schools, libraries, science and so on. This affects humans' cognitive abilities with the second wave of impacts: the needs for classification, theorizing, analyzing, synthesizing, and summarizing emerges.

---

[1] McLuhan, Marshall. (1994 [1964]). *Understanding Media*, p. 42.

Historically, each new medium brought some gains and caused some losses. A new society was formed that offers people new benefits, while the old society was dismantled. This process is always accompanied by disturbances, the breaking of traditions, and the disappearance of entire social classes or even entire nations (as McLuhan put it, “Every new technology necessitates a new war”[1]).

Now one can decide whether they like the services of media more than they dislike their disservices, not that their choice will make any difference. Media evolution moves forward according to its inner logic anyway. To incentivize humans to maintain the development of media, media evolution generally accommodates, in return, better extensions of humans in time and space. So, the ratio of the services and disservices of media remains “positive” – at least positive for media evolution.

[1] McLuhan, Marshall, and Fiore, Quentin. (1968). *War & Peace in the Global Village*, p. 98.

6. The features of orality

The literate bias

For a literate mind, the true nature of orality often remains in a blind spot. Orality is most commonly associated with folk songs, ballads, nursery rhymes, and so on. After giving it some thought, most people will find that orality is illiteracy – something incomplete in comparison to what literate individuals possess. To use Ong's metaphor, this view of orality is "like thinking of horses as automobiles without wheels."[1] Recognizing orality as not folk songs or illiteracy but the innate state of mind requires some effort and expertise.

As a state of mind, orality preceded literacy, but nothing preceded orality. Humans might have "invented" literacy, but they did not invent orality. It came with the factory settings of Homo sapiens as soon as implements and speech separated humans from animals.

Ong expressed a similar idea when he said that the world of sound is "the natural habitat of language."[2] But our concept of language is too "linguistic," too focused on verbal communication to understand the true nature of language in the conditions of orality. According to Ong,

> Fully literate persons can only with great difficulty imagine what a primary oral culture is like, that is, a culture with no knowledge whatsoever of writing or even of the possibility of writing.[3]

Frankly, it is similarly difficult for us to recognize what literacy is. Just as orality is often reduced to folk songs or illiteracy, so is literacy, in lay perception, often reduced to the ability to read and write. The fact that literacy is a way of seeing the world and operating in it is hard to comprehend. "The fish is not aware of the water" was one of the favourite proverbs of Marshal McLuhan. To recognize its environment, the fish must be pulled out into the antienvironment – the air.

Since we live in an environment shaped by literacy, it is invisible for us – we do not know its characteristics. Even less do we know about the

---

1 Ong, Walter. (2002 [1982]), *Orality and Literacy*, p. 12.

2 Ong, Walter. (2002 [1982]), *Orality and Literacy*, p. 8.

3 Ong, Walter. (2002 [1982]), *Orality and Literacy*, p. 31.

environment of orality. However, the absence of reflection on literacy or orality does not automatically imply the absence of experience. We surely have experience with literacy as a state of mind and a social order, but we also have experience with orality – an experience that is not only inherited but also lived through personally.

Some communities within even highly literate societies continue oral traditions dating millennia back to the time of primary orality. A pure example of this is the mafia. In other situations, people also revert to orality. This happens when social dynamics are regulated by means of oral communication. Collectives of hobbyists, fraternities, expeditions, field worker groups, political debates, prisons, and the entire Gulag Archipelago, along with some other social or professional groups or activities, still exhibit the features of residual orality to varying degrees.

Even a friends' gathering retrieves some features of orality as soon as people put down their cellphones and become immersed into oral practices, such as small talk or storytelling. And family reunions – certainly. They had not changed much since those evenings spent by families in caves around campfires and until the arrival of the TV at the family hearth.

The residual orality of literate people, however, gives only a glimpse of insight into the orality of people who never knew writing – such is the definition of primary orality suggested by Walter Ong. Contemporary residual orality, of course, differs significantly from the primary orality of preliterate people.

For a literate person, the comprehension of the oral mindset might be hard. For an oral person, the comprehension of the literate mindset is impossible. So, literate people have some advantage in understanding both conditions; they can deconstruct, with some effort, both literacy and orality. The trick is that orality can only be explored in its opposition to literacy and vice versa. They are perceivable only together as environment and antienvironment. To each other, orality and literacy are distorting mirrors in which their specifications can be seen through distortions. That is why the literate bias not only prevents but also *helps* to understand orality – after acquiring an awareness of what the literate bias itself is, of course.

Interestingly, the need for such dichotomic reflection was driven by changes in media. According to the already quoted Ong's observation,

> Our understanding of the differences between orality and literacy developed only in the electronic age, not earlier. Contrasts between electronic media and print have sensitized us to the earlier contrast between writing and orality.[1]

Another significant feature of this dichotomy is that, in a culture with writing and general education, literacy develops rapidly, perhaps within the span of several generations. Orality evolved over tens of thousands of years. Orality as a state of mind and culture started with oral speech as a communication device (we still use it) and developed it into a complex device of memorization. The memorizing function of orality has been replaced and suppressed by literacy and is mostly lost, though some residual forms of it (such as proverbs or idioms) persist and are now even being retrieved by digital orality in the forms of memes.

The multisensory nature of orality

Since orality operates with spoken words while literacy is based on writing, one might assume that the core sensory difference between orality and literacy is represented by the opposition "spoken word versus written word." However, this opposition is not about "listening versus reading" but rather about "immersion versus detachment."

Under the condition of orality, humans do not just talk "face-to-face" with each other – they directly face whatever they do, with their entire sensorium involved. Orality entails immediate presence not just for communication exchange but also for doing everything else.

Harold Innis was among the first who noticed that orality is not just illiteracy. It also has very peculiar sensory characteristics. He wrote in *The Bias of Communication* (1951):

> In oral intercourse the eye, ear, and brain, the senses and the faculties acted together in busy co-operation and rivalry each eliciting, stimulating, and supplementing the other.[2]

In orality, any sensory signal matters – any sensory signal *makes* sense. Perception is syncretic, and the sense of hearing works together with other senses.

---

[1] Ong, Walter. (2002 [1982]), *Orality and Literacy*, p. 2.

[2] Innis, Harold. (2008 [1951]). *The Bias of Communication*, p. 105

In analyzing the sensory differences between orality and literacy, McLuhan developed the dual concept of acoustic space and visual space. He turned to exploring the sensory features of orality and literacy because he was studying the effects of electricity. McLuhan proposed that electric media retribalize society precisely because they retrieve acoustic space – the sensory mode of perception typical for orality.

It might appear challenging to understand why television immerses the viewers in acoustic space. Television is "tele-*vision*" – we see it with our eyes. The point is that McLuhan's "visual space" refers not to vision per se but to vision as an *isolated sense*, which is precisely what vision becomes when we read. The most crucial sensory-cognitive effect of writing was that it isolated vision from the natural ratio of senses. All other senses are numbed when we write or read – vision remains "alone." The isolation of vision by literacy is the entry point for understanding McLuhan's dichotomy of acoustic vs. visual space.

Acoustic space represents the natural ratio of all senses in the sensorium, adjusted for operating in the natural environment. In acoustic space, a person is immersed in the "panorama of sensual experience."[1] McLuhan used the words "field" and "spherical" when describing acoustic space:

> The set of harmonic relations constitutes a field entity, which experimental psychologists refer to as acoustic space... Psychologists tell us that acoustic space is spherical because we hear simultaneously from all directions.[2]

Acoustic space is characterized by 360-degree immediacy and simultaneity – by the all-at-once-from-around perception of the world. "Acoustic space, always penetrated by tactility and other senses, is spherical, discontinuous, non-homogeneous, resonant, and dynamic," according to Marshal and Eric McLuhan's *Laws of Media*.[3]

In media ecology, acoustic space is a common metaphor for orality. Acoustic space is the sensory mode of orality. In a 1969 *Playboy* interview, McLuhan says:

---

[1] Havelock, Eric A. (1963). *Preface to Plato*, p. 254.

[2] McLuhan, Marshall. (1970 [1969]). *Counterblast*, p. 112.

[3] McLuhan, Marshall, and McLuhan, Eric. (1988). *Laws of Media: The New Science*, p. 33.

> The man of the tribal world led a complex, kaleidoscopic life precisely because the ear, unlike the eye, cannot be focused and is synaesthetic rather than analytical and linear. Speech is an utterance, or more precisely, an outering, of all our senses at once; the auditory field is simultaneous, the visual successive.[1]

Acoustic space delivers all signals from the environment. The processing of the "rich resonance of the tribal echoland"[2] keeps cognition busy. Environmental immersion in acoustic space is a full-time job that subjugates all leisure time and even sleep. Environmental immersion puts the sensorium into a state of permanent multitasking needed for 360-degree, here-and-now control over one's surroundings. This type of multitasking discourages cognitive concentration or specialization. You cannot afford to be distracted from your surroundings by any one thing for too long; otherwise, you might miss a crucial signal essential for survival. In the natural environment, something can harm or eat you, for example, if you stop controlling your surroundings. Acoustic space demands total immersion. This is why, according to McLuhan, before writing, "man lived in acoustic space: boundless, directionless, horizonless, in the dark of the mind, in the world of emotion, by primordial intuition, terror."[3]

The sensory-cognitive state of acoustic space is better understood when contrasted with the visual space created by literacy.

Visual space represents a cognitive perception shaped by the sensorium in which vision is detached from other senses and provides linear, one-at-a-time input of information, while other senses are numbed. It is important to note that, unlike spherical acoustic perception, vision is frontal. With the widest possible peripheral vision, eyesight remains unidirectionally focused. Unlike hearing, vision not just allows – it "calls" to be isolated and focused.

According to Walter Ong, sight situates the observer outside of what they see, at a distance; sight separates the viewer from the world. Sound, on the contrary, "pours into the hearer." "Sight isolates, sound incorporates," states Ong.[4] That is why orality submerges, whereas literacy detaches. Ong writes:

---

1 McLuhan, Marshall. (1969, March). "The Playboy Interview." *Playboy*, p. 59.

2 McLuhan, Marshall. (1969, March). "The Playboy Interview." *Playboy*, p. 59.

3 McLuhan, Marshall, and Fiore, Quentin. (1967). *The Medium Is the Massage*, p. 48.

4 Ong, Walter. (2002 [1982]), *Orality and Literacy*, p. 70.

> You can immerse yourself in hearing, in sound. There is no way to immerse yourself similarly in sight. By contrast with vision, the dissecting sense, sound is thus a unifying sense. A typical visual ideal is clarity and distinctness, a taking apart... The auditory ideal, by contrast, is harmony, a putting together... [1]

The centering action of sound, continues Ong, affects humans' sense of the cosmos: "The field of sound is not spread out before me but is all around me."

To highlight the idea that electric media retrieve the panoramic and simultaneous – all-at-once-from-around – perception of the world, McLuhan later extended his concept of acoustic space to audile-tactile space. As he clarified in 1969's *Counterblast*, "Tactility is not a sense but an interplay of all senses."[2] Whatever the ratio of all the other senses is, it is tactility that applies this ratio to the body's functioning. Tactility allows people to interact with the physical environment using data from all the other senses. Touch is the most *immediate* sense. It uses its own signals but also incorporates signals from all other senses.

Acoustic space confines humans within the environment, whereas visual space excludes humans from the environment. Visual space puts them outside and beyond, thereby allowing external observation. Acoustic space prioritizes reflexes, while visual space affords reflection. The mode of perception predefines cognitive "habits." This is how orality keeps humans immersed in the environment, while literacy detaches them from it.

Being always engaged with the environment through the rich signals of all senses favours situational thinking – the awareness of any situation through its tangible signals from inside, not outside. As Joshua Meyrowitz puts it, "Oral peoples are always at the center of their communication world, with few opportunities or perceptual tools to stand back from it and analyze it."[3]

In *Guttenberg Galaxy*, McLuhan refers to a paper, "Film literacy in Africa," published by John Wilson from the African Institute of London University in the journal *Canadian Communications* in 1961.[4] To combat

[1] Ong, Walter. (2002 [1982]), *Orality and Literacy*, p. 70.
[2] McLuhan, Marshall. (1970 [1969]). *Counterblast*, p. 23.
[3] Meyrowitz, Joshua. (2010). "Media evolution and cultural change", p. 57.
[4] "Film Literacy in Africa." Canadian Communications, vol. I, no. 4, summer, 1961, pp. 7-14.

malaria, sanitary inspectors created a 5-minute film explaining, in a slow and detailed manner, how to dispose of tins and how to prevent the accumulation of standing water, where mosquitoes breed. The film was shown in an African village with a high rate of malaria. However, when viewers were asked what they had seen, they answered that they had seen a chicken. The producers of the film were not even aware that there was a chicken in the movie. The preliterate mind could not see an abstract message amid the concrete details. The Western-style message, designed to exploit the isolated sense of vision, was not received. McLuhan comments:

> Literacy gives people the power to focus a little way in front of an image so that we take in the whole image or picture at a glance. Non-literate people have no such acquired habit and do not look at objects in our way. <...> Thus they have no detached point of view. They are wholly with the object. They go empathically into it. The eye is used, not in perspective but tactually, as it were. Euclidean spaces depending on much separation of sight from touch and sound are not known to them.[1]

"Non-literate societies cannot see films or photos without much training," concludes McLuhan.[2]

Interestingly, a similar effect was discovered by the Soviet psychologist Alexander Luria during his study of educational dynamics in Middle Asia in the 1930s. He sought to demonstrate how much the Soviet regime had improved the lives of the locals who lived in the conditions of an agricultural society, or, in media-ecological terms, in the conditions of orality.

Luria explored the cognitive differences between those who were illiterate and those involved in education and collective labor, meaning those already influenced by the Soviets. A series of surveys he conducted examined the receptiveness of the locals to optical-geometrical illusions, as this was a trending concept in gestalt psychology at the time. Luria found that non-educated participants could not perceive the "illusions" that were easily recognized by educated (meaning literate) people.[3]

---

[1] McLuhan, Marshall. (1962). *The Gutenberg Galaxy*, p. 37.

[2] McLuhan, Marshall. (1962). *The Gutenberg Galaxy*, p. 37.

[3] According to an anecdote told by Luria himself, he telegraphed in exaltation to Lev Vygotsky in Moscow: "The Uzbeks do not have illusions!" Vygotsky was frightened, as he thought that Luria was referring to "illusions regarding the Soviet regime," and the telegram

The capacity to isolate an abstract pattern or an intended message from the background full of tangible signals is a conditioned cognitive skill. It came with the development of writing. There is simply no need for it in the natural environment.

Acoustic space transmits signals for actions, interactions, feelings, emotions – for "spatial awareness" (McLuhan).[1] The acoustic space of orality creates perceptions, while the visual space of literacy creates conceptions. Describing the Homeric (meaning oral) type of consciousness, Havelock suggests avoiding the word "knowledge." Instead, he uses the notion of an "over-all body of experience" to refer to the sensory perception of the world in Homeric Greece.[2]

Acoustic space represents the natural ratio of the senses and keeps humans engaged with the natural environment.

Environmental immersion: experiencing the world live

In his 2017 *Media Ecology*, Lance Strate shares a gem he found in Max Frisch's 1959 novel *Homo Faber*: "Technology is the art of never having to experience the world."[3]

Strate writes:

> Whatever comes between us and our world, that is, whatever mediates between us and our world, becomes our world. Our mediations are what we know. They are all we know. They become our environment.[4]

---

was surely read by the political police. Allegedly, he telegraphed back in panic: "And Luria does not have brain!!!" It should be noted, however, that Luria's conclusion regarding the optical illusions of the illiterates was later disputed. See: Ясницкий, Антон. (2013). «'У узбеков ЕСТЬ иллюзий!'. Заочная полемика между Лурией и Коффка». / Yasnitsky. Anton. (2013). "'The Uzbeks DO HAVE illusions!'" The Luria-Koffka controversy." *Dubna Psychological Journal*. 2013-3, pp. 1-25.

[1] "Acoustic space as known by preliterates (and many non-alphabetic cultures), by contrast, is presumably the natural mode of spatial awareness, for it was not the side-effect of any technology." – McLuhan, Marshall, and McLuhan, Eric. (1988). *Laws of Media*, p. 31.

[2] Havelock, Eric A. (1963). *Preface to Plato*, p. 198.

[3] Strate, Lance. (2017). *Media Ecology*, p. 110.

[4] Strate, Lance. (2017). *Media Ecology*, p. 110.

If media mediate the world, then the less we use media, the more of the world we sense. Conversely, being fully immersed in media, we sense no world at all. And this seems to be the destination point for media evolution: when we completely merge with our media, they will become our only "natural" environment. At this point, media will lose their *mediating* function. The user, media, and environment will become one.

On the opposite side of media evolution, in its very beginning, there was a human being fully immersed in the world with no mediation, like all other living creatures. The Promethean gift of fire and tools started mediation, shielding humans from Nature but within Nature.

The metaphor shows that humans with speech and Promethean media (fire and implements) had no choice but to be immersed in the natural world. This condition was described as Stage A of Paul Levinson's "anthropotropic model" of media evolution.[1] At this stage, humans might have technologies in use (the mentioned Promethean tools), but communication itself is not mediated. *Unmediated* communication is *immediate* – it requires talking face to face.

Stage A, or orality, renders the world perceived naturally, as if it is sensed through biological sensors, even if extended or enhanced by tools. When smashing something with a hammer, humans still had the tactile perception of recoil in their hand. Action was mediated in space but immediate in time.

The rule "the less we use media, the more of the world we sense" has a corollary. If media extend humans, then the less we use media, the smaller our world is. The spherical acoustic space of a human experiencing the world only through talking and implements is the most this individual can reach out with their speech and implements. When considering the "longest-reaching" implements, such as arrows or throwing weapons, an oral person's spherical reach is approximately 50–60 meters in radius. Vision extends an individual's sensory perception to hundreds of meters, and so does hearing, if incoming sounds are loud enough. This observation can be questioned in terms of distance, but it implies a pattern: an oral person's experience of the world is physically limited by the reaching-out capacity of the sensorium, even when the sensorium is extended by tools.

[1] Levinson, Paul. (2017 [1978]). Human Replay: A Theory of the Evolution of Media. Connected Editions. P. 24.

Speech, without a doubt, can extend individual experience beyond physical reach. But for "practicing" speech, others are required. Oral experience, extended beyond personal reach, is the product of collective efforts. The world reached out to through speech is the world of the tribe, not of the individual.

As a consequence, an oral person does not endeavour to judge beyond personal or tribal experience – beyond the experience lived through, individually or collectively. This also was confirmed by Alexander Luria in his study. Luria asked illiterate participants to complete a syllogism: "In the far North, where there is snow, all bears are white. Novaya Zemlya is in the far North. What color are the bears in Novaya Zemlya?" The typical answers were, "I don't know, I have never seen them," or "You need to ask those who were there. Or the elders, they might know."[1]

Interestingly, when the syllogism was offered to a barely literate 45-year-old foreman of a collective farm, he answered: "To go by your words, they should all be white."[2] As Ong highlights in analyzing this case, being just recently made familiar with the literate way of thinking, this person still refers to the description of the researcher ("to go by your words").[3] He does not take responsibility for a speculative statement that has no base in his experience. Nevertheless, he appeared to be capable of completing the syllogism.

Illiterate people (or rather, people of primary orality) were not practically interested in what was beyond their reach. They were not capable of extracting such knowledge out of speculation (syllogism). Why would they want to do that? For this very reason, unlike literate individuals, they refrained from making statements about things they had not personally experienced.

Environmental immersion also has a rigid temporal dimension. All beings immersed in the environment are imprisoned in the eternal "now." Orality is always about "now," while literacy is always about "not now." Living in the "now" leaves no time for reflection. Orality incorporates an individual into events – into the world of the "here and now," while literacy

---

[1] Luria, Alexander. (1976). *Cognitive Development*, p. 108. See also: Mir, Andrey. (2022). "Media-ecological engineering of the Soviets." *Explorations in Media Ecology*, Volume 21, Issue 2-3, Oct 2022, p. 150.

[2] Luria, Alexander. (1976). *Cognitive Development*, p. 114.

[3] Ong, Walter. (2002 [1982]), *Orality and Literacy*, p. 52.

allows everyone to incorporate any time and any space of the world into the written – the induced reality.

While analyzing the TV replays used in news or sports broadcasts, McLuhan comes to a conclusion about the opposition between experience and meaning. The TV replay extracts meaning out of experience without experiencing. "In fact, such is the nature of experience that it is almost inevitable that we do miss the meaning," concludes McLuhan. Sports referees now rely on replays to render decisions about what really just happened. In this way, according to McLuhan, the instant replay exposes "the difference between cognition and recognition." [1] Living in the moment and through the moment and being immersed in the "here and now" obstructs the very possibility of recognition. Some media violence over the "normal" presence of time is needed to recognize what is happening. This is what recording media enabled, starting with writing and then further to TV: they replay reality, extending it in time and giving time for reflection.

The limitation of the world by spatial personal reach and the temporal eternal "now" is one of the features of primary orality that has been retrieved by digital orality. In digital media, this limitation of personal reach is known under the term "filter bubble," as coined by Eli Pariser in 2011.[2] The conditions, of course, are different: the digital bubble is not physical but social, and its range is limited not by senses or throwing implements, but by algorithms and the user's social graphs. However, the effect is similar: it is shaped in a fashion of audile-tactile space; it is simultaneous in a 360-degree sphere and strictly limited by "practical needs," now shaped by digital media.

Surprisingly (or not), the literate aptitude for speculative statements with no support in experience has survived digitalization. Physical distance is no longer an obstacle to "awareness" about polar bears. Media deliver the images of them – media induce the faked, simulated experience of seeing polar bears. Since social media encourage personal engagement, users can, or rather even have to, make judgments regarding events or processes of which they have no real personal experience whatsoever. They have only media experience regarding most of the things they encounter on the

---

[1] McLuhan, Marshall. (1974). "At the moment of Sputnik the planet became a global theater in which there are no spectators but only actors," p. 57.

[2] Pariser, Eli. (2011). *The Filter Bubble: How the New Personalized Web Is Changing What We Read and How We Think.*

Internet. Nevertheless, personal non-experiential judgment has survived literacy and flourishes on the internet. Such a judgment remains speculative but ceases to be syllogistic; social media judgment represents an oral-literate hybrid of speculation and immersion.

The environmental immersion of orality also means an immersion into the most important part of the environment – the collective.

Collective involvement: you'll never walk alone

In 1938, a small fire broke out in the stands of the Paris National Velodrome during a sports event. The panicking crowd rushed to the only exit. The situation was on the verge of becoming deadly. Luckily, there were two psychologists in the crowd who began to loudly chant: "Ne-pousse-pas! Ne-pousse-pas!" ("Do not push! Do not push!"). The rhythm was picked up by those around them, spread like a wave, and synchronized the chaotic movement of the crowd. The panic transformed into a coordinated action. The enthusiasm of coordinated efforts helped people safely leave the arena.[1]

The call not to push sounded reasonable; however, the crowd was not so much reasoned but rather resonated by rhythmic chanting. The content of the chant suggested a strategy, but the rhythmic chanting delivered it to everybody and made them comply. The rhythmic chanting was the medium of the message that induced cooperative behaviour that likely saved lives.

Rhythm was one of the primordial means of communion. Since communion is an evolutionarily beneficial strategy, synchronization – including synchronization through rhythm – was supported by a hormonal cocktail that induced pleasure. This produces the phenomenon of trance, which is often induced by rhythm in many people, especially in oral

---

[1] The case is recounted by Akop Nazaretyan in his book *Psychology of Spontaneous Mass Behavior* (2005 [2001]). Nazaretyan was the author of the principle of Techno-Humanitarian Balance; see: Nazaretyan, Akop (2017). "Mega-history and the twenty-first century Singularity puzzle." Social Evolution & History, Volume 16, Number 1, March 2017. Interestingly, as an expert in crowd control and the political psychology of the masses, Nazaretyan worked for the Central Committee of the Soviet Communist Party in the 1970s and trained revolutionary cadres for anti-capitalist resistance in the Third World. When visiting the guerrillas in Latin America, "Comandante Akopo", aside from his ideological work, also gathered a lot of ethnographic material for his later universal evolutionary theory, which somewhat resembles Teilhard de Chardin's theory of mega-evolution. See Akop Nazaretyan's profile on the Social Studies website.

cultures. Rhythm serves as the metronome of collectivity that is ingrained in humans physiologically. Synchronization through rhythm is physiologically reinforced by the feeling of being part of a larger organism, by the sensation of multiplied strength in unity. With the help of rhythm, you can organize any number of people, even without knowing their language; if you make the right rhythm, they will join in.[1]

We humans evolved not only through interactions with the environment but also, first and foremost, through interactions with each other. Others were the most crucial element of our environment, either beneficial or threatening. This is why environmental immersion also implies collective involvement: an individual cannot be not engaged with others. In an oral society, collective involvement is as total as environmental immersion itself.

The members of the collective had to emotionally tune into cohabitation. The series of oral acts people displayed to each other for tuning in had to be gestural, emotional, loud, salient, excessive in all aspects, and engaging in every possible way – something McLuhan called "empathic involvement."[2] For tribal cohesion to occur, it is necessary for everyone to be prominently present and signaling their readiness for connection and inclusion. Orality made people loudly and saliently exposed to each other for the sake of coordination and synchronization. Being an extravert is an organic condition of orality.

By filling shared spaces with the acoustic bubble of their self-exhibition, an oral individual asserts their level of integration into the collective, which also becomes a claim for status in the hierarchy. Those who are better "sensed" by the collective can demand greater social benefits. Individuals who are self-absorbed will likely lose in the competition for status and social benefits in a collective with a strong oral background. That is why an oral individual carries the cloud of their acoustic space with them like a smell – so that everyone around can get involved or be repelled. Loud and overtly affective speech may be

---

[1] In *Understanding Media*, Marshall McLuhan referred to radio as "the tribal drum," implying its ability to audially – immersively – synchronize nations into tribes of imperial scale. See: McLuhan, Marshall. (1994 [1964]). *Understanding Media*, p. 297. He underscored radio's crucial role in Hitler's regime (Ibid. p. 300). Through forming tribal unity at an unprecedented scale, radio, indeed, created all three major empires of the 20th century – the Communist, the Nazi, and the consumerist ones.

[2] McLuhan, Marshall. (1962). *The Guttenberg Galaxy*, p. 39.

considered ill-mannered in a literate culture, but in orality it is a survival strategy.

Empathic involvement can be seen as harmony: the community harmonizes its life through the total mutual exposure of its members. This harmonization comes at the cost of the total absence of private life. In orality, one cannot keep their life to themselves. It is always shared, exposed to others, and intertwined with the lives of others. You'll never walk alone. Individuals are involved in the exchange of obtrusive phatic signals (social grooming and requests for affirmation). Intimacy, in whatever sense of this concept, is likely impossible in an oral culture; intimacy is a side-effect of literacy.

The oral community would be a nightmare for an introvert. For a literate and self-absorbed person, just as for an electrician, insulation is better than earthing. It's quite possible that introverts are a by-product of literacy, too.

Some features of orality persist in our everyday interpersonal communication, though they are hardly recognizable. For example, the aforementioned phatic function of speech serves to establish and maintain social relations. When we meet a neighbour in the elevator, we chat about what a rainy day it is outside. The conversation conveys no useful information for either participant – both have just been outside and possess identical data about the weather. The meaning of the exchange is not to share valuable information but to reinforce our mutual statuses as neighbors and thus maintain tribal unity. Linguists assume that phatic interactions may comprise up to 30% of everyday conversations. The only purpose of these interactions is social grooming and establishing mutual statuses in social hierarchy, and through them ensuring collective coherence.

Small talk is inherently intrusive – we must show interest in someone's daily life. Contemporary urban culture imposes significant restrictions on such intrusiveness: you cannot ask a neighbour about their relations with their spouse after hearing some noise from their apartment. You cannot ask a coworker why he or she looks so pale today. Weather small talk is the safest. In an oral community, in a small village, there are no such restrictions. Everything will be asked and expected to be answered, driven by the survival strategy of "empathic involvement."

Under the conditions of orality, small talk was not actually small. They were of *Homeric* proportion and included vocal performance and pantomime. But there was also something atypical for the contemporary phatic exercises of literate minds. The exchange of information about the weather, recent hunts, family scandals, and other personal affairs held real meaning in primary orality. These talks were the news media of the oral era. The news has such a peculiar quality – it becomes and remains important as long as you follow it. Continuous news consumption fosters the habit of news: in an oral society, gossiping was an imperative that kept the tribe together.

And there was even more to it. The rapport provided by the phatic exchange served to tune up the collective mechanism of memorization. This effect of the phatic function is best explained in contrast to literacy. When writing emerged, it assumed the function of memorization. We can easily memorize or communicate information in writing – no rapport with our pen and paper, computer, or smartphone is required. Well, we still need to configure them in a certain way, but it's more of a technical customization. We don't need to get them to act in unison with us by imparting emotional and mental tones.

Now, imagine that the only medium for communication and memorization for everyone is not paper or a smartphone but another person. The only way to succeed in communication and memorization is by triggering their response, achieving their rapport, and inciting their contribution to collective coherence. Most communicative efforts have to be spent on tuning them in. The excessively affective speech of orality included efforts for achieving collective rapport and cohesion for coordination and memorization.

Writing and then printing allowed for collective coordination on a scale unimaginable in orality. And so did electronic media. However, while writing and print coordinated people by coopting them individually into shared ideas, radio and television coordinated people through shared emotions in a semblance of the tribal acoustic space – through "empathic involvement."

Social media deepened this reversal towards the emotional engagement of everybody with the collective. In McLuhan's words, said in 1967, 50 years before social media,

> Too many people know too much about each other. Our new environment compels commitment and participation. We have become irrevocably involved with, and responsible for, each other.[1]

The exposure of everyone to everyone on social media also serves as a request for others to resonate and acknowledge the existence and rightness of a user. These ongoing mutual exposure and constant communication requests make social media even more akin to the village than the global village of the television era, when people were emotionally engaged with collective issues but at least did not expose themselves.

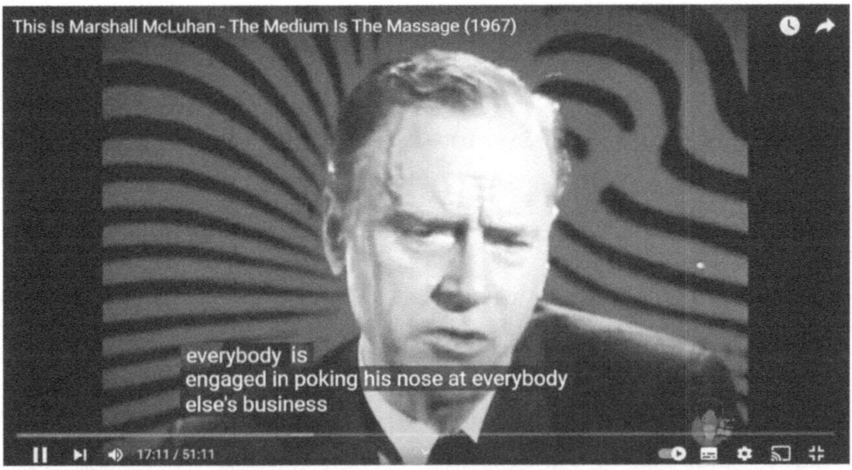

Figure 16. An excerpt from the movie: *This Is Marshall McLuhan: The Medium Is the Massage.* (1967). Directed by Guy Fraumeni and Ernest Pintoff.

In the movie *This Is Marshall McLuhan: The Medium Is the Massage*, made in 1967, McLuhan sounds as if he is describing the social media of the 2020s:

> The Global Village is at once as wide as the planet and as small as a little town where everybody is maliciously engaged and poking his nose in everybody else's business. The Global Village is a world in which you don't necessarily have harmony – you have extreme concerns with everybody else's business and are much involved in everybody else's life... It doesn't necessarily mean harmony, peace

[1] McLuhan, Marshall, and Fiore, Quentin. (1967). *The Medium Is the Massage: An Inventory of Effects*, p. 24.

and quiet, but it does mean huge involvement in everybody else's affairs.[1]

According to McLuhan, such relations emerge when "the spaces and times are pulled out from between people" by electronic media and people are exposed – "get close" – to each other. We can clearly see here the pattern of reversal from literacy to orality by electronic media and now digital media. They achieve it by removing the literacy-induced detachment of individuals from the environment and each other. As a result, "everybody becomes totally involved in everybody."[2]

Verbomotor intensity: orality as speech-behaviour

Non-symbolic communication does not convey meaning – it induces emotional states. Lev Vygotsky wrote that communication between animals that try to affect each other with evocative behaviour does not deserve to be called communication, as it rather resembles contamination. According to him, "The frightened goose, seeing danger and raising the whole flock with its cry, not so much communicates what it saw but infects the rest with its fear."[3]

Human speech evolved to convey symbolic meaning. However, this process had lasted millennia. In orality, spoken words were not the same semantic carriers as we use now, after 5000 years of literacy.[4] Emotions, tones, vocality, gestures, memes, voice and other extralinguistic factors carried information as well. Speech evolved from the vocal-pantomimic performance of primordial human. Initially, people just mimicked what they wanted to convey. According to Walter Ong, the oral framework is "performance-oriented rather than information-oriented."[5] In early orality, the lack of semantic means had to be compensated for by the intensity of expression that could provide "empathic involvement." We can still explain ourselves through pantomime, but it would require some acting and a lot

---

1 An excerpt from the movie: *This Is Marshall McLuhan: The Medium Is the Massage.* (1967). Directed by Guy Fraumeni and Ernest Pintoff. 17:00.

2 McLuhan, as quoted in: Chrystall, Andrew. (2015). "After the Global Village." First published in *The Canadian Journal of Media Studies*, 2011, 9 (1).

3 Vygotsky, Lev. (1934). *Thinking and Speech*, p. 11.

4 If counted from the invention of writing by humankind; in reality, different people might have from 0 to 20–30 generations of literacy in their cultural background, rarely more.

5 Ong, Walter. (2002 [1982]), *Orality and Literacy*, p. 167.

more emotional energy. Oral speech has always been more persuasion than informing. A conversation between fellow cavemen might appear to us very aggressive, as if they were about to get into a fight.

Humans eventually developed mimicking into symbolizing: speech mediated reality through symbols, which allowed engagement with the ideas of things. However, even when oral speech gained a sufficiently rich semantic arsenal to describe any objects or situations, the use of body language and tones of voice remained a compelling affordance. The intensity of expression served to capture attention and tune others into the message. Acting is a natural component of oral speech.

This is why oral speech is essentially an extralinguistic phenomenon. An oral utterance is an act of behaviour, not language. As strange as it may sound, speech as an isolated linguistic phenomenon did not exist in orality. It was quite difficult for the oral mind to isolate a word. Names, actions, and characteristics belonged to things, not to an utterance.[1] As an isolated verbal phenomenon, speech (not to mention language) was refined out of crude communication behaviour only as a result of alphabetic writing.

Speech as performance creates performative speech – speech that simultaneously is action. Any oral utterance is not a sentence but a speech act. Marshall McLuhan interpreted the term "utterance" as the "outering of all senses at once."[2] Oral speech in general is speech-behaviour. Mimicking, persuasion, emotionality, and often even emotional coercion are inherent parts of the "Psychodynamic of orality," as Ong titled a chapter in his *Orality and Literacy*. A section in the chapter is titled "Sounded word as power and action." Referring to writing as "autonomous discourse," Ong contrasted it with oral utterance, "which is never autonomous but always embedded in non-verbal existence."[3]

To describe orality, Ong used the notion of "verbomotor lifestyle." He borrowed the term *verbomoteur* from French anthropologist Marcel Jousse, who studied mimicry, rhythms, and gestures as mnemotechnics in oral cultures. Ong writes:

---

1 In *Thinking and Speech*, Vygotsky recalls a story: A peasant listened to a talk between two astronomy students and asked, "I understand that you can watch stars and measure the distance to them with your tricky devices – but how have you learned the stars' names?" – Vygotsky, Lev. (1934). *Thinking and Speech*, p. 311.

2 McLuhan, Marshall. (1969, March). "The Playboy Interview." *Playboy*, p. 59.

3 Ong, Walter. (2002 [1982]), *Orality and Literacy*, p. 157.

> The cultures which we are here styling verbomotor are likely to strike technological man as making all too much of speech itself, as overvaluing and certainly overpracticing rhetoric. In primary oral cultures, even business is not business: it is fundamentally rhetoric. Purchasing something at a Middle East souk or bazaar is not a simple economic transaction <...> Rather, it is a series of verbal (and somatic) maneuvers, a polite duel, a contest of wits, an operation in oral agonistic.[1]

However emotional and performative oral speech was, there was an even higher level of performativity – poetic speech, which was used for the "official business" of a tribe. According to Havelock, "Epic, despite its slightly esoteric vocabulary (actually, because of this vocabulary), represented significant speech."[2]

The skill of talking poetically and therefore persuasively was also a device of political legitimation. "You cannot flourish a document to command a crowd," writes Havelock. "But you can give an epic speech."[3] He points to an episode in the *Iliad*, when Achilles, a brutal warrior but also the commander over his Myrmidons, is described as "chanting the glories of heroes" with "a clear-toned lyre" in his tent. It is not because the warrior happened to also be a poet. The mastery of what we call now "poetic" speech was needed for ruling over people and doing politics with other nobles. Havelock writes:

> Poetry was not "literature" but a political and social necessity. It was not an art form, nor a creation of the private imagination, but an encyclopedia maintained by co-operative effort on the part of the "best Greek polities". This same technological situation was at least in part responsible for an interesting result: it tended to throw political power into the hands of the more cultivated members of the community - "cultivated", that is, in terms of an oral culture.[4]

According to Havelock, "the good performer at a banquet would be estimated not exclusively as an entertainer but as a natural leader of men." The ability to master an effective saying by employing the formulaic standards of epics could win a political debate; formulaic utterances

---

[1] Ong, Walter. (2002 [1982]), *Orality and Literacy*, pp. 66-67.

[2] Havelock, Eric. (1963). *Preface to Plato*, p. 135.

[3] Havelock, Eric. (1963). *Preface to Plato*, p. 127

[4] Havelock, Eric. (1963). *Preface to Plato*, p. 125-126.

themselves could also become the formulas of law, as exemplified in "an eye for an eye," for instance. Fluency in oral tradition, something that can be identified as "oral intelligence," also became an attribute or even a prerequisite of power, according to Havelock:

> The general effect was to put a great premium upon the intelligence in Greek social transactions and to identify intelligence with power. By intelligence we specifically mean a superior memory and a superior sense of verbal rhythm.[1]

In casual oral speech, acting is spontaneous; it's simply a side effect of emotionality and persuasion. Significant speech, on the other hand, demands a mastery of performance. In the conditions of orality, the poetic quality of significant speech was its means of effective delivery, impact, legitimation, and memorization. Poetic speech was a technical, not aesthetical, device. According to Havelock,

> The mental effort required is difficult for the literate mind wholly to imagine, but it obviously meant a total absorption, a mental immersion in the act of recital. Plato described it by the term *mimesis*, which in this context comes close to meaning the "miming" of a mythos, its acting out by sympathetic identification with the characters and actions described.[2]

In fact, despite Havelock's statement that this type of performative immersion is difficult to imagine, it is something familiar to everyone as a child or a parent. Telling a bedtime story in voices involves a somewhat similar impersonation and "sympathetic identification with the characters and actions described." Parents intuitively know how to do this because they are carrying on a millennia-old oral tradition.

Significant speech has survived in the conditions of literacy. The fluency in citing cultural formulas, whether in the form of quotes from the greatest minds or punchlines from popular movies, and especially the mastery of combining these formulas into new sayings, still confers a higher social status on a person. An elevated style of speaking is also recognized as a signal of significant speech on special occasions, such as celebratory toasts, political addresses, or memorial speeches.

---

[1] Havelock, Eric A. (1978). "The Alphabetization of Homer," p. 126.

[2] Havelock, Eric A. (1978). "The Alphabetization of Homer," p. 11

Digital media retrieve the affective verbomotor features of oral speech, but in new, digital forms. Smileys and emojis became digital equivalents of gestures and mimics. Sometimes, somebody STARTS SCREAMING ON SOCIAL MEDIA USING THE CAPS LOCK. A "lol" or "ha-ha" put at the end of a post simulate the vocal and mimic expression of laughter or sarcastic disdain. There are no such extralinguistic means of expression in literacy. An author of written text is obliged to affect others through the meaning of words – employing logic and metaphors expressed in written words only, without resorting to extra-linguistic means of affecting. (The exceptions are the exclamation mark, which mimics vocal intonation, or the ellipsis, which imitates a vocal pause – these are basically the only extra-linguistic tools literacy provides.)

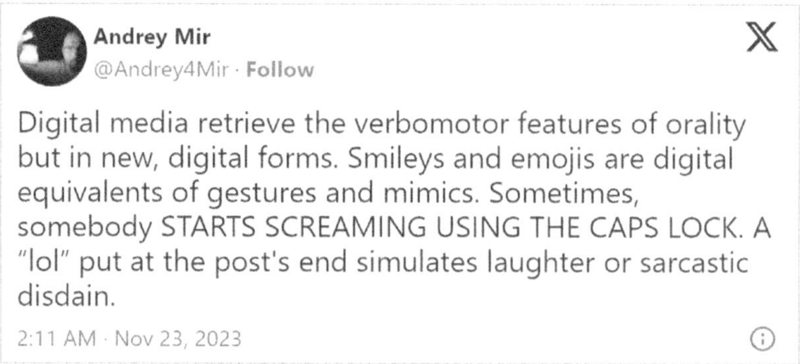

On top of retrieving the verbomotor intensity of orality, digital media have added some new qualities to it. In oral communication, emotional intensity and the intent to affect others could not go beyond the physical reach of the interlocutors or beyond the "here-and-now." On social media, on the contrary, the emotional intensity of conversation is not evanescent; it's recorded and can reach a however large number of interlocutors. Affecting and persuading instead of informing is not just a retrieved feature of orality but also a technological setting of social media platforms that encourage more active user engagement for profit.

The communicative aggression of cavemen casually yelling at each other to explain themselves and prove themselves right has been amplified by algorithms. The verbomotor and emotional intensity of primary orality served for better coordination, was fleeting, and did not often lead to animosity. The verbomotor and emotional intensity of digital orality suppresses rationalism, tends to disregard content, and contributes to polarization.

Relational bias and requests for affirmation

According to Ong, orality is "word-attentive in a person-interactive context rather than object-attentive."[1] To put it simply, orality is *relation-oriented*, while literacy is *object-oriented.* For a person with the mindset of primary orality, it is impossible to say, "Plato is dear to me, but dearer still is truth." Plato is dear to me – and that's it!

Collective involvement serves to maintain tribal loyalty. One needs to stick to their own folks regardless of whether they are right or not. Actually, the very notion of objective truth was not invented yet in primary orality: objective truth was a by-product of literacy.

The relational bias of orality had direct ethical implications. It put tribal loyalty into forms of selective, personally biased justice. In an oral community, Lady Justice would have neither blindfold nor scales. However, the relational bias of orality can not be judged from the standpoint of morality. Collective involvement – sticking together – was an evolutionary mechanism of survival.

Survival required not just collective unity but also hierarchy within the collective. People's benefits and responsibilities depended on their personal qualities. Physical strengths, skills, some other personal features, and, increasingly more, heritage formed individual statuses that shaped social hierarchy. From a survival perspective, hierarchy served to employ the best possible combination of individual qualities within the collective.

To meet the changing demands of survivability, social hierarchy needed to be adaptive. In early human groups, wealth or official rank did not yet define status. It was only speech that could serve as a means to balance the advantage of physical strength in a social hierarchy. Some anthropological theories even propose that one of the earliest functions of speech in groups of primordial humans was to enable beta males to form alliances, conspire against the alpha male, and kill him. This, in turn, led to a completely new group structure based on alliances among breeding males, with the corresponding distribution of responsibilities, benefits, and access to

---

[1] Ong, Walter. (2002 [1982]), *Orality and Literacy*, p. 66.

procreation.[1] Being the regulator of relations, speech also became the regulator of statuses in the hierarchy.

To maintain hierarchy and its adaptability, the oral lifestyle involved a constant status check. Any oral speech act, through its phatic load and emotional intensity, also conveyed this hierarchical message: to confirm or advance the status of the speaker and to confirm or challenge the statuses of others. This might not necessarily always manifest itself in open challenges or flattery, but status competition was always invisibly embedded in oral speech-behaviour. This psychodynamic persists in any collective that employs orality for social regulation.

The relational bias and status competition were the two opposites that provided a dynamic balance of mutual loyalty and constant mutual challenge in an oral community. In a sense, this balance created harmony in tribal relations as it protected people from outside threats while maintaining a better social hierarchy inside. This kind of harmony, however, could easily involve a peculiar combination of patronizing (matronizing) and bullying. The weakest were protected and bullied, while the strongest were revered and challenged.

Speech-behaviour was the primary venue for displaying this psychodynamic in all its shades. Each speech act carried the imprints of relational bias and status competition. The Hegelian struggle for recognition, which presumably runs society, unfolded in speech acts, each of which simultaneously served as a request for affirmation. When we talk, we still place ourselves within the social structure, expecting others to confirm our status. We also hope that relational bias can override the subject matter, especially if the subject mater is not favourable to us, and turn the judgment of others in our favour.

Relational bias, however, became irrelevant in writing, as writing is object-oriented. It deals with the meanings of things, not the relations between humans. Status competition persists in a literate society but takes the form of content competition. This is why literacy tends to disregard personal relations and focus on the subject matter.

Social media have not only retrieved relational bias and status competition but have also enabled an individual's request for affirmation at

---

[1] See, for example: Hunter, Donna. (2022, March 24). "Male-male alliances and the evolution of societal patriarchy." *Stanford School of Humanities & Science*.

an unprecedented scale. This is, perhaps, one of the most important features of digital orality and one of its most powerful retrievals from primary orality. Billions of users, anyone who goes digital, display their existence for others to react to and affirm. Everyone's demand for "empathic involvement" (McLuhan[1]) creates an incredibly intense environment of engagement, which is essential for the social media platform's business. The very design of digital platforms revolves around these primeval and archetypical motives of social participation, aimed at collective communion and status competition. Some people try harder, creating a presumably better-accepted digital version of themselves. Others may not even realize that their digital acts are subconscious requests for recognition, which social media also turn into requests for time.

Digital orality, however, has introduced some innovations. Now, not only other individuals but also algorithms, while collecting our personal data, serve as the judges to whom the request for affirmation is submitted. Digital media provide the service to satisfy the highest value in Maslow's pyramid, self-actualization, through the responses of others. The participation and increasingly growing role of algorithms in it make self-actualization deprived of the "self" – of agency. We are now "self-actualized" without even knowing it, while pausing in scrolling the newsfeed to watch something that caught our eyes, for example. But it will still be reflected in the way our newsfeed is shaped, influencing environmental signals that affect our actualization.

The new affordance for billions to submit their requests for affirmation reshapes the political, cultural, and ethical foundations of society. For example, a premise has emerged that someone "needs to be heard." After growing into an existential request, the need "to be heard" turned into a political demand. In a literate society, it is impossible to insist that someone "needs to be read." Not because literacy favours arrogance (though it does), but simply due to the absence of such an affordance. For the demand that someone "needs to be read" to emerge, this someone first needs to write something and, second, needs to write something worthy. Literacy, by default, due to its technical affordances, is selective and elitist. It selects those who can write something and whose writing can bypass the threshold of publishing. Neither of these limitations exists in digital orality.

---

[1] McLuhan, Marshall. (1962). *The Guttenberg Galaxy*, p. 39.

But electronic and then digital media created a new imperative of representation – the representation of "voices," not ideas.

The emancipation of authorship gave everybody access not just to information but also to self-expression. This affordance has turned into not only an obligation for everyone to expose some online activity, but also an obligation for others to react. The opportunity for oneself has turned into a demand for anybody else. The typically oral request for affirmation has been tremendously amplified, turning into energetic vampirism of a planetary scale and contributing to online agitation and polarization.

Prior to social media, physical distance separated people, deterring both friendship and enmity. The internet removed time and space between people and thus extended a person to the size of all humankind, allowing everyone to reach everyone else. Dunbar's number, which represents our brain's capacity to maintain relationships with 150 individuals, has been overridden; Facebook suggests it to be 5000 now.

With so many strangers, whom we can't help but invite to visit the intimacy of our solitude, digital media have become not only a platform for our explosion into the world but also a space for the world's implosion into each one of us. As McLuhan puts it,

> But whereas formerly the great clashes took place occasionally between groups geographically separated, there are no longer any geographic separations in the electric age. In terms of our daily knowledge and information about each other the human family now shares a very small global village. Our technology has enabled us to put all of our senses outside ourselves, with the result that we find our neighbor is inside, and not "out there" any longer. When the senses go outside, not only Big Brother but little brother goes inside.[1]

McLuhan reminds that "People leave small towns to *avoid* involvement. The big city *lined* them with its uniformity and impersonal milieu"[2] (italics are his). Big cities emerged with writing. Digital orality returns us to the village, now the global village, testing our tolerance for otherness by bringing others much closer and even more intrusively than oral communication did – right onto our most intimate space, our screens.

---

[1] McLuhan, Marshall. (1962). "8 mm in context: the modern media and externalized senses", p. 21.

[2] McLuhan, Marshall. (1997 [1967]). "The Hot and Cool Interview" to Gerald Stearn, p. 58.

Bragging

Robert Logan observes that the Hebrews were the first people who created a nonmythological and realistic history of themselves. The other literate cultures of the ancient world, from the Sumerians and the Egyptians to the Assyrians and the Hittites, recorded their historical events, but their historiography was crude, events were recorded in isolation, and, most importantly, they tended to record mostly their glorious moments.

According to Logan, it was alphabetic literacy that helped the Hebrews develop a historic sense. "The Hebrews connected the events and imbued them with purpose. They also had a measure of objectivity, recording both the events of which they were proud and those of which they were ashamed," writes Logan.[1] He also notes, implying the influence of the alphabet, that the Greeks developed a similar objective method of historiography.

Orality has no appetite for objectivity. On the contrary, all the functional features of orality – collective involvement, status competition, the request for affirmation, and environmental immersion with its imperative of occupying more or new space for greater benefits – emphasize the affordance and necessity of bragging. By its very psychological nature, bragging repels sober self-reflection that could be detrimental to tribal authenticity.

Bragging might not be encouraged in a literate society, but in orality bragging is a beneficial strategy or even a survival strategy. In an oral culture, everyone is exposed to the collective. Evolutionary selection developed these personal exhibitions into requests for recognition and appreciation. Everyone seeks to be exposed in a way that provides better "social security" – greater benefits from others. Such subliminal requests for affirmation simply have to project the importance of the speaker. Any speech act is inherently also a show-off.

Bragging, however, can involve not only tales of victorious deeds or significant events but also tales of great suffering, which grew in importance as social development led to the growth of empathy. Empathy provides benefits for the weak, and since weakness became a peculiar form of social capital, it needed to be shown off properly.

---

[1] Logan, Robert. (2004 [1986]). *The Alphabet Effect*, p. 102.

Through bragging, people contributed their victorious stories and the stories of great events to the collective body of individual tales. These tales also held instructive potential regarding acceptable behaviour and survival strategies. When hunters brag about a good kill, warriors brag about a victorious battle, or farmers brag about a good or bad year, they collectively supply and renew the standards of successful behaviour. Bragging is a collectively and mutually taught school of success and survival.

Another cumulative effect of individual bragging relates not just to maintaining behavioural standards but also to the accumulation of knowledge. Bragging stories were selected in accordance with their significance and, if worthwhile, reiterated or recited by others. If, at the individual level, bragging was a request for acceptance and appreciation, at the collective level, the multiplicity of individual bragging worked as a recording device within a family or a community. Bragging served the historization of personal and tribal events. The worthwhile individual, family, and tribal show-offs were poured into collective operative memory and fermented there. This collective processing of individual bragging defined and refined the significance of events for recording in the collective device of oral memory.

As Stuart Hall noticed regarding a similar function of television, "The event must become a 'story' before it can become a communicative event."[1] Bragging transformed significant events into significant stories and thus enabled cultural records that legitimized tribal hierarchy, conducted tribal indoctrination, and passed on tribal instructions containing outstanding experience. At the roots of any heroic epic lies banquet bragging. Bragging is the foundation of the "tribal encyclopedia," a term Eric Havelock coined to describe Homer's poems. If skilled individual show-offs amplified personal social capital, then proficiency in bragging on behalf of the community created the profession of bards as well as politics and diplomacy.

Until today, many stories shared among people can easily be interpreted as bragging about one's remarkable experiences. Bragging appears in casual conversations at friends' gatherings, in family anecdotes shared at the dinner table, in small talk at social events, or in presentations at business conferences. The exchange of bragging serves the same role as

[1] Hall, Stuart. (2012 [1980]). "Encoding/decoding," p. 138.

the phatic function: it establishes and maintains mutual relations for the speaker's benefit, but with special focus on the speaker's importance.

Since orality is relation-oriented and literacy is object-oriented, literacy mitigated the psychological intensity of bragging and afforded the emergence of modesty. The ultimate assault of literacy on bragging is represented in the juridical form of the non-disclosure agreement. The non-disclosure agreement is the ultimate killer of orality.

Digital orality has reversed that and retrieved bragging. It is not without reason that the design of social media platforms, whether Instagram, Facebook, Twitter, or TikTok, exploits and encourages different forms of bragging. This ranges from pictures of food and travel, geo-tagging check-ins, and name-dropping to listing personal titles in profiles, demonstrating meme proficiency, and posting intellectual exercises. What else are our posts and profiles if not requests for appreciation, or bragging, from its very primitive to very sophisticated forms?

Agonistic mentality

The total engagement and status competition are accompanied in orality by an agonistic mentality, as Walter Ong calls it. He writes: "Many, if not all, oral or residually oral cultures strike literates as extraordinarily agonistic in their verbal performance and indeed in their lifestyle."[1] Ong illustrates agonistic mentality through a story:

> In oral cultures a request for information is commonly interpreted interactively, as agonistic, and, instead of being really answered, is frequently parried. An illuminating story is told of a visitor in County Cork, Ireland, an especially oral region in a country which in every region preserves massive residual orality. The visitor saw a Corkman leaning against the post office. He went up to him, pounded with his hand on the post office wall next to the Corkman's shoulder, and asked, 'Is this the post office?' The Corkman was not taken in. He looked at his questioner quietly and with great concern: 'Twouldn't be a postage stamp you were lookin' for, would it?' He treated the

[1] Ong, Walter. (2002 [1982]), *Orality and Literacy*, p. 43. Conversely, people from oral cultures might perceive those from literate cultures as too pretentiously "nice" and smiley, which could be interpreted as a facade concealing hypocrisy and insincerity.

> enquiry not as a request for information but as something the enquirer was doing to him. So he did something in turn to the enquirer to see what would happen. All natives of Cork, according to the mythology, treat all questions this way. Always answer a question by asking another. Never let down your oral guard.[1]

In a literate culture, knowledge is detached from the person, and it is possible to establish status by possessing better information and sharing or withholding this information. In an oral culture, one establishes their status through others via either cooperation or rivalry with them. The oral utterance is designed to resonate, to be affective and to be engaging. Oral speech-behaviour is always intrusive. Emotionality, which is needed to convey affect for better cooperation and memorization, additionally intensifies the agonistic nature of speech-behaviour.

Since the function of an utterance in orality is not just to convey a subject matter but also to utilize the listener, everyone constantly decides whether he or she should comply with others' requests. Should one benefit from subordination or challenge them to maintain their own social status and respective privileges? The constant request for affirmation by everyone to everyone – the request for your time – creates psychologically quite an aggressive environment. Even compassion and empathy, which are innate in the conditions of total collective exposition, are agonistic and intrusive – they oblige.

The situation is exacerbated by the fact that everyone stands not just for themselves but also for the good name of their family or kin. Orality created a society regulated by honour, a regulative force opposite to both the concept of law and the concept of conscience (both emerged as effects of writing). If the relational bias of orality fostered loyalty and, to some extent, empathy, then the agonistic mentality fostered hubris, a personal and political trait much fought against by the Greeks as soon as they developed alphabetic literacy, as the Greeks believed that hubris underlies tyranny.

According to Ong, "By keeping knowledge embedded in the human lifeworld, orality situates knowledge within a context of struggle." Proverbs

---

[1] Ong, Walter. (2002 [1982]), *Orality and Literacy*, p. 67. The case is told with the reference to: Malinowski, Bronislaw. (1923). "The problem of meaning in primitive languages", in: C. K. Ogden, and I. A. Richards (eds), *The Meaning of Meaning: A Study of the Influence of Language upon Thought and of the Science of Symbolism*.

and riddles are used not just to store knowledge but also for engaging in verbal combat. Bragging about achievements or enduring is obviously a status-seeking speech-behaviour and as such is highly agonistic as well. Friendly or hostile name-calling is a legitimate sport in orality. In the same manner as a true sport, a name-calling contest sometimes substitutes for fighting. Or else, ritualistic insults legitimize real fighting that follows – they create the ground to morally justify escalation and physical altercation.

Ong writes that the name-calling contest is a "standard in oral societies across the world" and even has been fitted with a specific label in linguistics: *flyting* (or *fliting*).[1] Contests based on mutual insults were widely practiced on the battlefield or in public speech. After writing, they survived there and spread, though in rather more exquisite forms, in rhetoric, politics, jurisprudence, diplomacy, and beyond. Although Ong may not have witnessed it in his time, competitive name-calling also found artistic expression in rap battles, a descendant to oral poetry. Grand events in this genre are called "epic rap battles," as if keeping reference to primary orality.

On the opposite side of agonistic name-calling or vituperation is, according to Ong, "the fulsome expression of praise which is found everywhere in connection with orality."[2] From the point of view of literacy, the fulsome praise in oral or residually oral tradition sounds "insincere, flatulent, and comically pretentious," in Ong's words. Similar to name-calling, the oral tradition of fulsome praise survived the advent of literacy and holds on in some areas of social activity. Toasts, congratulations, and celebratory speeches are exceedingly praising and bombastic in cultures with strong residual orality. In others, their intensity is significantly reduced by literacy but still detectable.

Whether it is a song by an African *griot* or a toast by a *tamada* (the master of ceremonies) at a Georgian wedding, the praise carries its oral agonistic character anyway. It is still a status contest and a competition of competences.

Marshall McLuhan did not use the term "agonistic mentality," but he certainly saw it as an effect of retribalization. In a 1977 TV interview,

---

1 Ong, Walter. (2002 [1982]), *Orality and Literacy*, p. 43.

2 Ong, Walter. (2002 [1982]), *Orality and Literacy*, p. 44.

McLuhan dismisses the romantic expectations of the host regarding the Global Village:

> McManus: But it seems, Dr. McLuhan, that this tribal world is not friendly.
>
> McLuhan: Oh, no, tribal people… one of their main kinds of sport is a sort of butchering each other. It's a full-time sport in tribal societies... The closer you get together the more you like each other? No, there is no evidence of that in any situation we've heard of. When people get close together, they get more and more savagely impassionate with each other.[1]

The retrieval of the agonistic mentality has only intensified in the digital realm. On social media, everyone seeks affirmation from others on a scale unheard of in human history. Not only is the agonistic mentality making a comeback, but it also threatens representative democracy (by amplifying polarization) and people's mental health.[2]

Here is what McLuhan said about these conditions in 1967:

> The more you create village conditions, the more discontinuity and division and diversity. The global village absolutely insures maximal disagreement on all points. It never occurred to me that uniformity and tranquility were the properties of the global village. It has more spite and envy. <…> The tribal-global village is far more divisive – full of fighting – than any nationalism ever was. Village is fission, not fusion, in depth all the time.[3]

McLuhan sounded his proximity alert 50 years ago.

The syntax of orality: *doing* and not *being*

One of the pioneers of writing studies, Ignace Gelb, found it useful to look at child psychology to describe some features of the preliterate mind. Early preliterate drawings, as Gelb noticed, put objects in the picture

---

[1] Marshall McLuhan in Conversation with Mike McManus. (1977). 1:22.

[2] Se: Mir, Andrey. (2022, Winter). "The Medium Is the Menace." *City-Journal.*

[3] McLuhan, Marshall. (1997 [1967]). "The Hot and Cool Interview" to Gerald Stearn, p. 57-58.

randomly, with no regard for proportions or perspective, in the same way children would.[1]

Placing objects in a picture in a way representing their mutual positions and the general perspective of vision requires, indeed, a certain degree of abstraction. According to Jean Piaget's theory of early cognitive development, the ability of abstraction develops in children by the age of 8. Lev Vygotsky's school of psycholinguistic confirmed it by revealing that verbal associations in children 5–6 years of age are predominantly *syntagmatic*, for example: "dog" – "barks." Children think of a dog through what it does and how it looks in reality, not through how it relates to other objects in some abstract categories. The "situational" view of a dog prevails.

However, at around 7–8 years old, children begin to exhibit *paradigmatic* associations, such as "dog" – "cat."[2] The age of this cognitive development coincides with the acquisition of reading skills. When the object "dog" also becomes the word "dog," it assumes an abstract concept of a dog, allowing it to engage in abstract relationships with other concepts.

In linguistics, syntagmatic relations reflect the words' connection in sentences, while paradigmatic relations reflect the words' belonging to categories. Syntagmatic relations represent the sequential structure of speech, while paradigmatic relations represent the abstract structure of language. Paradigmatic relations embed dog not into situations but into abstract paradigms: "dog – owner," "dog – cat," "dog – man's best friend," and so on. Paradigmatic relations describe a dog through *what it is* (or isn't), while syntagmatic relations describe a dog through *what it does*.

A somewhat similar difference in syntagmatic-paradigmatic reactions was detected by Alexander Luria in his study of illiterate peasants in Soviet Middle Asia in the 1930s. In one instance, Luria asked the test subjects to exclude a "wrong" thing from a set of cards depicting a hammer, saw, log and hatchet. The literate mind would immediately recognize a set of tools – a "paradigm" of tools – and their "syntagmatic" relations to the log: tools

[1] Gelb. (1963 [1952]). *A Study of Writing*, p. 21. The comparison of primary-oral people to children does not imply that they are childlike. It simply means that both are preliterate. Words have not yet been disconnected from objects through writing. As writing eventually separated words from objects, it enabled the conceptualization of these objects and abstract operations with the concepts.

[2] See, for example: Лалаева Р.И., Серебрякова Н.В. (1999). *Коррекция общего недоразвития речи у дошкольников (формирование лексики и грамматического строя)*. СПб.: Союз.

can do something to the log. The piece of material, the log, does not belong with the set of tools.

But the illiterate mind sees objects in another, more practical light. As a 25-year-old illiterate peasant explained, "They're all alike. The saw will saw the log and the hatchet will chop it into small pieces. If one of these has to go, I'd throw out the hatchet. It doesn't do as good a job as a saw."[1]

"We got a surprising picture," reported Luria at a conference in 1974. "All categories that we were accustomed to deem natural, turned out to be social."[2] This, of course, supported the Marxist view that the materiality of social practice determines consciousness.[3]

When things are objects and not concepts, important are their syntagmatic (connectability) and not paradigmatic (selectability) relations. In the situational thinking of orality, it is important what a thing *does*, whereas explaining what a thing *is* might be quite challenging and, frankly, not needed.

For the oral mind, the world exists in doing, not being. "The Homeric Greek is innocent of any connection with the verb to be," writes Havelock.[4] After analyzing the predicative structures in the *Iliad*, he discovers that, "The fundamental units of the tribal encyclopedia are sets of doings and of happenings."[5] According to him, only a language of actions is amenable to rhythmic-mnemonic processing. Havelock writes:

> The only data which can live in the memory are experienced data with which we identify in act and in situation, and acts and events are "happenings"; they "become" or "are done."[6]

This is why an oral poem is always a dynamic narrative, an "event-series" in which heroes and gods always act and are not just present; or even their presence is syntactically expressed through verbs of acting.

---

[1] Luria. (1976). *Cognitive Development*, p. 56.

[2] Ясницкий, Антон. (2013). «'У узбеков ЕСТЬ иллюзий!'. Заочная полемика между Лурией и Коффка». / Yasnitsky. Anton. (2013). "'The Uzbeks DO HAVE illusions!'" The Luria-Koffka controversy." *Dubna Psychological Journal*. 2013-3, pp. 1-25.

[3] "It is not the consciousness of men that determines their being, but their social being that determines their consciousness" – Marx, Karl. (1859). *A Contribution to the Critique of Political Economy*. Preface.

[4] Havelock, Eric. (1963). *Preface to Plato*, p. 173.

[5] Havelock, Eric. (1963). *Preface to Plato*, p. 174.

[6] Havelock, Eric. (1963). *Preface to Plato*, p. 219.

Historical occurrences, such as a feud, a battle, a plague, or a storm, do not just exist but do something. Havelock notices that a plague or storm can "arise" or "perish" or "give up."[1]

Even when orality deals with listing something[2] – and a list naturally consists of items that just "are," – oral syntax transforms the mere existence of what is listed into doings or happenings. For example, in the famous Catalogue of Greek Ships in the *Iliad*, as Havelock points out, each contingent of the Greek federation is presented through mentioning what people dwell in what lands, or what captain leads what ships, or even through the short stories detailing the noble parentage of the commanders. The paradigmatic nature of the list is dismissed, and the items of the list develop their own "syntagmatic" narrative.

The Catalogue is presented through the syntax of happenings and doings because this is the only syntax known to orality. According to Ong, the Catalogue of the ships and captains in the *Iliad* is "not an objective tally but an operational display in a story about a war."[3]

It is interesting to observe the difference between Homer cataloguing ships and Hesiod cataloguing gods. Hesiod, presumably a contemporary of Homer, is believed to be the first writing author in Greek history. Both the Homeric catalogue of ships and the Hesiodic catalogue of gods are represented through doings and occurrences, not just listing. Hesiod, however, comes up with an unusual, for orality, idea to represent the ruling of gods in a paradigmatic way. Logan writes:

> Although he dealt with the same mythic material as Homer, Hesiod ordered his material into a definite pattern. Hesiod introduced the gods to the Pantheon systematically at the beginning of his Theogony and then went on to explain the creation of the universe.[4]

With Hesiod, writing had started influencing people's ways of seeing the world. According to Logan, Hesiod represented the beginning of the transition from the oral to the literate tradition.

---

[1] Havelock, Eric. (1963). *Preface to Plato*, p. 173.

[2] Listing actually is an invention of accounting and recording – of literacy. The appearance of the Catalogue in the *Iliad* always puzzled researchers. I will deal with it in Chapter 9.

[3] Ong, Walter. (2002 [1982]), *Orality and Literacy*, p. 97.

[4] Logan, Robert. (2004 [1986]). *The Alphabet Effect*, p. 111.

To highlight the nature of oral syntax, Havelock compares it to the syntax of literacy. Writing has introduced abstractions, and therefore the syntax of literacy needs to deal with them. Writing has also eliminated the need for memorization and thus removed the mnemonic requirements for syntax. An abstraction does not need to *do* anything. It simply *is*.

After stating that a thing, in order to be stored in the memory, has to happen, to become, or to be done, Havelock writes:

> Per contra, once the abstracted integration, the law or principle, has come into being, nothing can happen to it. It just is. It can be expressed in language the syntax of which is analytic; that is, terms and propositions are organised in relationships which are timeless. The angles of a triangle are two right angles; they do not gain possession of two right angles; they were not once three right angles and now have become two. They never did anything; they just are. Such a statement is totally divorced from the idiom and syntax of the saga.[1]

The oral syntax of *doing* and not *being* was formed under the pressure of environmental immersion and the lack of abstraction. However, as Havelock highlights, the syntax of *doing* also served memorization. This is one of the keys to understanding orality: all its features are defined by environmental immersion and eventually come to serve collective memorization.

Formulaic structures: oral speech as a memorization device

According to Jack Goody and Ian Watt, cultural heritage is passed on through the generations in three ways. First, the society passes its material assets. Second, "it transmits standardised ways of acting." Ways of doing something are passed through imitation and apprenticeship when pupils repeat actions after the master craftsman. Finally, heritage lives on through reciting and storytelling. Goody and Watt write:

> The transmission of the verbal elements of culture by oral means can be visualised as a long chain of interlocking conversations between members of the group. Thus all beliefs and values, all forms

[1] Havelock, Eric. (1963). *Preface to Plato*, p. 219.

> of knowledge, are communicated between individuals in face-to-face contact; and, as distinct from the material content of the cultural tradition, whether it be cave-paintings or hand-axes, they are stored only in human memory.[1]

However, as Goody and Watt highlight, the stories that convey heritage do not have "dictionary definitions." (As Hannah Arendt once noticed, "Storytelling reveals meaning without committing the error of defining it."[2]) Instead, according to Goody and Watt, "the meaning of each word is ratified in a succession of concrete situations, accompanied by vocal inflexions and physical gestures, all of which combine to particularize both its specific denotation and its accepted connotative usages."

Goody and Watt call this process "semantic ratification": "the totality of symbol-referent relationships is more immediately experienced by the individual..., and is thus more deeply socialised."[3] Semantic ratification is situational, collective, and affective: the members of an oral community "induce" in each other the experience described in the story through verbomotor speech-behaviour, in which meaning is created by persuasion through action rather than by information through data.

Verbomotor intensity filled oral speech with extralinguistic means, such as rhymes, rhythms, vocalization, and others as well as with metaphors, allegories, epithets, and all the tropes aimed at affecting. This made oral expressions, especially the expressions of poeticized and elevated oral speech, exceedingly colourful and emotionally charged.

For centuries, the *Iliad* and the *Odyssey* were regarded as outstanding examples of an otherwise primitive stage in poetry's development. Viewing these poems as masterpieces amidst naivety and primitivity was supposed to explain the richness of metaphors and characters, despite the structural inconsistency and stylistic redundancy of the Homeric poems. However, neither of these views turned out to provide an adequate understanding of Homer.

In the 1920s, Milman Parry[4] suggested that the poetics of Homer related not to the aesthetic choices of the author but to the specificity of

---

1 Goody, Jack, and Watt, Ian. (1963). "The Consequences of Literacy," p. 306.

2 Arendt, Hannah. (1970). *Men in Dark Times*, p. 105.

3 Goody, Jack, and Watt, Ian. (1963). "The Consequences of Literacy," p. 306.

4 Milman Parry (1902–1935), an American classicist, revolutionized the study of Homer in his 1928 dissertation and pioneered the study of oral tradition, which was further developed by Eric Havelock in *Preface to Plato* (1963) and Walter Ong in *Orality and Literacy* (1982).

collective oral memorization. The epithet "Hector of the gleaming helm" not only was a tribute to the might and nobility of the Trojan prince but, most importantly, gave a metric word-form suitable to be placed into hexameter. And so were the repetitive phrase "Achilles, dear to Zeus..." and many other idiomatic epithets and metaphors describing heroes or actions through formulaic structures.

Due to their formulaic nature, such fixed expressions were easily retrieved from the memory of the bard, quickly combined within the hexameter verse, and readily recognized by the listeners – in the same way that punchlines from widely loved movies become formulaic references and are easily recognized and often rephrased by people of the same culture, thus serving to preserve their collective identity.

As Havelock explains this technique, Homer had a "purely metrical pattern" that could be built out of interchangeable metrical parts. For this pattern to be filled in, the bard also had "a vast supply of word combinations or formulas of varying length and syntax rhythmically shaped so as to fit portions of the metrical line." These construction bricks also had "interchangeable verbal parts" so that the minstrel could change syntax while maintaining his meter. "His overall artistry thus consists of an endless distribution of variables where, however, variation is held within strict limits and the verbal possibilities, while extensive, are in the last resort finite," concludes Havelock.[1]

Havelock offers his analysis of Homer's mastery of playing with formulaic and repetitive patterns. He writes that "the easiest and laziest form of memorisation is sheer repetition":

> Hector is dead; Hector is dead.

Simple repetition automatically creates rhythm through the repeated phrasal emphasis, thus engaging the verbomotor faculties for memorization. Saying "Hector is dead" several times creates the affordance for rhythmic swaying, knocking, or clapping. However, as Havelock suggests, the poet can slightly increase the "output of energy" to keep the meaning unchanged but allow a formulaic variation of the word order:

> Hector is dead; dead indeed is Hector.

---

[1] Havelock, Eric. (1963). *Preface to Plato*, p. 92.

"Then the mind, growing bolder," writes Havelock, "will venture to place a further burden on itself" by coloring the image of a dead man within a certain rhythmic and formulaic pattern, affecting the listeners through the richness of both the recitation and the picture:

> Hector is dead; fallen is Hector
> Yea Achilles slew him
> Hector is defeated, Hector is dead.

This spirited manipulation with nevertheless formulaic structures and within formulaic rhythmic patterns are akin to jazz improvisation. It mesmerizes the listeners not just by the form of reciting and the content of images but also by the mastery of performance. Structurally, jazz is a distant cousin of oral poetry.

Havelock comments:

> Such devices can be pushed further and further to that extreme virtuosity found in the Homeric epic. The basic principle is however already revealed and can be stated abstractly as variation within the same. The mind's attention is continually bifocal: it preserves an identity, yet it makes room for a difference within this identity.[1]

The artistry of retrieving and stitching together formulaic passages was an important social skill in oral society. The masterful application of this skill distinguished professional bards. The metaphor of stitching the tissue from the patches was literally reflected in the description of the skill and profession of rhapsodist: the word was derived from ῥᾰ́πτω (rháptō, "to sew") and ᾠδή (ōidḗ, "ode; song"). The oral epic was a stitched song.

"Homer stitched together prefabricated parts," states Ong. "Instead of a creator, you had an assembly-line worker."[2] He writes:

> Basically the same formulas and themes recurred, but they were stitched together or 'rhapsodized' differently in each rendition even by the same poet, depending on audience reaction, the mood of the poet or of the occasion, and other social and psychological factors.[3]

The bard can not memorize the entire succession of words verbatim, word by word, but he memorizes themes and formulas that he likes and

---

1 Havelock, Eric. (1963). *Preface to Plato*, p. 147

2 Ong, Walter. (2002 [1982]), *Orality and Literacy*, p. 23.

3 Ong, Walter. (2002 [1982]), *Orality and Literacy*, p. 58.

that resonate with the audience. "He remembers these always differently, as rhapsodized or stitched together in his own way on this particular occasion for this particular audience,"[1] writes Ong.

This principle also reflects the use of formulaic expressions by ordinary people, who stitch their utterances from readily memorizable and retrievable patches that suit the situation. The richness and promptness of "rhapsodizing" created social capital in orality and is still valued in rhetorical speech, though the overuse of formulaic expressions would damage the originality of speech (and thought) valued in a literate society.

While the role of the bards was unique, the oral tradition has lived on and survived in everyday conversation. The stock of formulaic phrases and idioms that every one of us possesses is vast. The ability to intervene with a powerful idiom can be decisive in turning a conversation in one's favour or winning a debate. Also, we still memorize better the lyrics of a song that pleases us and resonates with us. This means the song conveys affect and what is now called "vibe" – formerly ritualistic trance, achieved by the rhythm of formulaic repetition and music.

Carrying on tribal wisdom by means of orality required almost mechanical individual contributions to collective efforts. The participants contributed the mechanics of their speech-behaviour by repeating proverbs or synchronizing their reactions while listening to the bard. It was a constant "live" verbomotor re-recording of the tribal encyclopedia in the minds of the tribe's members.

No one wants a recording mechanism to change anything in recorded material. Revisions might happen if certain stories or characters ceased to resonate with the parts of the collective verbomotor mechanism; they faded and died out. But it could not be someone's deliberate decision, as the story or characters belonged to nobody personally, only to the tribe. The tribe could vote for their continuing relevance only by telling or not telling certain songs and repeating or not repeating certain proverbs and other formulaic passages.

Goody and Watt underscore that the collective re-recording of tribal memory serves not only for memorizing but also for forgetting when the changed social reality requires it. They provide an example of such adaptation of the past to the needs of the present. The story of the origin of

[1] Ong, Walter. (2002 [1982]), *Orality and Literacy*, p. 143.

the state of Gonja in Northern Ghana held that the founding father, Ndewura Jakpa, travelled down the river Niger in search of gold, conquered the indigenous inhabitants, and enthroned himself as the chief of the state, with his sons inheriting to rule its territorial divisions. When the British first recorded this story at the beginning of the 20th century, Jakpa was said to have had seven sons, which corresponded with the number of tribes whose chiefs were eligible for the supreme office of the state by virtue of their descent from the founder of the particular chiefdom. Then, however, two chiefdoms disappeared through merging. Sixty years later, the story of the state's origin held that Jakpa had only five sons.[1] The oral tradition did not keep records of the previous version of the state's origin, so no controversy emerged. The new version of the federative legitimacy of the chiefdoms was as legally valid as the previous one. Only through the intervention of an external literate observation (the records by the British) was it possible to discern that the historical past changed according to the political present.

Goody and Watt suggest that such a mnemonic device served not so much to preserve historical records but rather to validate current social relations. They also assume that in Biblical Genesis, the twelve sons of Jacob represented the then-contemporary twelve tribes of Israel – the twelve sons referred "to contemporary groups rather than to dead individuals."[2]

In orality, the memorization of the past is needed to regulate the present; the past changes accordingly to the needs of such regulation. Goody and Watt highlight that an oral individual "has little perception of the past except in terms of the present."[3] (This oral capacity of having no other past than that one that validates the present has now to be retrieved by digital orality.)

Capturing an oral story by writing froze it. Any records made the past "original," or at least original in the state in which it was captured by the written record. Writing eliminated the oral capacity of "social amnesia," as Goody and Watt call it. In orality, "social amnesia" was a useful therapeutic mechanism for the tribe to forget the past that does not fit the present.

---

1 Goody, Jack, and Watt, Ian. (1963). "The Consequences of Literacy," p. 310.

2 Goody, Jack, and Watt, Ian. (1963). "The Consequences of Literacy," p. 308.

3 Goody, Jack, and Watt, Ian. (1963). "The Consequences of Literacy," p. 311.

Literate cultures have lost this blessing. According to Goody and Watt, literacy enabled the accumulation of records of the past that contradicted each other and the present. This led to the questioning of both the past and the present, which became a source of the "historical sense" and frustration. Literate individuals need to deal with the record of the past that does not conform to their view of the present or their place in the present.

Of course, literate cultures, too, use the past to validate the present through the dominant narrative. Nevertheless, literacy keeps all the records for alternative readings of history. This creates an affordance for seeing the past from different angles; this is why cultural wars are possible.

An oral culture simply lacks the technical affordance for alternative history. Since the tribal encyclopedia is needed not for the past but for the present, it must remember what is needed and forget what is not. Forgetting, or social amnesia, is achieved by not reciting. But remembrance requires an intricate collective mechanism of verbomotor reciting.

The structural and stylistic peculiarities of Homeric poems are explained not by the fact that this was outstanding poetry, or an outstanding exemplar of primitive poetry, but by the fact that this was not poetry at all – at least not in any sense that later epochs assigned to poetry as a literary art. Neither the dramatism nor style of oral poetry were aesthetic – they were purely functional. Homeric poems represented the collective mnemonic devices of oral culture. The stories told in such an elevated manner became engraved into collective memory through the efforts of the bard and the receptiveness of the listeners. They not only preserved the Greek identity but also served as a means of tribal indoctrination and instruction.

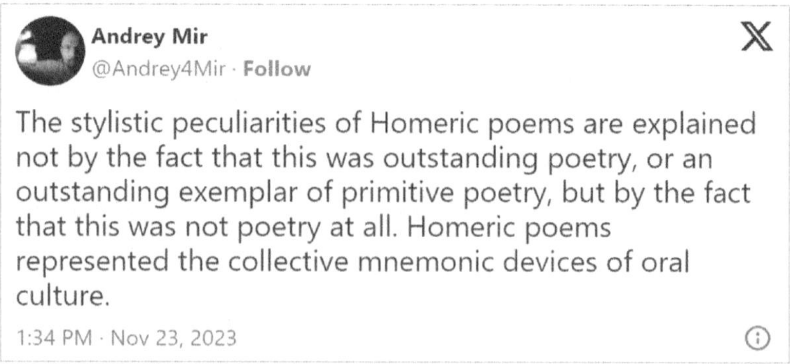
Andrey Mir
@Andrey4Mir · **Follow**

The stylistic peculiarities of Homeric poems are explained not by the fact that this was outstanding poetry, or an outstanding exemplar of primitive poetry, but by the fact that this was not poetry at all. Homeric poems represented the collective mnemonic devices of oral culture.

1:34 PM · Nov 23, 2023

Havelock thinks that epic poetry induced "emotional automatism"[1] in the response of the listeners, which caused a sort of hypnosis and pleasure. Emotional automatism helped the audience tune in. Something similar happens to people when they listen to a lullaby or a march – the genre is capable of inducing a reaction regardless of the content; the genre is the message because of the emotional automatism of reaction.

Havelock reminds that Plato often described this "non-philosophical" (read: Homeric, or oral) state of mind as "sleep-walking." Havelock writes:

> It is therefore to be concluded that the recital of the tribal encyclopedia, because of the technology of the recital, was also a tribal recreation. In more familiar terms, the Muse, the voice of instruction, was also the voice of pleasure. But the recreation was of a rather special type. The audience found enjoyment and relaxation as they were themselves partly hypnotised by their response to a series of rhythmic patterns, verbal, vocal, instrumental, and physical, all set in motion together and all consonant in their effect. These motor mechanisms were activated in as many ways concurrently as was possible.[2]

Interestingly, the same quality of "emotional automatism" is being recreated now in digital orality. Digital media afford the instant exchange of emotional and automatic responses that, at a sufficient scale, might create the *viral* effect. Virality is a new form of tribal synchronization that replaces, in the digital realm, the tribal drums and the rhythms of bardic poetry.

In digital orality, formulaic and idiomatic clichés, such as "Hector of the gleaming helm" and similar expressions, are represented by their distant heirs: memes. Those proficient in oral sayings were popular in oral culture, just as those skilled in memes are in digital culture. It results now in a higher number of likes and followers for those meme-proficient "digital bards".

Memes are recognized pieces of wit and wisdom aimed at maintaining our status as a smart and savvy person without producing any intellectual product except for references. But memes went way further than just retrieving the formulaic nature of orality. They completely reversed not

---

[1] Havelock, Eric. (1963). *Preface to Plato*, p. 190.

[2] Havelock, Eric. (1963). *Preface to Plato*, p. 152.

only literate writing but also oral rhapsodizing. Having allowed the use of memes, social media afforded a type of conversation that would have been impossible either in literacy or in orality. In orality, the utterance used verbomotor formulas for better memorization and affection. In literacy, the utterance valorized originality. But the utterance in digital orality can legitimately consist of *only a meme*, without stitching it with something else. Furthermore, the meme is designed to be used alone, as a complete and self-sufficient utterance. With a good meme and meme only, you can nail it. Complementing a meme with a verbal explanation or extension is dumb; it totally discredits the meme proficiency of the user.

Moreover, other interlocutors can post in the conversational thread variations of the same meme or even exactly the same meme and nothing else. They do not produce speech; they do not even stich prefabricated formulaic expressions. It can be compared to many bards stepping in one after another and, in their turn (or rather chaotically), calling the Trojan prince "Hector of the gleaming helm" and uttering nothing else. And each one would get some likes if the Trojan War is viral at the moment.

Posting just a meme and nothing else is functionally similar to leaving a hand stencil on a wall where others have already placed their hand stencils. This returns communication not to Homeric orality but to even earlier stages of orality contemporary to cave paintings. These are basically the digital-physiological signs of presence and authenticity.

The formulaic nature of orality was pushed by digital conversation to its limits and reversed into the seemingly pointless exchange of meme competences. However, even such exchange in digital orality still provides tribal synchronization and the preservation of tribal identity. People receive a slight hormonal hit of pleasure of communion when they insert their memes and especially when these memes are reacted to. Generally, this is only what such conversation does, as no other meaning is produced during the exchange of memes and no memorizing is involved. The interlocutors inform each other and the world that they are proficient in the memes of the tribe they belong to. By doing that, they also maintain the ongoing relevance of those memes, reproducing the tribal indoctrination of each other.

Analog thinking and magical consciousness

For a mind immersed in the environment, the prior experience defines and limits consciousness. The known cannot be extracted from the unknown; it can only be derived from or compared to another known. The experience-based consciousness of orality favours analog thinking: something is always similar to something else. Mimicking, the first mode of human interaction, formed not only oral speech but also its "software" – analog thinking.

In *The Lion King,* Simba learns that when the lions, who eat antelopes, die, they become the grass, and then the antelopes eat the grass. In this way, everything is connected in the Circle of Life. Thus, the question of life's meaning is answered: life is similar to circular movement, and your life is a part of this circle.

The analog explanation of life's meaning is typical in oral cultures. Life is often compared to something tangibly experienced: a circle, a river, a road, a journey, and so on. Metaphors like these represent the highest possible in orality level of abstraction (the circle is more abstract than the river but still tethered to physical experience).

When Alexander Luria asked the illiterate peasants in Soviet Middle Asia in the 1930s, "In the far North, where there is snow, all bears are white. Novaya Zemlya is in the far North. What color are the bears in Novaya Zemlya?" they lacked prior knowledge to extrapolate or draw analogies from; they also did not dare to speculate, so they chose to refrain from answering and redirected the inquiry to the elders.[1]

In oral consciousness, inquiries tend to seek analogies or precedents rather than speculations. If there are no direct precedents, the oral mind searches for analogies in other areas and employs them as metaphors. This is why orality is so good at producing allegories. Those who can establish corresponding relations between new occurrences and the known things are wise. Finding a good analogy in personal or collective experience (in sagas and proverbs) is finding wisdom. Good explanatory metaphors, once found, enter the inventory of metaphors and sayings that are ritualistically repeated on all proper occasions, referring to well-established wisdom, the

---

[1] Luria, Alexander. (1976). *Cognitive Development*, p. 108. See also: Mir, Andrey. (2022). "Media-ecological engineering of the Soviets." *Explorations in Media Ecology*, Volume 21, Issue 2-3, Oct 2022, p. 150.

power of which only grows with each repetition. A wiseman in orality is a person capable of finding the best references. Things are explained not through their essence (Platonic *idea*) but through their similarity to other things.

The cognition of the world in orality produces wisdom. The cognition of the world in literacy produces thinking. Wisdom has answers; it is a storage of precedents. Thinking has questions; it is an endless process of inquiry.

Answers born from wisdom are always complete and satisfactory. When Simba receives the answer that life is akin to a circle, he is awed but also satisfied with the revealed wisdom. The literate mind might appreciate the poetry of this metaphor but will never be satisfied with it. Finding the meaning of life in the Circle of Life implies that the life of the inquirer actually has no meaning.

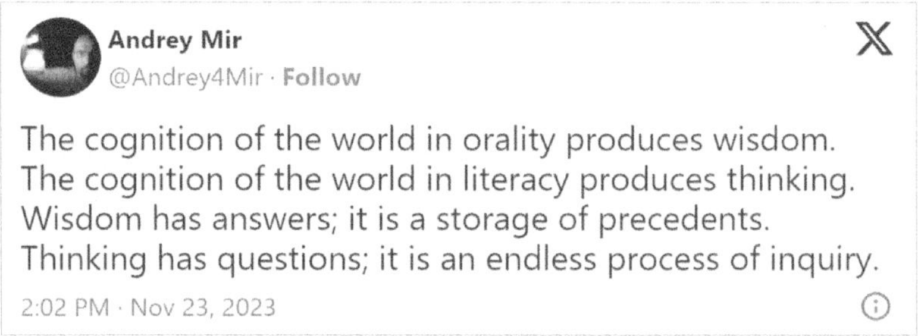
Andrey Mir
@Andrey4Mir · **Follow**

The cognition of the world in orality produces wisdom.
The cognition of the world in literacy produces thinking.
Wisdom has answers; it is a storage of precedents.
Thinking has questions; it is an endless process of inquiry.

2:02 PM · Nov 23, 2023

It is axiomatic for the literate mind that the question of life's meaning cannot be satisfactorily answered. This inherent inexhaustibility of enquiry is satirized in “The Hitchhiker's Guide to the Galaxy”: the answer to the “Ultimate question of life, the universe, and everything” is known – it’s 42. But what the question is exactly, nobody knows. (It also brings to mind an old joke. God summoned a man and said to him: “You have been granted the greatest opportunity. Ask me one question, but only one.” – “What question?”)

Metaphor is the transfer of meaning from one thing to another. Analog thinking is inherently magical – it transfers qualities from one thing to another. Being immersed in the environment, humans see all sorts of connections within the environmental assemblage and need to negotiate their place and fate with other “inhabitants.”

At earlier stages of these connections’ symbolization, humans identified themselves with Nature. The identification with other living creatures in

Nature led to totemism. With further development and the increasing complexity of symbolic and analog thinking, humans began to relate natural forces to their own activities. Likening Nature to the human world gave rise to animism/anthropomorphism. Both totemism and animism/anthropomorphism were the products of analog thinking and inevitably turned into magical consciousness.

Natural forces did not just exist – they were enacted. The oral syntax of *doing* and not *being* described by Havelock went hand in hand with analog thinking: doing requires a doer, an actor. If something is going on around, for instance, a thunderstorm or flood, it is not just *is* – it is *done* by someone who is mighty enough to act with such power.

Havelock writes:

> The psychology of oral memorisation and oral record required the content of what is memorised to be a set of doings. This in turn presupposes actors or agents. Again, since the content to be preserved must place great emphasis on public and private law, the agents must be conspicuous and political people. Hence they become heroes. All non-human phenomena must by metaphor be translated into sets of doings, and the commonest device for achieving this is to represent them as acts and decisions of especially conspicuous agents, namely gods.[1]

That is why natural forces were personalized and acquired divine agency. The magical consciousness emerged out of analog thinking, and the divine actors emerged out of the syntax of doing, the only predicative form of orality. Gods are the product of syntax. The responsibilities of gods for this or that matter played the role of causality. Havelock writes:

> They constantly provide an apparatus by which causal relations can be rendered in a verbal form with which the listener can identify. They become imitable and so memorisable. The complexity of the causative chain is simplified; the abstract factors are all crystallised as the interposition of powerful persons.
>
> Once viewed in this light, as a kind of recurrent metaphor for constant conjunction of causes and effects, polytheism can be seen to have a great descriptive advantage over monotheism.[2]

---

[1] Havelock, Eric. (1963). *Preface to Plato*, p. 171.

[2] Havelock, Eric. (1963). *Preface to Plato*, p. 170.

Polytheism was indeed the natural science of orality. But the explanatory power of the magical worldview had its limitations. When supernatural forces are anthropomorphized into divine beings, they end up in the same analog captivity as everything else: when everything is like something else, the cognition of the unknown is impossible because everything is metaphorically derived from something else that is already known. Cognition is not revelation of the essences of things but the discovery of the connections between them. Wisdom is proficiency in referencing. As Logan points out,

> Let us consider the personification of the natural forces in the form of the Greek gods as one example. This device, which made the Greek myths so vivid and hence easily recallable, severely limited the preliterate Greek's capacity to conceptualize natural forces. Consider how far science would have developed if the natural forces had never been abstracted, but continued to be personified and represented as gods.[1]

Another outcome of analog thinking is tolerance towards ignorance. When everything is connected to everything, everything can be explained through something else. If an individual did not have a proper analogy in the personal experience, he or she just ignored the inquiry, leaving all the tricky answers to the wisemen and elders. Invoking analogies or ignoring inquiries was a completely satisfying way of environmental comprehension.

Before the trauma of literacy, when Socrates revealed that he knew nothing, the negative value of ignorance simply did not exist. Instead, there was a real risk of invoking the wrath of gods (and people) by the incorrect divine attribution of events. So, it's better to refrain from passing judgment if it doesn't stem from your own experience or an analogy that has already been attested by the reaction of the tribe or gods.

Interestingly, both the situational exemplification of knowledge and the personalization of "science" are now being retrieved by digital orality. With print literacy losing its authority, anecdotal evidence is gaining validating power and replacing the abstract logic of generalization in public and even academic debates. Personal experience becomes legitimate content for dissertations, thus retrieving the epic practice of the personalization of

---

[1] Logan, Robert. (2004 [1986]). *The Alphabet Effect*, p. 108.

knowledge through the lives of heroes and turning academia into a "tribal encyclopedia." The risks of ignorance decline when arguments are backed by proper analogies, while the risks of wrong divine references grow. We are fortunate to witness a unique historical twist: the Homeric revenge on Plato, enabled by digital orality. Havelock would have been amazed.

Lay orality

In the communicative practices of an oral culture, Havelock distinguishes "significant speech" and "casual speech." Significant speech was inherently arranged in elevated poetic forms and "represented the maximum degree of sophistication." However, the verbomotor and idiomatic nature of orality manifested in everyday communication, too. According to Havelock, "The whole memory of a people was poetised, and this exercised a constant control over the ways in which they expressed themselves in casual speech."[1]

The use of oral speech as the only available means of memorization affected any instance of oral communication. As Havelock puts it,

> A minstrel would be a man of superior memory, and so also might be the prince and the judge. This automatically meant superior rhythmic sense, since rhythm was the preservative of speech. With superior memory and rhythmic sense would go also a greater virtuosity in the management of the formulas. The lesser memories of the populace would be content to use simpler and less elaborate language. But the whole community from minstrel and prince down to the peasant was attuned to the psychology of remembrance.[2]

We can assume that there were gradations of significance that were reflected in or supported by a certain degree of poetization/rhythmization of speech. Anything that should wield regulatory power was repeated, refined into formulaic structures, and passed on. Significant stories formed sagas, significant verbal resolutions were shaped into sayings and proverbs, and rhythmic accompaniments of activities turned into work shanties, nursery rhymes and the like.

---

[1] Havelock, Eric. (1963). *Preface to Plato*, p. 134.

[2] Havelock, Eric. (1963). *Preface to Plato*, p. 140.

While the oral recording of significant stories into epics was suppressed and replaced by writing, the less significant formulaic means of orality has survived after the proliferation of literacy. Walter Ong provides a contemporary example of using sayings as a legal means to resolve a dispute. His friend was about to embark on a long-distance car journey with his two sons. A conflict arose when one boy claimed the seat by the window and refused to give it up. Their father then said, "Turnabout is fair play," and the dispute quickly dissipated as the boys agreed to take the seat in turn.

Ong highlights the psychodynamics of the episode: the saying saved the youngster's face. He was moved out of a better seat not due to his weakness or lesser worth – one's status holds great significance in the "agonistically structured lifeworld of primary orality" – but because "turnabout is fair play." The saying was well-known and wielded regulatory power. Therefore, the young man gracefully yielded to the tribe's ruling rather than to the challenge from someone of "lower status."[1]

The regulatory power of sayings is maintained by the tribal convention, the convention is preserved in the tribal memory, and the memory is sustained by formulaic and verbomotor elements. Idioms affect through intonations, gestures, rhymes, and rhythms: "Deeds are fruits, words are leaves," "No pain, no gain," "Finders keepers, losers weepers," etc. The verbomotor qualities of idioms – rhythm, rhyme, parallelism – indicate that the utterance is the subject of memorization and, therefore, represent a tribally sanctioned ruling. The proficiency in formulaic references gives power not only to princes but to ordinary people, too.

Nowadays, the proportion of formulaic expressions in casual speech may indicate the level of literacy or residual orality: less formulaic casual speech reflects a stronger background of literacy. Nevertheless, proficiency in rhapsodising – in incorporating relevant oral formulas – still contributes to one's social capital.

While acquiring social capital might be seen as a purpose of using relevant idioms, there is also another goal. By using formulaic structures that embody significant verbal resolutions, individuals, in fact, re-record those idioms, keeping the collective mechanism of memorization rolling and simultaneously upholding the relevance of the selected idioms.

---

[1] Ong, Walter. (1980). "Literacy and Orality in Our Times," p. 202.

A similar mechanism of acquiring social capital, which also maintains the relevance of significant references, is used in literacy in the form of citations; the function of memorization, however, is not employed, as quotes are already written in their respective sources.

Digital orality utilizes this mechanism, too – in the form of meme proficiency. By posting memes, users demonstrate their wit and familiarity with tribal trends, simultaneously testing and upholding or refreshing the relevance of these "formulaic expressions," which now are often non-verbal. Memes and abbreviations have taken the place of traditional proverbs and sayings.

It is noticeable, however, that there are no epics in digital orality. All elevated forms in digital orality rely on literacy; all significant speech remains expressed by means of literacy. Digital orality is always lay orality.

Orality as a platform of mind

Both orality and literacy can be seen as platforms that reflect certain states of mind. Orality is not simply an oral means of conveying a message. It encompasses specific speech-behaviour, but it also represents the sensory and cognitive characteristics of individuals and, as a result, the specificity of oral culture and society. As Havelock puts it, the exploration of historical oralism involves "identifying a distinct mode of consciousness with its own rules."[1] On another occasion, Havelock states:

> The formulaic style characteristic of oral composition represented not merely certain verbal and metrical habits but also a cast of thought, or a mental condition.[2]

The cognitive distinctions between orality and literacy begin with differences in sensory input. The oral mind is immersed in the situation and receives signals from the surrounding environment simultaneously. There is no organized order: things rush into panoramic perception as they are, and the sensorium registers them accordingly, favouring impulsive reactions. Conversely, the literate mind is detached from what it observes and trained to receive ideas about the world in a linear and sequential way

---

[1] Havelock, Eric. (1986). *The Muse Learns to Write*, p. 40.

[2] Havelock, Eric. (1986). *The Muse Learns to Write*, p. x.

that favours rational perception. This is obviously an artificial way of interacting with the environment, created by writing (reading).

Sensory perception plays a crucial role in shaping our cognition ("Being determines consciousness" – Marx[1]). In the literate mind, things belong to certain concepts of ideal order. In the oral mind, things belong to the situation. Oral thinking is inherently situational and lacks the ability to theorize. Orality coordinates efforts in the situation and passes on successful situational experiences for future collective survival, but it does not favour extracting abstractions out of it. As Logan put it,

> Woven around the tales were the essential lore and wisdom of the culture. The customs of the society were taught by example, not by prescription.[2]

Reasoning in the oral mind is anecdotal rather than theoretical. It relies on past resolved situations or formulaic sayings accumulated from previous experiences to address new situations. To operate in this manner, the oral mind needs to constantly refresh its experiential knowledge. Orality functions as the continuous collective re-recording of experience.

It is not without reason that Innis deemed oral society to be time-biased,[3] akin to a society based on stone inscriptions or clay tablets. One would wonder, what is common between fleeting words that exist in the moment of utterance ("winged words," as Homer called it) and stones or fired clay tablets that preserve the message for millennia.

The songs about the Trojan War had lived 6–7 centuries before being written down in the *Iliad* and the *Odyssey*. Some folk songs or rhymes can be traced to their origin through millennia. The tale of the Beauty and the Beast, which is a highly romanticized bourgeois version of the oral "animal husband narrative," which in turn is a residue of the ancient rite of sacrificing a virgin to the divine elements of nature, has lived three hundred years in writing and four or five thousand years (or more) in oral form. Some oral narratives outlived, indeed, messages written in stone.

---

1 Marx, Karl. (1859). *A Contribution to the Critique of Political Economy*. Preface.

2 Logan, Robert. (2004 [1986]). *The Alphabet Effect*, p. 108.

3 The time bias is one of the few fundamental differences between orality and digital orality. Unlike time-biased primary orality, digital orality is highly space-biased, as it can instantly cover any distance but is transient in nature; but the content of digital orality does not last long.

As a method of communication, orality does not require a heavy carrier, such as stones or clay tablets, as a spoken word weighs nothing. Despite this, orality is not well-suited for covering long distances. For an oral story to travel, the entire tribe must travel, as the oral function of memorization does not exist within an individual carrier – a collective is needed. However, in time, an oral story can endure as long as people continue to tell and retell it, often adapting it to changes.

Special mechanisms helped make durable collective memories out of evanescent personal storytelling. Constant "live re-recording" involved communal gatherings with certain rituals. Storytelling involved the verbomotor performance of the bards or whoever assumed this role, who aimed to induce a "vibe" in the audience. This not only preserved useful survival expertise but also "kept a man in close psychological rapport with the ancestral tales," according to Havelock.[1] He writes:

> Oral verse was the instrument of a cultural indoctrination, the ultimate purpose of which was the preservation of group identity. It was selected for this role because, in the absence of the written record, its rhythms and formulas provided the sole mechanism of recall and of re-use.[2]

According to Havelock, "In such non-literate cultures the task of education could be described as putting the whole community into a formulaic state of mind. The instrument for doing this was to use the tribal epics as a paradigm."[3]

People had to constantly retell what they knew about the world to keep knowing the world. As a result, knowledge of the world acquired the features of its medium (it always does). Among these features were situational immersion, repetitive formulas, ritualization, analog thinking, content redundancy, the representation of communal experience and legal practices through the doings of people and deeds of heroes, magic explanation of natural occurrences as the doings of supernatural beings, anecdotal argumentation, collectivism, emotionality, empathic involvement, constant requests for affirmation, rhythm, poetical affectation and mannerism, and other mechanisms providing rapport, communion,

---

1 Havelock, Eric. (1963). *Preface to Plato*, p. 126.

2 Havelock, Eric. (1963). *Preface to Plato*, p. 100.

3 Havelock, Eric. (1963). *Preface to Plato*, p 140.

and memorization. The oral mind was shaped after the features of its media platform.

As a platform of mind, orality preceded literacy. Orality "emerged" about 100–150 thousand years ago[1] and completed the becoming of Homo sapiens. The first affordances of literacy appeared five thousand years ago and started the formation of humankind.

Ong admits that oral cultures produce "powerful and beautiful verbal performances of high artistic and human worth,"[2] but writing is "essential for the realization of fuller human potential and for the evolution of consciousness itself."[3] According to his evolutionary view, "orality needs to produce and is destined to produce writing."[4] Within the Jaspersian paradigm of the "universal history as a whole," it was all of us, humans, who have overcome orality and acquired literacy. As Ong puts it,

> Oral cultures today value their oral traditions and agonize over the loss of these traditions, but I have never encountered or heard of an oral culture that does not want to achieve literacy as soon as possible.[5]

Transitioning from the platform of orality to the platform of literacy brought humans significant benefits. One cannot make a vaccine out of storytelling; insisting otherwise is science denial in the most literal sense. But the transition to literacy also had its price. By suppressing orality, literacy suppressed environmental immersion, which is often mistaken for harmony with Nature, and collective involvement, which is often mistaken for social harmony.

Unlike orality, which mostly accumulated answers and not questions, literacy has developed significant critical traditions. Self-criticism, increasingly manifested by Western culture, is a side-effect of the "inward

---

[1] Some anthropologists move the origin of language farther into the depths of time, suggesting that this or that species of Homo possessed some form of proto-language that was more complex than the communication system of apes. These theories date the origin of language as early as 2.5 million years ago. But the orality of humans we discuss here certainly emerged some time after the "genetic bottleneck", an event from which a relatively small number of Homo sapiens 150–300,000 years ago appeared somewhere in East or North Africa and started colonizing Earth.

[2] Ong, Walter. (2002 [1982]), *Orality and Literacy*, p. 14.

[3] Ong, Walter. (1980). *Literacy and Orality in Our Times*, p. 199.

[4] Ong, Walter. (2002 [1982]), *Orality and Literacy*, p. 14.

[5] Ong, Walter. (2002 [1982]), *Orality and Literacy*, p. 171.

turn" enabled by literacy. This self-criticism had to eventually romanticize cultural settings associated with oral cultures, though in reality, nobody is willing to transition from literacy to orality, and rightly so, because living in the conditions of primary orality, with its environmental immersion and collective involvement, might be not very comfortable for people whose interaction with the world has already been mediated by literacy.

During the Enlightenment, when literacy was tremendously boosted by the printing press, the European critical tradition created the stock character of the "natural man" or "noble savage" – an individual uncorrupted by civilization. Havelock points out that, with this character, "the oral-literate problem entered the modern European consciousness."[1] According to him, the "noble savage" was essentially an oralist character, romanticised by Rousseau to highlight his "sincerity, simplicity, and moral integrity." However, drawing such romantic pictures "is no way to visualize a society of primary orality," according to Havelock.[2]

Indeed, little did Rousseau know about the real circumstances of oral life, let alone have any experience with living in oral conditions. He simply used such a character as a tool to condemn the cynicism, hypocrisy, and immorality of "civilized" society. And so did Voltaire in his philosophical-satirical novel *L'Ingénu* (1767). The story of a French boy who was raised by the Hurons in Canada and returned to France as a "child of nature" illustrated the conflict between his "natural" straightforwardness and the corruption of "civilized" society. *L'Ingénu* was intended to show "civilized" Europeans that their moral superiority over "natural people" was, in fact, a compendium of lies, sins, hypocrisy, and immorality.

Such depictions of cultures that we can distinguish as oral and literate became an even stronger tradition in critical theories after the West had tasted more of the benefits of technological advancement. Our understanding of the guilt and sins of "civilized" society has significantly advanced with it, paralleled by the continued romanticization of environmental immersion and collective involvement, inherent to oral cultures.

Nevertheless, however politically charged the debates about the moral aspects of orality and literacy may be, the emergence of digital media has

---

[1] Havelock, Eric. (1986). *The Muse Learns to Write*, p. 16.

[2] Havelock, Eric. (1986). *The Muse Learns to Write*, p. 68.

offered a completely different perspective. We have already started learning the hard way what happens to a society stripped of literacy. This perspective may encourage some to look at the conditions of orality and literacy, historical and oncoming, from a more realistic angle.

7. A catalogue of the effects of writing and the alphabet

Sensory effect: visual bias

All media effects start with the sensorium. The sensorium responds to the use of a medium by shaping a combination of senses that enables its most efficient use: the sensorium adjusts to a medium after we have done our best in adjusting the medium to our body. As John Culkin puts it, "We shape our tools, and thereafter our tools shape us."[1]

The natural state of the sensorium, McLuhan's acoustic space, is shaped by living in Nature. Acoustic space is characterized by the simultaneous and spherical perception of the world's signals through the equilibrium of all senses. Visual space, on the other hand, is "the space of detachment," as McLuhan puts it. Visual space relates to reading; it is created when the sensorium is trained by reading. In reading, the sense of vision is detached from the rest of the sensorium, while the other senses are blocked. (You can see this alienation in the eyes of guest stars on *Saturday Night Live,* for example, who pretend to be looking at the camera while, in fact, reading the teleprompter: their eyes focus not on the objects of surroundings but on the subject of the sketch.)

Focused and isolated vision dissects the sensorium. In the natural environment, such dissection of the sensorium would have been dangerous. But in the safety of the human community, isolating vision from the other senses gives the advantage of focusing on the written symbols and the ideas carried by them. If, in acoustic space, a person is submerged in sensing the environment, in visual space a person is submerged in processing meanings. Visual space transforms the *sensorial faculty* of vision into the *cognitive ability* of inner vision.

When an individual perceives the world through inner vision, a new reality is induced. On one hand, this reality is processed in the sensory pattern of vision: the things are seen in front of a person, forming a

[1] Culkin, John. (1967). "Each culture develops its own sense ratio to meet the demands of its environment", p. 52. The aphorism is so much McLuhanesque that is often mistakenly attributed to McLuhan. See an exploration on this matter in: *McLuhan Galaxy blog*, by Alex Kuskis (2013, April 1). "We shape our tools and thereafter our tools shape us."

subject-object positioning that favours detachment and perception from outside, not from within like in acoustic space. At the same time, this pattern of vision shapes cognitive perception in a way acquired from reading – as linear and sequential input of abstract meanings, with all other senses numbed.

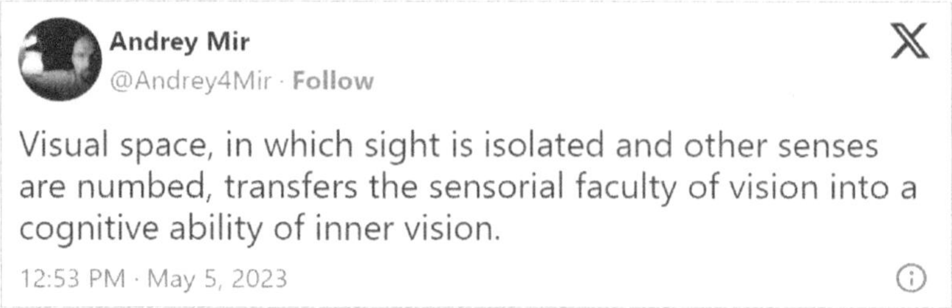
Andrey Mir
@Andrey4Mir · Follow

Visual space, in which sight is isolated and other senses are numbed, transfers the sensorial faculty of vision into a cognitive ability of inner vision.

12:53 PM · May 5, 2023

Eventually, such sensory conditions foster visual bias – the cognitive habit of ascribing linear and sequential order to the things we are thinking about. This sensory-cognitive operation breaks the holistic world into bits of information that are linearly, sequentially, and logically structured. Linearity and sequence imply not only the order in the world but also the delay of reflexes. This delay facilitates deliberating and reasoning, which are also supported by the detachment from the environment. The literate mind is immersed in the intelligible environment – the environment of reflection.

Visual bias causes all the other cognitive and social effects of writing. This is how Logan comments on McLuhan's concept of visual and acoustic space:

> Let us now turn to McLuhan's description of visual space, which he alleges arises from literacy and is the space of the phonetic alphabet, abstraction, deductive logic, Euclidean geometry and abstract Newtonian physics. The perceptual bias of visual space is linear, sequential, one thing at a time, objective, abstract, rational, deductive, fragmented, causal, and specialized, whereas that of acoustic space is non-linear, simultaneous, all directions at once, subjective, characterized by intense involvement, concrete, intuitive, all-embracing, mystical, inductive, and experiential. Visual space is characterized with patterns associated with the specialization of the brain's left hemisphere and acoustic space with those of the right.[1]

[1] Logan, Robert. (2013). *McLuhan Misunderstood*, p. 62.

In 2013 *McLuhan Misunderstood: Setting the Record Straight*, Logan suggests a set of dual notions that characterize visual and acoustic space through their opposite features. I took the liberty to rework Logan's chart a little, incorporating other oppositions he mentions and some additional ideas – Figure 17.

Acoustic space (a ratio of senses)	**Visual space** (isolated sight)
Natural	Artificial
Immersion	Detachment
Incorporates, unifies	Isolates, takes apart
Non-linear (spherical)	Linear
Simultaneous	Sequential
Concrete (situational)	Abstract
Holistic	Fragmented
Intuitive (emotional)	Rational
Percept	Concept
Affect	Deliberation
Analogy	Essence, thing-in-itself
Dynamic	Static
Subjective	Objective
Right-brain	Left-brain
Ground	Figure
Generalism	Specialism
Field, resonance	Particle

Figure 17. Acoustic and visual spaces. Based on the chart by Robert Logan in: Logan, Robert. (2013). *McLuhan Misunderstood: Setting the Record Straight*, p. 62.

Orality favours multitasking. Prolonged and focused attention was a rare professional skill in orality. Being focused on a subject for a long time might have been required for a hunter, for example. Otherwise, environmental immersion required "spherical attention," which led to constant shifts of focus in attention.

Staring at something for a long time might not have been entirely unknown to oral people, but staring at something or watching prey during a hunt still kept people immersed in the environment. Reading, however, is not just staring at something – it sends the mind of the reader into an internal confinement shared only with the content of the reading. This is something entirely unknown and simply not applicable in an oral culture. Literacy enhanced the human capacity for attention, increased the attention span, but also created a completely new psychomotor state – inner concentration. While reading, a reading person can stay concentrated on inner vision for hours, with all other senses numbed.

As a result of such evolution of the visual bias, humankind had, in the 20th century, several billion people capable of inner concentration. We were able to stay focused on linearly organized and logically ordered ideas without any verbomotor stimuli for hours. The attention span of humans likely achieved its historical maximum by the end of the 20th century. If, at the beginning of literacy development, it affected society by changing the cognitive abilities of the educated elites, in the 20th century, literacy affected cognition on a scale that encompassed the entire population in many countries.

What does it mean when the normal attention span of humans, i.e., the capacity of blocking all other triggers and focusing on one task, could reach hours? What does it mean for civilization when billions of people are capable of inner concentration for hours and able to diligently focus on an intellectual task?

These are interesting questions. But even more interesting is the question about what will happen when these capacities drastically decline on a planetary scale. Since digital orality returns us to acoustic space, we become multitaskers. We are now immersed in media consumption that emulates a simultaneous and panoramic mode of environmental perception. With this change, the attention span decreases and now averages only a few minutes.

As has been mentioned, McLuhan developed his dual concept of acoustic and visual spaces to explain the sensory nature of electronic media, not orality. In 1974, McLuhan observed that "Electronic and simultaneous man has recovered the primordial attitudes of the preliterate world."[1] As Logan explains, "McLuhan applied the concept <of acoustic space> to electric information because we are bombarded with electric

[1] McLuhan, Marshall. (1974). "At the moment of Sputnik...", p. 49.

information from all directions from across the globe more or less simultaneously."[1]

In the digital space, a person cannot stay concentrated on one thing for too long, as the environment sends signals to switch to something potentially more interesting and rewarding – hyperlinks, notifications, clickbaits, and so on, – enabling verbomotor-like reactions of clicks (taps, swipes, typing, etc.). Despite the availability of long texts on the internet, the digital environment simply does not favour isolating the sense of vision into inner vision. By allowing us to check and follow several sources of content simultaneously, digital media favour multitasking, thus activating a wider ratio of sensorimotor and cognitive reactions instead of isolated inner vision. As a result, digital media disrupt successive-linear perception, typical for literacy, and immerse us in simultaneous-panoramic perception, similar to acoustic space, the perceptual mode of orality, but inside digital reality.

The separation of the knower from the known

The essence of any symbolic activity is the representation of objects (and subsequently, ideas) in forms or materials other than the original. The signs of the objects are needed and used precisely as symbolic replacements. Symbols create the affordance of operating with the objects in their absence.

Oral speech had already fully employed this semantic function. By naming things, humans learn to operate with them in their absence. The doubling of reality had already occurred in oral speech. However, in oral speech, the symbolic representation of the absent belonged to the speaker in the moment of speaking. It did not extend beyond the speaker's physical reach in space and did not persist in time after the moment of utterance.

Writing revolutionized operations with the absent things by removing the speaker as the immediate carrier of symbolization. Writing separated the knower from the known, as Havelock puts it.[2]

Havelock contemplates the separation of the knower from the known in the context of the emergence of the concept of the psyche, or "soul," in the

[1] Logan, Robert. (2013). *McLuhan Misunderstood*, p. 60.

[2] Havelock, Eric. (1963). *Preface to Plato*, p. 197.

philosophy of Socrates. The separation of the knower from the known allowed an individual to break free from the collective mimetic practices of orality and acquire the self, or soul/psyche, that possessed all the characteristics of agency and personality we now see in it, from cognition to moral choice.

While Havelock focused on the knower, Ong focused on the known. What happens to the known when it breaks free from the knower? A lot.

Writing makes words visible, almost material objects. People can see and even touch inscribed words. It does not seem to be a big deal to the literate mind, but imagine the oral mind that suddenly realises that what was invisible and basically non-existing in the world of material objects was caught by somebody and made visible, material. For the oral mind, it was a disturbance that caused either an intellectual breakthrough (and further speculations on what language is and what I am) or schizophrenia, as Marshall McLuhan notes on many occasions.[1]

Besides the psychological shock this revelation delivers to the oral mind, it creates a simple material opportunity for carrying knowledge in space and time.

In orality, the known is always subjective, not only due to the fact that there is a certain person who utters it but also because this person always aims to affect others. "By keeping knowledge embedded in the human lifeworld, orality situates knowledge within a context of struggle," writes Ong, referring to the agonistic effect of orality. Being separated from the knower, "Writing fosters abstractions that disengage knowledge from the arena where human beings struggle with one another."[2]

The liberation of the known from the "egoistic" intents of the knower and from their constant struggle for affirmation has set up the conditions for objectivity. When there is no need to subordinate the known to the momentary needs of interaction, it becomes possible to focus on the essence of the known itself.

Finally, being separated from the knower and withdrawn from face-to-face agonistic interaction, the known acquires a sort of agency of its own. It starts functioning independently, attracting people to engage with it for further development, including selecting, classifying, accumulating,

---

[1] McLuhan, Marshall. (1962). *The Gutenberg Galaxy*, p. 22.

[2] Ong, Walter. (2002 [1982]), *Orality and Literacy*, p. 42.

combining, and employing. Being detached from the knower and becoming available to others as pure content, without any agonistic pressure from the knower, the known inspires others to generate the new known, as Ong notes in an essay whose title deserves quoting on its own: "Writing is a technology that restructures thought."[1]

Thus, the separation of the knower from the known not only radically enhances memorization and communication but also brings completely new affordances of generating knowledge, which did not exist in orality.

The objectivation of knowledge is a feature of literacy that appears to be reversed by electronic media. The reversal of knowledge objectivation would be the "subjectivation of knowledge." This epistemological comeback of orality can be described as a reconnection of the known with the knower. It transpires, for example, when right ideas are seen as wrong if they belong to the wrong persons, and wrong ideas are tolerated if they belong to the right persons. One's background becomes more important than one's content. As the agonistic mentality is back on social media in the form of everyone's constant requests for affirmation, the identity of an individual becomes the message.

The closure of the gap between the knower and the known leads, among other things, to the decline of irony. This becomes evident, for instance, in formerly satirical late-night TV shows. From irony, they have transitioned to mocking, the oral precursor of irony, thus slouching toward conditions that Jon Stewart,[2] the originator of the genre, could not survive.

The degradation of irony into mocking is accompanied by the "degradation" of hypocrisy into "new sincerity" or rather "new candidness." Both irony and hypocrisy were media effects of literacy. They emerged as a result of the detachment of the knower from the known and the accompanying affordance of doublethink.

Havelock writes about the preliterate Greeks:

> Another thing noticeable about them (ancient Greeks) in this period is their capacity for direct action and sincere action and for direct and sincere expression of motive and desire. They almost

---

[1] Ong, Walter. (1986). "Writing is a technology that restructures thought," p. 38.

[2] The most comprehensive analysis of the phenomenon of Jon Stewart and his contribution to postjournalism read in: Askonas, Jon. (2022, Summer.) "How Stewart made Tucker." *The New Atlantis*.

> entirely lack those slight hypocrisies without which our civilisation does not seem to work.[1]

Some ethnographers hypothesized that people of tribal cultures were unable to lie. However, there might be an issue with what counts as a lie or truth in tribal culture. Status competition favours exaggeration and bragging, both of which are fertile soil for lies. But an oral lie has to be natural and sincere, as there is no split reality in the oral mind. An oral individual genuinely believes in whatever they say in a situation. This is dictated by situational thinking and the inseparability of the knower and the known. The uttered reality belongs to the utterance "here-and-now," not to some abstract idea of reality. If there is no objective truth, there is no objective lie. But hypocrisy, deliberate and "rational" doublethink, seems unlikely to fit the oral mind indeed.

The merger of the known with the knower brings some other interesting outcomes. As electronic and now digital media emphasize concrete personal experience over abstract and detached speculations, a new hybrid state of mind has emerged that bestows the significance of objective knowledge upon personal experience. The abstract, literacy-type known can be justified by, or even extracted from, the personality of the knower. Among other consequences, this enabled, for example, such forms of academic pursuit as "autoethnographic" studies, through which scholars make a science out of their personal stories. In a similar vein, artists-scholars can get a PhD in humanities through artistic expression and scholarly reflection on it in the form of a "research-creation" dissertation, which can be seen as academic storytelling. The fundamental feature of literacy, the separation of the knower from the known, is shattered even in the bastion of literacy – academia.

Abstract thinking

When Gulliver traveled to Balnibarbi, he met a "scholar" who advanced a bill to abolish all words because they corrupt the lungs and shorten life. The "scholar" therefore proposed:

[1] Havelock, Eric. (1963). *Preface to Plato,* p. 158.

> Since words are only names for things, it would be more convenient for all men to carry about them such things as were necessary to express a particular business they are to discourse on.[1]

The proposal almost succeeded, but the women rebelled against it. However, "many of the most learned and wise adhere to the new scheme of expressing themselves by things." The only inconvenience was that such a wiseman needed to carry "a greater bundle of things upon his back, unless he can afford one or two strong servants to attend him." When such wisemen met each other, they would lay down their loads, open their sacks, and have conversations by showing things to each other.

Swift's allegory refers to the semantic structure of language: words stand for things or, more precisely, for the absence of things – for ideas. But the allegory also serves well to illustrate what our thinking would have been without the capacity for abstraction. We could "discuss" and think of only things at hand.

The so-called sensorimotor intelligence is available to higher animals and, according to Jean Piaget, infants. They can purposefully operate with the object presented in their environment. With further cognitive development, humans – as a species and as individuals – develop the capacity of abstraction.

"Abstract" is the opposite to "concrete" and "situational." Abstract thinking is the ability to deal with the *ideas* of things and events rather than with things and events themselves. Abstraction also entails pausing behaviour; abstraction is non-behaviour. By pausing behaviour and liberating the mind from the situation (through numbing the sensorium – that is what visual space does), abstract thinking unleashes inner vision, which is no longer a sensorial but a cognitive tool. Inner vision gets a chance to look at the essence of things and not at their situational, evanescent manifestations.

The oral mind was constrained by the situation (environmental survival) and by formulaic speech-behaviour (collective survival). These conditions predefined cognition, and cognition reproduced conditions. Plato's anti-Homeric rebellion targeted precisely this vicious cycle. Havelock highlights that Plato criticized Homeric poetry for its mimesis – the analog recreation of past experiences, where people's consciousness

---

[1] Swift, Jonathan. (1726). *Gulliver's Travels*, book III.

was emphatically submerged in the situations lived through by heroes and kings. This was the method by which the tribal encyclopedia reproduced itself. The re-recording of past experiences left no room for abstraction and reasoning.

The separation of the knower from the known by writing, among other things, liberated the mind from mimesis as the only transport of knowledge. Once situational immersion, whether immediate or poetically induced, loosened its grip on the mind, the affordance for abstracting emerged. Situational cognition yielded some space for abstract recognition.

By liberating minds from situations, abstract thinking fulfilled one of the main functions of Jaspers' move from prehistory to history. The divorce from situational thinking signified the divorce from an "entirely repetitive continuance of living, still closely allied to the processes of nature."[1] As soon as the mind breaks free from situational immersion, new horizons open before it. Innis wrote:

> Individuals applied their minds to symbols rather than things and went beyond the world of concrete experience into the world of conceptual relations created within an enlarged time and space universe. The time world was extended beyond the range of remembered things and the space world beyond the range of known places.[2]

All writing systems developed toward growing abstraction, along with loosing picturesque semblance with real objects.

Phonetization boosted the abstracting effect of writing even more. Logan highlights that the alphabet represents two levels of abstraction:

> All spoken words are abstractions of the things they represent. The written word is a further abstraction of the spoken word, and phonetic letters give it an even greater abstraction than ideographs or pictographs... A spoken word is first broken up into semantically meaningless phonemes or sounds, and the sounds are then represented by semantically meaningless signs – the letters of the alphabet.[3]

---

1 Jaspers, Karl. (2021 [1949]). *The Origin and Goal of History*, p. 32.

2 Innis, Harold. (1950). *Empire and Communications*, p. 11.

3 Logan, Robert. (2004 [1986]). *The Alphabet Effect*, p. 110.

According to Logan, "the Alphabet Effect is a subliminal phenomenon."[1] The ability to code the world in 20-something symbols that do not have any connection with or semblance to the world whatsoever trains the brain to operate at, perhaps, the highest level of abstraction, completely severing any environmental connections.

The alphabet had a tremendous impact on the Greek mind and culture because the Greeks moved to the most abstract state of mind, inherent in alphabetic literacy, directly from orality with its situational concretism.

According to Havelock, by the time of Plato (which means after three–four centuries from the introduction of the alphabet), even the syntax and semantic capacities of Greek language started changing. The syntax of *being* introduced a notion of "the thing *per se*"[2] – not what a thing *does* in a situation or what *happens* to a thing in a situation but what a thing *is* to itself in *all* situations.

This is where Plato's Theory of Forms is rooted, metaphorically described in Plato's Allegory of the Cave. Essentially, imprisonment in the cave represents an allegory of the human sensorium. Immersed in their environment, humans can perceive only the physical manifestations of things, offered by the sensorium, and cannot see the ideal and unchangeable essences of things. As Havelock interprets it, "Plato insists that his contemporaries must turn away from the panorama of sensual experience and focus instead upon the abstracted object *per se* which is the only possible object of thought."[3]

Homer would sing about beautiful clothes, beautiful armor, or beautiful people; Plato discovered the beauty – as Havelock specifies, "beauty per se,"[4] the very Form (essence) of beauty that exists in all situations, or, rather, regardless of any situation. The syntagmatic belonging of beauty to situational occurrences was abstracted into the isolated category of beauty, which could enter paradigmatic relations with other categories, such as dignity, honour, might, and so on. Any quality or action, which was previously incorporated and dissolved within a situational picture, became open to being thought of as having its own essence.

---

1 Logan, Robert. (2004 [1986]). *The Alphabet Effect*, p. 4.

2 Havelock, Eric. (1963). *Preface to Plato*, p. 224.

3 Havelock, Eric. (1963). *Preface to Plato*, p. 254.

4 Havelock, Eric. (1963). *Preface to Plato*, p. 226.

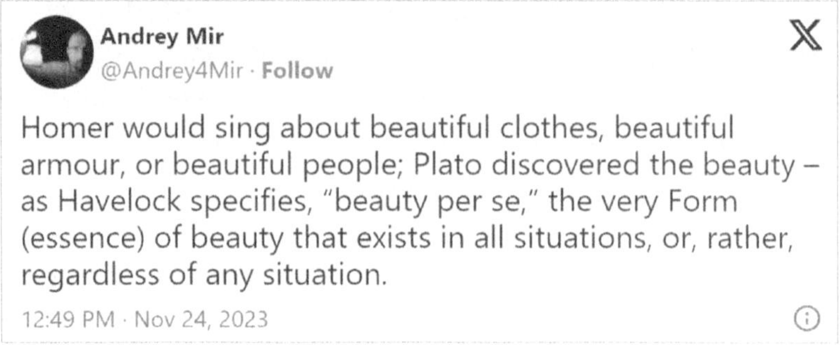
Andrey Mir
@Andrey4Mir · Follow

Homer would sing about beautiful clothes, beautiful armour, or beautiful people; Plato discovered the beauty – as Havelock specifies, "beauty per se," the very Form (essence) of beauty that exists in all situations, or, rather, regardless of any situation.

12:49 PM · Nov 24, 2023

Havelock discusses how Plato struggled to name his discovery of a "thing-per-se." Plato used the new meaning of the word "form," hence his Theory of Forms; he also used the word "idea," hence Platonic idealism. Alphabetic literacy compelled the Greeks to explore and invent not just the new syntax of *being* of things *per se* but also a new vocabulary that would reflect the world of ideas, not just things. According to Havelock, this led to "the invention of an abstract language of descriptive science to replace a concrete language of oral memory."[1]

Logan marks out the explosion of abstract concepts that emerged right after the introduction of the alphabet:

> Under the influence of alphabetic literacy, Greek writers created the vocabulary of abstract thought that is still in use to this day – notions such as body, matter, essence, space, translation, time, motion, permanence, change, flux, quality, quantity, combination, and ratio. These concepts became the language of philosophy.[2]

Havelock offers his reflection on the new vocabulary that emerged with abstract thinking, driven by alphabetic literacy, among the Greeks. He highlights its essentially paradigmatic and "counter-sensual" character:

> Goodness and rightness (with evil and unrighteousness), proportion and size, dimension and weight and shape, odd and even, the square and the diagonal, solidity, motion, velocity, and volume – what does this kind of terminology represent to us? As terms of a sophisticated vocabulary, these are many different things: they are moral values; they are also axioms; they are physical properties; and also relations. In combination with each other they furnish the

[1] Havelock, Eric. (1963). *Preface to Plato*, p. 236.

[2] Logan, Robert. (2004 [1986]). *The Alphabet Effect*, p. 110.

> terms in which we state both moral principles and physical formulas, both equations and laws. They bespeak the language of categories, and also of universals. The only modem term that would apply to all alike would be the word "concept". For these share the common characteristic that as categories, classes, relationships or principles or axioms, they have been coined by the mind to explain and to classify its sensual experience or have been extracted from that experience and have been inferred from it. As Plato says, the one thing you can say about them all is that you cannot see or taste or hear them. Some other faculty of man's brain is responsible for this kind of language. If we call them "concepts" it is to oppose them to the "image". If we call them "abstract" it is to oppose them to the concrete visualised event or the concrete visualised things that behave in an event. And it is fair to say that Platonism at bottom is an appeal to substitute a conceptual discourse for an imagistic one.[1]

This all happened historically instantly after alphabetic literacy spread among the educated Greeks. The literacy of a few created some distance, a gap, a breakaway, that allowed Plato to look at the oral state of mind, exposing the features of orality (he called them "poetry" or the "poetic mind," referring mostly to Homer) invisible before. With this change, according to Havelock, Greece entered "a dangerous and fascinating game, in which the combats of Homeric heroes found themselves being translated into battles between concepts, categories, and principles."[2] He writes:

> Europe still lives in their shadow, using their language, accepting their dichotomies, and submitting to their discipline of the abstract as the chief vehicle of higher education, even to this day.[3]

This resonates, of course, with the idea of Jaspers that the Greeks, Indians, Chinese, and other thinkers of the Axial Age discovered the universals through which humans still think about and see the world and themselves.

The invention of Nature

To deal with natural forces, humans created gods. Before gods, there were living supernatural entities, such as spirits, demons and the like, that

[1] Havelock, Eric. (1963). *Preface to Plato*, p. 261.

[2] Havelock, Eric. (1963). *Preface to Plato*, p. 302.

[3] Havelock, Eric. (1963). *Preface to Plato*, p. 305.

dwelled next to humans and did everything that the elements, natural objects, and places do. But then they acquired complex psychological characteristics and eventually became human-like gods organized in a human-like society, the pantheon, with their own hierarchies, kinships, alliances, dramas, and wars.

The totemization of humans (humans in the likeness of Nature) and then animation and especially anthropomorphizing of natural forces (Nature in the likeness of humans) were the spiritual forms of environmental immersion. They had significant explanatory power in an oral culture. Most importantly, when natural forces "behaved" like living things and especially like persons, their specific features were easier to follow and memorize in oral tradition. If the doings of heroes helped to memorize "social laws," the doings of gods helped to memorize "natural laws." Orality had to form a totemic unity with Nature and then transition to an alliance with animistic and anthropomorphic supernatural forces.

The explanatory power of living spirits and gods, however, prevented any further explorations of Nature. According to Logan, the personification of natural forces severely limited the preliterate Greek's capacity to conceptualize natural forces.[1]

Early writing had an analog nature and thus could not serve well the depersonification of natural forces. A sign system in which signs resembled real things carried inherent magical connections. Writing needed to transform into a rationally comprehensible code in order to break the magical associations between symbols and real objects. This transformation was enabled by phonetization and especially by the alphabet.

Remaining loyal to the gods as the Olympic guardians of historical legacy, the literate Greeks, nevertheless, began to replace those gods with principles in the domains of natural and civic regulations. A sort of competition even emerged among thinkers who sought to discover the best unified principle describing the nature of Nature. "This principle was different for each philosopher, but it established early in the history of science an important pattern," writes Logan. "From the beginnings of Greek science, an explanation for the operations of nature had been sought through some universal and unifying principle or principles."[2]

---

[1] Logan, Robert. (2004 [1986]). *The Alphabet Effect,* p. 108.

[2] Logan, Robert. (2004 [1986]). *The Alphabet Effect,* p. 115.

Different Greek thinkers put water, fire, matter, "apeiron," atoms, movement, the four elements, and other ideas into the foundation of the world. Some of their speculations happened to be insightful and were later validated by science. But what is more important, in this race for a universal principle (or set of principles), the Greeks set up Nature as an object of speculation and exploration. While replacing gods with principles, the Greeks accidentally discovered Nature.

From the 6th to the 3rd centuries BCE (the culmination of Jaspers' Axial Age), while trying to reveal universal principles of Nature, the Greeks made Nature the object of consideration and simply the *object*. This automatically positioned humans as the *subjects* – not solely due to their environmental activity (as they had been de facto the environmental subjects since Promethean media) but by their conscious attitude. The colonization of Nature by humans as a species was intellectually instrumentalized.

In "Alphabet, mother of invention," McLuhan and Logan write:

> The Greeks invented "nature" *(physis)* which is their classification of the objective external world. "Nature" does not include man or any of his artifacts such as the alphabet, which may explain why the Greeks never studied the *effects,* even of their own technology, a radical flaw in their objectivity. It was the separation of man from nature, perhaps that allowed Western thinkers to consider nature as an object to be studied, or a resource to be exploited.[1]

Logan develops this thought in *The Alphabet Effect*: "The objectification of nature by the Greeks has had implications in the West far beyond the development of natural science. It soon became an object to be exploited, subdued, and conquered for man's economic benefit."[2]

Logan parallels Greeks' objectification of Nature with the similar attitude of the Hebrews, "whose deity is quite separate from his creation" and "man is also considered separate from the rest of creation over which he was given dominion." The Hebrews, influenced by the proto alphabet, also sought a unifying principle and found it in monotheism. Perhaps, due to their historical quest for national identity, their universalism happened to be more concentrated on moral laws then on the laws of Nature.

---

[1] McLuhan, Marshall, and Logan, Robert. (1977). "Alphabet, mother of invention," p. 378.

[2] Logan, Robert. (2004 [1986]). *The Alphabet Effect,* p. 124.

The invention of Nature as something separate from humans, rather than something encompassing them, made humans also aware of their own separateness and their agency. Environmental immersion, often understood as harmony with Nature, was destroyed. The divorce with Nature allowed humans to discover themselves.

Individualism: the inward turn

The emergence of individuality was related to the invention of Nature, but the rise of individualism also reflected the disintegration of kinship-based collectivity, which was the "civic" platform of orality. Logan writes:

> What is important about this development, from the point of view of our study, is the parallel with the transformation that occurred in Mesopotamia, ancient Israel, Greece, and Rome in which the alphabet (or phonetic writing) was accompanied by three developments: (a) the demise of tribal society, (b) the rise of law based on the rights and the responsibilities of the individual, and (c) the creation of a universality of humankind that transcends family and tribal links.[1]

"The creation of a universality of humankind," of course, echoes the main idea of Jaspers' *The Origin and Goal of History*.

According to Jaspers, the formation of an individualistic spirit was one of the fundamental features of the Axial Age. Without delving into the immediate cause of individualism, Jaspers writes:

> Man proved capable of contrasting himself inwardly with the entire universe. He discovered within himself the origin from which to raise himself above his own self and the world.[2]

Contrasting oneself "inwardly to the entire universe" resonates with Walter Ong's idea of the inward turn. Ong, however, implies causality: the inward turn was enabled by writing.

According to Ong, the physical features of the spoken word – the sounds – united the speaker and listeners physically in common space: "When a speaker is addressing an audience, the members of the audience

---

[1] Logan, Robert. (2004 [1986]). *The Alphabet Effect*, p. 144.

[2] Jaspers, Karl. (2021 [1949]). *The Origin and Goal of History*, p. 10.

normally become a unity, with themselves and with the speaker."[1] The written word does the opposite: the readers enter their own "private reading world." The reader meets the words, not the writer, and is left alone to decode the meaning. This is how writing created the technical affordance for the inward turn.

The concept of the inward turn highlights that individualism, brought about by writing, did not just mechanically oppose "collectivism." The inward turn implies that the individualism of literacy opposed the immersion of a person into environmental conditions on one hand and the shared tribal identity on the other, both of which were innate to orality. Writing isolated individuals from their environment (through the invention of Nature) and from their tribe (through individualism).

Additionally, the inward turn has brought about a new type of spirituality that is rooted in personal, not totemic or tribal, relations with the divine. As Ong put it,

> By separating the knower from the known (Havelock 1963), writing makes possible increasingly articulate introspectivity, opening the psyche as never before not only to the external objective world quite distinct from itself but also to the interior self against whom the objective world is set. Writing makes possible the great introspective religious traditions such as Buddhism, Judaism, Christianity, and Islam. All these have sacred texts.[2]

It is worth mentioning that Jaspers counted the introduction of major religious doctrines as one of the main consequences of the Axial Age.

Havelock marks out that epic heroes certainly had individual characteristics but not self-awareness. As he writes, Achilles was a man of "strong character, definite personality, great energy and forceful decision," but we can hardly say that it would have occurred to him that he had a "personality apart from the pattern of his acts."[3] Havelock believes that the discovery of the self can only be made by the "thinking self." There is no self until abstract thinking separates a human from situational perception. As Havelock states,

---

[1] Ong, Walter. (2002 [1982]), *Orality and Literacy*, p. 72.

[2] Ong, Walter. (2002 [1982]), *Orality and Literacy*, p. 103.

[3] Havelock, Eric. (1963). *Preface to Plato*, p. 199.

> The "personality"... could not be that nexus of motor responses, unconscious reflexes, and passions and emotions which had been mobilised for countless time in the service of the mnemonic process.[1]

"As language became separated visually from the person who uttered it, so also the person, the source of the language, came into sharper focus and the concept of selfhood was born," states Havelock.[2] He concludes:

> At some time towards the end of the fifth century before Christ, it became possible for a few Greeks to talk about their "souls" as though they had selves or personalities which were autonomous and not fragments of the atmosphere nor of a cosmic life force, but what we might call entities or real substances.[3]

Hesiod (c. 750–650 BCE), perhaps a younger contemporary of Homer, is regarded as the first writing author who also was the first to mention himself in his works. The Greeks were the first, indeed, to invent the self. They even discovered the obsession with the self – as reflected in the myth of Narcissus.[4] One of the three Delphic maxims inscribed on the Temple of Apollo was "Know thyself" (presumably the 7th or 6th century BCE). Protagoras (c. 490–420 BCE) coined the phrase "Man is the measure of all things," and Socrates developed the idea of an inner entity of the person, the "soul." The explosion of interest in the self in Ancient Greece occurred in parallel with the adoption of the alphabet.

Being isolated from environmental and tribal immersions, humans became capable of uniting at a different level – politically, intellectually, and spiritually – as autonomous beings. Autonomy of the self became a new foundation for human cooperation, which was now based on consciousness rather than on verbomotor synchronization as seen in a tribe or a crowd. Ong writes:

> Writing introduces division and alienation, but a higher unity as well. It intensifies the sense of self and fosters more conscious interaction between persons. Writing is consciousness-raising.[5]

---

[1] Havelock, Eric. (1963). *Preface to Plato*, p. 199.

[2] Havelock, Eric. (1963). *Preface to Plato*, p. 113.

[3] Havelock, Eric. (1963). *Preface to Plato*, p. 197.

[4] The story of Narcissus and Echo was written by the Roman poet Ovid (43 BCE – 17 CE), but it was based on Greek characters and likely elaborated on the ancient Greek superstition that viewing one's own reflection would bring bad luck. Refining self-obsession out of it could be seen as an alphabet effect, indeed, even though the myth itself is much more ancient.

[5] Ong, Walter. (2002 [1982]), *Orality and Literacy*, p. 175.

In the Age of Reason, also known as the Enlightenment (the 17th–19th centuries), when alphabetic literacy was boosted by printing, the autonomous self became a fundamental prerequisite for the highest form of individuals' political unity – the social contract. The social contract incorporated individual rights and responsibilities into a new form of human cooperation: the republic with representative democracy, which eventually eliminated religious and political tyrannies in the West. In his treatise *On Crimes and Punishments* (1764), which formed the legal philosophy of Western constitutional law, Cesare Beccaria starts with an assertion of human autonomy:

> Laws are the terms under which independent and isolated men come together in society. ...They sacrifice a part of that freedom in order to enjoy what remains in security and calm. The sum of these portions of freedom sacrificed to the good of all makes up the sovereignty of the nation...[1]

For humans to consciously recognize their global political and historical unity, the disengagement of the individual from the environment and from the tribe or clan had to happen. As Vladimir Lenin said on another occasion, "Before uniting – and to unite – we must first decidedly separate from each other."[2] Jaspersian humankind is not a faceless mega-tribe or a hive-like collective; it is a political, cultural, and moral unity of autonomous nations made of autonomous individuals.

Has it been historically possible to progress towards the unity of humankind without isolating autonomous selves? Theoretically, it has; large collectives that do not appreciate individuality exist. But their sustainability might require a higher level of coercion. When Walter Lippmann introduced his concept of "manufacturing consent," he wrote that "Coercion is the surd in almost all social theory, except the Machiavellian,"[3] implying that the manufacture of consent among autonomous individuals is a less violent alternative to the otherwise inevitably coercive synchronization of the masses by political tyrannies, in which dissent and otherness – the features of individual diversity – are simply rooted out.

---

1 Beccaria, Cesare. (1995). *On Crimes and Punishments, and Other Writings*. p. 9.

2 Lenin, Vladimir. (1900). "Declaration of the editorial board of Iskra."

3 Lippmann, Walter. (1929 [1922]). *Public Opinion*, p. 295.

The inward turn, triggered by writing, spurred by the alphabet, and boosted by print, culminated in Dostoyevsky, Nietzsche, and Freud. They gazed into an abyss of the self in which any chances of synchronization with the environment, including the rest of humanity, could be lost.

The inward turn of literacy also made humans quieter – much quieter than expected under the conditions of orality. Quiet conversation with minimal phatic expressiveness is a side effect of literacy because it assumes the presence of the private spaces of others, who are immersed in themselves, not in the surroundings, too. The "quiet carriages" introduced by some public transportation companies are the last resort of the literacy-induced quietness under the assault of mobile phones and other digital devices.

Interestingly, digital media retrieve, or rather reinforce, the inclination of humans towards loud self-exposition, innate in orality and antonymous to the inward turn. For example, as has already been mentioned, talking on a cell phone with speakerphone on transforms phone conversation into speech-behaviour typical for orality. A phone conversation with the responder's voice being broadcast into the surroundings despite no practical need for it is a feature of oral outwardness with its absence of private spaces.

Digital media, by their very design, retrieve this verbomotor exhibitionism of orality. Any act of one's digital behaviour is by default exposed to others (and also to the algorithms). To succeed on social media, everyone has to "talk" loudly to somebody else while in public view. All virtual loudspeakers in these supposedly two-sided conversations are turned on, inviting everyone else to poke their nose in and amplify the divergences (the "agonistic mentality" of orality, as described by Ong). Digital orality gives rise to a new type of extrovert – the digital extrovert, who is often in fact an introvert in offline settings.

If digital orality is to reverse the inward turn and individualism of literacy, what would be the result of this reversal? Describing it as "collectivism" would be too mechanistic and simplistic. "Individual" means an indivisible, wholistic personality. While discussing corporate control in modern society, Félix Guattari and Gilles Deleuze introduced the concept of "dividuals"[1] – fragmented entities that represent individuals, for

[1] See, for example: Deleuze, Gilles. (1992). "Postscript on the Societies of Control," p. 7.

example, by an electronic code at a factory gate, a password at an ATM, or profiling characteristics in databases. Dividuals are abstracted identities that reflect a group affiliation of a person for the purposes of identification within the corporate and, by extension, social structure. The concept of "dividuals" illustrates a different logic of "collectivism" in a highly mediated society – the fragmentation of individuality into collectively shared identity markers.

Under the influence of electronic media, the modernist (meaning print-literacy) integrity of individuals became deconstructed by postmodernism and disintegrated into smaller features that represent the markers of identity: race, ethnicity, sex, gender identity, sexual orientation, age, economic class, disability status, education, religion, language, etc., with all possible "intersectional" combinations that bring even more focused identification. Unlike individuality, identity markers are not personal. They always represent belonging with a group; they are selectively shared individual features. However, from the postmodernist point of view, they constitute the core of personality.[1]

Developing this media effect of electronic media further, digital orality has enabled the identity race. On social media, both the struggle of users for recognition and the algorithmic customization for better advertising tend to amplify not individual but dividual characteristics of the user – the identity markers that affiliate the user with a political or customer tribe with an incredible automatic precision, a process in which individuals themselves have no say whatsoever. This marketing-control identification has been mirrored in the so-called "identity politics" that emphasizes identity markers for social stratification and political control.

Instead of individual originality, fostered in print literacy, a digitally retribalized society amplifies shareable and preferable identities. New totemism is emerging, compelling people to identify themselves (and others) with new totems of digital tribes that represent their shared identity.

Contrasting the inward turn incited by literacy, not with collectivism, but rather with tribal immersion offers a valuable perspective for exploring the features of literacy that are reversed when digital orality completes the suppression of print literacy started by radio and TV. Digital orality flips

[1] See: Mir, Andrey. (2020). *Postjournalism and the death of newspapers*, p. 313

the inward turn of literacy inside out in a peculiar way, twisting individuality like a Möbius strip, making it challenging to discern what is still individual and what has become identical (and therefore tribal).

From percept to concept. Objectivity, or rather objectivation, of knowledge

No, literacy did not create objectivity. For the concept of objectivity to emerge, it was necessary to have the scientific method, which appeared only as a by-product of printing approximately 4500 years after the invention of writing.

People did not become "objective" with writing. But writing, by separating the knower from the known, created subject-object relations between the thinking subject and the object of thought. Havelock called this a "discovery of intellection."[1]

The scholars of literacy attribute the discovery of the self to the Greeks, so the "objectivation" of thought can also be dated to the Greek alphabetic breakthrough. Havelock writes:

> ...as the existence of the self was progressively clarified, there occurred a parallel and simultaneous effort to bring the self into relation with what is not self. The existence of the subject in short, for the Greek, came to presume the existence of the object.[2]

The personalization of the knower logically entailed the depersonalization of the known. The known ceased to be recorded in verbomotor practices of a living recording mechanism – humans. As Ong put it, "Writing separates the knower from the known and thus sets up conditions for 'objectivity', in the sense of personal disengagement or distancing."[3]

In orality, most of the cognitive energy was expended on achieving rapport and synchronization. However, as soon as writing assumed the function of memorization, not only was the known separated from the knower, but a significant amount of cognitive energy was released, as seen by Havelock, and redirected toward "intellection" rather than mere

[1] Havelock, Eric. (1963). *Preface to Plato*, p. 201.

[2] Havelock, Eric. (1963). *Preface to Plato*, p. 216.

[3] Ong, Walter. (2002 [1982]), *Orality and Literacy*, p. 45.

repetition. Another factor contributing to the process was the detachment of humans from situational thinking. Instead of submersion into the didactic stories of the tribal encyclopedia, people started thinking about the principles underlying those stories.

Orality carried tribal wisdom and had answers; literacy had wisdom written down and freed up the mind for deliberation and questioning. Storytelling and formulaic sayings in orality aimed to heal disruptions and fix communities by providing closure; thinking in literacy inevitably disrupts the wholeness of whatever it addresses and disturbs communities by endless inquiring. Questioning became the starting point for conceptualizing.

In analyzing Plato's rejection of epic poetry, Havelock writes:

> He asks of men that instead they should examine this experience and rearrange it, that they should think about what they say, instead of just saying it. And they should separate themselves from it instead of identifying with it; they themselves should become the 'subject' who stands apart from the 'object' and reconsiders it and analyses it and evaluates it, instead of just imitating it.[1]

Most vividly, this new way of thinking was represented by Socrates' dialectic method: Socrates would question any utterance of his pupils by asking: "What do you really mean by that"? The purpose was to replace commonly held and mechanically repeated beliefs with true philosophizing – critical thinking. Havelock suggests that the Socratic method of repetitive questioning and chain-reasoning destroyed the very morphology of poetic narrative: "Here was the tribal encyclopedia, and to ask what it was saying amounted to a demand that it be said differently, nonpoetically, non-rhythmically, and non-imagistically."[2] Havelock explains:

> To say, 'What do you mean? Say that again', abruptly disturbed the pleasurable complacency felt in the poetic formula or the image. It meant using different words and these equivalent words would fail to be poetic; they would be prosaic. As the question was asked, and the alternative prosaic formula was attempted, the imaginations of speaker and teacher were offended, and the dream so to speak was disrupted, and some unpleasant effort of calculative reflection was

---

[1] Havelock, Eric. (1963). *Preface to Plato,* p. 47.

[2] Havelock, Eric. (1963). *Preface to Plato,* p. 209.

> substituted. In short, the dialectic, a weapon we suspect to have been employed in this form by a whole group of intellectuals in the last half of the fifth century, was a weapon for arousing the consciousness from its dream language and stimulating it to think abstractly. As it did this, the conception of 'me thinking about Achilles' rather than 'me identifying with Achilles' was born.[1]

The break-up with the verbomotor recording of the oral tradition allowed not just alienating the known from speech-behaviour but also making it an object of intellection. The affordance emerged for the known to exist on its own, with certain detectable characteristics and not just as an immediate experience of the prisoners in Plato's cave. This was not yet objectivity, but the objectivation of knowledge, a prerequisite for objectivity.

The objectivation of knowledge not only emancipated thinking from the sensual and verbomotor shackles of oral tradition but unleashed its own elements related to the necessity to somehow organize objectivated knowledge, as it was no longer organized by rhythmic formulae, poetic narrative, and the collective verbomotor speech-behaviour. Essentially, philosophising allowed re-recording of the tribal world in a new language, the language of objectivated knowledge instead of verbomotor formulae. Havelock describes this new intellectual challenge:

> Thus the autonomous subject who no longer recalls and feels, but knows, can now be confronted with a thousand abstracted laws, principles, topics, and formulas which become the objects of his knowledge. These are the essences, the *auta ta*, the things *per se*. Are they a heterogeneous and random collection? Or do they in their turn exhibit a new kind of mutual organisation, some sort of counterpart to the old narrative organisation of the great poem?[2]

Logan illustrates how the objectivation of knowledge affected the structure of knowledge. In Egypt, geometry was quite elaborate but practical in nature. The priest-administrators knew how to establish boundaries for farmers' lands after flooding and employed sophisticated calculations for this purpose. Empirical science sufficed for these tasks, and they did not come up with theorems. Logan writes:

---

[1] Havelock, Eric. (1963). *Preface to Plato,* p. 209.

[2] Havelock, Eric. (1963). *Preface to Plato,* p. 220.

> Egyptian geometry is not derived from a set of axioms. There are no theorems or proofs, or propositions. There are merely a set of rules that are used strictly for practical applications such as land measuring or construction calculations.[1]

It took phonetic writing and, specifically, the alphabet to develop abstract laws and general principles out of applied knowledge. When the knowledge of geometry became an object of thinking and not just a *techne* (a practical art), an epistemological shift happened. Knowledge has acquired its own specific structure and logic, common now for all scientific disciplines.

To summarize, the separation of the knower from the known enabled discerning of the cognising subject and the cognised object; with this, attention began to be paid to what are the innate qualities of the object. Percept yielded the way to concept in comprehending the world. An epistemological breakthrough occurred: scientific laws, principles, axioms, and theorems began to emerge. Thus, phonetic writing and the alphabet begat science. Abstract science – thinking in abstract concepts – is a media effect of the alphabet.

The formation of conceptual thinking occurred precisely in the time of Jaspers' Axial Age and, according to Jaspers, was a constituting part of the Axial Age. This gives us a solid link between the causes of the Axial Age, which Jaspers was unable to disclose, and the alphabet effect as a candidate to be named among the causes of the Axial Age.

Digital media reverse the conceptual view of the world, typical for literacy, to perception, typical for orality. "What's on your mind, Andrey?" Facebook asks me. Does it want me to express my thoughts or feelings? It is not clear, as both possibilities are open. But when users engage in digital conversation, there is not much room for conceptual exchange. The viral collective recording of trending topics, which also serves as a constant referendum regarding the relevance and significance of what is happening in the community, captures people's attitudes and emotional reactions, not thoughts.

[1] Logan, Robert. (2004 [1986]). *The Alphabet Effect*, p. 113.

Fragmentation of the flow and completeness of text

Biologically, life is immersed in the flow of natural cycles and structured by them: day and night, summer and winter, flood and drought, the bodily cycles of hunger and satiation, reproductive cycles, and so on. Animals and primordial humans just went with the flow; Jaspers called this state the "entirely repetitive continuance of living, still closely allied to the processes of nature."[1]

To isolate and preserve valuable experiences that happened in the flow of life, the oral mind fragmented it into events and turned events into stories, which could be recorded through collective reciting. Arresting and capturing the flow of occurrences in separate stories became an important mechanism for extracting, accumulating, and sharing valuable experiences. The fragmentation of reality turned out to be a beneficial strategy: disassembling the flow of events into stories allowed, to some extent, the assembly of new instructions.

The medium – the oral reciting of songs, tales, and proverbs – gave its form to perceived reality. The selected and mythologized fragments of the past natural occurrences shaped their own flow, the flow of oral tradition.

However, the fragmentation of reality by means of orality was also limited by the technical parameters of the medium. The sizes of chunks that could be cut out from reality were defined by the natural "cycles" of the flow of oral speech: by the turn-taking between interlocutors in conversational exchange or by the time allocated for speaking or singing at the campfire or during a festival.

Writing tremendously boosted the fragmentation of reality. Not only did writing arrest the flow and capture it in tiny fragments of records – words – compatible with each other, but it also alienated them in the material form of inscribed signs. The alphabet naturally became the ultimate form of this fragmentation, as reality became available for disassembling into the tiniest meaningless quanta, the letters, which could be afterward reassembled into any new meanings. In writing, and especially in alphabetic writing, names that previously belonged to things became words belonging to speech.

---

[1] Jaspers, Karl. (2021 [1949]). *The Origin and Goal of History*, p. 32.

Havelock writes:

> The feeling for spoken tongue as a stream flowing (as in Hesiod) was replaced by a vision of a fixed row of letters, and the single word as written, separated from the flow of the utterance that contained it, gained recognition as a separate "thing."[1]

As Ong puts it (referring to Jack Goody), "An entirely oral language which has a term for speech in general, or for a rhythmic unit of a song, or for an utterance, or for a theme, may have no ready term for a 'word' as an isolated item, a 'bit' of speech."[2]

Ignace Gelb also observes that oral minds can grasp such parts of speech as utterances and phrases, but "it is frequently with some difficulties that they can recognize individual words."[3] He writes:

> The ability to divide a word into its component syllables is a great step in their understanding of speech and it frequently must be learned through outside influence. The division of syllables into single sounds usually lies beyond their capacity.[4]

Furthermore, Gelb refers to a multitude of observations indicating that syllabic systems of writing are more readily accepted by oral people when introduced by educational missionaries. Isolating syllables represented the natural limit of fragmenting the flow of speech in an oral culture. It was most likely because the syllabic fragmentation could be more or less supported by a natural cycle – the cycle of breathing. Isolating phonemes into letters was almost impossible for the oral mind. Up until the present, children learn alphabetic writing through the syllabic division of words.

Curiously, even after the invention of alphabetic writing, the mind shaped in orality still could not easily detach itself from the patterns of flow. Early alphabetic writing knew no spaces between words and no punctuation. The punctuation signs indicating the end of a phrase emerged, in no small part, due to the use of writing for oral performance: the Greek playwrights of the classical period (the 5th to 3rd centuries BCE) began using marks indicating the end of a sentence to show the actors where to pause.

---

1 Havelock, Eric. (1986). *The Muse Learns to Write*, p. 113.

2 Ong, Walter. (2002 [1982]), *Orality and Literacy*, p. 59.

3 Gelb, Ignace. (1963 [1952]). *A Study of Writing*, p. 203.

4 Gelb, Ignace. (1963 [1952]). *A Study of Writing*, p. 203.

The fact that alphabetic script itself struggled to detach from the continuity of flow is best illustrated by boustrophedon, an early style of alphabetic writing in which letters shaped a sort of "uninterrupted" flow of speech. The letters would be written from left to right in the first line, then u-turned on the second line and continued in the reverse order from right to left. This was an "analog" style of alphabetic writing – it simulated the way in which a farmer plowed a field with an ox. The word "boustrophedon" (βουστροφηδὸν) in Ancient Greek meant "like the ox turns [while plowing]."

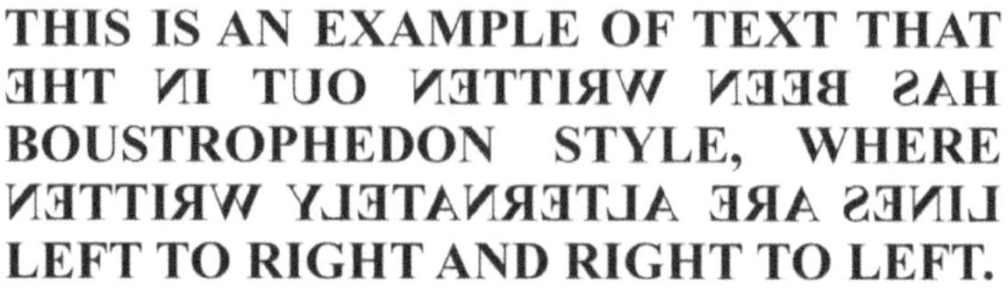

Figure 18. An example, in English, of boustrophedon as used in inscriptions in ancient Greece (lines 2 and 4 read right-to-left). Source: Wikipedia, "Boustrophedon."

Thus, the fragmentation of the flow of reality by writing was not a natural mental faculty. The natural state of mind resisted it. From my teaching experience, modern students have a hard time fragmenting their writing into paragraphs. I cannot tell if this is an impact of digital media or just due to a lack of writing experience. But it is evident that the segmentation of the flow of speech (and thoughts) into isolated parcels of meaning requires significant cognitive effort that does not come naturally.

With writing, eventually, the natural flow has lost its power over humans. Highly literate society has become capable of not living by the natural cycles of day and night, summer and winter, flood and drought, hunger and satiation. Even reproductive cycles have become manageable. The fragmentation of reality by writing contributed to the divorce of humans from the environment.

The fragmentation of the natural flow was a necessary prerequisite for analytical thinking: it allowed the division of things and ideas into parts in the same way as a child tears apart a toy to see what is inside.

Jack Goody and Ian Watt write that there was "some fairly convincing evidence to suggest a more directly causal connection between writing and logic."[1] They point out that the Greek word for an "element" was the same word as for a "letter of the alphabet." They refer to *The Statesman*, in which Plato compared the first basic principles of his philosophy with the child's first contact with the alphabet: "each principle or letter is the key to an infinitely greater number of words or ideas than the particular ones through which it is learned."[2] Furthermore, in *Theaetetus*, Plato develops this idea, "when Socrates compares the process of reasoning to the combination of irreducible elements or letters of the alphabet into syllables which, unlike their constituent letters, have meaning."[3]

Letters, the primary elements of the however complex whole, provided a model of fragmentation. The alphabet effect of fragmentation was not just subliminal; the Greeks recognized it consciously and almost immediately, perhaps due to their historical shock with the alphabet. Fragmentation naturally led to the idea of the world's inner structures. What the alphabet did to speech gave a pattern of what thinking could do to the world. As Postman noticed, "Nature was God's text, and Galileo found that God's alphabet consisted of 'triangles, quadrangles, circles, spheres, cones, pyramids, and other mathematical figures'."[4]

Logan writes:

> In addition to serving as a paradigm of abstraction and classification, the alphabet serves as a model for division and fragmentation. With the alphabet every word is fragmented into its constituent sounds and letters. The Greeks' idea of atomicity - that all matter can be divided up into individual distinct tiny atoms - is related to their alphabet: "Atomism and the alphabet alike were theoretical constructs, manifestations of a capacity for abstract analysis, an ability to translate objects of perception into mental entities" (Havelock 1976[5]).[6]

The fragmented nature of the alphabet and the fragmentation caused by the alphabet to the flows of reality led Marshall and Eric McLuhan to refer to it as the "atomist revolution":

---

[1] Goody, Jack, and Watt, Ian. (1963). "The Consequences of Literacy," p. 331.

[2] Goody, Jack, and Watt, Ian. (1963). "The Consequences of Literacy," p. 331.

[3] Goody, Jack, and Watt, Ian. (1963). "The Consequences of Literacy," p. 331.

[4] Postman, Neil. (1992). *Technopoly*, kl 507.

[5] Logan refers here to: Havelock, Eric. (1976). *Origins of Western Literacy*, p. 44.

[6] Logan, Robert. (2004 [1986]). *The Alphabet Effect*, p. 112.

> The change in perception brought about by the spread of the alphabet provided the visual bias necessary to support the atomist revolution and pushed aside the inclusive, audile-tactile orchestration of the senses.[1]

From then onward, the ways people cut reality down into pieces depended on the material production of texts. Scrolls, clay tablets, Roman wax tablets, vellum and parchment codices, printed leaflets, pamphlets, posters, books, and newspapers dictated the size and structure of the fragments of worldview.

Fragmentation as disassembling entailed re-assembling – intellectually organized structuring. Structuring became the secondary effect of fragmentation. A general structural pattern appears common to all texts: introduction, body, and conclusion. It emerged naturally in the environment of writing but was reflected upon in categories, starting with Aristotle's *Poetics* and extending to the modern Freytag's pyramid of a dramatic arc: introduction, rising action, climax, falling action, and resolution. Similar structures emerged in other literate activities. Official documents or academic writing follow the same pattern: intro/preamble, main arguments, application/conclusion. In journalism, the principle of the inverted pyramid prescribes putting the most important information upfront, followed by important details, and then background information.

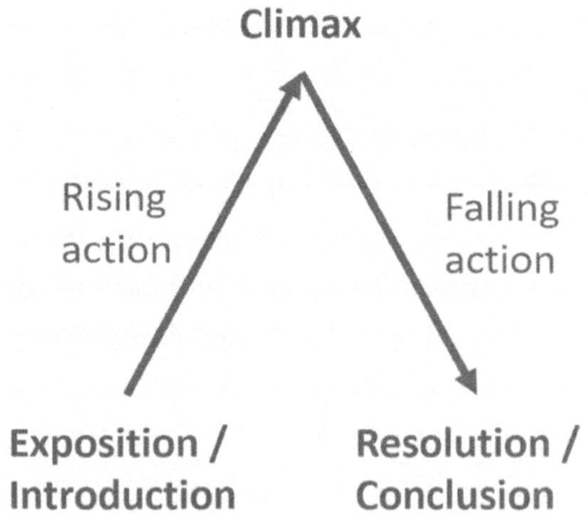

Figure 19. Dramatic structure based on Freytag's pyramid.

[1] McLuhan, Marshall, and McLuhan, Eric. (1988). Laws of Media: The New Science, p. 33.

Figure 20. The inverted pyramid of journalistic news was developed during the time of the telegraph. Telegrams were paid by the word, and the cost was quite high. This shaped the structure of news for the next 150 years. Source: Wikipedia, "Inverted pyramid (journalism)."

This structural pattern shaped not just the written reflection of reality but also other human activities. Any meeting, conference, or even sports workout reproduces the structure of "introduction/opening – main part – conclusion/closure." There is nothing like this in the natural flows of reality, which do not have a beginning, an end, and some logical structure between them. The deliberate structuring of reality is a media effect of writing.

Parchment codices and especially printed books brought about the next effects of fragmentation reality by writing – the *selectiveness* and the *completeness* of the story. For a book to be published, the author and the editor must select the ideas and complete the text. Similarly, newspapers had limited paper space and demanded the selection of news. Printing industrialized the fragmentation of reality. Any text should be completed by the time of printing and encompass the amount of fragmented reality suitable for physical delivery and selling for a certain price.

The ripple media effects piled up. Space limitation and selectiveness led to the emergence of editorial policy, which eventually formed the patterns of political and cultural agenda: "breaking news – politics – economics – entertainment." Radio and TV shows, the products of "secondary orality" (orality based on literacy – Ong), had their own limits of scheduled airing and followed the rules of fragmenting the flow of reality into the selected and complete stories.

The very materiality of the medium drove the selection and refining of content as the corollary of fragmentation. The necessity to complete the text trained the Gutenberg mind to perceive reality in logically structured and complete fragments – news, novels, documents, conferences, meetings, projects, programs, etc. Fragmentation, the selection of fragments, and the completeness of selected fragments were rarely noticed but crucial mind-shaping effects of literacy. Percept shaped concept: the world was seen, and human activity was organized, through well-structured and complete patterns.

This is now being reversed by digital orality. Digital media returns us to the natural state of the flow. Text and pictures published on websites – the residue of Gutenberg culture – may have represented Gutenberg's completeness, but they are consumed as a digital stream in the process of web surfing. The digital orality of social media is a stream, literally – one just cannot find the end of the newsfeed to stop scrolling. The newsfeed flows. It has no beginning and no end.

The quantum theory of media

Before the Internet, the very technology of print production and delivery cut the natural flows of news and thoughts down to deliverable parcels, which became books, newsletters and newspapers.

The internet made it possible to deliver content in smaller 'parcels' of separate articles, video clips, etc.

Now, the news teaser, not even the article, is the quantum of media content. As McLuhan once said, "The future of the book is the blurb." The present of journalism is the news teaser. The necessity to attract turns news teasers into news bits and news baits in one.

Morphologically, the flow of news on social media represents the flow of news in the world in the most relevant way. The parcelling of news has finally caught up with the natural pace of events by means of quantization into the tiniest news pieces.

The news bits (teasers, recaps, headlines, etc.) act as particles when representing pieces of the world picture mosaic. However, when reassembled in a personal newsfeed, they act as the flow, with resonating waves that enable the viral behaviour of news on social media.

From: Andrey Mir. (2020). *Postjournalism and the Death of Newspapers.* Available on Amazon.

Since social media engagement is stimulated by hormonal rewards that are instigated by the promise of recognition, as in real communication, the issue of digital addiction emerges. The user cannot break free from digital immersion in the same way as the oral individual cannot exit the natural environment. These are just two different types of environments – the natural and the digital – but the totality of immersion is almost identical. The only reason for a user to interrupt the immersion in the digital stream is the user's willpower or physical exhaustion. Or Wi-Fi shutdown.

However, there are distinctions in fragmenting the flow of speech between primary orality and digital orality. Real oral communication was naturally constrained by time and space; the digital flow is not. Having become digital, tribal conversation escaped the time limitations of oral talks; but it also escaped the spatial limitation of the physically present audience, as digital speech reaches out instantaneously to any corner of the globe to any number of users. Digital orality transcends the "streaming" affordances of primary orality. Digital orality is even "more oral" than primary orality due to technical facilitation of the communication exchange by the time- and space-ignorant medium of the social media platform.

Curiously, the merging of oral and written speech into digital speech alters the structural capacities of traditional written language. The ways people "speak" on social media have already affected punctuation, for example.

Punctuation served alphabetic fragmentation and was a substitute for essential, yet unavailable in written form, verbomotor means of expression (for instance, such are exclamation and question marks). Modernist prose and poetry have already experimented with punctuation. In postmodernity, the rejection of punctuation became a tool of disruption in the revolt against power structures. Some authors, for example, reject capital letters or quotation marks for ideological reasons.[1]

Capital letters and full stops are indeed tools of mandatory thought structuring, and they have become increasingly omitted not only for artistic or ideological reasons but also in regular written – or rather digitally typed – communication. This trend is especially noticeable among younger

[1] See, for example: *CBN NEWS*. (2021, September 9). "'Capitalization is oppression': Canadian Univ VP says 'Reject the symbols of hierarchy', especially capital letters," or: Kappler, Maija. (2023, October 3). "Why are so many authors abandoning speech marks?" *The Walrus*.

individuals who subliminally perceive capital letters or full stops as signs of passive aggression.

However, punctuation's demise, whether it is due to an ideological manifesto, subliminal psychological avoidance, or simply a result of naturally growing illiteracy, also reflects a general environmental tendency of the reversal of written speech, inherently structured, back into an unstructured flow.

The affordance for writing to become an unstructured flow of communication emerged on social media. But now it proliferates into other forms of writing. The trend is further propelled by the fact that the digital orality of social media and all other forms of writing use the same technology of text production – keyboard typing. The customs of digital orality are becoming the norms of digital literacy. On top of this, keyboards are now virtual, and they actively suggest using emojis and pictograms instead of words, thus often replacing text with digital verbomotorics.

With the reversal of fragmentation, selection, and completeness, digital orality dismantles logical structures brought about by literacy. Without fragmentation and structuring of the flow, content returns to the natural forms of storytelling, social grooming, and quarrel – the forms of tribal exchange. Literate structuring and fragmentation fostered completeness and distancing; without them, the mind submerges into the digital flow of occurrences and becomes shaped by it. In the newsfeed environment, the reaction delay needed for deliberation is not encouraged. As a result, less and less we see what things are *per se* but focus instead on their situational display – on the shadows in Plato's cave.

Classification – primary and secondary effects of writing

Curiously, Homeric poems, being among the most significant creations of oral poetry, represent the mind-shaping power of literacy in their structure. When they were written down, both the *Iliad* and the *Odyssey* were divided into 24 books in the likeness of 24 letters of the Greek alphabet. This is the best illustration of Logan's statement that "Not only has the alphabet performed admirably as a tool for literacy, it has also served as a model for classification."[1]

[1] Logan, Robert. (2004 [1986]). *The Alphabet Effect*, p. 2.

The case of classification helps to explore the ecological "cascading" of media effects. Writing enabled and demanded for humans to develop the capacity of classification twice, at different levels – cognitive and social.

Classification is not needed in practical or situational thinking. Objects are used according to their practical compatibility (which represent "natural" syntagmatic relations). The need for classification emerges when objects are referred to symbolically and those references need to be stored and otherwise operated with. It is convenient to store tokens representing sheep in one box and tokens representing amounts of grain in another. Or to store in one box tokens of sheep and grain received from farmer Hadad and in the other those received from farmer Dakiya. Thus, the classification of objects by their essence (what they are, not what they do) began as soon as the objects were represented in other material, i.e., by symbols.

In the first written civilizations, the need for classification led to the invention of lists or catalogues that priests-administrators used to register offerings, dynastic facts, or celestial events. However, as soon as a classification of objects stores a sufficient amount of knowledge about reality, referencing to this knowledge requires another level of classification. The priests-bureaucrats needed to store their records in groups according to the type of content, transaction, names, time, or place. Any storage of records entails such a classification because the very purpose of records is their use – future referencing.

This is a secondary media effect that rearranges the social use of knowledge for better referencing. This effect brings an institutional change – the emergence of archives and libraries as the foundation of the monopoly of knowledge, on which the power of the temples-palaces in ancient civilizations rested. The further development of classification led to the structuring of knowledge itself.

It is interesting to observe how digital media retrieve the principle of referencing innate to the preliterate mind. The storage of content on early websites was organized according to Guttenberg logic. Home pages looked like the table of contents in a book. With the advent of touchscreens, the design of navigation mutated toward rectangular tiles with headlines and pictures that users needed to touch manually, as if they were not a line in a book but a physical object. A digital version of the operational tactility has emerged. Classification in the form of lists changed visually. No longer was it a list but rather a "columbarium" with "tombstones" for different items.

Digital-tactile usability led to the logical demise of literate list-based classification. The structure of the list could no longer represent the structure of content because content delivery itself turned from complete parcels to the infinite flow.

The final blow to the Gutenberg systematization of content was delivered by contextual search.

In a print culture, referencing was based on the table of contents. A user had to go to a library, search through a catalogue, find the book, and, in the table of contents, find a link to the chapter with the needed information. Before that, in an oral culture, finding information was similar to contextual search. The “user” asked a storyteller, the keeper of the tribal encyclopedia, to tell the desired story. The bard was the voice assistant of orality, the Alexa of the tribe. At an oral gathering, people would ask a bard to sing a song about the battle between Achilles and Hector. Similarly, a child asks a parent to tell a bedtime story about Pooh and Piglet going to find some honey. The user makes prompts, not a selection.

The same method of extracting needed data is used in Google search. The digitally all-permeating data storage allows one to use contextual prompts to find exactly the information that one needs, without thematic searches in catalogues and tables of contents.

The table of contents gradually becomes an obsolete tool and an obsolete cognitive pattern. We, digital migrants, most likely still organize our computer files in folders and directories similarly to library classification. Observing digital natives, I would assume that their competence of cataloguing is less used and therefore weakens. Digital natives might create some folders for their files, but they increasingly rarely use them for navigation in digital storage. Instead, they use the file search function embedded in the file manager. Why remember the structure of folders and which file *should be* located in which folder if you can easily access the needed file by searching with keywords? It saves the time and effort of memorization and searching through the directory tree in the file manager. It also represents a different logic of “classification” and the search for information – essentially, the oral logic. Instead of systematizing and expecting the things to be systematized, one should ask the “elders” or those who carry relevant competence.

This started with the transformation of memory caused by smartphones. Why remember or keep John's phone number written in a notebook if you can just tell your device to call John? You need to talk to John, not to remember his phone number, right? Contextual search is so much more convenient than cataloguing that it dismisses the need for a table of contents and for the entire content organization that the table of contents represented.

Since knowledge and data storing have become interactive, classification is losing its logistic value. You do not need to have and use the skill of classification, when, in order to find data or a story, you can ask the search box in the file manager, Google, community, Siri, Alexa, or Chat GPT, thus reproducing the oral mode of data retrieving: asking somebody who knows better. You need to know whom to ask and how to ask. Instead of the skill of classification, the skill of prompting becomes more and more required. It is now prompting that needs to be taught at schools and universities as an essential element of digital media literacy.

Will the cognitive ability of classification, the primary effect of writing, be weakened after the classification of data, the secondary and social effect of writing, is replaced by contextual search? It is likely so: the cognitive faculty of classification becomes increasingly less trained and gradually atrophies. Or, to use a neurophysiological metaphor, if it is not fired, it is not wired ("use it or lose it" – in a mundane translation).

If you do not need a file structure, you do not need to think about how to classify certain files to put them in a proper folder. You also do not need to have an inner vision of the paradigmatic tree of your folders, which is a sort of archival scaffold of your personal knowledge and your cognition. Classification used to serve as a pattern for structuring reality in which all knowledge was paradigmatically assigned to certain departments of reality. Now, the entire (digital) reality switches from an alienated paradigmatic pattern to a flow in which the user is immersed and can navigate by picking over and testing items or asking others (including AI).

The digital reversal goes even further back in history and dismisses not only the table of contents but also the tagging system of early scroll-based writing. Tags were used, and perhaps even invented, by Zenodotus (the early 3rd century BCE), the first chief librarian of the Alexandrian library, the greatest library of the ancient world. Since scrolls did not have covers or spines, one had to unroll a scroll and read it to see what it was about. To streamline the process and expedite search, Zenodotus began attaching tags with names or descriptions to each scroll.

The early internet and the blogosphere had their own system of tagging that retrieved the practice of Zenodotus. However, contextual search spares you from the necessity to tag your text. The classifying function of tagging becomes obsolete, too.

Tags are still used on social media, but their function is now completely different. Hashtags on Twitter are aimed at the possible "viralization" of the topic. Users tag their posts with a special symbol (#) for cross-referencing – to synchronize with their online tribe and join viral events in the hope of gaining more exposure. Influencers use hashtags as battle cries, uniting and mobilizing their followers for viral assaults on trending topics. You still need to guess a better classification when creating or joining a hashtag, but its lifespan and nature are highly situational and evanescent. It doesn't serve for classification and subsequent navigation but rather enhances immersion in the current flow of events to gather better responses.

Codified law

Customs, taboos, and the norms of punishment had existed before the first codes of laws emerged. However, as with everything else in orality, they were immersed in concrete situations. According to Ong, "Pre-Socratic Greeks thought of justice in operational rather than formally conceptualized ways."[1]

This syncretism of environmental thinking led also to the inseparability between political and legal judgements. As Havelock puts it,

> But in such a society where oral debate and decision is the sole vehicle for the transaction of public business, the line between political and legal decision, between political direction and legal judgment, would be thin.[2]

What was supposed to be a legal decision (from the point of view of a literate culture) was affected by political considerations and personal attitudes. Havelock highlights that orality required "significant speech" (i.e., "political and legal speech") to be metrical and formulaic; otherwise,

[1] Ong, Walter. (2002 [1982]). *Orality and Literacy*, p. 48

[2] Havelock, Eric. (1963). *Preface to Plato*, p. 108.

the statements of leaders would not be considered "the voice of the Muse"[1] and would lack divine legitimizing power. To excel in governing and diplomacy, kings and princes had to be able to wrap their statements in eloquent poetic speech, with all its formulaic passages and flamboyant epithets. Even Achilles, not much of a politician but rather an audacious warrior, was rehearsing the chants of the glories to heroes with a "clear-toned lyre" in his tent while making his lieutenant Patroclus wait.

The implementation of a political-legal judgment relied heavily on the capacity of this judgment to "please the ear," resonate with the listeners, and be introduced into the repository of oral instructions. Havelock characterizes the princes' proficiency in bardic speech as "the art of seduction." Since the medium shapes the message it conveys, the verbomotor qualities of statements were an important virtue of political-legal regulation. Legal judgments consisted more of persuasion than consideration.

When Innis characterized the first empires that emerged from the monopoly of knowledge maintained by writing, he wrote that "The sword and pen worked together."[2] I cannot tell if Innis paraphrased Al Capone, who allegedly said that you get more with a kind word and a gun than you do with a kind word alone; likely not. But Capone's saying represents the verbomotor nature of oral judgement (with the mafia being the best-preserved exemplar of orality in a literate society). Innis' formula of literate power, "the sword and the pen," clearly mirrors Capone's formula of oral power, "the gun and the kind word", in which "kind word" means, in Havelock's language, the seductive poetic word authorized by the Muse. What Al Capone knew about orality was the idea that persuasion by force and persuasion by talking worked better together. The legal-political judgment had an inseparable coercive and poetic power; both aspects reinforced and legitimized each other.[3] This syncretism of the poetic, the coercive, and the legal was an effect of the environmental-tribal immersion.

---

1 Havelock, Eric. (1963). *Preface to Plato*, p. 109.

2 Innis, Harold. (1950). *Empire and Communications*, p. 11–12.

3 "But you don't ask with respect. You don't offer friendship," says Don Corleone to Bonasera, who is seeking retribution for his daughter. Bonasera's request is not "seductive": he separates the essence of the matter from personal engagement – he tries to buy Corleone's service of violence with money and without offering "respect" and loyalty, thus insulting him. Essentially, Don Corleone points out that Bonasera disrupts the legitimizing syncretism of the legal and "poetic," inherent in orality.

As with everything else in orality, the governing speech-behaviour was intimately connected to specific situations, leaving no room for the generalization required for true law. The codes of laws brought a legal revolution. First, they separated, or at least indicated the separation of, legal judgment from political judgment. Second, they shifted legal regulation from situational judgments, based on relations, traditions, and wisdom, to judgments based on generalized principles.

In the article "Alphabet, mother of invention," McLuhan and Logan write:

> The Babylonian syllabary, like the alphabet, encouraged the development of classification. The reform and simplification of the Babylonian syllabary from 600 signs to 60 signs occurred at the same time that the Hammurabic legal code was introduced.[1]

Logan develops this thought in *The Alphabet Effect*:

> The Age of Hammurabi marks the culmination of the regularization and reform of both the writing system and the legal system in the form of the Hammurabic code. These developments were not coincidental. Both reforms promoted the paradigms of abstraction, classification, and universality and thus encouraged the development of scientific activities.[2]

Hammurabi was a king who ruled in Babylon from 1792 to 1750 BCE. He was not the pioneer of codified law. The first known code of laws was created by King Ur-Nammu of Ur (2112–2095 BCE). Several other Mesopotamian collections of laws survived, but the Hammurabic code was the most structurally developed and complete among them. Its structure clearly reflected the literate way of thinking, as it contained an abstract statement of divine justice in the "introduction", followed by a catalogue of crimes and punishments classified into "chapters" by types of crimes and offenses.

As noted by McLuhan and Logan, the codification of laws coincided with the development of Mesopotamian syllabic writing. As mentioned in chapter 5, it is also plausible to assume a connection between the codification of laws and librarian classification. Librarians needed to

---

[1] McLuhan, Marshall, and Logan, Robert. (1977). "Alphabet, mother of invention," p. 376.

[2] Logan, Robert. (2004 [1986]). *The Alphabet Effect*, p. 82.

organize records and knowledge according to principles that would facilitate their further use. This created a cognitive pattern of classification similar to that employed in the codification of laws.

The issuance of the law code was also, or primarily, a political statement of centralized authority. Orality did not possess such a tool for political centralization. The oral epic as the tribal encyclopedia might serve tribal unity and indoctrination but not centralization. As Logan emphasizes,

> Hammurabi set a pattern - one that was to be repeated by future administrators of large empires. Therefore, codified law represents a bifurcation from a set of local laws to govern a city state to one that could govern and administer an empire consisting of diverse cultures.[1]

In a paradoxical way, the strengthening of the state through codified law simultaneously marked the emergence of the individual legal subject. The autonomy of an individual, whether a perpetrator, victim, complainant, or plaintiff, was singled out and, at once, legitimized for the first time in history. As an individual obtained legal status, it ensured not only legal responsibility but also, at the same time, legal rights. The Mesopotamian codes de jure acknowledged human rights 3700 years before this concept became the focus of global politics in the 20th century.

Legal codification went hand in hand with the phonetization of writing, i.e., higher-level abstraction and classification. The Mosaic Biblical Law, which includes the most refined form of a legal code – the Ten Commandments, was likely connected with the Mesopotamian tradition but also grounded in the alphabetical experience of the Hebrews. The Draconian code of laws, despite its modern connotation, introduced the legal principle in Athens near the end of the 7th century, when the alphabet started affecting Greek culture. Interestingly, both the Ten Commandments and Draco's code aimed, in part, at dismantling oral tradition: the Ten Commandments rejected the polytheistic cults, while Draco's code unified legal principles against the loose interpretations of oral customs by the Athenian aristocracy.

The legal judgment in orality and literacy can be examined through the distinction between common law and civil law. Common law (case law,

---

[1] Logan, Robert. (2004 [1986]). *The Alphabet Effect,* p. 88.

precedent law) is based on past rulings – essentially, on *stories*. A bard – a judge – decides which exemplary story, carrying tribal instructions from the past, should be applied today. In civil law (statutory law), it is still the judges who implement legal decisions, but they use codified laws passed by legislatures. Legal ruling does not go "after" the situation but precedes it in the rulings of legislators. If precedent law is based on the classification of cases, civil law is based on the classification of principles.

The impartiality and "inhumanness" of civil law are reflected in the principle *Dura lex, sed lex*. However harsh the law is for someone to accept, it is the law, and no personal or situational consideration can affect the law unless the law itself is changed in the political process. The law should be implemented no matter what. Interestingly, common law prevailed in the former Roman peripheries, which were mostly oral at the time of the Roman Empire. In a paradoxical way, the essentially oral tradition of legal judgment (precedent law) survived in Britain, despite a subsequent significant increase in literacy, perhaps, because the country continued to oppose the Papacy in Rome both legally and politically.

Digital media have not reversed the codification of law, at least not yet; however, the retrieval of certain features of legal judgment inherent in orality is underway. On social media platforms, a hybrid oral-literate form of legal ruling has emerged, the "community guidelines" and the "rules of community." Formally, they inherit the literate tradition of law codification, as in civil law, but often rely on individual judgments, as in common law. It is, in a sense, inevitable, as the fluidity of digital orality and the multiplicity of possible cases cannot be grasped with the codified set of laws. Subjective expertise of implementation is unavoidable, but it also carries the flaws of subjectivity, sometimes at the systemic level, considering the amplification of judgements by algorithms.

Besides, unlike the judges of common law, the judges of social media "rules of community" have a doubtful authority. In contrast to the true laws, which are introduced publicly by elected legislators, the "rules of community" are easily bent toward situational needs and political pressure, as became evident in the notorious "Twitter files" in 2023, the exposure of the "Censorship Industrial Complex" that amalgamated political interests of the ruling elites with the regulatory power of the digital platforms. In particular, the "Twitter files" exposed the mechanism of censoring so-called "malinformation," a newly invented notion that describes information that is true but might be potentially harmful in the view of the self-proclaimed regulators of digital speech.[1]

Regulation that is based on rejecting truth due to its "misleading" character is a direct reversal of the principle *Dura lex, sed lex.* Some signs of the weakening of this principle can be observed in general legal practices, too. The political influence has to re-emerge in legal practices and not in the form of corruption as would have been the case in a literate culture, but in the form of societal expectations and public pressure as would fit an oral culture. In the same way as with the political-legal judgments of the princes in the *Iliad,* the legal judgments in the increasingly retribalized society are expected to "please the ear." Legal adjudicators have to keep an eye on the latest tendencies in bardic speech and tribal indoctrination and make sure their lyres are "clear-toned."

Thinking about thinking: logic and theorizing

The awakening of thinking about thinking that happened to the human mind 2500 years ago is somewhat similar to a hypothetical self-awakening of AI, a much-discussed topic in 2024. The mind recognized itself and started exploring its own mechanisms and principles beyond the mundane tasks of practical applications. The awakening of the mind's self-reflection was the main characteristic of the Axial Age, as described by Jaspers.

"Oral Greek did not know what an object of thought was," writes Havelock.[2] For a thought to be caught, the flow of words needed be arrested and words needed be captured and separated from a thinking individual. Writing made it – it put captured words in front of an individual for contemplation. Looking at a sign entailed thinking of what this sign means and why.

The necessity to consider the relations between signs and objects became even more apparent in the scribal schools. Pondering the meanings of signs in the process of writing or reading could occur by chance—it was not necessarily a deliberate process. However, when teaching someone else to write, contemplating the meanings of signs became unavoidable.

[1] Mir, Andrey. (2023, March 16). "'Malinformation' and the wrong truth. By accepting the concept of 'misleading truth,' democratic society departs from its foundations." *Discourse.*

[2] Havelock, Eric. (1986). *The Muse Learns to Write*, p. 97.

Alphabetic writing visualized not the objects or the ideas of objects but speech itself. Viewing recorded speech meant seeing the "footprints" of thinking. When observing a string of written words, a reader sees a sequence of recorded thoughts. Thus, recorded speech exposed thinking to a detached observation. McLuhan called the alphabet the "means of arrested visual analysis."[1] Writing separated the known from the knower, but the alphabet afforded further fragmentation – the separation of knowing from the known.

Since the Greeks were particularly affected among other Axial cultures by the abrupt transition from the sensory experience of primary orality directly to the most abstract level of alphabetic literacy, it didn't take them long to objectify not only knowledge but also thinking itself.

Figure 21. A popular internet meme.

Havelock highlights that, "Along with the discovery of the soul, Greece in Plato's day and just before Plato had to discover something else – the activity of sheer thinking." He emphasizes that "the same sources which testify to a sort of virtuosity in the use of the words for 'soul' and 'self' testify also to the same kind of virtuosity in the words for 'thinking' and 'thought'." According to Havelock, something novel was in the air at the

[1] McLuhan, Marshall. (1962). *The Gutenberg Galaxy*, p. 23.

end of the 5th century BCE, and this novelty was the "discovery of intellection."[1]

The discovery of thinking about thinking and its relation to literacy is best exemplified through the succession of the philosophical method from Socrates through Plato to Aristotle.

Socrates (circa 470–399 BCE) was still an oral thinker. He knew writing and rejected it because written words were dead thoughts whereas speaking represented live thinking itself.[2] But he was already affected by the alphabet. This could be seen in his philosophical and pedagogical method of dialectics – the exploration of thinking by questioning the essence of what was said. Such questioning was unthinkable in an oral culture – the listeners were supposed to memorize, recite, and pass on what they heard, not question it. Socratic dialectics represented a cultural and pedagogical revolution, a blasphemy against the foundations of the oral society. This resulted in the death penalty for Socrates himself on the charge of "impiety" by the citizens of Athens.

Plato (circa 428–347 BCE), Socrates' student, transitioned to writing, but most of his legacy consists of the recordings of presumably oral conversations. This is evident even in the genre of his writings, the dialogues. In these dialogues, he also recorded much of the Socratic legacy, often mixed with his own observations. It is symptomatic that, after transferring thinking from oral to written forms, Plato fiercely attacked the old Homeric mind shaped by poetry, or the oral state of mind, as interpreted by Eric Havelock in *Preface to Plato*.

Aristotle (circa 384–322 BCE), a student of Plato, was perhaps the first philosopher of literacy. He wrote not only dialogues but also moved to philosophical prose and wrote in the genre of the treatise, which has remained the main genre of philosophy since then. (As Logan notes, "With the alphabet a new style of writing developed – namely, prose – with which it is possible to create analytic statements. Abstract science without prose and analytic statements would be impossible."[3]) Aristotle established the foundation of literate philosophy in many areas, from politics to poetics.

---

1 Havelock, Eric. (1963). *Preface to Plato*, p. 200-201.

2 In Plato's *Phaedrus*, Socrates affirms Phaedrus' assumption that spoken words are "the living word of knowledge which has a soul, and of which written word is properly no more than an image."

3 Logan, Robert. (2004 [1986]). *The Alphabet Effect*, p. 117.

Other great Greeks, of course, had their share of merits in shaping Greek, Western and world philosophy during the transition from orality to literacy. However, these three, as it were, impersonated the transition of thinking from orality to alphabetic literacy in a clearly sequential manner and in an incredibly compressed historical period (compared to the overall very slow pace of history in ancient times). During the combined lifespan of this trio, the axis of the Axial Age occurred in Greece.

Instead of being satisfied with magical formulas and explanation through analogies, the philosophers started digging into the essence of things and eventually revealed that thinking itself is a tool. Enquiry about the world logically led to an enquiry about enquiry, i.e., about thinking. In his 1951 *Bias of Communication*, Innis suggests the media direct our focus of attention. He expressed this idea with the question: "Why do we attend to the things to which we attend?"[1] This is the ultimate Socratic question, indeed. According to Innis, media are the answer.

According to Marshall McLuhan, "Lineal, alphabetic inditing made possible the sudden invention of 'grammars' of thought and science by the Greeks."[2] This grammar of thought and science manifested in two interconnected but separated intellectual faculties – theorizing and logical thinking. Theorizing and logical thinking were not just characteristics of some other intellectual activities – they were intellectual activities that recognized, reflected upon, and cultivated their own nature, in the same way as the grammar of language became the subject of grammar as a discipline.

Havelock highlights that Aristotle tied his definition of thinking to the metaphors of vision:

> The words he chooses to describe their intellectual enterprise are *theoria* and its verb *theorein*, both referring to the act of looking at something. The choice may be a better pointer toward the real truth of what had happened. Why choose vision as the metaphor for an intellectual operation, unless guided by the subconscious recognition that the operation had arisen out of viewing the written word rather than just hearing it spoken?[3]

---

[1] Innis, Harold. (2008 [1951]). *Bias of Communication*, kl 608.

[2] McLuhan, Marshall. (1962). *The Gutenberg Galaxy*, p. 23.

[3] Havelock, Eric. (1986). *The Muse Learns to Write*, p. 111.

The "means of arrested visual analysis,"[1] as McLuhan called the alphabet, allowed one to see – with the eye – thoughts captured by writing. The isolated sense of vision created inner vision, and inner vision created an affordance of intellection. But theorizing became more than this. It started dictating its own rules, its "grammar," demanding the creation of theories – complete and logically organized explanations of the world based on some universal principles. Theorizing completed the transition from perception to conception and the transformation of thinking from an oral to literate state.

Theorizing replaced rhapsodizing or "stitching songs together." The deritualization of mind was a side effect. But for a theory itself to be stitched, a new tool of intellection had to be devised – abstract logic. Logic had nothing to do with sensorial experience. If magical (oral) thinking matched the supernatural with natural phenomena, logical (literate) thinking matched ideas with one another. In the oral tradition, moving forces were personified in gods within narratives intended to affect perception for better memorization. When the burden of memorization was taken from humans by writing, these were no longer gods that represented the moving forces of the universe but ideas that engaged in their own intricate interplay. As Havelock puts it, "These are not men and women but rather words and thoughts which cluster in competing formations and manoeuvre to challenge us and win our attention while they seek to elbow each other off the boards."[2]

Instead of seeking analogies in past experiences or the natural environment, logical thinking employed its own "natural" analogy: it adopted the linearity and sequential unfolding of meanings from alphabetical writing. As Logan puts it:

> The use of the alphabet serves as a model for matching – an activity crucial for the development of logic. Each letter of the alphabet is matched with a sound and vice versa. Every time a word is read, a match between a visual sign and a spoken sound is made. Matching forms the basis of rationality or logic. Rationality grew out of the concept of ratios, which in turn involves matching. A is to B as C is to D is an example of a ratio achieved by matching.
>
> The linking together of the elements of the alphabet – the letters –

[1] McLuhan, Marshall. (1962). *The Gutenberg Galaxy*, p. 23.

[2] Havelock, Eric. (1963). *Preface to Plato*, p. 276.

> to form words provided a model for the linking together of ideas to form a logical argument. Arguments are linked together in order to reach a conclusion. The deductive reasoning implicit in formal logic and geometry also formed the basis of early Greek science, which attempted to derive its description of nature from first principles.[1]

Theorizing and logical thinking represented a completely opposite approach to forming and expressing knowledge as compared to orality. To ensure better affect and therefore memorizing, oral knowledge required excessive means of expression, redundancy of epithets, numerous repetitions of important formulas, verbomotor activities (rhyme, tone, mimicry, gestures), and emotional engagement. This all would be a failure in logical reasoning. Logical thinking excludes repetition as a fallacy. Epithets are needless. Brevity and clarity are virtues in logic and in literate expression in general.

The capacity of literacy to facilitate theorizing relies, in no small part, on the "atemporality" of reading, as Corey Anton calls it. According to him, "books allow one to read at one's own pace." The content of reading is "seamlessly worked into the flow of consciousness" because "the text does not 'go on' without us."[2] Anton suggests distinguishing between *self-paced technologies,* such as books, and *auto-paced technologies,* such as podcasts, films, and videos. He writes:

> Communication technologies that run at a pre-set rate, which *flow* as it were and thereby demand that consciousness attend to them as they are flowing, are more psychically constraining and confining than self-paced technologies.[3]

The temporal constraints imposed by electronic formats that simulate orality immerse the user in an external environment, controlled by the source of broadcasting. Anton even implies that this submission to *auto-paced technologies* can explain the frustration often accompanying the consumption of electronic and digital media:

> Could it be that there is an undiagnosed stress – an oppression of the mind – that comes from having to spend time within simulated environments that unfold at a rate not endemic to one's own

[1] Logan, Robert. (2004 [1986]). *The Alphabet Effect,* p. 113.

[2] Anton, Corey. (2023). "Reading good books, further defended," p. 122.

[3] Anton, Corey. (2023). "Reading good books, further defended," p. 122.

> consciousness? Could it be that people have unconsciously trained their minds to obediently align to of auto-paced technologies and now experience a vague but pervasive sense of moving to other people's rhythms instead of their own?[1]

Reading, on the contrary, adjusts the pace of information intake to the reader's personal thinking rather than to someone else's broadcast, thus integrating the content of what is read "seamlessly" into the inner space of the reader's thought. Among all media, only books possess this quality, as Anton highlights. Reading is morphologically compatible with thinking.

Not only did literacy enable theorizing, but it also facilitated the accumulation of theoretical knowledge through the phenomenon of quotability embedded in reading and writing. Scholars would read what their predecessors wrote, pick up worthy quotes, and reassemble them in new theories while adding new ideas. The next generations would do the same, thus constantly refining and developing the best ideas in the chain reaction of theorizing, as it were. Each scholarly reading entailed writing.

Electronic media cannot do that. The content of TV or radio programs might be astonishingly intelligent, but it will unlikely be reworked in a new TV or radio program through quoting and adding ideas. This content may trigger some thoughts, but it is not quotable, as one cannot capture a worthy thought from TV and embed it in their own reflection to make it available for the next iterations of quoting and adding ideas. On TV, radio, and podcasts, any idea dies in the moment of broadcasting, resulting, at best, in viewers' affection for the speaker. Likeability beats quotability. Electronic media refine and accumulate attitudes, not knowledge.

The internet made the world repository of texts available for quoting and adding upon. But the issue is that, unlike print literacy, digital orality fosters quick exchange, not prolonged reading and reflection. Books made bookworms, but digital consumption favours switching between sources while shortening the span of concentration. Digital media users quote memes, not thoughts. Memes are funny and sometimes witty, but they do not coalesce into theories. In the digital environment, the scholarly effort of reading and then quoting and adding ideas in subsequent writing may be maintained by personal willpower but is clearly disfavoured environmentally.

---

[1] Anton, Corey. (2023). "Reading good books, further defended," p. 122.

From collective indoctrination to personal inquiring

Before writing, there were two main forms of education: apprenticeship and storytelling. Apprenticeship submerged trainees into practical trade situations, while storytelling submerged listeners into mimetically recreated situations with moral and instructional exemplars from the heroic past. Walter Ong writes:

> All thought, including that in primary oral cultures, is to some degree analytic: it breaks its materials into various components. But abstractly sequential, classificatory, explanatory examination of phenomena or of stated truths is impossible without writing and reading. Human beings in primary oral cultures, those untouched by writing in any form, learn a great deal and possess and practice great wisdom, but they do not "study".
>
> They learn by apprenticeship – hunting with experienced hunters, for example – by discipleship, which is a kind of apprenticeship, by listening, by repeating what they hear, by mastering proverbs and ways of combining and recombining them, by assimilating other formulary materials, by participation in kind of corporate retrospection – not by study in the strict sense.[1]

As Havelock puts it, "The learning process was not learning in our sense but a continual act of memorisation, repetition and recall."[2] The tribal encyclopedia could be learned, but it was not about learning. Its re-recording served to incorporate people into tribal identity.

Apprenticeship and epic storytelling, both aimed at the practical training and indoctrination of youth, were immersive. They sucked pupils into practical or mimetic situations.

This started changing when the necessity emerged to learn a new trade – the craft of writing. The scribal schools must have started like any other trade education – with the diligent repeating of the simplest actions after the master scribe. But the skill of writing included also the skill of reading, which cannot be mechanically repeated. Reading requires understanding the meanings of symbols, which can come only as an intellectual exercise with significant effort on the side of the learner.

---

[1] Ong, Walter. (2002 [1982]). *Orality and Literacy*, p. 8.

[2] Havelock, Eric. (1963). *Preface to Plato*, p. 157.

The growing complexity of symbols led to the emergence of the separate rules of semantics and grammar, which described why certain symbols represent certain meanings and why certain symbols join others in a certain fashion. The rules could not be grasped by mechanical repetition after the craftsman. They needed to be explained and understood. For the first time in history, the affordance and therefore necessity to sit and learn emerged.

The question "What does it mean?" is essential to reading. Literacy legitimized questioning, an intellectual activity that could not be employed during mechanical repetition after a tradesman or in verbomotor resonance with a storyteller. Questioning the meaning of signs supplied a pattern for questioning the meaning of everything. If orality fostered mutual indoctrination, literacy inaugurated personal inquiry.

Goody and Watt write that Herodotus, the first literate author and the founder of historiography, invented the method of *historia* – "personal inquiry or research into the most probable versions of events as they were to be found in various sources."[1] In ancient Greek, the word *ἱστορία* meant "learning through research, telling of what is learned," from *ἱστορέω* – "to learn through research, to inquire."

Before writing, no teacher would ever have been interested in what a disciple thinks. All of a sudden, Socrates started asking pupils about what they really mean when they say something. Interestingly, while reflecting on this transformation, Havelock employs the same metaphor of awakening that Jaspers uses to characterize the Axial Age:

> If the educational system which transmitted the Hellenic mores had indeed relied on the perpetual stimulation of the young in a kind of hypnotic trance, to use Plato's language, how did the Greeks ever wake up?
>
> The fundamental answer must lie in the changing technology of communication. Refreshment of memory through written signs enabled a reader to dispense with most of that emotional identification by which alone the acoustic record was sure of recall. This could release psychic energy, for a review and rearrangement of what had now been written down, and of what could be seen as an object and not just heard and felt. You could as it were take a second look at it. And this separation of yourself from the

[1] Goody, Jack, and Watt, Ian. (1963). "The Consequences of Literacy," p. 324.

> remembered word may in tum lie behind the growing use in the fifth century of a device often accepted as peculiar to Socrates but which may well have been a general device for challenging the habit of poetic identification and getting people to break with it. This was the method of dialectic, not necessarily that developed form of logical chain-reasoning found in Plato's dialogues, but the original device in its simplest form, which consisted in asking a speaker to repeat himself and explain what he had meant.[1]

Havelock highlights how offensive the act of re-asking must have been for oral tradition, as it would dismantle the formulaic structures and their power of hypnotic resonance. With it, old authorities were undermined. Ong writes:

> By storing knowledge outside the mind, writing and, even more, print downgrade the figures of the wise old man and the wise old woman, repeaters of the past, in favor of younger discoverers of something new.[2]

The habit of inquiring, acquired by the learned individuals of the literate era, corrupted oral indoctrination. Stories were replaced with theories, and storytelling was replaced with theorizing. Grounded in questions rather than answers, theorizing deritualized the mind.

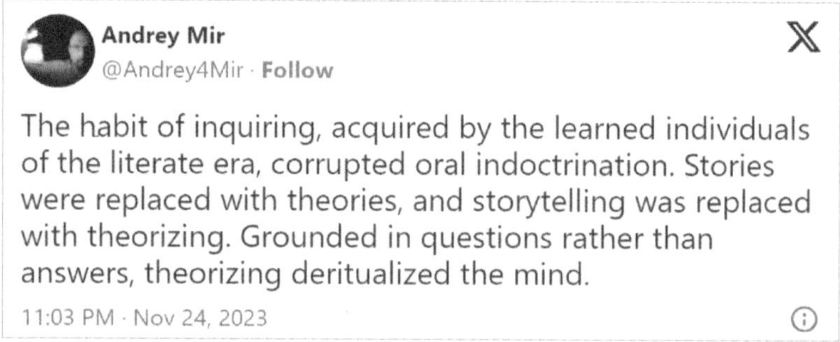
Andrey Mir
@Andrey4Mir · Follow

The habit of inquiring, acquired by the learned individuals of the literate era, corrupted oral indoctrination. Stories were replaced with theories, and storytelling was replaced with theorizing. Grounded in questions rather than answers, theorizing deritualized the mind.

11:03 PM · Nov 24, 2023

This all began to reverse with electronic media. Amusement, induced by electronic media, undermined the conditions favourable for inquiry. Radio and especially television made emotional rapport the commodity that deeply permeated all spheres of public life, including politics, as revealed by Neil Postman in his 1985 *Amusing Ourselves to Death: Public*

[1] Havelock, Eric. (1963). *Preface to Plato*, p. 208.
[2] Ong, Walter. (2002 [1982]). *Orality and Literacy*, p. 41.

Discourse in the Age of Show Business. When people are absorbed into emotional resonance with the tube, less and less room remains for rational inquiry. People just join and resonate in the fashion of the verbomotor communion of the audience with the bard, cheering or booing certain parts of the story, thus verifying the story's relevance. In TV-watching, even when questions do arise, they often fail to persist and transform into inquiries; instead, they come and go with the TV schedules.

To combat the influence of television and, in a broader sense, postmodernism, Postman in his 1999 book *Building a Bridge to the 18th Century* suggested restoring the educational principles of the 18th century, the Age of Reason and Enlightenment. The idea of countering postmodernism with the educational principles of modernity is both logical and unfeasible. Books, lengthy texts, are far superior to TV in fostering intellectual self-immersion and inquiry. However, books require a level of environmental detachment that is not possible on a statistically significant scale when electronic amusement is available. Electronic immersion became so panoramically rich that it sucked in people's time and attention, leaving less time and attention for deep reading.

Even more so do digital media now. To activate inner vision, gadgets must be prohibited, and books reinstated. It might be doable within a family policy but impossible at the statistical scale – at the level of the entire society. Media evolution can reverse media effects and retrieve media functions, but it never reintroduces media devices. Books may still exist as physical objects or e-texts, but lengthy reading has ceded its share in media diet to immersive digital multitasking – to the temptation of a single click redirecting attention to things that are more captivating than exhaustive and time-consuming lengthy reading.[1]

Not only has the idea of reinstating print literacy in education been broadly ignored, but the most progressive educational theories themselves have advocated for the so-called "immersive education," which is an inherent practice of primary orality and the direct opposition of alphabetic and print literacy. Immersive education is a marshal at the parade of orality retrieval; immersive education is the enemy and gravedigger of literate education.

---

[1] Mir, Andrey. (2002, winter). "The medium is the menace. Ubiquitous digital media offer potent rewards - but at the price of eroding our sensory and social capacities." *City Journal*.

Paradoxically, Marshall McLuhan played a part in this by coauthoring the 1977 book *City as Classroom: Understanding Language and Media.* The main idea of the book suggested to follow the changes in the cultural environment and "to get students in small teams to go outside, to study the setup of the situations that they live with every day and to discover what they're made of," as McLuhan explained it in an interview.[1]

Though McLuhan was logically consistent: electric and now digital media reversed the detaching effect of literacy and submerged humans back into situational living. Education just followed media evolution. It should be understood, however, that immersive education provides entertainment and, at best, exploration, but not studying. In the practices of immersive education, what students really learn is being immersed into the media that entertain them. Learning through entertaining teaches being entertained. Learning by alleviating the efforts of learning teaches effortlessness. True studying does not entertain the sensorium, only the intellect.

The listeners of Homer were well trained in verbomotor and emotional resonation with the stories of political quarrels between gods, kings, and heroes; they could recite sayings, but they did not learn the concepts of politics, history, or morality. Moreover, they lacked an opportunity to inquire about such subjects. In the collective-environmental immersion, one needed to resonate, not to question. Those who questioned were swiftly ostracized, the best example being the death sentence for Socrates.

The lack of conditions for personal enquiry in the collective-environmental immersion summons the other side of the same coin: indoctrination. Of course, indoctrination has always been a part of education. Literate education, however, assumed the solitude of reading, the source of contemplating, theorizing, and enquiry. To indoctrination, solitary reading was an eternal source of constant challenges (this is how the Protestant Revolution commenced, for instance). Immersive education, on the contrary, disfavours the solitude of reading and thus creates a new, additional affordance for indoctrination simply due to its environmental, technical settings. Pupils are expected to join some activities so that their own verbomotor activity has educational value. When pupils are encouraged to contribute their identity, not inquiry, to the tribal resonance

---

[1] McLuhan interview on *The City as Classroom*. (1977). McLuhan's New Sciences blog.

of immersion, "identarian" indoctrination becomes inevitable. The self-criticism innate to literacy fails to check this failure, as critical theories themselves have reached their limits in filling the theoretical space and reversed into normative theories impervious to critical thinking.

Mutual indoctrination is amplified evermore by the environmental effects of social media, which are designed to extract users' requests for affirmation in pursuing the resonance of virality, the most desired (both by people and social-media platforms) outcome of collective-environmental immersion. Digital orality recreates an environment in which collective indoctrination is encouraged while personal inquiries are suppressed.

Monotheism, absolute, and the universal law

Neil Postman recollected that his interest in media was stirred by a "prophet far more formidable than McLuhan, more ancient than Plato." He refers to the Decalogue, the Second Commandment of which "prohibits the Israelites from making concrete images of anything: 'Thou shalt not make unto thee any graven image, any likeness of any thing that is in heaven above, or that is in the earth beneath, or that is in the water beneath the earth'."[1]

Postman wonders, why "the God of these people would have included instructions on how they were to symbolize, or not symbolize, their experience." He ponders that such an ethical instruction assumed a connection "between forms of human communication and the quality of a culture." He writes:

> We may hazard a guess that a people who are being asked to embrace an abstract, universal deity would be rendered unfit to do so by the habit of drawing pictures or making statues or depicting their ideas in any concrete, iconographic forms. The God of the Jews was to exist in the Word and through the Word, an unprecedented conception requiring the highest order of abstract thinking. Iconography thus became blasphemy so that a new kind of God could enter a culture.[2]

[1] Postman, Neil. (2006 [1985]). *Amusing Ourselves to Death*, p. 9.

[2] Postman, Neil. (2006 [1985]). *Amusing Ourselves to Death*, p. 9.

So, if the First Amendment means to protect media from the government, the Second Commandment meant to protect God from media.

The development of monotheism among the Hebrews was influenced by a combination of many factors. Some prerequisites for monotheism related to the nomadic and seminomadic lifestyle of the Semitic tribes. Normally, the gods were derived from natural forces and attached to certain places or natural elements, which made them specialized in certain activities. This was not the case for nomads. Their deities traveled with them and tended to be attached to the people, not places or elements. People became important enough to be considered "chosen." As Logan points out, "Their idea of a wandering god, a god of no fixed place, was incorporated into the monotheistic notions of god developed later by Moses under the influence of literacy."[1]

Nomadism, however, was typical for many tribes and thus could not become the key for developing monotheism. Something else was required. The alphabet, of course.

Moses was educated in Egypt, but he also lived among the Midianites and even married the daughter of their leader. As Logan points out, the biblical Midianites are the very same Seirites who were Sinai miners under the Egyptians and who borrowed phonetic signs form them. Therefore, Moses had to be familiar with both hieroglyphics and the proto alphabet.

Moses went to Mount Sinai and received "two tables of testimony, tables of stone, written with the finger of God" (Ex. 31:18). Logan proposes that these events,

> ...represent the historic transition of three separate innovations in the cultural and religious life of the Israelites:
>
> 1. Their first use of an alphabetic script
> 2. Their first adherence to a codified system of law and morality
> 3. Their first acceptance of a true and complete form of monotheism
>
> The concepts of codified law and alphabetic writing were ideas that the Hebrews borrowed from other cultures but the introduction of monotheism at Mount Sinai represents a historic first for all of mankind.[2]

[1] Logan, Robert. (2004 [1986]). *The Alphabet Effect,* p. 94.

[2] Logan, Robert. (2004 [1986]). *The Alphabet Effect,* p. 96.

Logan does not insist on a causal link between those three innovations. But he states that their simultaneity was not coincidental; they at least reinforced each other. He supports his view with a quote from Innis:

> The written letter replaced the graven image. Concentration on the abstract in writing opened the way for an advance from blood relationship to universal ethical standards, to the influence of the prophets in opposition to the absolute power of kings, and to an emphasis on monotheism.[1]

Thus, the intellectual capacity for abstraction, evidently fostered by the alphabet, facilitated an ethical pattern wherein the prophets' knowledge of God became true knowledge able to overcome the will of kings. The ethical supremacy of the prophets over kings held significant political implications for the Hebrews, as it could "legitimize" their exodus from slavery. While it may appear unusual today, the transition from slavery to freedom demanded some sort of "legal" validation. If the God of slaves outperformed the gods of the mightiest Earth king, the Pharaoh, then the Hebrews deserved to be free, and the Pharaoh could not demand them back. The universal God-moralist turned out to be mightier then specialized gods, who were essentially mythical craftsmen with restricted competencies.

Interestingly, according to the Bible, the supremacy of one God over many gods was proven through a series of "practical" miracles that still adhered to the oral and polytheistic-magical method of verifying divine powers. Unlike polytheistic beliefs that are proven by miracles (which are not miracles but rather a regular divine engagement in everyday life) the monotheistic faith has to be proven by faith itself. In the Bible, however, we still can see the struggle between the practical magic of orality and abstract worldview of literacy: sometimes faith requires miraculous proofs and receives them, while at other times faith has to be verified only by the strength of believing and nothing else.

This is the point: under absolute morality and absolute faith – under the Absolute – one has to believe despite having or not having practical situational gains. The practical gains of absolute faith do not belong with this world. Therefore, no miracles are necessary for true faith. True faith simply "knows." It is "rational" knowledge of the special privilege of being

[1] Innis, Harold. (2008 [1951]). *Bias of Communication*, p. 39.

the "chosen people," or, later, with the further development of literacy, "rational" knowledge about salvation in the afterlife.

The fact that the ever-mightier God promised the Hebrews their own fate and their own land had to be recognized by the Pharaoh and, therefore, by all others. In a sense, the supremacy of monotheism over polytheism bought the Israelites their way out of Egyptian slavery.

Monotheism was not merely an arithmetic reduction of the number of gods to one. It was a completely different intellectual and ethical concept. The multiplicity of gods allowed humans to choose between them for different practical purposes. When you can select a god-protector for various daily needs, the power of such a god and loyalty to him or her are relative. Under polytheism, there is no absolute, and everything is negotiable, including truth. In polytheistic beliefs, it is quite possible that things happen against the will of the gods.

In monotheism, one God becomes the absolute power, the cause of everything. Monotheism automatically brings the concept of absolute and final truth. Being the cause of everything, absolute God demands absolute loyalty. This is why, with the shift from orality to literacy, the notion of personal morality emerged, allowing for the development of law as abstract moral guidance rather than simply a set of arbitrary and practical punishments.

What was so special about the alphabet that contributed to the emergence of monotheism? It was that "highest order of abstract thinking" noticed by Postman. A God that does not need representation in any visible form and can be contemplated only through the "invisible" Word must be of superior power. He also can be only one, as he fills in all the space of the divine. Nobody sharing power can possess absolute power; therefore, absolute power is non-shareable.

The coding of meaningful words and ideas by meaningless signs representing invisible and meaningless sounds elevated the cognitive faculty of abstraction to the height at which the notion of absolute abstraction had to emerge. Absolute abstraction enabled the abstract absolute. The emergence of monotheism was a peculiar and unique cognitive tweak caused by the alphabet and supported and amplified by the ethnographic and political circumstances.

So, the might of a single God "authorized" the freedom of the Israelites and obliged them with the covenant. "The Ten Commandments are without a doubt a unique element, which created a new level of morality not previously known to humankind" writes Logan.[1] The single and almighty God brought to the Jews and to humankind the utterly abstract concept of the moral absolute, which entailed an entire universe of previously unknown ethical rules and philosophical principles. The Greeks, who invented the first fully-fledged alphabet, "absolutized" the concept of the absolute and abstraction even more and passed it on to the Romans and eventually to Western civilization.

As the alphabet elevated religious mysticism to the highest possible level of abstraction, the magical connections between the supernatural and the natural were severed, thus completing the detachment of humans from Nature. Prior to that, symbolic practices of early humans were bound to the material world through symbolic resemblances. Magical thinking relied on analogy, where everything acts like something else. Finding the appropriate analogies was the leading scientific, ideological, and ethical principle. The true absolute, however, does not require concrete exemplification through analogies. Any analogies would have degraded it and undermined its transcendent universality, the source of its power. The true absolute is solely grounded in itself and encompasses everything else in the world. It also cannot be confined to an image; hence, any reduction of the divine to an image is blasphemy.

Logan connects his analysis of the invention of monotheism by the Hebrews to the search for universal law. He writes:

> Before Hebrew monotheism, the law or rule of a god was limited to the geographical zone over which he held sway. With the advent of an omnipresent god whose law applied everywhere, the idea of a universal law developed.[2]

The Hebrews were the first to introduce monotheism, but other cultures found their own paths to the universal principle governing the world. It is perhaps safe to say that the alphabet, as the ultimate abstraction, provided the shortest route. However, writing in general, at the stage of phonetic abstractions, incited abstract thinking anyway. This

---

[1] Logan, Robert. (2004 [1986]). *The Alphabet Effect*, p. 99.

[2] Logan, Robert. (2004 [1986]). *The Alphabet Effect*, p. 116.

led to the pursuit of universal laws in all cultures that had advanced sufficiently in their development of writing.

Like the Hebrews after adopting the phonetic elements, the Greeks directed their intellectual effort to the search of the absolute immediately after adopting the alphabet. Unlike the Hebrews, however, the Greeks had a range of competing universal principles, including atomism or the abstract concept of motion. Among these competing concepts, the notion of Logos, which is closely associated with the idea of a monotheistic god, eventually gained prominence. Logan writes:

> Explicit in the systems of Anaximander and Heraclitus and implicit in the other Ionian systems is the notion that nature is ruled by law or Logos: "All things come to pass in accordance with this Logos" (Heraclitus, fragment).

The Hebrews' God and the Greeks' Logos were morphologically compatible as an opposition to tribal relativism and the multiplicity of gods. God and Logos, however, had their inner frictions. God was transcendental; the early God often even assumed verification by a miracle, i.e., magical evidence in concrete situations, which was obviously a residue of orality. Logos, on the contrary, was rationally comprehended and knew no miracles; it was a phenomenon of reasoning, not transcendence. In the Age of Reason, Logos rebelled against God and established its power in secular life.

The other great Axial cultures developed their own universal principles, too, as soon as the major effects of writing came into play. For example, Ong directly connects the emergence of major religions to the "inward turn" enabled by literacy, calling Buddhism, Judaism, Christianity, and Islam "the great introspective religious traditions" and pointing out that they were made possible by writing and all of them had sacred texts.[1]

In various "introspective" philosophical and religious teachings, the notion of universal law may not be articulated as explicitly as in the Hebrew concept of one God or the Greek concept of Logos. Nonetheless, concepts such as Karma, Nirvana, Samsara, Tao, and others represent the same search for universal principles. Some of these concepts still retain elements of analogies, as seen in Samsara, which represents the cosmic

---

[1] Ong, Walter. (2002 [1982]). *Orality and Literacy*, p. 103.

cycle of life common to many mythological systems, or Tao, the concept of the world order that is analogous to a way or path. However, developing concepts like Karma, Samsara, Tao, and others required a level of complexity and abstraction inherent in writing systems that abolished the resemblance of symbols to material objects and themselves developed a significant level of abstraction, for which phonetization is likely a necessary attribute. Most importantly, despite possible vestiges of analog thinking in these concepts, they represent universalism, which is impossible, or rather impractical, in magical thinking.

The transcendental was well-known to oral and magical cultures with all their mysticism, but it was primarily related to sensory perception. The transcendental could be attained through spiritual practices involving specific bodily exercises or the use of substances. However, such transcendence would come from perception, not conception. In oral cultures, the altered state of consciousness was pretty much an altered state of the body. Literacy enabled interaction with the transcendental without altering the physio-chemical processes in the body.

The literate universality directly claims its ultimate level of abstraction, whether it be the Christian God or the East Asian Tao. It may never be fully comprehended, but it calls for cognition. Some spiritual practices, including bodily exercises, may be employed to reach or approach the absolute in a literate culture, but these could be seen as residues of oral spirituality and magical mysticism. The absolute, however, is the subject of contemplating, not experiencing – or, rather, contemplating it is the highest form of experiencing it. Just as abstraction separates thought from sensory experience, the absolute does not require any involvement of the body. Inner vision, a secluded sense of vision that transcends from the sensory to the cognitive realm while numbing all other senses, serves as a sufficient conduit for an individual towards the absolute. No absolute, whether it be God, scientific truth, or a moral imperative, can depend on an individual's state of mind or body – they would not be absolute with such a dependence.

The leap of humans to the ultimate edge of abstract thinking and to universal principles were the cornerstones of Karl Jaspers' concept of the Axial Age. This leap happened in the main Axial regions during the 8th to 3rd centuries BCE. As quoted earlier, Jaspers writes:

> The Mythical Age, with its tranquillity and self-evidence, was at an end. The Greek, Indian and Chinese philosophers were unmythical in their decisive insights, as were the prophets in their ideas of God. Rationality and rationally clarified experience launched a struggle against the myth (*logos* against *mythos*); a further struggle developed for the transcendence of the One God against non-existent demons, and finally an ethical rebellion took place against the unreal figures of the gods.[1]

Jaspers did not relate this transformation of thinking to writing, leaving the mystery of the origin of the Axial Age unsolved. However, a view from the media ecological perspective connects these changes in thinking to the development of writing, with a special focus on the affordances for abstraction triggered by phonetization.

Print literacy strengthened the absolute through standardization. However, the mass media with their necessity to accommodate the interests of niche audiences, and especially electronic media, initiated the process of the reversal of the absolute. The concept of the absolute had began being undermined by the application of relativism to any matter under consideration.

The first who noticed this was Walter Lippmann. In his 1922 *Public Opinion*, he wrote that the Darwinian theory of evolution coincided with technological progress and became a "general term." He predicted that the same would happen with the theory or relativity, which gained popularity in science at about that time. He wrote that, "Relativity, like Evolution, after receiving a number of intelligible but somewhat inaccurate popular expositions in its scientific aspect, will be launched on a world-conquering career."[2] He even predicted that the new phenomenon would be called "relativismus."

Perhaps, as Darwinism coincided with industrial progress in the late 19th century, the Einsteinian theory of relativity coincided, indeed, with something in the first third of the 20th century – namely, with the development of the mass media, mass culture and "mass man" (Ortega y Gasset) – that eventually led to the dissolution of the abstraction of the absolute.

Mass culture even produced a caricature of polytheism: the pantheon of superheroes. Comic books represented the antiliterate perversion of print

[1] Jaspers, Karl. (2021 [1949]). *The Origin and Goal of History*, p. 10.

[2] Lippmann, Walter. (1998 [1922]). *Public Opinion*, p. 106

literacy. Unlike ancient gods or Christian archangels and saints (which represented a polytheistic/oral element within monotheistic religion), superheroes lacked specialized trade patronage. But they possessed individual divine attributes in the form of superpowers.

Interestingly, right after his interpretation of the Second Commandment as a cultural and media transition from analog imaging to abstract wording, Neil Postman highlights a cultural reversal incited in the 1980s by television: "People like ourselves who are in the process of converting their culture from word-centered to image-centered might profit by reflecting on this Mosaic injunction."[1] Comics and TV were image-centered indeed. By reconnecting the world with the emotional expectations of viewers, television undermined the objectivity fostered by literacy and the cultural authority of the absolute with it.

The fragmentation of previously monolithic universal values began with the split of culture into mass culture and high culture, as they were better commodified separately. In general, the niche value-based commodification was propelled by the mass media, the first and exemplary commodity of industrial capitalism, which was capable of not just satisfying but also inducing demand. Niche commodification taught society that values are relative, thus enabling the shift from object-oriented information (inherent in literacy) to subject-oriented information (inherent in orality).

The mass media's shift towards niche relativity legitimized the fragmentation of previously monolithic universal values and paved the way for postmodernism, which purposefully and conceptually attacked the concept of the absolute and anything homogeneous. It is no coincidence that the development of postmodernism accompanied the TV boom. This revolution was indeed televised.

By the time digital media arrived, the relativity of the absolute as a social construct had become conventional wisdom. The absolute, one of the pillars of alphabetic and then print literacy, has lost its power. In highly literate societies, which suffer from digital reversal the most, the absolute is routinely challenged in science and morality; it holds on in religion, but religion itself is weakened, in no small part due to being the main stronghold of the absolute.

---

1 Postman, Neil. (2006 [1985]). *Amusing Ourselves to Death*, p. 9.

Objective truth: from the relativism of tribal morality to the absolutism of personal moral duty (and now back)

Objective truth did not exist before literacy. The right and the wrong were defined by applying beliefs in concrete situations. Truth was verified by how well it comported with Nature and its divine moving forces.

In the oral state of mind, the world was run by various supernatural forces. Polytheism was the natural science of oral culture. Polytheism also formed the moral imperative of orality. To deal with Nature and gods, people were to make respective arrangements with supernatural patrons controlling this or that resource or activity. Better arrangements lasted longer and conferred better benefits. The same was applied to relations between people: truth was established by talking, by the agonistic competition of statuses. Prehistoric pantheism and then oral polytheism favoured the relativity and practicality of truth, so the truth could and should be negotiated with the support of good offerings, skills of persuasion, or simply by force. Preliterate truth was conditional, negotiated, and tested by outcomes.

Havelock points out that Plato uses the word *doxa* to describe the "non-abstract state of mind."[1] *Doxa* was not just a random opinion or belief; it was an opinion or belief sanctioned into truth by "poetic" use. It is worth reminding that "poetic" did not mean "artistic" – it meant "authorized by the tribal reciting". The medium of poetic expression was the message of truth. Havelock highlighted that *doxa* was not a product of individual consideration but "the state of mind of the many" and a "state of mind hostile to thinking."[2] The word *orthodoxy* – right and correct beliefs held by many, the ancient concept of political correctness – might explain well the power of tradition as collective sanctioning. In modern terms, *doxa* was an opinion or belief whose power was authorized by viral distribution.

The collective live re-recording of important knowledge was maintained by the effect stories and sayings had on their users, both the speakers and the listeners. For the sake of affect and better memorization, any "poetised statement must be designed and recited in such a way as to

---

[1] Havelock, Eric. (1963). *Preface to Plato,* p. 248.

[2] Havelock, Eric. (1963). *Preface to Plato,* p. 280.

make it a kind of drama within the soul both of the reciter and hence also of the audience," writes Havelock. Making drama – the emotional experience – out of knowledge was an essential technique of orality aimed at coordination and memorization. Drama led to "reliving experience in memory instead of analyzing and understanding it," according to Havelock.[1] For Plato, it was the enemy of true civic education.

Dramatic – verbomotor – speech-behaviour made everything spoken sensory experienced and lived through and thus created a situational truth "proved" by the personal experience of everyone involved. Similarly, on social media, one's "likes" correlate with what one believes is true. And vice versa: "liked" means "true." The more "liked" something is, the "truer" it is for everyone who liked it. Truth has a variable value; there is no absolute truth in this epistemological paradigm. The verbomotor investment of everyone strengthens truth through everyone's personal contribution. Truth is a referendum by likes.

Andrey Mir
@Andrey4Mir · Follow

On social media, one's likes correlate with what one believes is true. The more "liked" something is, the "truer" it is for everyone who liked it. The verbomotor investment of everyone strengthens truth through everyone's personal contribution. Truth is a referendum by likes.

12:02 AM · Nov 25, 2023

The joint solidarity of verbomotor involvement with the collective shapes the epistemological scaffolds of consciousness. As Havelock puts it,

> You threw yourself into the situation of Achilles, you identified with his grief or his anger. You yourself became Achilles and so did the reciter to whom you listened. Thirty years later you could automatically quote what Achilles had said or what the poet had said about him. Such enormous powers of poetic memorisation could be purchased only at the cost of total loss of objectivity.[2]

---

[1] Havelock, Eric. (1963). *Preface to Plato,* p. 45.

[2] Havelock, Eric. (1963). *Preface to Plato,* p. 45.

It took centuries of writing for humans to detach the truth from situational, collective, and dramatic immersion. Through the separation of the known from the knower and expressing reality in abstractions, writing taught humans that the essence of things could exist independently of practical validation or collective sanctioning: the essence of things has its own true value in the space of intellection. The emergence of objective truth as one of the universal laws was a part of the general "evolution out of the concrete towards the abstract" (Havelock[1]) enabled by writing and completed by the alphabet.

The literate truth is ideal and absolute – it cannot depend on situational development or tribal sanctions. Of course, the majority in a literate society still complies with commonly held *doxa*. But literacy, especially the alphabet, extracted truth from the realm of relationships and placed it into the realm of intellection, where no relations with gods or other humans can affect truth.

Monotheism played a specific role in the emergence of objective truth. By displacing the multiplicity of gods, monotheism deprived humans of the opportunity to negotiate their fate with a variety of divine patrons. Monotheism "trained" humans to accept the only – the absolute truth. This way, monotheism introduced the moral imperative – the allegiance not to tribe but to a rationally established abstraction. As Logan puts it, "A new form of truth emerged based on rationality and differing from traditional values of tribal solidarity."[2] The relativism of tribal morality was replaced with the imperative of personal moral duty.

This change in ethical regulation brought by literacy was noticed by Harold Innis. Thirty-five years before Postman's analysis of the Second Commandment, Innis wrote:

> The importance of sculpture to large-scale political and religious organizations was shown in the prohibition of images by the Hebrews. The written letter replaced the graven image. Concentration on the abstract in writing opened the way for an advance from blood relationship to universal ethical standards, to the influence of the prophets in opposition to the absolute power of kings, and to an emphasis on monotheism.[3]

---

[1] Havelock, Eric. (1963). *Preface to Plato*, p. 63.

[2] Logan, Robert. (2004 [1986]). *The Alphabet Effect*, p. 128.

[3] Innis, Harold. (2008 [1951]). *Bias of Communication*, p. 39.

The jural principle of the Romans, *Dura lex, sed lex,* applies also to the concept of truth. Orality valued subjective relationships above all, but literacy learned to value objective truth over subjective relationships. Literacy created weird and unnatural conditions in which an individual can even go against traditions, beliefs, and relationships if the truth this individual has revealed does not comply with the tribal worldview.

This is how Aristotle came up with his "Plato is dear to me, but dearer still is truth." Aristotle's rejection of loyalty to the elder and the teacher and pledging loyalty to some abstract notion of truth was the greatest ethical revolution in the history of humankind. Claiming that "truth is still dearer" was a truly axial event, the ethical epitome of the Axial Age, the historical axis between ancient and modern humans, between orality and literacy.

The difference in ethical regulation imposed by oral and literate truth is often recognizable in everyday life. A person significantly affected by literacy will be more likely to step forward against the collective if the truth requires it. For example, in self-officiated sports, when players themselves need to apply rules to concrete situations, an individual with a significant literate background will admit a rule violation even if the ruling is detrimental to the team's progress, while a teammate with a significant oral background will try to negotiate the ruling – despite eye witnessing the violation – and will deem the first individual a traitor. One can see similar ethical differences in professional sports when a player engages in an altercation with the referee after the decision has been made as if the application of the rules is a matter of persuasion or, even more strangely (for the literate mind), a matter of post-factum persuasion.

The objectivation of truth came from the fact that literacy materialized truth just technically. The fleeting truth of orality was captured and pinned down in writing. The truth inscribed in the Book was uniformed and absolutized. In different times, the Book was the scripture, the code of laws, the textbook; all of them contained absolute truth. As a result, in written cultures, truth can not be arbitrated by experience. It belongs solely to the highest abstract authority and can only be interpreted.

The contemplation of the abstract absolute, however, was long available solely to the most learned few. The abstract absolute became accessible to many only through print. The main effect of printing was uniformity. Printing accustomed readers to uniformity as a "tangible" manifestation of the absolute: various books had this in common – they all were the medium of some higher authority. The "material" uniformity of the book replaced the sanctioning power of oral *doxa*. The printing press democratized objective truth and inaugurated its epistemological superiority to all who could read.

Since then, law, science and rational logic, all of which are based on the imperative of absolute truth, have come to dominate the West. The United States was built upon this epistemological principle: the social contract was literally established in writing – by written documents – not by accumulated customs. It does not mean that irrationality or tribalism were fully eliminated, but they were suppressed by literacy, especially after the introduction of compulsory education.

Throwbacks to the oral epistemology of truth and the corresponding ethical regulations had already occurred in history. For example, Logan notes that, after the fall of Rome, the Roman civil administration based on the law was replaced by a "new form of government based on the older oral traditions of the Germanic tribes."[1] In that system, the subjects pledged their loyalty to the tribe and warlord through a verbal oath of allegiance. The codified and systemic law of literate culture yielded to social regulation based on personal loyalty. From being at the core of the law, truth was demoted to serve the transient everyday needs of the tribe and became once again open to negotiation or being taken by force. The feudal setback of orality lasted until Gutenberg brought literacy back with reinforcement from printing.

But now the Gutenberg Galaxy is collapsing, exposing objective truth to retribalization. The de-objectivation of truth can be traced back to the early 20th century, to two main sources. On one hand, linguists began to explore the differences between language and speech and endeavoured to overcome structuralism via pragmatic theories. On the other hand, the "pragmatic" redesign of truth had its roots in mass media. After society achieved mass literacy, mass media approached their natural limits in reaching out to the masses. Since that moment, maintaining the media business meant learning what the mass audience wanted. This endowed the masses with agency, enabling universal suffrage on one hand and further structuring the masses into more identity-specific audiences on the other.

---

[1] Logan, Robert. (2004 [1986]). *The Alphabet Effect*, p. 164.

Electronic media turned the imaginary agency of audiences into the criterion of worthiness, edging out the elitist views of authors. Postmodernism, Barthes' "death of the author," and the respective critical theories were adaptations of cultural software to changing media hardware. From linguistics and philosophy, the "pragmatic" epistemology of truth became an object of cultural studies – a new discipline that emerges to serve precisely this process of truth customization – and, by the mid-2010s, reached journalism, having transformed it into postjournalism.[1]

This anti-platonic turn was perhaps best represented in George Lakoff and Mark Johnson's debunking of objective truth in 1980:

> We do not believe that there is such a thing as *objective* (absolute and unconditional) *truth*, though it has been a long-standing theme in Western culture that there is. We do believe that there are *truths* but think that the idea of truth need not to be tied to the objectivist view. We believe that the idea that there is absolute objective truth is not only mistaken but socially and politically dangerous. As we have seen, truth is always relative to a conceptual system that is defined in large part by metaphor. Most of our metaphors have evolved in our culture over a long period, but many are imposed upon us by people in power – political leaders, religious leaders, business leaders, advertisers, the media, etc. In a culture where the myth of objectivism is very much alive and truth is always absolute truth, the people who get to impose their metaphors on the culture get to define what we consider to be true – absolutely and objectively true.[2]

Lakoff and Johnson "revealed" that truths are the products of beliefs:

> We base our actions, both physical and social, on what we take to be true. On the whole, truth matters to us because it has survival value and allows us to function in our world. <...> In order to aquire such truths and to make use of them, we need an understanding of our world sufficient for our needs.[3]

According to them, we inevitably make "true statements" in human categories, i.e., based on our experience. Therefore, "true statements made

---

1 Mir, Andrey. (2020). *Postjournalism and the death of newspapers. The media after Trump: manufacturing anger and polarization*.

2 Lakoff, George, and Johnson, Mark. (1980). *Metaphors We Live By*, p. 159-160, *italics* are theirs.

3 Lakoff, George, and Johnson, Mark. (1980). *Metaphors We Live By*, p. 160.

in terms of human categories typically do not predicate *properties of objects in themselves* but rather *interactional properties* that make sense only relative to human functioning."[1]

By tethering truths to human needs and functioning, they accidentally revived the Homeric state of mind, in which environmental and collective immersion leaves no room for abstract absolutes. For example, according to Lakoff and Johnson's logic, language does not exist – it simply should not exist. Only concrete language usages – speech acts – exist; or, at best, the summary of usages. Therefore, within this logic, our use of language for our needs and within our beliefs is the only way to know the language. Grammar is also impossible and, when introduced forcibly, is "socially and politically dangerous," as it conveys the power of those who imposed the rules of grammar. Such views should have appeared in this line of thought – and they have eventually appeared.

The scholars of literacy had a different opinion regarding the objective truth. "It is only with alphabetic literacy that timeless analytic statements emerge that can express universal truths independent of the context in which they occur," writes Logan.[2] He mentions the statement "Two plus two is four" as a common and simple example of universal truth that cannot be disavowed by any context. Indeed, "Two plus two is four" will remain true even if Hitler says it. However, with the proliferation of digital orality, even the statements of math and other sciences become "contextualized." In orality, "Two plus two equals four" does not exist. In literacy, "Two plus two equals four" no matter what. In digital orality, "Two plus two equals four" is doubted if said by Hitler. In some radical forms of digital orality, "Two plus two equals four" *is* Hitler.

The imperative of combatting "political, religious, and business leaders" by rejecting objective truth plunges the mind back into Plato's cave, where the prisoners now "rationally" inaugurate their sensory experience as the only real truth. But in the abyss of this cave, identarian tribalism reigns, inhabited by chthonic creatures ranging from Trump to intersectionality, the tribal form of social scoring.

Similar to oral tradition, the truth of digital orality is verified by practical outcomes; however, these practical outcomes occur not in

---

[1] Lakoff, George, and Johnson, Mark. (1980). *Metaphors We Live By*, p. 164, *italics* are theirs.

[2] Logan, Robert. (2004 [1986]). *The Alphabet Effect*, p. 110.

physical reality but in digital reality. Since digital reality presents the world through the views of others, the truth of everyone is defined by the truths of others. It has no even situational tethering in "objective," material reality.

> **Andrey Mir**
> @Andrey4Mir · **Follow**
>
> In orality, "Two plus two equals four" does not exist.
> In literacy, "Two plus two equals four" no matter what.
> In digital orality, "Two plus two equals four" is doubted if said by Hitler.
> In some radical forms of digital orality, "Two plus two equals four" is Hitler.
>
> 1:08 AM · Oct 3, 2023

After the emancipation of authorship[1] by the Internet, millions of people entered the business of meaning production. This was not their intent, but the very design of this new environment has destroyed the monopoly of absolute truth. Scriptures and textbooks forfeited their power. The caste of priests-interpreters (scientists, philosophers, journalists, etc.) was replaced by the multiple crowdsourced interpretations of reality. Such an environment can't help but challenge the monopoly of knowledge, logically leading to what Martin Gurri called the "crisis of authority" in his book "The Revolt of the Public."[2]

Digital media completed the "shift of agency" from the author to the audience by making the audience the author. It did not lead, though, to the reinstating of Homer, as Homer is an authoritarian figure, too. Instead, in digital media, Homer was crowdsourced.

Social media have legitimized crowdsourced truths as a side effect of their design. Since online engagement is built on responses, digital orality demands that everybody relates to the truths of others.[3] The practical outcomes that verify truth are still environmental, but the environment is digital and consists of others (and algorithms).

---

[1] Miroshnichenko, Andrey. (2014). Human as media. The emancipation of authorship.

[2] Gurri, Martin. (2018). *The Revolt of The Public and the Crisis of Authority in the New Millennium.*

[3] Mir, Andrey. (2023, Spring). "The Viral Inquisitor. Social media have unleashed a culture of instant judging." *City Journal.*

The *doxa* of the Homeric mind is back, now without any poetry as a carrier; the carrier is the newsfeed on social media. The collectivism of *doxa*, the social power of *orthodoxy*, is now technologically amplified by viral distribution and, most importantly, by everyone watching over the compliance of everyone due to the instant exposure of everyone to everyone on social media. It is becoming harder to withstand the "peer pressure" of the tribe when objective truth does not align with the truths of the tribe.

People now vote for truth with clicks, which are the digital surrogates of cheering at a bardic performance. Truth is again up for negotiation. "Tribal solidarity" is back as a moral regulative, suppressing the literate moral imperative of truth. Had Aristotle had a Twitter account, he would have said that "Truth is dear to me, but dearer still is Plato." Digital orality rejects absolute truth, affecting even science and jurisprudence. A scholar needs to adjust their methodology to get preapproved results. Lady Justice needs to lift her blindfold and carefully watch what she is weighing. Truth is dear but dearer still are right people, so pick the right truth.

Andrey Mir
@Andrey4Mir · **Follow**

Orality values subjective relations over objective truth, while literacy values objective truth over subjective relations.
Digital orality reverses the latter and retrieves the former.

11:41 AM · Jun 8, 2023

8. Differences between the effects of writing and the alphabet

The alphabetic bias in studying literacy

What is the difference between the effects of writing in general and the alphabet?

All forms of writing obviously opposed oral speech. But writing itself had different forms whose features and effects differed significantly. Scholars of literacy implied those differences but not always articulated them because they were mostly preoccupied with the opposition of literacy to orality, in which the alphabet played the key role. The alphabetic bias, of course, exposes the Western proclivity of literacy studies.

Marshall McLuhan and Robert Logan (1977) focused on the alphabet and considered earlier forms of writing as precursors that eventually led to and were encompassed by the alphabet effect. Eric Havelock (1963), Jack Goody and Ian Watt (1963), Walter Ong (1982) and many others focused on the Greeks' transition from orality to literacy, but the Greek history of literacy was unique, as the Greeks adopted the alphabet directly without developing the prior stages of writing. Consequently, the earlier stages of writing were not central to their explorations. It was sufficient for Havelock, for example, to acknowledge the general "evolution out of the concrete towards the abstract"[1] in the development of writing.

As a result, it is sometimes difficult to differentiate between the general effects of writing and the specific effects of the alphabet. Phonetization, linearity, fragmentation, and abstraction began to emerge prior to the alphabet in syllabic writing. Literacy obviously progressed gradually, amplifying some earlier effects and introducing new ones. So, what was the specific contribution of the alphabet to the development of literacy and suppression of orality? The effects of literacy also continued to develop after the introduction of the alphabet, leading to a similar question concerning print: What were the specific effects of the printing press?[2]

---

[1] Havelock, Eric. (1963). *Preface to Plato,* p. 63.

[2] It needs to be mentioned here that Robert Logan explores the further development of the

The distinctions between the effects of alphabetic literacy and print literacy, along with the specific effects of other forms of writing, gain practical significance for exploring the reversal of literacy and the retrieval of orality by digital media. It might be useful to learn what exactly we are about to lose or have transformed, how, and with what outcomes.

The question of the specific alphabet effect grows even more practical as it allows reflection not just on the Greek (or Judeo-Christian) past of the West but also on the Chinese future of the East and, perhaps, the world, if the dominance of alphabetic literacy, indeed, is coming to an end.

Recording speech, not events: an eye for an ear

While defining boundaries between the effects of writing can be challenging, the overall trajectory of writing's development is clear: it progressed from concrete to abstract, from pictorial to phonetic, and from recording events to recording speech.

The more primitive the means of communication were, the more they relied on recognizable features of the situation, which were mimicked in various ways. The speech of early humans likely involved a dance-vocal performance with pointing gestures, mimicking the sounds of Nature, and expressing emotions that were relevant to the described situation. Primordial speech most likely aimed to induce the described situation by imitating it.

Such *mimesis* persisted when communication switched to "materials other than the human body" (one of McLuhan's descriptions of technologies[1]). Drawings directly depicted situations. As Gelb puts it, drawings represented events, not speech.[2] Tallies (counting notches and pebbles) also exhibited a similarity to what they represented: the items being counted.

Some degree of abstraction had already emerged at this stage. Drawings were not perfect and represented objects more and more

---

alphabet effect by printing and computers in his 1986 *The Alphabet Effect*.

[1] In the chapter "Narcissus as Narcosis" in *Understanding Media*, McLuhan wrote: "...men at once become fascinated by any extension of themselves in any material other than themselves." – McLuhan, Marshall. (1994 [1964]). *Understanding Media*, p. 41.

[2] Gelb, Ignace. (1963 [1952]). *A Study of Writing*, p. 74

schematically and, eventually, symbolically. Recognizing three fish in three pebbles or three warriors in three notches started training human perception's cognitive capacity for abstraction.

Each subsequent stage of writing – tokens, pictograms, cuneiforms and hieroglyphs (logograms and ideograms), syllabograms, and alphabetic signs – represented a further progression from iconic signs (imitations of what is represented) to symbolic signs (learned associations with no visual cue).

The general schema of writing's development can be represented in a diagram – Figure 22.

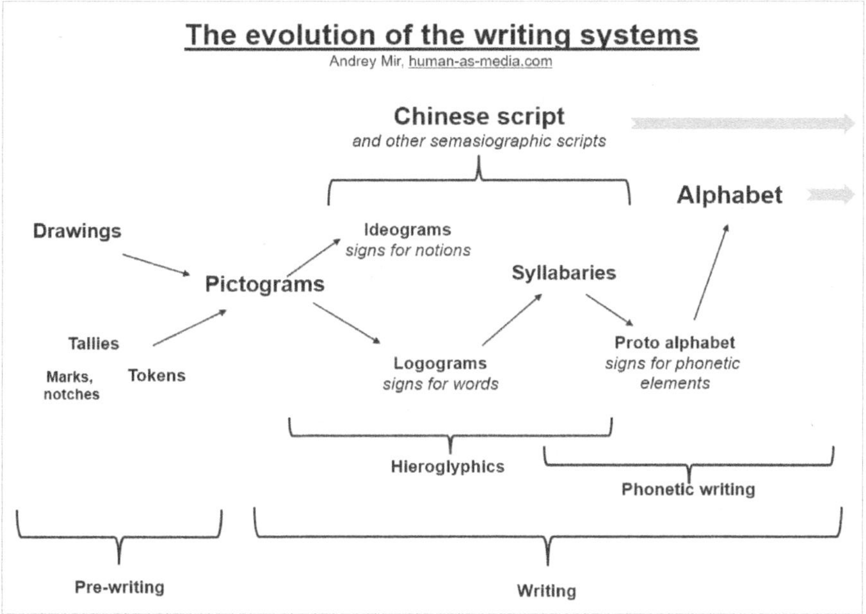

Figure 22.

The crucial turn happened when signs began representing not objects or events but sounds of speech. At the stage of phonetization, writing isolated vision by allowing an eye to recognize the signs for isolated sounds of speech, thus enabling an unnatural sensorial state, which media ecology calls "an eye for an ear."[1] As Marshal and Eric McLuhan put it,

[1] For example, McLuhan: "Only the phonetic alphabet makes a break between eye and ear, between semantic meaning and visual code; and thus only phonetic writing has the power to translate man from the tribal to the civilized sphere, to give him an eye for an ear." –

> Oral, resonant speech is broken into irreducible (uniform) bits of meaningless sound, each connected to a sign by arbitrary association, and by uniform orthography. By means of a continuous linear sequence of signs, the bare sounds that compose speech are re-presented and re-cognized through a single sense in isolation.[1]

The initial means of phonetization, such as syllables and phonetic determinatives, had already introduced some degrees of this sensorial disturbance that, in general, facilitated the transition of cognition from perception to conception. But the alphabet completed the disintegration of the natural equilibrium of the senses. The alphabet enabled the precise recording of speech.

From this unique property, all other features of the alphabet emerged, defining the specificity of the alphabet effect. As McLuhan put it, "For to translate the audible into the visible by phonetic means is to institute a dynamic process that reshapes every aspect of thought, language, and society."[2]

Fluency, fullness, richness, precision

It is only through the alphabetic script that a reader can precisely restore an utterance they have never heard and have never had situational clues about. "Phonetic efficiency meant the removal of that ambiguity of recognition which had limited all previous writing systems in their application," writes Havelock.[3]

If speech is the most natural and the most elaborated form of human communication that allows expression of thoughts of any complexity, then the alphabet fulfilled the very idea of writing – the precise recording of spoken communication. With alphabetic script, situational supports or contextual prompts were no longer needed for communication. The alphabet allowed conveying speech without any necessity to guess or interpret pictorial analogies.

By recording speech and not events or situations, the alphabet also assumed some qualities of speech, such as fluency, for example.

McLuhan, Marshall. (1962). *The Guttenberg Galaxy*, p. 27.

[1] McLuhan, Marshall, and McLuhan, Eric. (1988). *Laws of Media: The New Science*, p. 18.

[2] McLuhan, Marshall. (1959). "Myth and Mass Media," p. 339.

[3] Havelock, Eric A. (1978). "The Alphabetization of Homer," p. 4.

As Havelock puts it,

> An act of vision was offered in place of an act of hearing as the means of communication, and as the means of storing communication. The adjustment that it caused was in part social, but the major effect was felt in the mind and the way the mind thinks as it speaks. The crisis became Greek, rather than Hebrew or Babylonian or Egyptian, because of the alphabet's superior efficiency. Fluency had always characterized orally formed communication. To achieve a complete transfer to a system of visual recognition required a comparable visual fluency.[1]

The fluency of written records comparable to the fluency of speech also caused other "recording" properties of the alphabetic script, such as fullness and richness. In "The alphabetization of Homer," Havelock conducts an interesting study. He compares "A flood recorded in cuneiform" (a passage from the *Epic of Gilgamesh*) and "A flood recorded in the alphabet" (a passage from the *Iliad*).

The chosen passage from *Gilgamesh* "achieves a degree of narrative vividness not to be matched elsewhere in the poem." The flood is described in an "unusually rich vocabulary"[2] because the author of the epic provides many concrete and specific details. Nevertheless, Havelock detects a significant level of repetition as compared to the flood recorded in the *Iliad*. The percentage of non-unique words to the total is 23.3% in the *Epic of Gilgamesh* and 14% in the *Iliad*.

The same applies to the expressions that are not necessarily equivalent but still paraphrase each other. In the *Epic of Gilgamesh*, "the verbal 'originality' of composition begins to exhaust itself, and we get the following series of repetitive sequences..."[3]

This is predefined by the limitation of scripts. Cuneiform was a logo-syllabic script, as it included both logograms (signs for words) and syllabograms (signs for syllables). However rich the oral version of the *Epic of Gilgamesh* was, a scribe who recorded it was limited by a certain number of logographic signs and also by the complexity of combining syllabic signs to express words. Even though the repertoire of cuneiform writing reached

[1] Havelock, Eric. (1986). *The Muse Learns to Write*, p. 100.

[2] Havelock, Eric. (1978). "The alphabetization of Homer," p. 5.

[3] Havelock, Eric. (1978). "The alphabetization of Homer," p. 6.

hundreds of signs, it could not record all expressions likely employed in the oral version of the saga. When recording the saga, the scribe was forced to reduce the richness of the narrative to the capacity of the script. As Havelock suggests,

> The deficiencies of cuneiform as an instrument of acoustic-visual recognition have discouraged the composer from packing into his verse the full variety of expression which such a description calls for.[1]

And yet that was an unusually detailed passage full of rich expressions. Typical cuneiform records were much more reductive: they conveyed the basics of a story as they were unable to deliver its entirety to the reader. Neither Mesopotamian cuneiforms nor Egyptian hieroglyphs were capable of recording poetry as-is. This also means that the richness of their original epics was lost forever. We have only a reduced version of verses that the scribe managed to record.

Unlike with the Mesopotamian epic, the recording of the Homeric texts represented the precise records of the oral narrative. We know this because the written records convey the hexameter of the poems. It perfectly preserves the original story in all its richness and vividness. The alphabetic arsenal, containing only 24 signs, allowed recording of all the words precisely as they were uttered by Homer or whoever composed and dictated them to the scribes.

Havelock highlighted that the Greek description of the flood is still tautological and ritualized. This was predefined by the formulaic and repetitive nature of oral poems devised for memorization. Yet, the alphabet did not reduce the richness and diversity of the vocabulary further, as cuneiforms did.

Having compared "the so-called 'literatures' of Sumer, Babylon, and Assyria, as well as versions of Egyptian wisdom literature," with the Homeric poems, Havelock concludes:

> A stark contrast appeared between the sheer richness of Greek orality as transcribed and the caution of its competitors. A wealth of detail and depth of psychological feeling contrasted with an economy of vocabulary and a cautious restriction of sentiment which seemed to be specific properties of all Near Eastern and Hebrew literature. It

[1] Havelock, Eric. (1978). "The alphabetization of Homer," p. 9.

> occurred to me that the true orality of these non-Greek peoples was not getting through to us – had in fact been irretrievably lost, because the writing systems employed were too imperfect to record it adequately.[1]

"The primary advantage offered by the alphabet over previous writing systems was to provide the power to document the oral report fluently and exhaustively," concludes Havelock in his comparison of the epic floods reported in the cuneiforms and the alphabet.[2]

Being incapable of recording poetry because it could not record live speech, early writing also did not record prose because prose had not been invented yet. Early writing, beyond simple inscriptions, recorded just the main features of events and practical inventories of different kinds.

The alphabetic *recording* of oral narratives, such as Homeric poems, allowed preservation of all the redundancies needed for oral memorization and thus delivered all the oral richness. But *composing* something new in the alphabetic script dictated a completely different approach. Formulaic redundancy and repetitive elements were gradually abandoned, along with such mnemotechnic means as rhythm and rhyme. Alphabetic composing allowed a focus on creating a written speech that would represent an inner narrative or, in Vygotsky's terms, speech thinking.

Being freed from the formulaic requirements of memorization, written speech thinking could not help but focus on meaning. This became the essential feature of prose. In alphabetic *composing,* the affecting of readers became possible not through verbomotor attacks on their perception but through engaging them with concepts. The efficiency of message delivery shifted from formal affectation to logic and argumentation. (Interestingly, the non-alphabetic scripts, such as Chinese, have come to prose in their own ways, but likely without Platonic rebellion against poetry, which was one of the formative events for Greek and Western rationality.)

Ong: literacy as an enhancement of orality

Literacy and orality coexisted, but literacy also enhanced orality, with rhetoric being the pinnacle of this enhancement. The affordance to write down an oral speech before delivering it at an assembly, according to Ong,

---

1 Havelock, Eric. (1986). *The Muse Learns to Write*, p. 9.

2 Havelock, Eric. (1978). "The alphabetization of Homer," p. 10.

contributed to the emergence of rhetoric, an essential element in political and legal practices in Greece and then Rome. Ong suggests that rhetoric, despite being an oral practice, "was and had to be a product of writing." The Greeks were fascinated with the art of rhetoric, and this fascination turned rhetoric into the "most comprehensive academic subject in all western culture for two thousand years."

This led Ong to a conclusion:

> Thus writing from the beginning did not reduce orality but enhanced it, making it possible to organize the "principles" or constituents of oratory into a scientific "art", a sequentially ordered body of explanation that showed how and why oratory achieved and could be made to achieve its various specific effects.[1]

The logic of this observation is supported by another Ong coinage, the concept of *secondary orality*. Writing, indeed, not only enabled literacy but had a rebound effect on orality. First, rhetoric emerged, then, in the era of electronic media, literacy affected the oral speech of people talking on the telephone, radio and TV. Ong described this effect as "the 'secondary orality' of present-day high-technology culture, in which a new orality is sustained by telephone, radio, television, and other electronic devices that depend for their existence and functioning on writing and print."[2]

Secondary orality represented the oral speech of highly literate societies, where people's brains were trained in literacy for at least several generations. Therefore, despite its oral format, secondary orality was affected by the rules of written speech. It tended to represent linear and subsequential thinking, fostered by print literacy.

In a sense, rhetoric as oral speech affected by writing was a precursor for secondary orality. Rhetoric developed as the art of oratory, but it also infiltrated the educated speech of the literate era. The secondary orality of the electric age can be seen as a "democratized rhetoric," or a rhetoric emancipated by electronic media and employed, in simplified forms, by educated people. Secondary orality was literate oral speech.

Ong's view of literacy as the enhancement of orality was supported by his observations of secondary orality on radio and TV. According to him, "Electronic media do not tolerate a show of open antagonism." Despite

[1] Ong, Walter. (2002 [1982]). *Orality and Literacy*, p. 9.

[2] Ong, Walter. (2002 [1982]). *Orality and Literacy*, p. 11.

cultivating spontaneity on air, he writes, electronic media were dominated "by a sense of closure which is the heritage of print."[1] In his view, a show of hostility "might break open the closure, the tight control" and therefore was avoided on TV.

Perhaps these characteristics suited the TV of the 1970s, with its talking-head news announcers, pundits in the studios, and innocent game shows. Television of that era still inherited from print a tight control over emotions. Tabloid talk shows that focused on scandals and controversies developed only by the end of the 1970s.

But with a growing focus on viewership and not on content, electronic media eventually became less object-oriented and more relations-oriented, thus signifying the beginning of the reversal from literacy to orality. In this process, electronic media simply had to retrieve Ong's "agonistic mentality" and McLuhan's "tribalization." And so they did.

By creating *CNN* in 1980, Ted Turner essentially televised the telegraph, the first electronic medium that served newspapers and was strictly factually based. The effect of print literacy on early *CNN* still was strong. But it was Roger Ailes who completed the making of true television by creating *Fox News* in 1996. He fully unveiled the specific and unique capacity of TV: the delivery of an affirmative emotional world picture that would talk to the viewers at their homes and within their value systems.

Television stopped being news-centered and started being viewer-centered.[2] This move reversed the print-induced control over emotions and retrieved the agonistic mentality both on the air and in the viewers, starting the process of cultural and political polarization (which skyrocketed 15 years later with the advance of social media).

The shift of television towards orality has particularly transpired in game shows. In the 1970s, on the *$10,000 Pyramid*, a word association game, the players mostly prompted their partners with antonyms, synonyms, and dictionary-style definitions, which were appropriate for a literate culture with its paradigmatic conceptualization. Fifty years later, players more often try to "induce" the sought word using interjections and gesticulation, as if they want to "persuade" their partners by affecting them

---

[1] Ong, Walter. (2002 [1982]), *Orality and Literacy*, p. 134.

[2] See: Mir, Andrey. (2023, April 26). "Past Their Prime (Time). Fox News and CNN enter the last stage of their parallel history." *Discourse*.

rather than explaining the word's meaning. Their prompts retrieve the vocal pantomime of speech-behaviour. Celebrations are hysterical. Electronic exposition to the invisible distant audience exaggerates participants' self-expression into theatrical hyperbolization. Since regular people have no skills for it, they just agitate themselves into screaming interjections. The prizes have increased (now it's the *$100,000 Pyramid*), but players' average score has decreased, both representing certain kinds of inflation.

Verbomotor intensity on modern TV is incomparable to that of the 1970s. The emotionality and exaltation on TV would have made Ong reconsider his view of television. On-air scandals or even brawls have become genre specials on some TV shows, disproving Ong's thesis about electronic media's intolerance for open antagonism.

Electronic media, and television first of all, have become the main enabler of the so-called "affective economy," in which the circulation of affect connects people and objects in the manner of Marx's capital. It became the business model of television: money – affect – money. The more intensive the communication exchange, the more affect is produced. [1] Television profited on affect in the same way as social media now profit on engagement.

Interestingly, similar to how digital media use algorithms to amplify engagement, television learned to use laugh tracks, controlled or prerecorded applause, and other techniques of "sweetening," as they call it, to simulate or induce "empathic involvement" (McLuhan[2]), inherent in orality. We see such sound design as natural for TV, and it is. But it also is the verbomotor synchronization of the listeners, a feature artificially – *technologically* – retrieved from primary orality.

Despite Ong's 1970s expectations, the secondary orality of electronic media could not manage to preserve the legacy of literacy. Electronic orality developed its immanent traits, which were more tied to orality than to literacy. Nevertheless, Ong's implication to see literacy as a linking element in the succession of oralities can offer a useful optic. The same line of succession in oral-literate hybridizations that underlays secondary, or electronic, orality, has eventually led to digital orality ("tertiary orality" as

---

[1] Ahmed, Sara. (2004). "Affective Economies," p. 120.

[2] McLuhan, Marshall. (1962). *The Guttenberg Galaxy*, p. 39.

Logan originally called digital orality, following Ong's idea of the secondary orality of electronic media).

Digital orality can be seen as rhetoric, "democratized" by digital media even further, to a level where literacy and educational pretensions play an ever-fading role, while the verbomotor intensity of primary orality grows in significance.

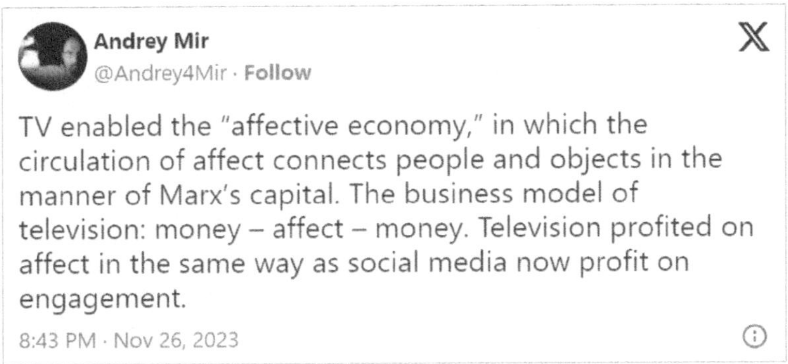
Andrey Mir
@Andrey4Mir · Follow

TV enabled the "affective economy," in which the circulation of affect connects people and objects in the manner of Marx's capital. The business model of television: money – affect – money. Television profited on affect in the same way as social media now profit on engagement.

8:43 PM · Nov 26, 2023

The evolution of interpersonal and mass communication can be seen, indeed, through the lens of the sequential "enhancement" of oral communication, as prompted by Ong. Primary orality was succeeded by writing, which refined the high form of orality – Havelock's "significant speech" – into rhetoric. Then, the development of writing led first to electronic communication and secondary/electronic orality and then to digital communication and tertiary/digital orality.

Literacy, therefore, was a historically short but very intense period in the evolution of interpersonal and mass communication, historically enclosed between the era of primary orality and the era of electronic media. The print culmination of this period is sometimes called the "Gutenberg Parenthesis," a 500-year period of print literacy between mostly oral and mostly electronic/digital eras. The idea of a "parenthesis" implies that McLuhan's "Gutenberg Galaxy" had not only a beginning but also an end. The Gutenberg Parenthesis is closing. Orality, in the meantime, continues in new forms.

Havelock: the alphabet as an erosion of orality

Focusing on the rebellion of Plato against epic poetry (the Homeric state of mind), Havelock implies that the introduction of the alphabet led to the replacement of the oral mind by the literate mind. He writes:

> More accurately, rather than speak of destruction, we should say that what set in with the alphabetization of Homer was a process of erosion of "orality," extending over centuries of the European experience, one which has left modern culture unevenly divided between oral and literate modes of expression, experience, and living.[1]

Orality did not quickly disappear, of course; orality and literacy coexisted, clashing ("Plato" vs. "Homer"), but also affecting and enriching each other. Literacy started developing on the platform of orality. As Havelock puts it,

> In the Greek case then we face the paradox that, whereas the alphabet by its phonetic efficiency was destined to replace orality by literacy, the first historic task assigned to it was to render an account of orality itself before it was replaced.[2] Since the replacement was slow, the invention continued to be used to inscribe an orality which was slowly modifying itself in order to become a language of literacy.[3]

Early writing even reinforced the positions of orality to some extent. Pre-phonetic writing was based on the similarity of signs to objects, and this gave the caste of scribes magical power over reality. This was what Havelock meant when he wrote that early writing added in records "ritual dignity at the cost of omitting the complexities of physical and psychological response."[4] Orality kept the practices of early writing within the environmental, immersive, and magical state of mind.

Orality and literacy might coexist as modes of communication, but as a state of mind, literacy started suppressing orality after the "alphabetization of Homer" (Havelock[5]). The main and unique effect of the alphabet was the obliteration of the monopoly of analog thinking, which could not have happened under earlier writing. Analog thinking was based on matching anything unknown to something known, thus constituting the power of magic, tradition, and wisdom. The alphabet destroyed the pattern of

---

1 Havelock, Eric. (1978). "The alphabetization of Homer," p. 4.

2 Interestingly, the "first task assigned" to the printing press was, of course, the printing of the Bible and indulgencies, the main forms of chirographic literacy at the time.

3 Havelock, Eric. (1986). *The Muse Learns to Write*, p. 90.

4 Havelock, Eric. (1986). *The Muse Learns to Write*, p. 91.

5 Havelock, Eric. (1978). "The alphabetization of Homer," p. 3.

matching to other things and introduced the pattern of matching to the thing's own true meaning, as in Plato's Theory of Forms. As McLuhan puts it,

> The interiorization of the technology of the phonetic alphabet translates man from the magical world of the ear to the neutral visual world.[1]

When things were analogical to each other, their interconnection created a large but nevertheless closed circuit of overlapping mutual encompassment. But when each thing is expected to match its own essence, all things in the Universe gain freedom. Without analogical similarity to something else, each thing became orphaned and demanding adoption. Each thing became filled with its own meaning, akin to alphabetically written words, which had no resemblance to anything else and proudly carried their meaning on their own. The scariest consequence was that human life itself turned out to be free from satisfactory explanations through the circle of life or totemic/tribal belonging.

Immediately, the questions of meanings arose. What is the true meaning of a thing if it is not another thing? What is the meaning of life if it is not an analogy with the circle of life and "entirely repetitive continuance of living, still closely allied to the processes of nature"[2]? By destroying the pattern of matching things to other things and introducing the pattern of matching things to their true meaning, the alphabet incited the eternal search for the true meaning of things. That is why literacy is centered around questions and never satisfied with answers.

The assault of the alphabet on analogical thinking did not fully dismiss mysticism and the awe of humans before the power of Nature and the unknown. Mysticism, however, was reworked from magic to faith.

The shift from magic to faith brought not just a switch from many specialized gods to one almighty God. It was also a shift from superstitions to religion, from spells to prayers, from incantations to scriptures, from shamanism to priesthood, from outward to inward, from primitive metaphysics to elaborated ethics. In magic, truth was negotiated; in faith, truth was prescribed. Magic allowed for manipulations and arrangements fitting the needs of the situation; faith dictated moral duties that disregarded situational needs.

---

[1] McLuhan, Marshall. (1962). *The Guttenberg Galaxy*, p. 18.

[2] Jaspers, Karl. (2021 [1949]). *The Origin and Goal of History*, p. 32.

Religious faith might have freed humans from the magic of the natural/supernatural, but it obliged them to universal moral law. The switch from magic to faith was also a shift from the bodily to the moral and, as such, from spatial to temporal. Non-historic and prehistoric beings sought safety in space; historic beings seek salvation in time. Media evolution started with facilitating the human biological conquest of space and has eventually turned into the post-biological request for time.

The shift from magic to faith also shaped the precondition for scientific thinking. Magic, however, retained its power in the West until the time of modernity when print literacy asserted the advantages of the alphabet and inaugurated scientific logic.

From this perspective and accepting Havelock's idea of the alphabet as the ultimate assault on orality, the specificity of the alphabet effect can be defined through the exclusive property of the alphabet – recording speech, not events or images. This property evoked the following specific effects of the alphabet (the list is open):

- Speech-like fluency, precision, and the richness of writing,
- The relinquishment of verbomotor affect in favour of more elaborated content (persuasion by argumentation),
- The emergence of prose,
- The dismissal of analog thinking and, as a consequence,
- The dismissal of magical thinking.

To this list, the effects of the alphabet revealed by Robert Logan need to be added:

- Codified law,
- Monotheism,
- Abstract science,
- Deductive logic,
- Individualism.

Finally, the distant effects of the alphabet include:

- The printing press as an industrial technology (resulted in capitalism, socialism, and representative democracy)
- The electric and electronic technologies
- Coding and the digital technologies.

The primary and secondary effects of writing and the alphabet

When used by a person, a fence is an instrument to protect and defend, a further extension of the skin beyond clothes and huts. However, when used by a culture, a fence is an environmental force that transforms a nomadic tribe into a sedentary society. Similarly, what seemed to be just the instrumental use of a medium in an isolated act (or a series of acts) becomes an environmental force when the user is not an individual but an entire culture.[1]

When used as tools, media extend our physical or psychological capacities in time and space. These extensions, however, require the sensorium to adjust to new capacities. To exemplify: a fisherman does not sense a fishing rod, he senses a fish. The rod delivers the sense of the fish to the hand and the brain of a fishermen and thus extends the sensorial and cognitive perception of a fisherman to the fish itself.

Through this mechanism of extension, any medium, when it becomes successful and habitual, reshapes the sensory and cognitive faculties of the user to harmonize the use and maximize the utility of use. This can be characterized as the *sensory-cognitive effect* of media.

If a medium is successful, many start to use it, and the medium becomes an environmental force. It produces social changes. This is *the social effect* of media; it manifests through the changes in social institutions and rules. For example, writing led to the accumulation of records, and the accumulation of records became the accumulation of knowledge.

Both sensory-cognitive and social effects of media can be primary and secondary. For example, visual bias, the linear and sequential perception of data through inner vision, is *the primary sensory-cognitive effect* of writing. However, when writing produces a social effect in the forms of accumulated knowledge, a new environment emerges that affects sensory-cognitive perception again. Cognition needs to learn to classify records and develop the skill of classification. This is *the secondary sensory-cognitive effect* of writing.

---

[1] See: Miroshnichenko, Andrey. (2021). "Media and responsibility for their effects: instrumental vs. environmental views". *Laws*, 2021, 10(2), p. 48.

Classification that emerges out of the need to organize the storage of records also has further social effects. The classification of records, for example, leads to the classification of knowledge. Out of it, the division of science emerges as the next institutional change caused by the social effect of writing. The division of knowledge can be seen, therefore, as *the secondary social effect* of writing. In addition, stored and classified records create archives, libraries, and the entire palace-temple economy. These all are the secondary social effects of writing, too.

The systematization of the primary and secondary sensory-cognitive and social effects of media allows structuring of the ripple effects of media. It describes how exactly media cause the overlapping changes in the sensorium, cognition, and society.

The ripple effects of media can be presented through a set of interconnected definitions.

- **Primary sensory-cognitive media effect:** the use of a medium adjusts the sensorium and cognition to maximize the efficiency of this medium as an instrument.
- **Primary social media effect:** the collective instrumental use of a medium turns into an environmental force that shapes certain social institutions and rules.
- **Secondary sensory-cognitive media effect:** the environment with the changed institutions and rules requires further adjustment of the sensorial or cognitive faculties of the users who live in the environment created by the medium as an environmental force.
- **Secondary social media effect:** the environment, changed by the medium, and the additionally adjusted sensory or cognitive capacities of the users create new environmental forces and cause further readjustments of social institutions or rules.

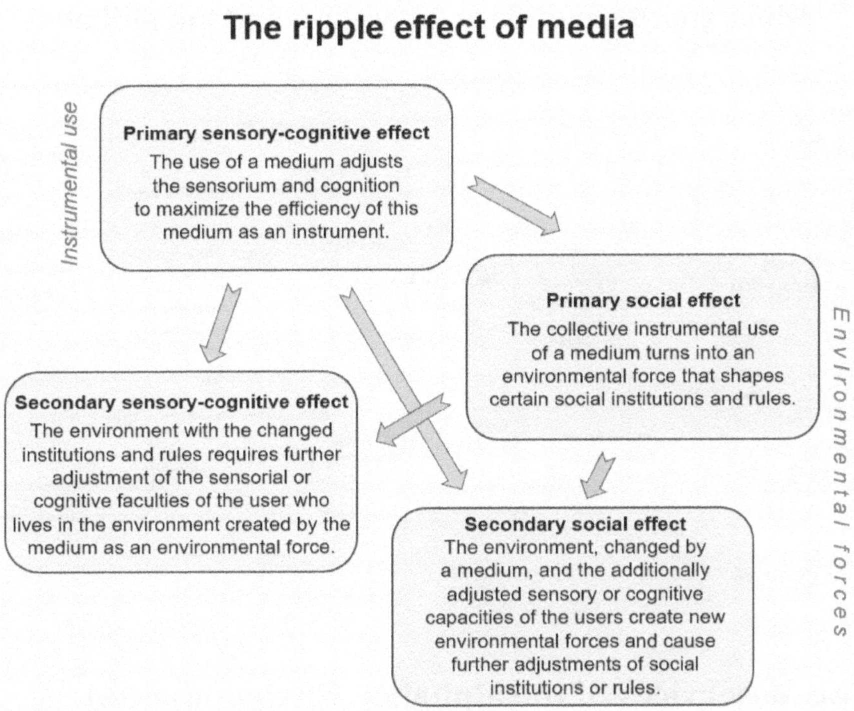

Figure 23.

Of course, the chain of effects can continue further, as the ripples of media effects can overlap again and again, but for the purpose of a simple systemization it seems sufficient to single out the primary media effects – both sensory-cognitive and social – while identifying all the subsequent effects as secondary, whether they are sensory-cognitive or social.

The taxonomy of sensory-cognitive and social media effects, primary and secondary, gives another optic for looking at the effects of writing and the alphabet, with an opportunity to identify the specific effects of the alphabet.

The sensory-cognitive and social effects, primary and secondary, of writing and the alphabet

Figure 24.

The disservices of the alphabet. Environmental withdrawal.

One of the disservices brought by any new medium is the disruption of the services provided by the old medium. Literacy not only offered new affordances but also discontinued the affordances of orality. By isolating the sense of vision and remodeling vision into a cognitive faculty, literacy disturbed the natural equilibrium of the senses.

In general, orality provided the environmental coherence of mind that kept humans within the environmental assemblage, while alphabetic literacy forced inquiring minds to disassemble reality. The result was the withdrawal of humans from the natural environment and the demise of environmental thinking. According to McLuhan, the alphabet extracted humans from "the tribal trance of resonating word magic and the web of kinship."[1]

The sensory-cognitive and social effects of the alphabet can also be seen as cognitive and social trauma. Cognitive trauma was a downside of the

[1] McLuhan, Marshall. (1994 [1964]). *Understanding Media*, p. 82.

rejection of analog thinking and magic. The revelation that things were not necessarily related to other things but could also be a physical embodiment of their own ideas shattered the habitual world into incongruent pieces in which an individual, also a shattered piece of the former tribal unity, can easily be lost. Marshall McLuhan often highlighted this when he spoke about the alphabet, such as in the passage: "It follows, of course, that literate man, when we meet him in the Greek world, is a split man, a schizophrenic, as all literate men have been since the invention of the phonetic alphabet."[1] McLuhan then quotes Bertrand Russell:

> Not all of the Greeks, but a large proportion of them, were passionate, unhappy, at war with themselves, driven along one road by the intellect and along another by the passions, with the imagination to conceive heaven and the wilful self-assertion that creates hell.[2]

The social trauma of the alphabet involved the dissolution of society based on tribal unity and kinship. This, again, can be seen as a two-sided process involving both gains and losses. Social regulation based on kinship, honour, and sacred knowledge was replaced with regulation based on codified law, economy-based stratification, and individual moral duties. In a literate society, well-being and social security became available to a larger number of people; this was one of the alphabet's affordances. But the gap in technological advancement between cultures, boosted by the alphabet, also amplified the scale of colonialist conquests and wars.

Touching upon the disservices that the alphabet brought specifically to the Greeks, Robert Logan states that the specialization and fragmentation induced by the alphabet eventually turned into tunnel vision. The separation of concept from percept ended up in abstract rationality that was often divorced not just from the environment but also from common sense. Starting with Parmenides, Greek thinkers were forced to "choose between trusting their senses and trusting logic."[3] They chose logic. As Logan puts it,

---

[1] McLuhan, Marshall. (1962). *The Guttenberg Galaxy*, p. 22.

[2] McLuhan, Marshall. (1962). *The Guttenberg Galaxy*, p. 22. The quote used by McLuhan is from: Russell, Bertrand. (1967 [1945]). History of Western Philosophy, p. 39.

[3] Logan, Robert. (2004 [1986]). *The Alphabet Effect*, p. 118.

> The abstractness of the phonetic alphabet promoted a divorce of brain and hand, a disdain of empiricism, and excessive adherence to logical rigor among Greek thinkers, each of which inhibited the development of modern science.[1]

The Greeks developed philosophy and theoretical thinking to heights that remained unparalleled through millennia until the modern day. But it came at the cost of neglecting empiric knowledge.

Logan specifically highlights that abstract logic, fostered in the Greeks by the alphabet, also prevented them from discovering zero, a fundamental concept for theoretical and practical knowledge based on calculations. As Logan explains it,

> Although Greek science contained many of the elements of modern abstract science, it took 2,000 years for a fully mathematical description of nature à la Newton to develop. Because two major factors were missing from Greek science, full flowering was held back until the European Renaissance. One factor was the lack of an experimental orientation, and the other was the absence of the concept of zero. Paradoxically, the same rational, logical way of thinking that contributed to the early development of abstract science also inhibited both these factors.
>
> The importance of zero to science is twofold. First, it led directly to a place number system (Arabic numerals) and, as a consequence, to simpler arithmetical calculations. Second, zero also encouraged the development of algebra. The Greeks precluded the possibility of inventing zero when they accepted Parmenides' arguments for the impossibility of non-being.[2]

This disdain for empiricism is evident in Plato's Allegory of the Cave. The world of sensory perception, according to Plato, represents the lowest realm inhabited by the cave prisoners who can only observe shadows on the wall. The prisoners of the empirical world assign names to the shadows but are unable to see the true world of ideal forms that cast those shadows into the darkness of the cave. These ideal forms can only be comprehended through reason, not through sensory experience.

---

1 Logan, Robert. (2004 [1986]). *The Alphabet Effect*, p. 166.

2 Logan, Robert. (2004 [1986]). *The Alphabet Effect*, pp. 117-118.

With such an ethos of abstract logic, the Greeks' brightest minds deprived themselves of any interest in technological applications. This is not to say the Greeks, Romans, and those after them did not make any technological advancements. They did, and those advancements inevitably exceeded the technologies of non-literate cultures. But the primary focus of alphabetized Greece was on the rational, not empirical, cognizing of life, the universe, and everything.

It was not until the early modern period when technological inventions and scientific discoveries from the Chinese, Indians, and the Islamic world, including printing, paper, gunpowder, the compass, and others, along with the advancements in algebra, medicine, and alchemy, began to reach Europe. These contributions merged with the rigorous logic of Greek reasoning, European technologies, and the media effects of the printing press. All together, this enabled the European breakthrough in both abstract science and applied technologies – the Technological Revolution.

The environmental withdrawal – the separation from Nature – is commonly perceived as a loss of harmony. After Rousseau, who used the stock character of "noble savage" to expose the fellow Europeans, this natural harmony has often been viewed in a romantic light as an ideal for human relations with Nature and each other. However, the natural harmony of the senses that humans possessed as a biological species did not automatically provide a harmonious or comfortable life in natural settings. Very few locations on Earth can offer a more or less safe life for humans in the wilderness without a 24/7 fight for survival. After all, the Promethean gift of technology was bestowed upon humans precisely because of the harshness of Nature – to ensure their survival.

The same holds true for the loss of social harmony: harmony as an ecological equilibrium is often confused with harmony as a desired quality of life. Social "harmony" in orality excluded any identity other than totemic or tribal identity with which everyone had to comply. The harmony of "empathic involvement"[1] also meant the total absence of personal space and constant requests for status affirmation resulted in both (and often simultaneously) caring and bullying; or, else, caring that obliges. For example, within such "empathic involvement," compulsory hospitality cannot be refused under the threat of hospitality turning into hostility.

[1] McLuhan, Marshall. (1962). *The Guttenberg Galaxy*, p. 39.

Such social "harmony" works well as a collective survival strategy, but it is not that sort of harmony that aims to please or give some sort of environmental or moral "closure".

Nevertheless, even though the environmental and social harmony of orality might often be misunderstood, the cognitive, social, and environmental balance of the preliterate mind and preliterate society was certainly disturbed by the alphabet, as always happens when a new medium takes over. The environmental withdrawal, amplified by technologies, has eventually led to catastrophic consequences, such as environmental pollution. However, it also must be noted that ecological awareness and ecological initiatives themselves are distant effects of the alphabet and a logical response to the same environmental withdrawal that led to ecological distress in the first place. Eco-movement logically emerged as a byproduct of alphabetic literacy, with its aptitude for analysis and self-reflection.

The environmental withdrawal, however, was not the only disservice of the alphabet. The alphabet also fostered a new sort of intolerance in humans – ideological intolerance.

This is not to say that hostility had not been known in preliterate cultures. Ancient narratives are full of stories of murder and genocide, along with slavery, infanticide, torture, misogyny, and other terrible things. If we compare the "culture" of violence in orality and literacy, we will find that environmental detachment made "literate violence" more technological and less physiological; it is more focused on "efficiency" and less on the physiology of pain. Conversely, orality, with its agonistic mentality, status competition, and bragging, favored the personal and "bodily" attitude toward harm and murder. Tribal collective involvement required collaborative-competitive personal devotion in everything, including bullying, animosity, and victimization. In oral violence, causing pain was not a "side-effect" of some other solutions – it was the sought solution. The inventiveness in tortures, rape, and killing was normalized into ritualistic communication of such stark ingenuity that would be seen as sadistic in a literate culture.

What was new after the introduction of the abstract absolute by the alphabet was a rationally elaborated ideological provision for violence. It was not without reason that Postman called Plato not only the "most luminous intellect" of antiquity but also "the world's first systematic fascist."[1]

The alphabet contributed to ideological intolerance through the invention of monotheism and universal principles. The very idea of the absolute is exclusive and exceptionalist. If in orality, hostility and murders were a matter of otherness or rage, alphabetic literacy added ideological intolerance to the list of "motivations" for violence.

On the other hand, the emergence of codified law instead of regulation by honour and blood kinship introduced efficient measures of controlling violence by forming a monopoly on violence and assigning it to special institutions ruled (ideally) by law. Overall, while one side-effect of the alphabet was the introduction of a new "reason" for violence, other effects eventually led to restraining violence through new regulations.

The environmental withdrawal of humans by the alphabet was reversed by electronic media – electronic media retrieved a simultaneous and spherical perception of reality. McLuhan uses the metaphor of Sputnik to show that the entire planet, as a physical space, became the space of new electronic enclosure. As he puts it,

> Perhaps the largest conceivable revolution in information occurred on October 17, 1957, when Sputnik created a new environment for the planet. For the first time the natural world was completely enclosed in a man-made container. At the moment that the earth went inside this new artifact, Nature ended and Ecology was born. "Ecological" thinking became inevitable as soon as the planet moved up into the status of a work of art.[2]

Observing the turn of Nature to Ecology by means of human technologies, McLuhan comes up with a beautiful quote:

> On Spaceship Earth there are no passengers; everybody is a member of the crew.[3]

Because of electronic media, we became the crew of Spaceship Earth in the same way as preliterate humans were the crew of the tribe enclosed in

[1] Postman, Neil. (2000 [1999]). *Building a Bridge to the 18th Century*, p. 13.

[2] McLuhan, Marshall. (1974). "At the moment of Sputnik the planet became a global theater...," p. 48.

[3] McLuhan, Marshall. (1974). "At the moment of Sputnik the planet became a global theater...," p. 50.

the situational environment and the listeners of the *Iliad* were the crew of Homer. All of them, and now us, have their part in this theatre, now the Global Theatre; the late McLuhan switched from the Global Village to the Global Theatre to underscore not just total connectivity but also "empathic involvement" and the practical engagement of everyone in the global performance. "We all are the crew on Spaceship Earth" is not so much a call for ecological action, as some think (moral calls were atypical for McLuhan), but rather an assertion of the fact that we are now enclosed in the new global environment.

The difference is that it is no longer the natural environment given to us by virtue of our biological origin. It is the technological environment, an environment induced by our alphabetic activity (as both coding and electronic media were created by the alphabetic mind).

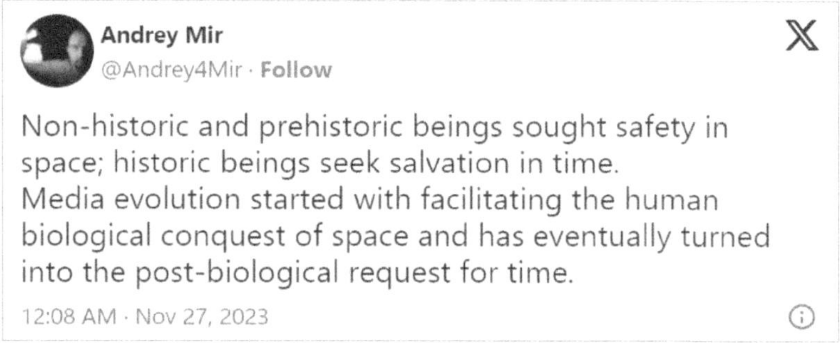

9. The mystery of Greece: the pirates and the alphabet

Pirates and the opportunistic mentality

In 20 years of the Trojan War and a drawn-out return home, Odysseus encountered more events and endured more suffering than agrarian men would have experienced in 20 generations. While Odysseus' journey back home was indeed particularly outstanding, as he found himself between a rock and a hard place of gods' favour and wrath, a high frequency and intensity of events in the life of a seafarer was not unusual. The lives of Odysseus, Sinbad the Sailor, and Robinson Crusoe were full of remarkable adventures. Odysseus was a king, Sinbad was a merchant, and Robinson was a commoner, but seafaring dragged them into ventures involving looting, the slave trade, and banditry – in one word: piracy.

For a pirate, a change of scene was an essential prerequisite of the trade. However, it wasn't just a change of scenery; it was also a change of prospects. The gains in the business could be plentiful, but the losses could also be ultimate, leading to captivity, slavery, or death. Such a variability of outcomes made the seafarer a venture capitalist investing in a risky business, where his main assets consisted of his luck and inventiveness and his stakes were his own fate and life.

Soviet philosopher Mikhail Petrov (1923–1987) advanced a theory about the role of piracy in the "Greek Miracle." In his 1966 essay *Pirates of the Aegean and Individuality*, Petrov suggested that the ancient pirates introduced a new type of mentality principally contrarian to the mentality of cultures based on irrigation.

According to Petrov, the first agrarian civilizations, including those of Ancient Egypt, Babylonia, China, and Minoan Crete, were the "Olympian civilizations," as he called them. Unlike the previous clan systems, in which tribe members received their names as professional and social instructions, the more developed agrarian societies dissociated the names-instructions from individuals, granting people a bit more freedom. Instead, the names-instructions were assigned to gods, who became responsible for various trades. The variety of gods, with their divine attributes, covered the entire spectrum of natural occurrences and human relationships.

Olympus, the mountain where the Greek gods dwelled, represented the division of labour and also the division of knowledge. As a pantheon, Olympus was, according to Petrov, "a mnemonic device that helps society orient its members in the world-cosmos and raise new generations in accordance with the legacy of the past."[1]

In other words, Olympus (or any developed pantheon of gods-specialists) served as a device of memorization, instruction, and indoctrination and was clearly another "tribal encyclopedia," as Eric Havelock called the Homeric poems just three years before Petrov wrote his essay (with Petrov, a Soviet WWII veteran and philosopher-dissident, having not a single chance to know about Havelock's existence).

Havelock, by the way, also noticed that natural and human relationships were "recorded" in the relationships of gods. He writes:

> So the gods do indeed become a kind of apparatus organised in families on the analogy of men, and they have personal attributes that remain fairly constant. For a given phenomenon, a given god becomes appropriate (though Homer shows some flexibility in his choices) and these divinities in order to be remembered with constancy themselves become incorporated in their own saga, so to speak. They love and quarrel, rule and obey, in situations and stories which imitate the human political drama. Their stories thus in turn become paradigms of the operation of the public and private law which it is the business of the saga to preserve. They constitute a second society superimposed upon the society of the heroes.[2]

Looking for an explanation for the "Greek Miracle" – the Greek Enlightenment of the 5th–3rd century BCE – Petrov tried to detect in Greece something that wouldn't conform to the rigid patterns of Olympian divine instructions. Petrov writes:

> Examining the skills of a Greek in the Homeric period, we need to exclude most of them as inherently ritualistic due to their cyclic and repetitive nature, fixed in the patterns of experience, and therefore oriented towards the past. The only exceptions are seafaring and

---

[1] Petrov, Mikhail. (1995 [1966]). *Pirates of the Aegean and Individuality*, Ch. 2.

[2] Havelock, Eric. (1963). *Preface to Plato*, p. 170-171.

> piracy. Here, repetition, rigid patterns, and a lack of originality and initiative in handling situations would be a straight way to die. In essence, each raid becomes an act of creativity, where traditional and novel approaches are combined in new ways, each time derived from the circumstances.[1]

Seafaring and piracy, therefore, were exceptions from the otherwise ritualistic division of labour in ancient societies.

Despite all irrigation civilizations belonging to the same Olympian type, Petrov contrasted the Minoan civilization of Crete with China. The distinction was "geo-political." The inland isolation of China decreased the risks of invasion; also, the centralized administration learned to deal with invasions when they occurred, as evidenced by the construction of the Great Wall some time later. Seashores, on the contrary, were open to pirates who appeared and vanished momentarily. Piracy did not require organizing large armies. A ship with 50–60 oarsmen, who were also well-trained and well-armed bandits, could easily rob a village and escape before the arrival of the regular forces.

Therefore, as Petrov writes, the Chinese statehood was "hydrotechnical": it focused on harnessing seasonal and river cycles for agriculture. Minoan statehood focused on the protection of agricultural products from looters coming by the sea. This is why the Minoan leader was a warrior, while the leading figure in Ancient China, as well as in Egypt and Babylonia, was the "minister of solar eclipses," as Petrov calls it – a high priest responsible for the due cyclicity of natural processes.

Additionally, river behaviour, the main concern of the inland civilizations, was a highly regular phenomenon. The knowledge of the past and the successful past patterns of behaviour determined success in the future. This necessarily past-based regularity was at the core of agrarian ritualism.

On the other hand, the main concern of the coastal civilization was sea behaviour. While the sea itself could be predictable to a certain extent, piracy was a highly irregular factor. Nobody could know when and where the pirates would strike again. This environmental specificity disfavored any ritualistic cyclicity and rituals in general. Piracy, according to Petrov, was the only trade that could not be ritualized. The irregularity of piracy

---

[1] Petrov, Mikhail. (1995 [1966]). *Pirates of the Aegean and Individuality*, Ch. 6.

affected the mentality of both coastal dwellers and the pirates themselves. Moreover, they were often the same people: the defender of a seashore village against pirates could easily go on a pirate raid the next month.

Minos, the semi-legendary ruler of Crete, was reportedly the first historical figure to build a navy; he was also known for suppressing piracy. However, some accounts suggest that these so-called efforts to suppress piracy were rather attempts to simply regulate it. Sea nations would make treaties not to raid the shores and ships of each other. Otherwise, occasional or professional piracy was a usual occupation of seafarers. The kings in the Homeric poems habitually bragged about past raids and rich booty.

The innovative state of mind was the distinctive feature of people living at sea and by the sea. Petrov notices that inventive Odysseus could plot, with equal facility, the capture of Troy with the use of a giant wooden horse, the escape from the Cyclops by tying himself and his men under the bellies of the Cyclops' rams, and the killing of Penelopa's suitors after a contest manifesting his true king's right. Along the way, Odysseus would not forget to steal some rams and goats from the Cyclops.

The common epithet for Odysseus was "cunning"; his cleverness was often highlighted. In Greek, however, the main quality of Odysseus was referred to as *polytropos*, which meant not so much "smart" or "clever" but "of many turns." The intellectual qualities the Greeks valued in Odysseus were his outstanding inventiveness and versatility, his ability to elaborate a winning strategy for an unprecedent task.

Thus, the repetitive nature of inland life and the adventurous character of life at sea contributed to the formation of ritualistic or opportunistic mindsets, respectively. The virtue of the agrarian mind was following tradition, while the virtue of the seafaring mind was versatility and opportunism.

This wasn't solely a matter of choice or cultural legacy; such were the environmental affordances of life inland or on shore. The environmental affordances of coastal and inland living were both natural and technological. The natural affordances were formed either by inland isolation or by seashore openness. The technological affordances were formed either by season-based agrarian technologies or by the technologies of sea travel.

In Innis' terms, irrigation civilizations were time-biased, as they sought to preserve successful patterns of the past over time, while sea civilizations were space-biased, as it was "afforded" for them to explore new opportunities overseas, and the temporal parameter of cyclicity did not play a significant role.

Coastal and inland cultures

Natural environmental affordance	Technological environmental affordance	Time-space bias	Type of mentality
Coastal setting, openness to "the other"	Technologies of navy transportation and warfare	Space-biased	Opportunistic, agile, innovative
Inland setting, comparative isolation	Technologies of seasonal agriculture (such as river control) – repetitive and cyclical	Time-biased	Conservative, tradition-based, ritualistic

Figure 25.

The division between continental and coastal mentalities can fuel large geopolitical theories, such as a conspiracy theory about the perpetual conflict between "Atlanticism" and "Eurasianism," popular among Russian conspiracists ranging from the émigré Nikolai Trubetzkoy in the 1920s to Alexandr Dugin, an alleged ideologist within Putin's regime. Some Western geopolitical theorists, like Zbigniew Brzezinski with his "geostrategics"[1], also expressed compatible ideas. According to this theory, for example, the astute Atlanticists deliberately pitted two major inland powers, Germany and Russia, against each other in both World Wars. The Cold War can also be seen as a continuation of the conflict between Atlanticism (the coastal mentality) and Eurasianism (the inland mentality).

Signs of the opposition between continental-ritualistic and coastal-opportunistic mentalities can be traced even in American elections: the

[1] See, for example: Brzezinski, Zbigniew. (1997). *The Grand Chessboard: American Primacy and Its Geostrategic Imperatives.*

inland so-called "square states" lean more towards traditions and conservatism, while the "coastal states" tend to be more progressive.

The ancient Greeks belonged to coastal cultures and leaned towards the opportunistic mentality developed by seafarers and pirates.

Pirates and horses

Interestingly, the versatility of the pirates parallels the opportunism of the Eurasian Steppe horse riders. The people of the Steppe lived deep inland and therefore might have been expected to exhibit a "continental" mentality. However, their primary occupation – herding – was not as cyclical as farming. Most significantly, the domestication of horses in the 4th millennium BCE made them fast moving nomadic herders.

Horse riding allowed for the herding of larger flocks across larger territories. The climate was changing: the Steppe was becoming drier, compelling herders to move more actively across greater distances in search of better pastures. Consequently, the ability to travel faster and over larger expanses increased the frequency of encounters with "the other" and others. New horizons widened the spectrum of opportunities and opened new avenues for migration and economic strategies. The conditions were somewhat similar to that of the sea. The introduction of the wheel further intensified the military application of horses: chariots appeared. Alongside the increased contacts with others, the technologies of horse riding and the wheel created, for the Steppe people, once peaceful herders, the affordances of militarism and banditry. These affordances pushed the Steppe herders to become inland pirates.

In the 2nd and 1st millennia BCE, Eurasian nomads radiated outward from the Great Steppe in all directions, reaching Europe, India, and the Near East. This historical expansion is evident in the proliferation of Indo-European languages, horse riding, and chariots. The invasive opportunistic mentality of horse riders clashed with the indigenous ritualistic mentality of the first agrarian civilizations with their palace economies. This led or contributed to the so-called Late Bronze Age collapse of civilizations everywhere from India (Harappan civilization of the Indus valley, 2500–1700 BCE), to the Hittites in Anatolia (1600–1200 BCE), the Minoans of Crete (3500–1100 BCE), and others.

Perhaps upon their arrival in the East Mediterranean, the Eurasian horse riders adopted a new means for raids and migration – ships. This could potentially explain the appearance of the so-called "Sea Peoples," a wave of invaders of unknown origin who attacked the shores of the East Mediterranean during the late Bronze Age (1300–1000 BCE).

The Mycenaeans (1750–1050 BCE), who were likely a part of this migration process, adopted the palace culture from the Minoans. However, they themselves were unable to withstand the global turmoil of raiding and piracy they likely contributed to. Raiders overthrew palaces everywhere. Opportunism beat rituals, stability was swallowed by chaos, and space-biased strategies disrupted the time-biased consistency of the ancient civilizations.[1]

The early agrarian civilizations of Sumer, Egypt, and Minoan were driven, both literally and symbolically, by oxen, an agrarian medium. The murals of Knossos, the Minoan capital of Crete (which I enjoyed observing myself), are centered around oxen in a style reminiscent of Egyptian or Sumerian. However, sometime during the transition from the Minoan to Mycenaean civilization, the totemic monopoly of oxen over the Mediterranean was interrupted by horses. The culture of the Mycenaeans was replete with horses, as witnessed by Homer. The subsequent Greek, Assyrian, and Roman cultures followed suit. Zeus still occasionally turned into a bull, but Heracles was already raised by a centaur,[2] a half-man, half-horse creature.

Horses and ships happened to be different media with similar media effects. The nomad-making power of horses was transformed into the pirate-making power of ships. Apart from literally being embarked on ships, horses became ships. In terms of media ecology, when the Steppe people reached the Mediterranean, ships became horses 2.0, and the sea became a new Steppe.

Both horses and ships gave their masters opportunistic ("tip-and-run") superiority over sedentary cultures. Both horses and ships were the media of extended discovery and conquest that fostered the masculine culture of

---

[1] Except Egypt and the Assyrian Empire in Mesopotamia – they survived but were weakened, which gave more autonomy and space for the advance of some younger and less rigid (less "palace") cultures, such as the Phoenicians, for example.

[2] Paradoxically, the Greek word κένταυρος contains the root *tauros* – bull, though it might specify rather gender attribution.

war, robbery, enslaving, agility, and military-political brotherhood with respective heroico-tragic epics.

Many sources point to close associations between horses and ships in the late ancient Mediterranean cultures. Poseidon was the god of the sea, earthquakes, *and*, somehow, horses. He patrolled the sea on a horse-drawn chariot. The Phoenicians, the Mediterranean's finest seafarers, built their ships with horseheads on the bows: their ships were totemized into horses. There is even a theory that the Trojan Horse was actually a ship. It was a common tradition to offer retribution to local gods after a retreat in a war, and the retreating Achaeans leaving behind a ship with a horsehead would make much more sense than a giant wooden horse. This could explain why the Trojans so routinely "accepted" the gift on behalf of their gods, as they were also familiar with the tradition.[1]

The invasion of Eurasians was an ethnic migration, but the transformation of nomadism into piracy reflected a sort of media migration. When nomadism-turned-piracy proved its military superiority and economic efficiency, this technology began spreading on its own, across nationalities, by involving more people in practicing it.

This double strike of ethnic and media migrations ended several palace civilizations in the North-East Mediterranean. In Greece, the Late Bronze Age collapse led to the Dark Age (1100 to 750 BCE), roughly the period between the Trojan War and Homer.[2] The Dark Age in Greece was marked by the reign of piracy and political chaos but also by the vague memory of the great palace cultures of the past, with the beautiful but abandoned ruins that triggered imagination and provoked fantasies about gods and heroes, supported also by the incredibly rich oral tradition, that culminated in Homer. The Greeks forgot writing and returned to primary orality, but with a strong pirate-opportunistic state of mind, which was rather unusual

---

[1] The theory of the Trojan Horse as a ship is based on the fact that the Homeric poems do not provide explicit descriptions of the Trojan Horse. Instead, the detailed narrative of a wooden horse as a gift to the Trojans is found in the *Aeneid*, a composition by Virgil that dates many centuries later. It is possible that the *Aeneid* contains a poeticized misreading of the "historical" events that developed into a fascinating story about the wooden horse. This theory was advanced by Italian scholar Francesco Tiboni and others; see, for example: Burger, John. (2018). "The Trojan Horse might not be what you think it was." *Aleteia*.

[2] In India, the period between the urban Harappan civilization of the Indus Valley and the second urbanization in the Ganges Plain lasted, roughly, from 1700 to 600 BCE and ended just in time for Jaspers' Axial Age.

for the orality of highly ritualistic agrarian cultures in which writing emerged.

The nomadic opportunism of the horse riders and the Odyssean versatility of seafarers and pirates might have played a significant role in the incredibly rapid adoption of the alphabet by the Greeks. After all, it is known for sure that the phonetic script of the Phoenicians was delivered to Greece by sea.

Pirates and the tragic spirit

As previously discussed, the life of agrarian people was a repetitive cycle of prescribed activities. They were instructed by rituals on what to do each season or even each day. This does not mean that their lives were easy; however, everything that might happen was normalized by rituals. An agrarian individual could live his or her entire life without experiencing any unexpected event.

A nomad, on the contrary, could not rely on pre-established routines. Making choices to navigate unfamiliar situations was "business as usual" for nomads. Wrong choices led to disastrous outcomes. The possibility of dramatic and tragic developments always loomed as a real probability in the life of a nomad. Coupled with the constant pressure of individual decision-making, this contributed to the emergence of the "tragic spirit," as Jaspers called it, in nomadic people.

Looking for a possible cause for the Axial Age to begin, Jaspers considered the so-called equestrian theory – the arrival of the Steppe horse riders to all the key Axial regions. Indeed, the introduction of the opportunistic and tragic mentality of nomads into the ritualistic and traditionalist agrarian lifestyle was disruptive. After the nomadic invasion, agrarian people recognized that the old rituals, the foundation of routine and safety, could no longer ensure their security. The priests, their armies, and their gods might not be able to provide reliable protection. People revealed, in frustration, that they were exposed to the ups and downs of fate. An individual tasted a bit of, not individualism yet – individualism came later with literacy – but autonomy, mostly the autonomy of suffering. Jaspers writes:

> Here the conception of that autonomy is now elevated to a plane where the soul attains its full self-realization in the power to think and to know. This is its supreme faculty; in the last resort its only one. Man is "a thinking reed".[1]

This is how the expectation of the unexpected in nomadic consciousness could transform, after clashing with the rituals and knowledge of agrarian cultures, into thinking about the meaning of life, which can be seen as a key feature of the Axial Age.

The tragic spirit brought by the nomads found especially fertile soil in Greece. There, the tragic spirit was elevated from a form of frustration to a sense of heroic self-actualization and the noblest dramatic genre. The classical reading posits that the genre of tragedy represents the conflict between feelings and duties, between desire and destiny. Tragedy highlighted the principal unresolvedness of life for a concrete heroic character. By no means could reality "coagulate into a dogmatic fixity of definitive institutions and notions, neither into life under a caste-system nor into life under a cosmic order," Jaspers writes.[2] Tragedy shattered dogma and ritual.

For their tragedies, the Greeks used the stories from their myths but reshaped them in a way that put the tragic occurrences with heroes front and center. In tragedies, epic stories were no longer "articles" from the "tribal encyclopedia." They rather became explorations of human solitude and contemplations of human destiny. As Jaspers puts it,

> Still creating myths out of the primeval substance of tradition, and rendering them more profound in the image, the tragic poets, despite the fact that they drew their intuition from original sources, lived by questioning and interpreting. They heightened the content and were on the road to its dissolution. They were the creators of the most profoundly significant configurations of the myth, and at the same time of the end of the myth as all-embracing truth.[3]

He concludes: "Greek tragedy stands at the transition from myth to philosophy."[4]

---

[1] Jaspers, Karl. (2021 [1949]). *The Origin and Goal of History*, p. 205

[2] Jaspers, Karl. (2021 [1949]). *The Origin and Goal of History*, p. 75.

[3] Jaspers, Karl. (2021 [1949]). *The Origin and Goal of History*, p. 270.

[4] Jaspers, Karl. (2021 [1949]). *The Origin and Goal of History*, p. 270.

But why Greece? Songs with various forms of grievance and even the tragic spirit were known to all other cultures. Why were the Greeks the ones who refined the tragic spirit into tragedies, the examples of which have remained unparalleled up to the present day?

The answer is piracy.

A seafarer, especially a militant seafarer – a pirate – had to be prepared to face a radical "shift of fate," as Petrov called it.[1] Death or enslavement were the flip side of the trade. The high probability of such "eschatological moments" created a "psychological tension" that fostered "strong feelings," according to Petrov. He implies that the Greek mentality was affected by this constant expectation of the "shift of fate" underlying life on the shore and at sea.

The Greeks distilled the pure tragedy out of the tragic spirit and embodied it in a genre that did not aim to recite a tribal instruction but rather used heroic characters and events to deliver the purified tragic emotion – what Petrov referred to as the "strong feeling" of "eschatological moments." The purified tragic emotions were supposed to lead to catharsis and the comprehension of the eternally unresolved conflict between essence and existence, to use the terms of the 20th century's French existentialism. Recognition of this conflict was a part of fostering the noble spirit in an individual, a phenomenon that attracted Shakespeare, Dostoevsky, Nietzsche, London, Sartre, and many others, proving Jaspers' idea that the Axial Age created universals in which we continue to think.

The genre of tragedy formed and reached its exemplary form in Classic Greece (the 5th – 4th century BCE). Tragedies were composed in poetic meter and theatrically performed and thus followed the oral tradition. However, they were written before performing, and thus they were written compositions. This is how piracy met the alphabet – via tragedy that emphasized human autonomy through the struggle with destiny.

Piracy and the alphabet

Despite all the similarities between pirates and nomads, there is an aspect that distinguishes them. However adventurous and dangerous a nomad's life could be, it was impossible for him or her to remain alone for a

[1] Petrov, Mikhail. (1995 [1966]). *Pirates of the Aegean and Individuality*, Ch. 6.

long time. Even if an individual was abandoned or expelled by their tribe, or captured and enslaved by another tribe, he or she would inevitably become part of a new collective.

Being lost at sea radically differs from being lost in the steppe or forest. At sea, there's always the possibility of ending up on a desert island or an abandoned ship or sailing a boat alone. All the exemplary pirates/seafarers – Odysseus, Sinbad, Robinson Crusoe, even Jack Sparrow – find themselves completely alone at some point in their lives. For days, months, or even years.

The prospect of being caught in complete solitude added to the tragedism of the seafaring mentality. But it also tested the resourcefulness of a seafarer and mobilized his ingenuity. The "probabilistic affordance," so to speak, of complete isolation provided by sea was the ultimate trial of an individual's autonomy and universalism.

Nomads, with all their opportunism and autonomy of choices, remained collective beings that counted on the presence of others, whether friendly or hostile. Seafarers had to possess universal skills that could be required for survival when nobody was around. For Odysseus to be *polytropos* meant not only to be opportunistic but also self-reliant. Odysseus was capable not only of savvy political games but also of ruling the kingdom and ploughing the soil. He was well-versed in cattle husbandry and dairy production. He knew cooking and medicine. He single-handedly built a boat and navigated the sea back home completely alone after losing all his men. Most importantly, he was morally ready to encounter all these tasks and challenges on his own. Athena sympathized and helped him, but there was also Poseidon, whose wrath neutralized her divine support, causing Odysseus endless problems at sea. All in all, no matter what games the gods play, a seafarer has to rely on himself.

Even if not all sailors can actually end up in solitary adversity, the level of autonomy and universalism of a seafarer is incomparable to that of an inland inhabitant. As Petrov puts it,

> In a typical "Olympian" civilization, there were no situations in which a man, willingly or not, needed to accumulate universal skills, reflect on his own fate, and manage his life on his own.[1]

[1] Petrov, Mikhail. (1995 [1966]). *Pirates of the Aegean and Individuality*, Ch. 6.

The seafaring Minoan civilization of Crete and the succeeding Mycenaean civilization, with their leaning toward piracy, consisted of individuals with such a level of autonomy and universalism that was unparalleled at the time. Petrov highlights that the Cretan-Mycenaean[1] statehood was the first in the history of humankind that pirates-explorers devised as a system that formed "men-states" – self-determining and well-rounded individuals possessing individual civic virtues.[2]

In a sense, piracy had a similar effect of individualization as writing – but piracy came first. This is why Petrov's essay is titled *Pirates of the Aegean and Individuality*. Petrov explores the effect of piracy on forming the autonomous mentality, comparing it to the effect of literacy.

Quite in tune with Havelock and Ong (and practically at the same time: Havelock – 1963, Petrov – 1966, Ong – 1967, 1982), Petrov analyzes the transformation of consciousness under the development of writing from the bureaucratic craft of the few (Havelock's "craft literacy") to the literacy of many. In the Cretan-Mycenaean epoch, writing was integrated into the palace management and had not yet revealed the "blind creative power of text," as Petrov writes. During the Greek Dark Age (1100–750 BCE), palace writing was abandoned and forgotten. But then the alphabet triggered the explosion of literacy. "Writing transformed from a registry craft into an individual-universal skill – a written speech," as Petrov sees it. "The Greeks were forced into the position of compulsory creativity."[3] This is where the similarity with piracy transpires.

Since Petrov was not translated in English, it is worth giving an extended quote from his 1966 *Pirates of the Aegean and Individuality* that shows his advanced understanding of media ecology before the term itself was even introduced by Postman in 1969. On the transition of writing from bureaucratic registry in temples-palaces to the individual skill of written speech, Petrov comments:

> The enormity of this event is evident; all other cultural revolutions fade in comparison, as this is not about, for example, imparting in everyone the skill of swimming across medium-sized rivers, but

[1] Petrov belonged to the tradition that saw the Mycenaean civilization as Cretan-Mycenaean, implying that the younger Mycenaeans from mainland Greece subjugated the older Minoan culture of Crete Island and borrowed much from its palace culture, thus becoming factually the "Cretan-Mycenaean" civilization.

[2] Petrov, Mikhail. (1995 [1966]). *Pirates of the Aegean and Individuality*, Ch. 6.

[3] Petrov, Mikhail. (1995 [1966]). *Pirates of the Aegean and Individuality*, Ch. 1.

> about instilling in each person an individual attitude towards reality – an attitude principally original and distinct from others. Writing, as a universal individual skill – as literacy – is inherently a blind creative force that mobilizes the entire population of the literates, whether they want it or not, for theoretical creation.[1] Literacy sets up minds in mutual non-conformity and mismatching, forbids them to repeat each other, and requires each literate mind to produce a new text, a new opinion on any subject that has already been touched upon by the opinions of others. The transition of writing into literacy signifies an automatic transition to a new psychological disposition, a disposition toward seeking novelty, for each literate mind now has to identify the pre-existed attitudes towards reality, reject them as a-priory false or incomplete, and elaborate its own views completing "truth" – meaning constantly being in a creative mode of analysis of the present and a synthesis of the new.
>
> In this way emerges private ownership over thought and its products: theoretical relationships with the world. This private ownership over thought monopolizes the right of truth-seeking and becomes an aggressive-creative mental force incapable of being satisfied by any existing theoretical system, constantly suspecting that truth – ultimate certainty – lies somewhere beyond the established system of relationships, beyond ritual. A never-ending ancient discord, the Hobbesian "war of all against all," bursts out, in which the only victor is social memory which absorbs all newly arriving texts, meaning new theories of the world, unless it is trimmed or fenced by a Great Wall of censorship or policing measures such as the canonization of texts into a sacred scripture.[2]

After the transition from a craft to a skill, a former bureaucratic nature of writing transformed into a "civic" feature of a writing individual, according to Petrov. This civic feature happened to be also quite a restless and aggressive source of societal turbulence. Instead of social regulation by the pre-established ritualistic mechanisms managed by temples-palaces, it became possible and inevitable to constantly balance the living social organism with the active participation of autonomous and universal citizens. Petrov points out that one of the main concerns of the classic Greek philosophical thought was fostering civic virtues not in a prince but in an ordinary citizen.

---

[1] Essentially, Petrov here describes the concept of *affordance*, knowing nothing about Gibson, who coined the term and the word "affordance" in the very same year – 1966.

[2] Petrov, Mikhail. (1995 [1966]). *Pirates of the Aegean and Individuality*, Ch. 1.

The very concept of citizenry emerged. People were recognized as "equally gifted and equally competent" to such degree that political positions in Athens were filled at some point by sortition, not election: the Athenians were concerned that elections could be corrupted by oligarchs, while the random appointment of officials by a lottery (resembling the selection of jurors nowadays) would preserve the political system from the influence of oligarchs. But such a system also meant that literally every citizen was deemed to be autonomous and competent enough to fulfill political duties on behalf of the polis.[1] Each free Greek was expected to be a *polytropos* – an Odysseus – in civic matters.

Petrov calls this transition "Ariadne's thread in our journey in the labyrinth of the Mediterranean from Minos to Solon." The autonomy and universalism of the seafarers and pirates, already unusual for the times when human agency was often delegated to gods and rituals, turned into the civic autonomy and universalism of the Greek citizens, exceptional then and no less today.

Piracy prepared the Greek minds for the effects of the alphabet. This might explain why the alphabet effect in Greece was so instant and so transformative. The Greeks were ready for the alphabet. The rapid adoption of the alphabet itself was a result of this same preparedness.

Direct clash between orality and the alphabet

It took thousands of years for writing to develop from pictograms to logograms and syllabaries with phonetic elements in Egypt, Mesopotamia, and China. But in Greece, due to the effect of borrowing, orality jumped right to the alphabet in the period between the 8th and the 5th centuries BCE. That is why, perhaps, Greece gave the purest examples of those transformations that Jaspers ascribed to the Axial Age.

In the oral tradition, huge psychic energy was directed to the creation and reproduction of formulaic expressions. With the advance of writing,

[1] This reminds one of Walter Lippmann's objections against the "romantic view of democracy" in his 1922 *Public Opinion*. In fact, as Lippmann insisted, people are not omnicompetent in civic matters – they are rather shortsighted and rarely know anything beyond their daily routine. Therefore, a special political class of communication experts is needed to guide both people and politicians and "manufacture consent" in society.

and especially the alphabet, this energy was released and redirected to attend to a completely different matter. If a bard shaped “mental images” to fit rhythm and metre, a writing author chose words so that their meaning would fit a concept. After Plato, who was one of the first to write in prose, nobody cared about the rhythmic properties of words. What the author cared about was whether the word had the right meaning that represented the right idea. The psychic energy was directed from the form to the content and, most importantly, from preserving the old to creating the new.

However, between the bard and the author, there were the priest-administrator and the scribe who recorded events but not speech. They recorded reality but were not yet creating it. Pre-phonetic writing did not dismantle rituals but empowered them. The first writing systems served the temples-palaces and themselves tended to turn into sacred rituals (the Greek word “hieroglyph” means “*sacred* carving <on stone>”). The ritualistic potential of early pictography smoothed and mitigated the transition from the oral to the literate state of mind in the “normal,” sequential process of writing’s development.

The Dark Age destroyed the Aegean palace cultures and relieved Greece from a “historical necessity” to develop its own writing as a sacred craft. As Harold Innis puts it,

> Greece escaped the problem of worship of the written word which had embarrassed oriental empires. The delay in the introduction of writing until possibly as late as the beginning of the seventh century, the difficulties of securing large and regular supplies of papyrus from Egypt, and the limitations of stone as a medium combined to protect the oral tradition. No energy was lost in learning a second language and monopolies of knowledge could not be built around a complex script.[1]

The Greeks forgot the Linear A and Linear B scripts used by the Minoans and Myceneans and at once encountered a highly developed phonetic script. Their oral culture was the first to directly collide with the alphabet. Somewhere between 700 and 550 BCE, the Homeric poems were “committed to writing,” as Havelock calls it in “The Alphabetization of Homer.” “It was something like a thunder-clap in human history… It laid

[1] Innis, Harold. (2008 [1951]). *The Bias of Communication*, p. 41.

the basis for the destruction of the oral way of life and the oral modes of thought," he writes.[1]

Since Greece avoided the lengthy development of its own writing system, the changes brought by the alphabet were incredibly rapid and traumatizing. The Greeks managed to survive, perhaps because of the opportunistic mentality developed by seafarers and pirates. They adopted the alphabet and made a new tool of exploration out of it. They even reworked the mental and cultural trauma resulting from the sudden alphabetization of orality into tragedy and philosophy. Plato's recognition of the archaic nature of the Homeric mind was part of a culture-wide psychotherapeutic process led by a cohort of exceptional thinkers who were awakened by the alphabet, precisely in the sense of the Jaspersian awakening of humankind in the Axial Age.

The phantom literacy of Homer

All Homeric scholars tripped over an element of the *Iliad* that should not be there – the Catalogue of Ships.

For decades, scholars debated if a catalogue can be part of an oral tradition at all. Walter Ong, who was also puzzled by the Catalogue of Ships, writes: "Orality knows no lists or charts or figures."[2] Perhaps only the genealogy of gods and nobles could have been preserved in oral tradition through sorting out, though it would have been more like a chanted story than a list per se: "Abraham begat Isaac; and Isaac begat Jacob; and Jacob begat Judas and his brethren..." The cataloguing of reality is a function of a bureaucrat, not a bard. The catalogue is a product of writing, more specifically, the product of bureaucratic registry.

A bureaucratic catalogue typically does not contain sentences with regular syntax. Its logic dictates it to be a list of nouns. The elements in the list do not form a syntagmatic sequence and cannot be narrated as a story in oral speech. In the meantime, according to Havelock, in oral tradition all things and characters *do* something, they cannot just *be*. This is needed for memorization and affectation – things and heroes need to be embedded in action; otherwise, there is no *story*-telling. In a catalogue, items just *are*.

[1] Havelock, Eric. (1978). "The alphabetization of Homer," p. 3.

[2] Ong, Walter. (2002 [1982]). *Orality and Literacy*, p. 96.

They are listed, and there is no need for them to do anything. The very presence of an item in the list stood for its predicate.

The Catalogue of Ships in the *Iliad* contains a list of 29 contingents from different Greek lands sailing to the war with Troy. The scholars counted that these 29 contingents with 46 captains represent more than 1100 ships with more than 140,000 warriors. This is basically a "constitutional" register of the Greek confederation.

Puzzled by the appearance of such a "bureaucratically" detailed catalogue in an oral epic, Havelock assumes that Homer might have been familiar with the original Mycenaean document, the muster list of lands whose kings and warlords must stand under the hand of High King Agamemnon of Mycenae in a war.

Havelock suggested that Homer reworked the list into syntax-fitting oral storytelling. Each contingent is represented through the short stories of their leaders with accounts of their ancestry, the descriptions of the procedure of embarkment or sailing. As Havelock puts it, "The summons to war and the Mycenaean muster list turn partly into a sailors' guide to the Aegean as it was perhaps about 700 b.c."[1] This way, the listed *beings* of items was turned into their *doings*, as was appropriate for oral syntax.

Even if Homer did not see the muster list himself, he must have been familiar with this kind of registration of reality, which is a direct product of palatial bureaucratic writing. This means that the orality of Homer was not so much innocently "primary orality". According to Ong, primary orality is "that of persons totally unfamiliar with writing."[2] It appears Homer might have been familiar with writing or at least with its product, a catalogue.

The *Iliad* also contains a direct mention of writing. The poem tells the story of prince Bellerophon. A king, whose wife fell in love with Bellerophon, sent the prince away, to his father-in-law, and give him "baneful tokens, graving in a folded tablet many signs and deadly"[3] – a secret letter to the father-in-law with the suggestion to kill the prince. Although this is the only direct mention of writing in the poem, it allows the record to be set straight: Homer was aware of writing.

---

[1] Havelock, Eric. (1963). *Preface to Plato*, p. 123.

[2] Ong, Walter. (2002 [1982]). *Orality and Literacy*, p. 6.

[3] Homer, *Iliad*, Book 6, 167-170.

Seeking to explain the Greek mystery, Havelock hypothesizes that Greek orality in the Late Bronze Age developed in parallel with the writing of the dying Mycenean palaces. This fact must not "obscure the vital importance of the oral technology both in the Mycenaean age and after," as Havelock suggests. The systems of writing at the time were "very clumsy weapons of communication."[1] He highlights that they were "too specialised to serve general social needs."[2] But even this clumsy Mycenean script had died out, and so Greeks were forced to perfect their mastery in acoustic, verbal, and musical rhythms. In Havelock's view, "Their supposed disadvantage in the competition for culture, namely their non-literacy, was in fact their prime advantage."[3] The importance of oral efficiency made eloquence and poetic skills a political virtue pursued by all Homeric heroes. All this reasoning allows Havelock to draw a conclusion:

> We can hazard the guess, in short, that that specific and unique Hellenic intelligence, the source or cause of which has baffled all historians, received its original nurture in communities in which the oral technique of preserved communication threw power and so prestige into the hands of the orally more gifted. It made the competition for power, endemic among all human beings, identifiable with the competition for intelligence. The total non-literacy of Homeric Greece, so far from being a drawback, was the necessary medium in which the Greek genius could be nursed to its maturity.[4]

All of this is undoubtedly true. But what does it have to do with the Greeks' uniqueness? In all oral cultures, eloquence is always associated with intelligence and thus brings social capital and is used in the competition for power.

The uniqueness of the Homeric mind was not in its orality but, on the contrary, in its residual literacy, inherited from the Mycenaean palaces with their bureaucratic writing (Linear B). The residue was very weak, almost faded, so it can be called *phantom literacy* – the phantom literacy of Homer. It formally displayed itself in the Catalogue of Ships and the mention of writing in Bellerophon's story. But most importantly, it carried

[1] Havelock, Eric. (1963). *Preface to Plato,* p. 118.

[2] Havelock, Eric. (1963). *Preface to Plato,* p. 118.

[3] Havelock, Eric. (1963). *Preface to Plato,* p. 128.

[4] Havelock, Eric. (1963). *Preface to Plato,* p. 127.

on the millennial cultural legacy of the palace cultures represented in a highly elaborated pantheon of gods, very atypical for a "primary-oral" culture.[1]

Olympus – the tribal wikipedia of the Greeks

All mythological systems start with the natural elements: earth, heavens, winds, waters, fire and so on. The older deities in Egyptian, Sumerian, Greek and many other theogonies are the primary elements representing the natural forces.

With the development of imagination and symbolical culture, the divine morphed into totemic forms. More concrete metaphors of spiritual animistic ancestors emerged that would connect people with noble living creatures, such as wolves, bears, eagles, and so on.

Further symbolic development led to anthropomorphizing: gods appeared. They were, essentially, human-like persons with divine abilities and responsibilities. Human-like gods created nuclear and extended families and, eventually, formed the divine society. This stage of gods' civilizational development mirrored the human stage of palace civilization. For gods to have Olympus, humans needed to have palaces.

The Greek pantheon, Olympus and its cosmic outskirts (Hades, seas, pastures, and so on), enveloped all the theogony in 4–5 generations of deities. The oldest ones, the primeval deities, represent natural elements: Chaos, Erebus (darkness), Gaia (earth), Uranus (Sky), Tartarus (underworld), Eros and some others. The next generation are Titans – they are a sort of pagan, pre-civilized deities or still some derivative natural

---

[1] The true mystery of Homer, in fact, lies not in the Catalogue of Greek Ships but in the Trojan Battle Order. Homer mirrored the Mycenaean muster list with the catalogue of Trojan commanders and allies, though less extensive. It is probable that Homer saw the muster list of the Mycenaeans 300 plus years after the war or heard about it. But could he see the registry lists of both fighting sides? It is very unlikely. Theoretically, knowing about one catalogue, he could have grasped the idea and created the second one. However, the factual material, the list of the actual Trojan contingents, would have needed to be passed to him through oral tradition. While oral tradition can depict the might of both warring parties in an epic, can it do so with such bureaucratic detail? How did the Greeks manage to do that? Anyway, the presence of such complex catalogues in the epic suggests that Homer was familiar with the format of bureaucratic registries. Coupled with the mention of a tablet in Bellerophon's story, the hypothesis stands: Homer was aware of writing, and his orality was not so much innocently "primary" orality.

elements (such as Cronus – time). Then follows the third divine generation, the "civilized" gods that have their palatial society with Zeus at the helm. They also beget many other divine creatures, which may represent minor natural forces (such as nymphs, for example) or mythic characters (such as cyclopes or centaurs), and also semi-gods and immortal heroes. This very diverse population of the immortals absorbed all the derivations of the previous and current divine history of antiquity. It all was ruled from the palace, Olympus, by king-god Zeus.

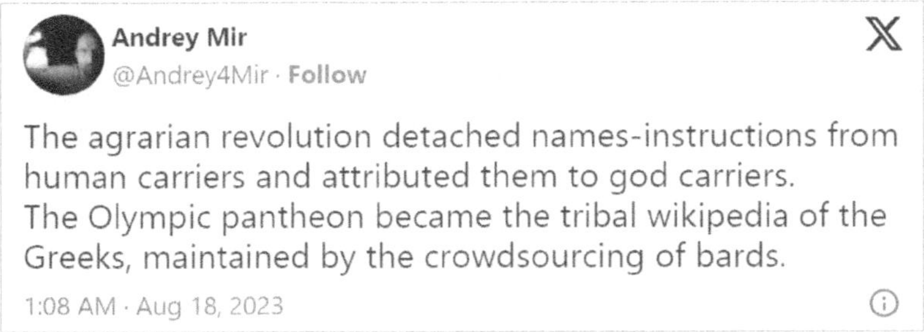
Andrey Mir
@Andrey4Mir · Follow

The agrarian revolution detached names-instructions from human carriers and attributed them to god carriers.
The Olympic pantheon became the tribal wikipedia of the Greeks, maintained by the crowdsourcing of bards.

1:08 AM · Aug 18, 2023

Petrov called Olympus a "mnemonic device." Through the gods-specialists and their relationships, Olympic mythology contained all cosmic, metaphysic, scientific, social, and professional knowledge and instructions.[1] If the Homeric poems were, according to Havelock, the tribal encyclopedia, then Olympus was the *tribal wikipedia* of the Greeks. It not only contained all possible knowledge and instructions, but it was also crowdsourced and properly maintained by the best experts: the priests, bards, and wisemen constantly revisited and rewrote it in the process of reciting and preserving.

The Olympian type of culture and, respectively, the Olympian state of mythology were common for agrarian – or palace – civilizations, including Ancient Egypt, Babylonia, Egypt, Minoan, and others. The unique quality of the oral Greeks in the Dark Age (1100–750 BCE) was that they had a palatial-level Olympian mythology without having a "proper" palatial civilization. The preceding palatial and written culture, that of the Mycenaeans, had already sunk in the Lethe long ago before Homer, leaving him without writing – with alleged "primary orality." But the content of the

[1] This Olympian polytheism of oral mythology was preserved, to some extent, in the Christian institutions of apostles, archangels, and saints. They have different magic duties, being "saint patrons" to something or somebody. Their names kept fulfilling the function of names-instructions typical for oral and polytheistic tradition.

Homeric message was Mycenaean, and his primary orality turned out to be not very "primary."

It was not the Catalogue of Ships or the mention of a tablet in the *Iliad* but the Olympian legacy that rendered the main effect of *phantom literacy* on the Homeric mind. The Greeks might inherit some fading cognitive and social effects of writing from the Mycenaeans, which transpires in the capacity of classification and bureaucratic registry, as exemplified in the Catalogue of Greek Ships and the Trojan Battle Order. This residue of literacy did not have any practical tethering in the Dark Age and the time of Homer – the Greeks did not write and totally lost Linear B, the script of Mycenaean palaces. But this *phantom literacy* provided the Greek orality with a cultural link to the highly elaborated palatial-level mythology of the Mycenaeans and, through them, to the Minoans and, through them, to the Egyptians and Sumerians.

In total, the length of the palatial cultural legacy accessible to Homer through this unique *phantom literacy* contained 2000–2300 years of historical development of several written civilizations. No "primary-oral" culture could boast of such an incredible heritage accumulated by preceding cultures with a higher level of development, as attested by them having palaces and writing.

Through their *phantom literacy*, the oral Greeks acquired access to the cultural legacy that exceeded their level of social development in the Dark Age. The opportunism and tragedism of pirates, coupled with the alphabet, did the rest for the Greek miracle to appear.

10. The Mystery of China and the Axial Age

The expected failure of this book

This book had two tasks:

1. To employ Jaspers' concept of the Axial Age and Logan's Alphabet Effect in exploring the transition from orality to literacy in ancient times while pondering how the retrieval of orality in the digital era might unfold – for future exploration of the new phenomenon of digital orality. The hypothesis is that the global effect of digital media will be somewhat similar to Jaspers' Axial Age but replayed backward.

2. To speculate on whether the alphabet effect could serve as an explanation for the Axial Age since Jaspers did not offer such an explanation and mostly overlooked the effects of media, while the timeframe of the Axial Age perfectly coincides with the initial proliferation of the alphabet and the main features of the Axial Age align with the effects of the alphabet.

The book has failed in this second task but failed in a controllable, so to speak, manner. It was clear from the very beginning that ancient China, one of the three Axial cultures, does not fit the explanation of the Axial Age through the effect of the alphabet for a simple reason – China has never had an alphabet.

What a beautiful and perfectly coherent hypothesis it would have been if not for China.

Frankly, ancient India, another Axial culture, according to Jaspers, does not support the speculation of the alphabetic origin of the Axial Age either. The Indian script Brāhmī, which is said to be influenced by the Aramaic script, another descendant of the Phoenician proto alphabet, fully developed by the end of the Axial Age, around the 3rd century BCE. Meanwhile, Jainism, Buddhism, and other fundamental Axial contributions from ancient India date back to the 6th century BCE or even earlier.

Jaspers likely underestimated the Vedic legacy in India: the Vedic period lasted for a millennium from c. 1500 BCE to 500 BCE. Being a much more extended tribal encyclopedia than the *Iliad* and the *Odyssey* together, the *Vedas* elaborated a rich moral and metaphysical tradition that lasted and partly transformed into the later teachings of Buddhism and Hinduism. However, some significant historical events in India did coincide with Jaspers' timing of the Axial Age: the end of the Vedic Age in the 6th century BCE, the rise of Jainism and Buddhism, and the beginning of the second urbanization in the Ganges Plain.[1]

There is still a possibility to speculate that the early development of the Brāhmī alphabetic script might have influenced Jainism and Buddhism. It is believed that the Vedas were first written down sometime after 500 BCE. Some pre- or proto-alphabetic writing was certainly known in India by the middle of the 1st millennium BCE and might have contributed to the rise of the Axial consciousness. Moreover, as the correct pronunciation of sacred sounds of the Vedas was highly valued and, in the late Vedic period, professionally studied in the oralist Vedic schools, sages and scholars managed to isolate the sound structure of words, which itself was a fascinating oral achievement in abstract grammar. It is reported that the sounds of sacred texts were even visualized in *mudras*, ritual gestures. Thus, phonetic abstractions and even some degree of phonetic visualizations were present before and during the Axial Age in India – regardless of the early alphabetic development – and could have contributed to the Axial breakthrough.

However, the case of China eliminates any chance of saving face for the alphabetic explanation of the Axial Age anyway. But this is not a point worthy of fighting for. This book already contains enough bold assertions. The point is that the concept of the Axial Age, proposed by Karl Jaspers in 1949, and the alphabet effect, revealed by Robert Logan in 1986, provide ample material to set up the historical and media framework for exploring the ancient shift from orality to literacy and its contemporary reversal in

[1] The first instance of urban settlements in India with a palace economy and the earliest inscriptions of an economic nature related to the Indus Valley, or Harappan, civilization (3300 BCE to 1300 BCE), which assumedly declined because of an Arian invasion and/or climate change, leading to the Vedic period of the Indo-Arians (1500–500 BCE), resulting in the second urbanization in the central Indo-Gangetic Plain and the rise of Jainism and Buddhism.

the form of digital orality. If China does not fit into it, let's call it the "China mystery" and leave it as is.

But one outcome of these speculations still stands firm: the alphabet effect perfectly describes the contributions of the Hebrews and especially the Greeks to the Axial Age. The ethical teachings of the Hebrew prophets and the philosophy of the Greek thinkers, along with monotheism, codified law, deductive logic, and abstract science, provided humanity with the universal principles that continue to shape our understanding of the world today.

Meanwhile, the key features of the Axial Age, which originated in the East Mediterranean, India, and China, as well as the subsequent development of the Axial message in the history of various cultures and humanity as a whole, strongly resonate with the effects of media, even though the alphabet turned out to be not capable of taking all the credit. While working on the interplay between the Axial Age and the alphabet effect and trying to deal with China being an outlier, I have accumulated some circumstantial observations regarding China's past and future role in delivering the Axial message. To the explanatory power of media determinism, only the sky is the limit, so there is still a chance to approach the Celestial Empire with media deterministic optic.

In fact, sensing the "excessive" otherness of China, a "usual suspect" in representing the complete opposition to the West, Jaspers himself addressed the question of whether China belonged with the Axial Age. He referred to the views of Alfred Weber (whose equestrian theory he tested as a possible cause for the Axial Age). According to Weber, China and India remained bound to magic and therefore should be placed alongside Ancient Egypt and Babylonia, who did not make it to the Axial Age. Jaspers rejects this view. He argues that Egypt and Babylonia may be set alongside early China and the Indus Valey (Harappan) civilization,[1] but Confucian China and Buddhist India certainly belonged with the Axial civilizations, "not only because they lived on, but also because they accomplished the breakthrough."[2]

Confucianism was one of the main factors of the Axial transformation in China. It was an indigenous phenomenon that elaborated the universals

[1] The Harappan civilization, the first urban civilization in India that collapsed circa 1700, perhaps because of the same all-pervasive invasion of horse riders.

[2] Jaspers, Karl. (2021 [1949]). *The Origin and Goal of History*, p. 62.

that influenced the global culture for millennia. China found its own way to the historical "awakening" (Jaspers) and the "inward turn" (Ong), perhaps by focusing more on ethics than on abstract logic. The magical was reworked into the metaphysical. So, the question of whether the Axial Age happened in China should be taken off the table.

When I first presented the idea of examining Jaspers' Axial Age through the alphabet effect to Robert Logan, I complained that the theory would have been perfectly coherent if not for China. Logan suggested exploring whether there were any cultural connections between China and alphabetic cultures that could have affected China and brought the Axial transformations there.

For example, the Silk Road, a network of Eurasian trade routes that connected the East and West, surely provided strong economic, cultural, political, and religious exchange between civilizations and might bring the ideas and mindsets, affected by the alphabet, to the countries that did not use the alphabet. The Silk Road had existed since approximately the 2nd century BCE, but similar trade connections might have preceded it. At the very least, it is certain that such trade and cultural contacts existed between India and the Near East before and during the Axial Age.

Luckily (or sadly), Jaspers examined the possibilities of cultural exchange when he explored the hypothesis of the Axial Age originating from a single source. And no – he insisted that Axial events happened in three different and distant regions (the Near East, India, and China) simultaneously and independently. So, he rejected the idea of infusion from a single source.

Jaspers writes:

> These developments were originally independent of one another. Real communications and stimuli must be ruled out. Only after the penetration of Buddhism into China, which took place at the end of the Axial Period, did a profound spiritual communication between India and China come into being. Though there had always been relations between India and the West, these only became extensive during Roman times, via Alexandria.[1]

The only transmitter of Axial phenomena in China from outside, which Jaspers could agree to consider, could have been Buddhism. Jaspers

[1] Jaspers, Karl. (2021 [1949]). *The Origin and Goal of History*, p. 22.

admits that India experienced "the transmutation of the magico-metaphysical into ethicism by Jainism and by Buddha" and that this transmutation by Buddhism also happened in China.[1]

However, the main Axial doctrines in China, Confucianism and Taoism, emerged circa the 5th–4th centuries BCE, while Buddhism, a potential carrier of both the Axial mindsets and "second-hand" alphabet effects, arrived in China later, sometime in the 3rd century, when all the major Axial features in China had already been shaped.

All in all, any external cultural and phonetic-script influence on Chinese Axial events was too little and too late, if it existed at all. China made it on its own (as did India, too). So, the alphabet effect remains a coherent and time-matching explanation for the Axial Age only in the Near East and Mediterranean, further impacting the entire development of the West. But alas (for this book), it had nothing to do with China and little to do with India.

Maybe some other scholars, with good expertise in Chinese writing and history, will be able to find some media ecological connections between the possible phonetic development of Chinese writing in the 8th–3rd centuries BCE and the Axial "awakening" in China. If the emergence of phonetic elements in Chinese writing (or the isolating of phonetics in oral tradition, as it likely happened in India) had increased the level of abstraction in thinking and thus contributed to the Axial Age, it would be a life preserver thrown to the alphabetic hypothesis of the Axial Age, which is otherwise sinking in China.

Until then, the beauty of the alphabetic hypothesis of the Axial Age exceeds its plausibility. Sometimes, it is good enough for pattern recognition. A quote from Cixin Liu's novel *The Three-body Problem* comes to mind: "But from the perspective of aesthetics, I must be right and the universe must be wrong." Anyway, I will leave it here as it is and will no longer attempt to Tetris China into the alphabet effect or the alphabet effect into China.

[1] Jaspers, Karl. (2021 [1949]). *The Origin and Goal of History*, p. 71.

Nevertheless, the role of China in *The Alphabet Effect*

In a sense, Robert Logan owes the discovery of the alphabet effect to China. A physicist from Toronto, he wondered why abstract science developed in the West and not in the East, despite China being the homeland to so many crucial technological inventions, from gunpowder and rocket propulsion to the compass and printing. Logan was thinking about monotheism and the codified law of the Hebrew and the formal logic of the Greeks and brought this question to Marshall McLuhan, who immediately identified the alphabet as the primary underlying factor for the mindset open to monotheism, codified law, formal logic, and abstract science. (McLuhan asked: "Bob, what else do we have in the West that is not present in China? The alphabet, of course!"[1]).

Thus, the alphabet was Logan and McLuhan's answer to the question of why abstract science commenced in the West and not in China. In a 1977 article co-authored by Logan and McLuhan (in which they laid the ground for Logan's concept of the alphabet effect), they wrote:

> Western alphabetic and Chinese literacy represent the two extremes of writing. The alphabet is used phonetically to visually represent the sound of a word. Chinese characters are used pictographically to represent the idea of a word. Consequently, they are less abstract and less specialized than alphabetic writing. Eastern and Western thought patterns are as polarized as their respective writing systems.[2]

Posing China as the "significant other" helps Logan identify the specific effects of the alphabet and, subsequently, the distinct features of the Western mentality formed under the influence of the alphabet. His view is, of course, that of a Westerner (as is this book). It would be interesting to see if the Chinese would agree with the features of their mentality "assigned" to them in the set of East-West cultural dichotomies, as represented in Logan's *Alphabet Effect.*

---

[1] Robert Logan recollects the details of that and other conversations with McLuhan in his short memoir: Logan, Robert K. (2020) "'The alphabet, of course': How I met Marshall McLuhan." *The New Explorations Blog*.

[2] McLuhan, Marshall, and Logan, Robert. (1977). "Alphabet, mother of invention", p. 374.

Comparison of Chinese and Western Cultural Patterns

By Robert Logan

China	Europe
Logograms	Alphabet
Right-brain oriented	Left-brain oriented
Nonlinear	Linear
Acoustical	Visual
Analogical	Logic
Inductive	Deductive
Concrete	Abstract
Mystical	Causal
Intuitive	Rational
Generalist	Specialist
Decentralized	Centralized
Local	Universal
Integrative	Fragmented
Space oriented	Time oriented
Traditional	Progressive
Cyclic time	Continuous time
Algebraic	Geometric
Concrete science	Abstract science
Order and pattern	Natural law
Craft	Technology
Invention	Exploitation
Technique	System
Customs-mores (Confucius)	Codified law
Harmony of nature (Tao)	Monotheism
Relativity	Absolutism

Figure 26. Source: Logan, Robert. (2004 [1986]). *The Alphabet Effect,* p. 62.

Chinese explosion of literacy and its effects

Ignace Gelb, a pioneer in the study of writing systems, stated in 1952 that complex and rigid logo-syllabographic script tended to preserve the privilege of the ruling bureaucracy, as ordinary people usually could not use it in their daily lives. After explaining the rigidity and decline of Egyptian hieroglyphs, Gelb turns to the Chinese writing system. He writes:

> The almost unbelievable development of logography in the Chinese writing is a well-known phenomenon. Due to its marginal geographic position in the Old World, China was not affected by foreign invasions to the extent that the Near Eastern areas were. For that reason, the evolution of the Chinese writing progressed through thousands of years undisturbed by foreign influences, resulting finally in a type of writing which perfectly suited the needs of a small bureaucratic clique, but was totally inaccessible to 90 per cent of the population.[1]

Gelb wrote this in 1952, a time when the literacy rate in China was at 15–20%.[2] The political bureaucracy preserving their privilege through the complexity of writing might have been a factor allowing the analogy with Egyptian hieroglyphs, which endured thousands of years but were mostly inaccessible to ordinary people. However, Gelb ignored or dismissed another factor – the tonal character of Chinese language (more accurately, the group of languages) that made the alphabetic principle considerably less suitable for Chinese as compared to Indo-European languages. Once again, China did not fit into the general model, and Gelb was content with a rather simplistic explanation for the preservation of the logographic nature of Chinese writing by the bureaucratic elites securing their privileges.

For almost 3000 years, Chinese writing, indeed, developed in its own stew and accumulated complexities. Egyptian hieroglyphics eventually did not survive their incidental offspring, the alphabet. In China, however, the political will, perhaps coupled with the strong influence of Confucian statism, eventually brought a completely opposite outcome. Since the communist modernization in China, the Chinese script has become "accessible" to the entire population – something that Gelb could not have imagined.

Something similar had happened in the USSR a half century before, and it affected the entire world. The Bolshevik's "liquidation of illiteracy" program increased literacy in the USSR from 20–30% in 1918 to 99% in 1959. This allowed the Soviets to make a scientific and technological breakthrough resulting in the first Sputnik and the first man in space, with

[1] Gelb, Ignace. (1963 [1952]). *A Study of Writing*, p. 203.

[2] See, for example: "The single greatest educational effort in human history," *Language Magazine*.

the USSR becoming one of the two greatest world powers.[1] The USSR "overproduced" more than 100 million literates in 40 years, and the media effect of this explosion of literacy in a single previously mostly illiterate country shaped the world in the second half of the 20th century.

In China, during communist modernization and under the leadership of the new bureaucracy, a similar task of fighting illiteracy was completed in the second half of the 20th century. Literacy was defined there as knowledge of 1500 characters for rural residents or 2000 characters for urban residents.[2] The literacy rate, which was about 20% in the 1950s, reached 98% in 2020.[3] Therefore, China "overproduced" more than 1 billion literates in 70 years – ten times more than the similar breakthrough of the Soviets. What does it mean when an "extra" billion people become proficient in a writing system that was so complex that no more than 20% of the population were able to employ it for centuries?

Learning the alphabet typically takes months at the age of 5–7 years, and then children in alphabetic cultures use reading to learn everything else. Everything else settles in the mind with the structure provided by the alphabet. Furthermore, historically, everything else is structured by the alphabet in the process of knowledge accumulation.

Achieving full fluency in reading Chinese might take years. In parallel, the Chinese learn everything else while perfecting their writing and reading. The way of acquiring knowledge by an individual is structured differently from that in alphabetic cultures; and so is knowledge itself – its is structured differently. Logo-syllabographic writing might not favour abstract logic or individualism, but it certainly fosters diligence. Diligence is the primary cognitive effect of prolonged and focused learning. Knowledge can eventually be acquired through various methods, but diligence is a product of persistence and sustained concentration, which must be applied to the study of complex and numerous logographic characters.

In the meantime, the ease of learning the alphabet (and acquiring knowledge through the alphabet) in the West is approaching its ultimate degree, at which point, as we already know from McLuhan's Laws of Media,

---

[1] Mir, Andrey. (2022). "Media-ecological engineering of the Soviets," p. 147.

[2] "The single greatest educational effort in human history," *Language Magazine*.

[3] See: "Adult literacy rate in China from 1982 to 2018," *Statista*, and: "Literacy Rate in China (2018 – 2021)," *Global Data*:

it reverses its effect. The ease of learning itself becomes the content of educational institutions. Many progressive learning methods include gamification, multimedia learning, and other forms of interactive engagement, which aim to ease the burden of the learning process. This often comes at the cost of rejecting lengthy individual reading, which was the primary educational method in times when Western education yielded its most significant fruits in the form of scientific and technological revolution. Essentially, immersive education and any form of interactivity, whether in-class or digital, replaces reading.

Education was once a product and a bastion of reading. The demotion of reading is a media effect of electric and digital media, of course, but education, paradoxically, leads the process. It becomes a norm in schools and universities to assign for reading selected chapters and fragments, not entire books. The systemic source of diligence and completeness of task-performing – lengthy and complete reading – is being obliterated in favour of interactivity. Methods with more digital or group interactions and less individual reading are systematically being preferred. Paradoxically, by introducing more verbomotor activities that replace individual, silent, and comprehensive reading, education is spearheading the reversal from literacy to orality without realizing that orality did not know formal education at all – only apprenticeship and tribal indoctrination.

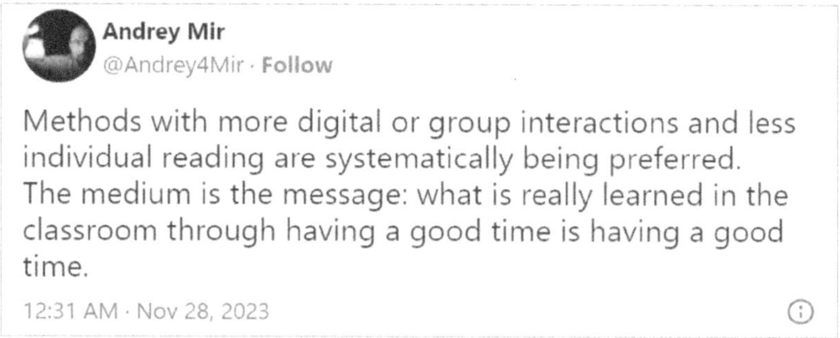

The medium is the message: what is really learned in the classroom through having a good time is having a good time. The demand for having a good time and being entertained persists further on into students' lives. Not supported by the "hostile" environment of adult life with its demands for commitment and diligence, this leads to anxiety and frustration, which extends into various far-reaching psychological, political, and cultural implications, reflected, for example, in labelling youth "snowflakes," etc.

In the meantime, the design and outcomes of educational systems have "geopolitical" consequences. In 1957, the Soviet breakthrough in literacy and, subsequently, science appeared in the American night skies in the form of a tiny glaring and beeping star. Sputnik shocked the Americans. Such a cumulated and distinct shock, however, had a curative effect on American education. Prior to it, American education aimed mostly at religious and moral indoctrination. Sputnik (read: the Bolshevik's program of fighting illiteracy) changed this. American education was revamped to produce more and better "rocket science" – literally. In 1958, just a year after Sputnik, Congress passed the National Defense Education Act, a "$1-billion spending package to bolster high-quality teaching and learning in science, mathematics and foreign languages."[1] Additionally, in 1958 the USA created the Advanced Research Projects Agency, also known as ARPA, later DARPA, which eventually became the progenitor of the Internet. This all occurred because millions of peasants and workers in Soviet Russia learned to read 20 years before.

Interestingly, "in the first half of the 20th century, U.S. educators shunned homework," a source reports. Sputnik changed that, too.[2] Homework became regular at schools. More homework meant, among other things, more individual reading.

The USA won both the Space Race and the Cold War. Now, digital media are pushing education to return to religious-type moral indoctrination through interactive verbomotor formats innate to orality, replacing reading.

In the meantime, in China, the acquisition of literacy by a billion people within a highly complex cognitive paradigm of logographic writing provides not only a billion literates but also a billion diligent and persistent individuals who have already become a part of both Chinese and global culture. This might have significant implications, especially amid the lowering of the requirements of assiduousness in Western education.

Chinese assiduousness, of course, will be mitigated by Western consumerism, the mightiest secret weapon against all anti-Western, anti-capitalist, and anti-democratic encroachments. (Consumerism, by the way,

---

[1] Roos, Dave. (2019, August 13). "How the Cold War Space Race led to US students doing tons of homework." *History.com.*

[2] Roos, Dave. (2019, August 13). "How the Cold War Space Race led to US students doing tons of homework." *History.com.*

through individualism and industrial capitalism, is a distant by-product of the alphabet, too; so, consumerism is intrinsically an agent of westernization and globalization.) Consumerism crushed classical Marxism, the labour movement, and the Soviet Empire. But whether the power of consumerism appears to be sufficient to "neutralize" the diligence and persistence of the billion of those carrying the "logographic" mentality remains to be seen.

Digitalization of logography

A culture based on logo-syllabographic writing is likely less susceptible to a reversal from literacy back to orality under the influence of digital media. The provision of diligence in a logographic culture may help it endure the "liberating-from-literacy" effect of digital media longer, as learning logograms still requires significant and prolonged efforts – something completely opposite to what digital orality fosters.

Moreover, digital media may add new cognitive advantages to a culture based on logo-syllabographic writing. The way the Chinese use computer and smartphone keyboards is amazing. Pinyin, the method of alphabetical spelling of logographic characters, has married, at last, the alphabet with the Chinese script. Introduced in the 1950s to help overcome illiteracy, it was also used for teaching Chinese to foreigners. But perhaps the utmost effect of Pinyin was achieved in digital typing.

The user types, with Latin letters, a syllable that could represent Chinese characters but without marking a vocal tone, as there is no such capacity in Latin letters. The algorithm does the rest: it "summons" a set of Chinese characters it thinks the user has in mind, sorted by the frequency of their use, and the user then selects the needed character. That's it – the word is typed in Chinese script using alphabetic input.

Pinyin's effect on the mind is yet to be fully comprehended. In short, Chinese culture, especially the younger generations, has experienced the birth of a new system of writing.[1] This novelty is certainly detrimental to

[1] In general, Chinese digital input methods can be divided into two types: phonetic-based and shape-based. Phonetic-based methods use letters to type syllables and "summon" characters, as Pinyin does, thus combining the alphabet and logography. The shape-based methods assign different keys on the standard keyboard to represent certain shapes or strokes, thus "summoning" needed characters by partially drafting their shapes. The phonetic-based methods introduce alphabetic atomization and abstraction into the mind by "typing"

the traditional skill of logographic writing because the users do not need to pull the right character out of their memory. The algorithm "remembers" all the words-characters and handily suggests the most probable on the screen for the users to choose. The users still have to learn the characters to be able to recognize them, but the faculty of the independent selection of characters "on the go" – in the process of writing – is not practiced in Pinyin typing and can be weakened or even lost. As always, the service of a medium comes with a price – with a disservice.

Pinyin IME for Simplified and Traditional Chinese

Pinyin IME is a phonetic input method.

As you type pinyin, e.g., "hao", you'll see a list of candidate characters that map to your input.

hao
1. 号 2. 好 3. 豪 4. 浩 5. 郝

You can choose a candidate from the list by taking any of the following actions:

- Press SPACE to select the highlighted candidate,
- Click on it,
- Type the number next to the word,
- Navigate the list of candidates in a page with LEFT / RIGHT arrow keys. Flip pages with UP and DOWN or , and . or - and = keys.

Press ENTER to type in English (i.e., the letters you type).

Figure 27. Alphabetic input of Chinese characters. Source: Google Input Tools.

At the same time, in the background of all those captivating digital activities that enslave us, the brain that employs Pinyin performs, routinely and unconsciously, an entirely new type of task. Using the alphabetic keyboard for logographic characters involves intricate translation between logical and metaphorical, digital and analog, providing the brain with subtle but constant exercise – in addition to the diligence that a culture based on the logo-syllabographic script still naturally fosters. It might require further examination, but I would advance the hypothesis that

logograms with alphabetic signs. The shape-based methods preserve the analog and metaphorical tradition of the logographic script while also developing it through new categorizations of characters.

digital media do not degrade logographic literacy as significantly as alphabetic literacy. Pinyin, the method for the alphabetical input of logographic characters on digital devices, will further develop metaphorical and analog thinking while incorporating "alphabetic" (atomistic, highly abstract) features into it.

New environment for an environmental mentality

While it is from difficult to impossible to record spoken speech in logography, the Chinese learned instead to record thoughts, notions, and images, and, as we may assume, achieved perfection in it, as the Chinese language is the oldest written language in the world.

Alphabetic cultures made their way there through the technological objectivation of nature, while non-alphabetical cultures preserved, at least to some degree, an environmental mentality that includes people into the world instead of instrumentalizing it. In the meantime, digital media create an environment into which all human activity is now resettling. The environmental thinking naturally preserved by the non-alphabetic mind may happen to be better suited for this new environment than the instrumental thinking fostered by the alphabet.

The technological advantage that Western culture gained after the amplification of the alphabet effect by printing led to the invention of digital media. Coding is the highest form of the alphabet.[1] At the same time, alphabetic culture may approach its limits. McLuhan's law of reversal, which suggests that any medium or technology, when pushed to the limits of its potential, reverses its effects or characteristics, might apply to a culture, too. Environmental detachment and the objectivation of Nature formed one of the main cultural characteristics of the West: its excellence in appropriation. After reaching its limits, the European aptitude for cultural appropriation is reversing into self-deprivation.

Such a risk does not seem to pose a threat to the non-West. In the meantime, as humankind moves towards more uniformity, any knowledge is becoming available to everyone, regardless of this knowledge's country of origin. Jaspersian Axial expansion and digital media provide everyone, including the non-West, with access to knowledge and technologies created

[1] Paradoxically, the ultimate development of the alphabet – coding – engendered its gravedigger, digital orality. This is another example of a media reversal.

by everyone, including the West. The rest is a matter of determination, resources, and diligence. Strengthened by environmental thinking, which is better preserved in non-alphabetic cultures, and coupled with digital alphabetization (Pinyin), China's digital endeavours may succeed, in certain ways, more than anyone else's.

The environmental thinking of the logographic mind does not mean ecological thinking. It is not that kind of "environmentalism" that saves the planet: China is unlikely to lead in fighting environmental pollution. The environmental mentality of logographic culture will likely unfold not in the natural environment but in the new digital environment of social involvement – specifically in digital social regulation.

Now that the environment is digital, human existence will transform to fit its most "natural" features, such as the environmental "harmonizing" of society by social scoring or the most meticulous form of capitalist surveillance – communist surveillance, which serves both corporations and the state. For the cultures that preserved a significant level of environmental and collective immersion, personal exposure is not as unacceptable as it is for alphabetic cultures that fostered the inward turn and, subsequently, the high value of private life. Without individualism, compliance with social digital regulation is more easily achievable.

Therefore, surveillance and social scoring are more likely to be tolerated in a logographic culture. It's not merely a political matter; it's a technological imperative. In fact, environmental immersion even *dictates* the observation and "harmonizing" of private lives. The most significant advancements in the digital technologies that "immerse" private lives in all-pervading regulation will likely occur in China.

The AI race will add a new dimension to this digital development (if China manages to withstand the AI chip export restrictions introduced by the US [1]). International competition in the area of AI will amplify the technological imperative: the inevitability of AI's rule. The affordance,

[1] In 2022–23, the US barred exports of AI training chips, a crucial element of AI hardware, to China. Experts say that "US chip restrictions may have helped boost China's domestic chip industry, which is thought to lag behind that of the US, Taiwan, and South Korea by many years." – Knight, Will. (2023, October 17). "The US just escalated its ai chip war with China." *Wired*. The question is whether these "many years" will be enough for the US to widen the gap due to the accelerating development of AI or China will manage to rapidly build its own chip production and establish AI sovereignty to sustain its own AI future, which most likely will be very distinct from the AI perspectives in the West.

imposed and dictated by the future AI, will certainly not be generating texts or pictures for humans instead of humans. It will unleash its own terraforming power. After integrating AI with social scoring and surveillance, the affordances of this new medium will create a very specific version of human unity. The impending uniformity of humankind bears not only romantic connotations.

A corollary of both Jaspersian historical theory and media evolution is that wherever a technology emerges, its application will pave its way everywhere. Nobody remembers where horses were domesticated or where the wheel was invented. Once a technology proves its efficiency in extending humans in time and space, it proliferates on its own. At different stages of historical development, different cultures contributed differently to the "history of humankind as a whole," but now it all belongs to humankind.

Regardless of what appears in the rearview mirror, what is more important is the path lying ahead. Computer coding, the highest symbolic form of alphabetic culture, is already shared to all and available to both alphabetic and non-alphabetic cultures. The environmentalism of non-alphabetic cultures (as well as the reversal of alphabetic literacy) will create opportunities for the next advancements toward human unity, though not all of them will please the alphabetic minds.

11. The meaning and goal of history when the medium is the message

On historical linearity again: the question of progress

McLuhan was often criticized for focusing on the technicality of media and disregarding the social factors behind media use. For example, Raymond Williams, one of the founders of cultural studies and a renowned British Marxist, wrote that McLuhan "desocialised" all media operations. At the same time, he accused McLuhan of an ideological cover-up, suggesting that such concepts as retribalization or the global village project images of society "welcomed by the 'media-men' of the existing institutions."[1] Williams eventually even comes to a conclusion that McLuhan's analysis *is* an ideology: "The initial formulation – 'the medium is the message' – was a simple formalism. The subsequent formulation – 'the medium is the massage'[2] – is a direct and functioning ideology."[3]

Such criticism, implying that McLuhan's "techno-determinism" deliberately neglected ideological factors or even creates an ideological screen in the guise of ideological agnosticism, was similar to the reception of McLuhan in the Soviet Union. For instance, Aleksandr Kukarkin in his 1978 *Bourgeois Mass Culture*, which delivered, perhaps, the first review of McLuhan's ideas to the Soviet readers, wrote:

> The views of "electronic era oracle" M. McLuhan regarding various means of mass cultural communication exhibit an extreme and even extravagant approach in their efforts to define the driving forces of bourgeois mass culture entirely within the realm of technical means of information and through the differences on their impact on human senses. However, precisely because of their extremes and extravagance, these views serve well as a cumulative sample of the general bourgeois-idealistic tendency to de-ideologize the phenomenon of mass culture and deprive it of its true class nature.[4]

---

1 Williams, Raymond. (1975 [1974]). *Television: Technology and Cultural Form*, p. 127.

2 The title of Marshall McLuhan and graphic artist Quentin Fiore's experimentally designed 1967 book.

3 Williams, Raymond. (1975 [1974]). *Television: Technology and Cultural Form*, p. 127.

4 Kukarkin, Alexandr (1985 [1978]). *Bourgeois Mass Culture*, p. 49.

In the chapter titled "The theology of Technocratia," Kukarkin formulates his verdict:

> The secret of McLuhan's popularity is simple: McLuhan pleased the powerful, for all the spirit of his "works" is defined by the desire to prove by all means, even the most preposterous ones, that the famous thesis from the Communist Manifesto – "The history of all hitherto existing societies is the history of class struggle!" – should be replaced by the thesis "The history of all hitherto existing societies is the history of the struggle of mass media of communication."[1]

It is hard now to tell if McLuhan successfully completed the assignment given to him by the bosses from Madison Avenue and distracted the masses from class struggle. The distraction was mainly accomplished by an agent far more formidable than even McLuhan – by media themselves (the class struggle was enabled by printing and ended by electronic media – they fostered consumerism that aligned with the well-being achieved in capitalist society). But the morphological similarity between McLuhan's view and Marxist historical determinism seemed to have been caught accurately.

Accusing media determinism of ignoring ideology evokes the essential distinction between media ecology and other communication theories: they focus on what (powerful) people do with media, while media ecology explores what media do to people, powerful or not. After all, Karl Marx himself was a media determinist when he proposed that the base predefines the superstructure (ideology) or that "The hand-mill gives you society with the feudal lord; the steam-mill society with the industrial capitalist."[2] Media evolution reflects historical materialism in a quite Marxist sense: productive forces are media, and relations of production are media effects. Extending Marxist historical materialism, media ecology explores the struggle of media, which predetermined, indeed, the ideological struggle – among all other struggles of humankind.

One can choose any optic to look at the historical process. But looking at history through the prism of power relations or ideological struggle is nothing short of calling for presentism and selectiveness. Even Marx

---

[1] Kukarkin, Alexandr (1985 [1978]). *Bourgeois Mass Culture*, p. 54.

[2] Marx, Karl. (1847). *The Poverty of Philosophy*. Chapter 2.1, Second Observation, Para 2.

himself, while analyzing the historical dynamics of ideologies and power struggle, based his analysis on the development of media – on the evolution of productive forces. Georgi Plekhanov (1856–1918), the first Russian Marxist, who was highly appreciated as a Marxist philosopher by Lenin despite their irreconcilable political differences, directly associated the development of productive forces with media evolution, implying, along the way, that media are "the extensions of man" – 70 years before McLuhan. In 1895, Plekhanov wrote:

> In the implements of labour man acquired new organs, as it were, which changed his anatomical structure. From the time that he rose to the level of using them, he has given quite a new aspect to the history of his development. Previously, as with all the other animals, it amounted to changes in his natural organs. Since that time, it has become first of all the *history of the perfecting of his artificial organs, the growth of his productive forces.*[1]

By linking socio-economic history to the evolution of media, Marx and Marxists built up an impeccable logic of historical linearity and social evolution in which each historical stage accumulated prerequisites and controversies to flip to the next one.

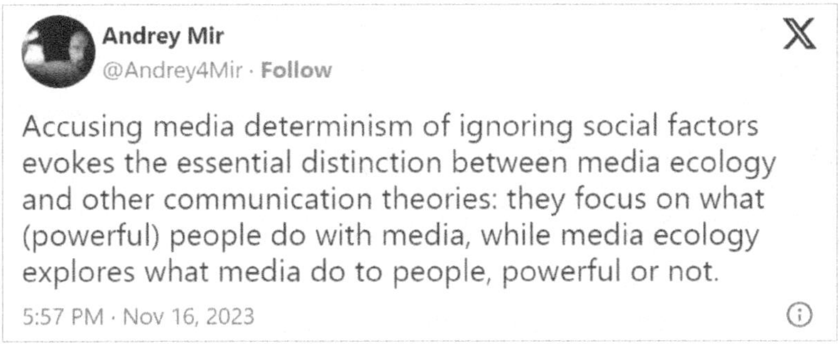

Andrey Mir
@Andrey4Mir · **Follow**

Accusing media determinism of ignoring social factors evokes the essential distinction between media ecology and other communication theories: they focus on what (powerful) people do with media, while media ecology explores what media do to people, powerful or not.

5:57 PM · Nov 16, 2023

Media evolution gives us an optic to see history for what it really is – a process coherent in time. The timeline of history itself is neither fragmented nor disrupted nor accentuated. History was filled with events that followed each other, with the previous ones affecting and contributing to the subsequent ones. Accusing historical media determinism of ignoring ideology, power dynamics, and human intents in general is, in fact,

---

[1] Plekhanov, Georgi. (1895). *The Development of the Monist View of History*, Ch. 5 (*Italics* is his).

praising it. Within the paradigm of media determinism, history unfolded according to the objective logic of media evolution and not a logic assigned to it by an observer. Therefore, the task of *historia*, Herodotus' inquiry into the succession and meaning of human events, is to determine the logic of media evolution, which resonates well with Jaspers' motive behind *The Origin and Goal of History*.

Media evolution certainly provides a linear view of history. Immediately, another question arises: has this linearity been progressive? Has humankind socially, morally, and spiritually developed, regressed, or remained at the same stage?

Media evolution inevitably represents progressive linearity because evolution favoured media that allowed for the "better" extension of human capacities – further in time and space. The spaceship extends the human capacity of transportation "better" than the horse. Zoom extends the human capacity of communication "better" than papyrus. The linearity and progression between horse and spaceship or papyrus and Zoom are obvious and can be reconstructed step by step with exact historical timing and periodization.

If we tie the historical stages of human development to the horse and the spaceship as the means of transportation or papyrus and Zoom as the means of communication, we will get the linearity and progression of human history regardless of whether we like some parts of it or not. The media effects are embedded; they may be extremely negative for us but "positive" for media as they enable their further development. For example, print and telegraph facilitated huge scientific and economic progress and tremendously increased people's well-being, but they also enabled the bloodiest wars in history, the religious and imperialist ones. As McLuhan once said, "Every new technology necessitates a new war."[1] A war, in its turn, always spurs technological advancement even more. Media effects do not ask Raymond Williams for ideological approval; media evolution remains linear and progressing and imposes these qualities on human history regardless of someone's appraisal.

As soon as the logic of media evolution is accepted, the history of humankind is presented in its entirety, not in a selection of preferred fragments. Just as media predetermine human perception and action, so

[1] McLuhan, Marshall, & Fiore, Quentin. (1968). *War & Peace in the Global Village*, p. 98.

do they predetermine the linearity and progression of human history. The logic of media evolution serves as the most effective historiographic cement solidifying the logic of history.

Media as equalizer

Besides providing historical linearity and progress in social development, media also serve as a historical equalizer.

The Axial Age signified the "awakening" of humankind – the discovery of basic ethical and metaphysical universals in which all humans eventually come to think. We can call it the Axial imperative: the thinkers of the Axial Age revealed universals common to humankind as a whole – the universals to which all cultures and peoples arrive, whether naturally or forcibly.

The Axial imperative also means that all Axial discoveries or achievements, regardless of their origin, become common assets of humankind. Whatever was invented in this global cultural movement by the Hebrews, Greeks, Persians, Indians, Chinese, or other cultures that joined the Axial movement later – became the property of all when humankind transitioned from many local histories to one world history.

Jaspers claimed, in 1949, that this stage – world history – had just commenced. This became evident even at the formal level: the first global planetary government in history was created – the League of Nations (1920), followed by the United Nations (1945). Notably, both were established in the aftermath of the World Wars, which were also global events confirming Jaspers' "Schema of world history."

As people generally seek the same living conditions due to their biological and social nature, all advanced technologies, which supposedly provide these conditions, become eventually distributed across the planet by market forces or governments. Every country possesses electricity, medicine, a financial system, computers, and abstract science. The cultural and technological differences between countries may be significant but they are incomparable to those of the past. Important events in any country will resonate in the global news agenda. Some events are innately global, such as financial crises, big internet innovations, or pandemics.

What makes them global? Media. Media of transportation made trade, wars, and epidemics global. There were no global wars or pandemics before transportation connected all continents. Communication media created a global economy in which a sneeze at the Tokyo or Hong Kong stock market can turn into a fever in Johannesburg or Toronto. Capitalism, a media effect of the printing press, takes care of developing new drugs and distributing them worldwide. The producers of new movies and musicals dream of a world premiere.

The synchronization of global history has been happening from its beginning, very slowly at first, and increasingly accelerating recently. It took millennia for writing to spread, centuries for printing, and decades for electricity. The internet and social media seized the world historically in an instant. AI will not care about geographically seizing the world at all, as the entire world is already delivered to it in the form of the internet. Digital media have completed the synchronization of world history.

In the process of media synchronization, all surviving cultures joined the common patterns of historical development – the Axial imperative. Electronic and especially digital media made the origin of knowledge no longer matter. Digital media have become the final and ultimate historical and cultural equalizer.

The total unity might not have happened yet, but the trend is evident, and this trend is accelerating. The unity of the world, as Jaspers predicted, is becoming increasingly apparent, despite news' portrayals of the world being shattered. Furthermore, the very impression of the world being shattered is evidence of its burgeoning unity.

Nativist or progressist backlashes to global media synchronization – to globalism – still persist here and there. Also, calls for cultural diversity maintain an impression of the deep divide between people on the basis of their personal, ethnic, religious, or cultural identities. In full compliance with the law of reversal, universalism is denied by the very people who contribute to it the most; besides, denying the universalism of others itself is a perversive form of universalism. It does not affect the synchronization of the world by media anyway, as all people seek the same media extensions.

Media synchronization does not make people and cultures similar, but it makes them connected into humankind. A view from any point of the past or from a distant planet will immediately expose how insignificant any divide is amid the growing oneness of the all-humankind agenda.

Jaspers believed that the unity of humankind could materialize either as a "world order" or a "world empire." In the mid-20th century, following the defeat of Nazi Germany and during the victorious expansion of the Soviet regime, the fate of humankind was envisioned as either democratic or totalitarian. However, when the future has arrived, it turns out to be much more complex and mixed.

Electronic media facilitated retribalization, and digital media boosted it even more. Under the pressure of digital orality, the influence of literacy weakens in highly literate societies and vanishes in societies with strong oral backgrounds. Additionally, electronic and digital media informed societies with a strong oral residue about better opportunities abroad and enabled the new global wave of migration, comparable to or even exceeding the previous waves of migration triggered by the printing press and telegraph/radio. Those migration waves were the carriers of literacy, but the latest one represents rather a massive movement of people from societies with a strong oral tradition, as this wave comes predominantly from cultures with 2–3 or fewer generations of full literacy.

Since digital media have equalized the global pace of history, some of those cultures have skipped the print, television, or sometimes even desktop PC stages of literacy development and joined the Axial imperative outright at the stage of smartphones. These cultures experience a unique amalgamation of primary orality with digital orality, thus "outperforming" the Greeks, who jumped from primary orality right to alphabetic literacy, with all the shocks this rapid transition entailed. As a result, a new global mix of orality and literacy has emerged. The positions of print literacy are challenged by the conjoining efforts of digital orality, on one hand, and the migration of strong oral tradition, on the other. Having many cultural differences, digital orality and oral tradition, nevertheless, are morphologically compatible in their assault on print literacy.

Since we are all now connected, the global retrieval of orality is leading to global balkanization, a weird type of cultural fragmentation that in fact is uniting all of humanity. The impending uniformity of humankind appears less structured than what world democracy or world totalitarianism in Jaspers' predictions might have implied. Instead, humankind seems to be facing *tribal globalism* with its very chaotic political and cultural unity provided by digital media. Global swarming may turn out to be more disastrous than global warming.

The second Axial Age? The Axial Parenthesis

While pondering the uniqueness of the Axial Age, Jaspers argues that no similarly significant epoch existed in human history. He considers other candidates for this distinction, such as the emergence of the first agrarian civilizations in Egypt, Sumer, and the Indus Valley in the 3rd to 2nd millennia BCE as well as the Technological Revolution in 18th-century Europe. However, he asserts that they fall short of being recognized as equally Axial events in history due to their lack of synchronicity, density, and originality.

Jaspers returns to the possibility of the next Axial Age time after time. In his view, the Axial Age followed the period that laid foundation for detaching human life from the animal kingdom: the Promethean Age. He assumes that the second Promethean Age – the Technological Revolution – could lay the groundwork for the next Axial Age, "which would constitute a single, world-embracing reality."[1] The contours of this next Axial Age are "beyond our powers of imagination," as he sees it.

We now have enough power to unleash our imagination beyond the horizons available to Jaspers in 1949.

Fantasizing about the next Axial Age, Jaspers foresaw, essentially, the "world-embracing reality" of the Singularity, the ultimate outcome of the Technological Revolution. The Singularity also perfectly fits his idea of the "goal of history" – "the greatest inclusiveness and the most categoric unity of human history," when humankind eventually becomes one.

However, it will not be an Axial *Age*. Due to the compression of historical time, it will be rather an extended Axial Decade. The digital revolution started with the internet and condensed into the Digital Axis, which commenced in the late 2000s with social media (and similar digital platforms for human activities) and will culminate in AI that acquires something akin to self-consciousness either through self-awakening or through merging with the human will via a cognitive interface. This event will signify the Singularity. The futurological consensus regarding its timing commonly refers to Ray Kurzweil's 2005 prediction:

> I set the date for the Singularity – representing a profound and disruptive transformation in human capability – as 2045. The

[1] Jaspers, Karl. (2021 [1949]). *The Origin and Goal of History*, p. 110.

> nonbiological intelligence created in that year will be one billion times more powerful than all human intelligence today.[1]

Considering the progress of generative AI, the forecast can be moved a little bit closer to the present – sometime in the 2030s. To determine a more precise date, we need to follow the news about the development of AI and cognitive interfaces, such as Elon Musk's Neuralink and others. Neuralink received U.S. Food and Drug Administration approval for its first human clinical trial in May 2023.[2]

So, history is linear and progressive, until it is not. Linearity does not move on the time axis after the curve of progress goes vertical (see the "Portrait of the Singularity"). On the axis of time, the curve of progress condenses into a dot at the moment of the Singularity.

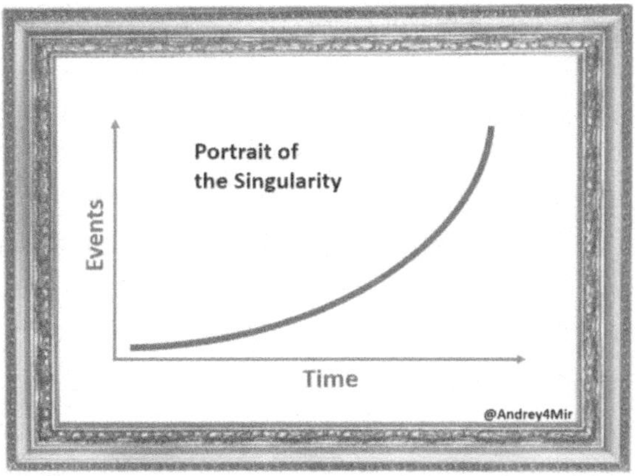

Figure 28.

As McLuhan noticed in 1969,

> An electrically imploded tribal society discards the linear forward-motion of "progress." We can see in our own time how, as we begin to react in depth to the challenges of the global village, we all become reactionaries.[3]

---

[1] Kurzweil, Ray. (2005). *The Singularity Is Near*, p. 136. Kurzweil, however, kind of demoted the phenomenon of the Singularity by stating: "Despite the clear predominance of nonbiological intelligence by the mid-2040s, ours will still be a human civilization. We will transcend biology, but not our humanity" (p. 136).

[2] Mir, Andrey. (2023, July 6). "The final merging of humans and their media has begun." *Discourse*.

[3] McLuhan, Marshall. (1969, March). "The Playboy Interview." *Playboy*, p. 70.

The Digital Decade becomes the closing parenthesis for the period that began with the Axial Age. Will it be the long-promised end of history? Due to the decline of alphabetic literacy, it certainly may be the *Decline of the West*, as predicted in Spengler's 1918 book. However, the parentheses[1] can also be closed at a larger scale. The Axial Age was characterized by the awakening of humans as humankind. The Digital Axis may end up in the awakening of the next, non-biological iteration of intelligence in the place of humankind. So, yes, the period from the Jaspersian Axial Age to the Digital Axis can be seen as enclosed into the Axial Parenthesis. Or else, as the Digital Axis reverses literacy, it can even be seen at a larger scale – as the end of the history of humankind, which commenced with the writing of the first agrarian civilizations.

The Digital Axis can be interpreted in terms of Jaspers' *goal of history*: humankind will become one, but it will become one with its medium and its environment when all three merge into the ultimate medium – a networked cognitive interface with AI. Unless another reversal will happen – self-destruction, according to the so-called Great Filter hypothesis,[2] which posits that it is very hard for intelligence to transcend its biological form. Basically, the technological imperative leaves humankind no choice: singularize or die. Humankind is the biological embryo of AI; but it can die in birth or short before.

Media evolution will continue in the digital era until the end – until the user merges with its ultimate medium, which is also its environment. After that, mediation will no longer be needed. Media are a species that comes to extinction when it succeeds. The Singularity is a mere continuation of media evolution by other means.

---

[1] In his 2023 *The Gutenberg Parenthesis*, Jef Jarvis explains that in the US "parenthesis" means the symbols themselves, but in British English, in which the term was coined, "parenthesis" also means what is inside, between parentheses. – Jarvis, Jeff. (2023). *The Gutenberg Parenthesis*, p. 4.

[2] A theory called the "Great Filter hypothesis" explains why we cannot detect any signs of extra-terrestrial civilizations and are not contacted by them, despite the vast number of potentially habitable planets and the potentially more advanced development of their habitants. The Great Filter theory posits that alien civilizations may have progressed to a certain point where they were unable to handle the immense power unleashed by their technologies, ultimately leading to their extinction or regression after an ecological or technological cataclysm.

Media platforms of mind

In a popular 2011 YouTube video, a 1-year-old girl tries to pinch and swipe a picture in a glossy magazine, but it does not work. The baby girl gets frustrated and demands her iPad back. At the end of the video, a parent types a caption:

> For my 1-year-old daughter, a magazine is an iPad that does not work. It will remain so for her whole life. Steve Jobs has coded a part of her OS.

Steve Jobs might have coded the iPad, but it was the parents who coded the OS of this baby girl with the iPad.[1] The point, however, is that media, indeed, train our sensory and cognitive capacities – our operating system.

The human operating system follows the media it uses – why would it have been otherwise? For example, the hardware of writing necessitated the software of literacy. The sensory-cognitive operating systems form the platforms of mind – the platforms on which respective cultures and societies are based. Before the conclusion, I'd like to outline those main media platforms of mind.

Primary orality

Walter Ong, who coined the term, called primary orality "that of person totally unfamiliar with writing"[2] and "untouched by writing in any form"[3]. Therefore, a primary oral culture is a "culture with no knowledge whatsoever of writing or even of the possibility of writing."[4]

Havelock, however, had a slightly different definition of the original orality of humans. He stated that, "Orality, by definition, deals with societies which do not use any form of phonetic writing."[5] Indeed, for orality to be offset, the oral speech needs to be recorded "as is." This can be done only by the alphabet. Non-phonetic writing systems got along with orality. Logographic writings and, to a lesser extent, syllabaries not only coexisted but also collaborated with orality. They might have initiated the inward turn and visual bias, but they did so gradually, generally preserving

---

[1] Mir, Andrey. (2023, March 08). "Screen time is stolen time." *City-Journal.*

[2] Ong, Walter. (2002 [1982]). *Orality and Literacy*, p. 6.

[3] Ong, Walter. (2002 [1982]). *Orality and Literacy*, p. 8.

[4] Ong, Walter. (2002 [1982]). *Orality and Literacy*, p. 31.

[5] Havelock, Eric. (1986). *The Muse Learns to Write*, p. 65.

rather than dismissing magic and analog thinking because they themselves were analog systems.

Craft literacy

The term "craft literacy" was introduced by Eric Havelock to describe the state of literacy when writing skills were a trade practiced by certain craftsmen.[1] The first literate persons were the scribes and priests-administrators in the temple-palaces of the agrarian civilizations of Sumer, Egypt, Minoan and those following them. The craft literacy of the priests was also sacred literacy, as it was used for "divine accounting": recording gods' deeds, calendars, dynastic genealogies, etc.

Later and until the early modernity, craft literacy became a trade for hire, as with any other craft. People would hire scribes to write a letter or a document, "as they might hire a stone-mason to build a house, or a shipwright to build a boat," as Ong explained.[2]

Phantom literacy

I suggest the term "phantom literacy" to characterize the specific state of mind in Homeric Greece. It is widely acknowledged that the Greeks at the end of the Ancient Dark Age (1100–750 BCE) lived in the conditions of primary orality. However, the view of the Greek conditions as primary orality does not align with the notion of primary orality as a state of mind totally unfamiliar with writing. The Homeric Greeks actually had some vague memory of writing. This is evident not only in the mention of a tablet in the *Iliad* (the Bellerophon story) and the Catalogue of Ships (a typically bureaucratic document) but also in the possession of the highly elaborated Olympic Pantheon, the apparent legacy of the palace civilization of the Mycenaeans and, through them, the Minoans, Egyptians, and Sumerians. Palaces implied writing: any legacy of palace civilization was inevitably influenced by writing.

Therefore, the primary orality of Homeric Greeks was not so much "primary"; it was "contaminated" by writing – by phantom literacy. Nobody could write and read, these skills had been lost, but some of their effects impacted the orality of the Homeric Greeks, thus contributing to their unique role in history.

---

[1] Havelock, Eric. (1963). *Preface to Plato*, p. 47.

[2] Ong, Walter. (2002 [1982]). *Orality and Literacy*, p. 92.

The idea of phantom literacy corresponds with a notion of residual orality, or oral residue, used by Ong. The Homeric Greeks retained some residue of palace writing culture so minuscule and indistinct that it was phantom. Nevertheless, the alleged "primary orality" of the Homeric Greeks existed not before writing but after it.

Perhaps, the conditions of phantom literacy were also specific to the early Vedic culture in India (1500–500 BCE). While rooted in an extremely rich oral tradition, this culture also could have been affected by the Harappan civilization of the Indus valley (3300 to 1700 BCE). Being the first urban-agrarian civilization in India, the Harappans left a significant body of inscriptions, mostly economic records. Their writing was lost with the collapse of the civilization – a clear parallel with the Minoans-Mycenaeans. However, it is also possible that the vague memory and evidence of writing affected the subsequent long oral tradition that influenced the Vedic culture.

Semi-literacy

This term was introduced by Eric Havelock: "Greece was passing from non-literacy through craft literacy towards semi-literacy and then full literacy."[1] He writes:

> In short, in considering the growing use of letters in Athenian practice, we presuppose a stage, characteristic of the first two-thirds of the fifth century, which we may call semi-literacy, in which writing skills were gradually but rather painfully being spread through the population without any corresponding increase in fluent reading.[2]

Semi-literacy may be seen as a development of craft literacy beyond the trade of temple scribes or scribes for hire. Craft literacy is made of and by the scribes, while semi-literacy is made of and by the learned authors. Semi-literacy is, therefore, a stage when writing already ceased to be solely a trade, but the number of readers does not significantly exceed the number of writers. Readers are still mostly those who regularly write.

Semi-literacy is a dynamic state: both the number of literates and the gap between readers and writers expand. Semi-literacy assumes the emergence of a significant number of literates among ordinary folks and the full literacy of the elites. The state of semi-literacy lasted from classical

[1] Havelock, Eric. (1963). *Preface to Plato*, p. 47.

[2] Havelock, Eric. (1963). *Preface to Plato*, p. 40.

Greece, where even some slaves and mercenaries could write, to the introduction of general education, when semi-literacy grew into full literacy (the 18th –19th centuries in Europe).

General literacy

General, or full, literacy means that everybody above a certain age (7–9 years) can read and write. This is obviously an outcome of general education, which is normally introduced at a certain stage of media development in society. Wherever it came, it came after industrialization, urbanization, and the emergence of mass newspapers – the third element of this triad.

Describing the development of literacy in classical Athens, Havelock points out that the condition of Classic Antiquity in Greece "depended on the mastery not of the art of writing by a few, but of fluent reading by the many."[1] The citizens of Athens (citizens, not the entire population) achieved full literacy almost immediately, 2–3 centuries after the alphabet's introduction.

Both writers and readers are needed in all forms of literacy, but full literacy is defined by the number of readers, not writers. The priests of craft literacy made notes for themselves, for the circle of their kind. The authors of full literacy write for an extended circle of readers. As Havelock puts it:

> But writers in order to fulfil the full potentiality of their writing require readers, just as minstrels require an audience. ... In short, the "literacy" which a writer can exploit depends on whether the educational system creates readers for him.[2]

It is an important factor of literacy, worthy of emphasizing in the modern conditions: writers emerge after the introduction of writing by themselves like mushrooms after a rain, but readers can only be created by education. Literacy as a state of mind and a state of culture relies on an educational system that supplies readers.

Another factor underlying full literacy is the simplicity of the writing system. In many countries, this simplicity was brought by the alphabet. According to Havelock, "syllabaries were too clumsy and ambiguous to

---

[1] Havelock, Eric. (1963). *Preface to Plato,* p. ix.

[2] Havelock, Eric. (1963). *Preface to Plato,* p. 293.

allow fluency or encourage general literacy."[1] He also states that "One cannot build up a habit of popular literacy on a fund of inscriptions."[2] (To mirror this statement in modern conditions: one cannot build up a habit of popular literacy on a fund of TikTok.)

However, after industrialization and urbanization, literacy became a must for any society, alphabetic or not. This is why China developed full literacy despite having a complex writing system. The bureaucracy, typically seeking to preserve its privileges through a monopoly of knowledge and restricted access to information, for which a complex writing system is an essential element, in China became an instrument of the political will aimed at promoting general literacy, which made China so unique.

Residual orality

Walter Ong uses the notion of "residual orality" or the "residue of orality" to describe the legacy of oral practices that continue to permeate any literate society. Orality stays with us in the forms of storytelling, sayings, proverbs, nursery rhymes, formulaic jokes, repeated anecdotes, folklore, and small talks.

Orality regulates family relations and persists in communities that do not use writing for communication and tends to reproduce the tribal-type of collective – hobbyist groups, fraternities, prisons, the mafia, etc.

Residual orality is not about audial expression. It is a cultural, not vocal, phenomenon that keeps emerging in any temporary or lasting collective, even if the members are literate, when the relationships and statuses are maintained by oral communication.

Secondary orality (electronic orality)

The concept of secondary orality was introduced by Walter Ong in the 1970s to contrast this state with primary orality. Secondary orality was brought by "the electronic transformation of verbal expression."[3] This new orality was "sustained by telephone, radio, television, and other electronic devices that depend for their existence and functioning on writing and print."[4] The secondary orality of experienced TV and radio personalities

---

[1] Havelock, Eric. (1963). *Preface to Plato,* p. 135.

[2] Havelock, Eric. (1963). *Preface to Plato,* p. 40.

[3] Ong, Walter. (2002 [1982]). *Orality and Literacy*, p. 132.

[4] Ong, Walter. (2002 [1982]). *Orality and Literacy*, p. 11.

tends to replicate vocabulary proficiency, syntax, and structural completeness of written sentences.

According to Ong, "Secondary orality is both remarkably like and remarkably unlike primary orality."[1] The resemblance to primary orality is "in its participatory mystique, its fostering of a communal sense, its concentration on the present moment, and even its use of formulas."[2] Ong writes:

> Like primary orality, secondary orality has generated a strong group sense, for listening to spoken words forms hearers into a group, a true audience, just as reading written or printed texts turns individuals in on themselves. But secondary orality generates a sense for groups immeasurably larger than those of primary oral culture—McLuhan's "global village".[3]

Ong marks out that, before writing, oral individuals were group-minded because they simply did not have any alternative for presenting themselves. "In our age of secondary orality, we are group-minded self-consciously and programmatically. The individual feels that he or she, as an individual, must be socially sensitive," writes Ong.

Ong describes the reversal effect of secondary orality on the "inward turn." Secondary orality reversed the reversed – it turned the inward turn back outward. Ong writes:

> Unlike members of a primary oral culture, who are turned outward because they have had little occasion to turn inward, we are turned outward because we have turned inward. In a like vein, where primary orality promotes spontaneity because the analytic reflectiveness implemented by writing is unavailable, secondary orality promotes spontaneity because through analytic reflection we have decided that spontaneity is a good thing.[4]

The reversal, however, was only partial. The inward reversed into the outward, but reflectiveness reversed into spontaneity in a controllable way, as Ong notes. The professionals of electronic orality indeed simulate their spontaneity on TV, radio, or in other electronically mediated oral venues in

---

[1] Ong, Walter. (2002 [1982]). *Orality and Literacy*, p. 133.

[2] Ong, Walter. (2002 [1982]). *Orality and Literacy*, p. 133.

[3] Ong, Walter. (2002 [1982]). *Orality and Literacy*, p. 133.

[4] Ong, Walter. (2002 [1982]). *Orality and Literacy*, p. 134.

order to fit the requirements of the genre for the better electronic delivery of affect. As Ong sarcastically concludes, "We plan our happenings carefully to be sure that they are thoroughly spontaneous."[1] So, secondary orality is "essentially a more deliberate and self-conscious orality,"[2] according to him. Writing and print, on which this orality depends, have left their marks on it.

There are other differences between secondary and primary orality. Due to the electronic extension over time and space, secondary orality allows one to reach farther, longer, and to an incomparably larger audience. In a paradoxical way, this removes the audience from the equation. The audience is never present in electronic orality but always assumed. In Ong's words, "The audience is absent, invisible, inaudible."[3]

Since Ong's time, however, the presence of the audience has increasingly been faked – as in political debates or TV game shows – in order to simulate the collective engagement and empathic involvement innate in orality. But it is a simulation – the performer in secondary orality always addresses the distant, meaning absent, audience, which is always much bigger due to electrical outreach.

Emancipated authorship

It is commonly acknowledged that the internet gave the masses access to information while bypassing traditional gatekeepers, and this changed the world. More crucial, however, was the access to unsanctioned and unfiltered self-expression afforded to millions and now billions of people.

Before the internet, humankind had had about three hundred million authors, meaning people capable of delivering their messages beyond their physical reach.[4] The internet emancipated the authorship of ordinary people, irrespective of their capacity to produce meaningful content. We are living through an unprecedented explosion of authorship.

The emancipation of authorship was an affordance created by the internet, the blogosphere, and now social media. The burden of filtering content was transferred from editors of all kinds to the collective

---

[1] Ong, Walter. (2002 [1982]). *Orality and Literacy*, p. 133.

[2] Ong, Walter. (2002 [1982]). *Orality and Literacy*, p. 133.

[3] Ong, Walter. (2002 [1982]). *Orality and Literacy*, p. 134.

[4] I roughly calculated the number of authors in human history in: Miroshnichenko, Andrey. (2014). *Human as Media. The Emancipation of Authorship*.

mechanism that I call the Viral Editor.[1] If a traditional editor filters content before publishing, the Viral Editor filters content after posting – in the process of delivery through the efforts of people who like, repost, comment, etc.

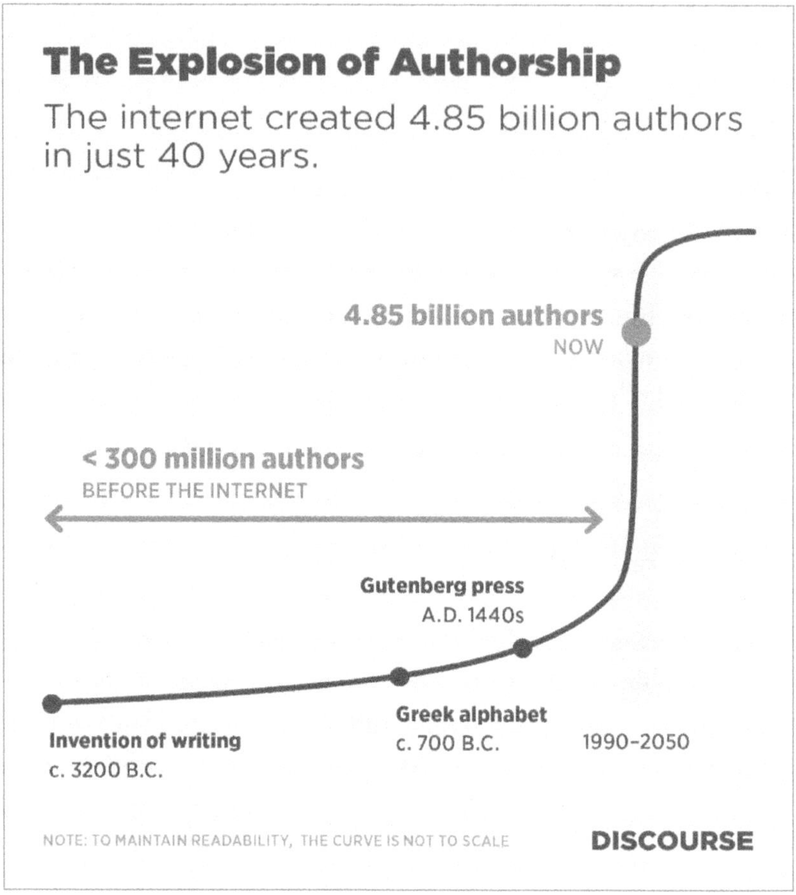

Figure 29. Source: Mir, Andrey. (2022, January 13). "Social media emancipated authors, but to what end?" *Discourse*.

This alone created a completely new type of society, which emergence was signified by the chain of upheavals in the 2010s, beginning with the progressive antiestablishment movements (the Arab Spring, Occupy Wall Street, and others) and continued by the conservative antiestablishment movements in the late 2010s.

[1] Mir Andrey. (2013, November 13). "The Viral Editor as a distributed being of the Internet. The Manifesto of the Viral Editor." *Human as Media Blog*.

In the blogosphere, emancipated authorship still adhered to the rules of literacy. Blog posts typically comprised a few hundred words, necessitating creative effort and logical organization on the part of the writer. Essentially, blog posts were the last texts of the Gutenberg era. However, with the advancement of social media, emancipated authorship opened the gates for orality to encroach into writing (typing).

The emancipation of authorship boosted the number of writers and almost equalled it with the number of readers. All 4.8 billion social media users are active prosumers: they consume and produce content. Of course, most of them produce content of vanishingly little significance and merely contribute their minimal activity, sometimes even non-verbal, to the work of the Viral Editor. Nevertheless, even when a user likes something or pauses while scrolling the newsfeed, it still contributes to filtering, as now algorithms consider even these personal "contributions" and shape the world picture out of it.

At the level of statistical pattern, the equation of the numbers of writers and readers is a move back to craft literacy. It is another, though quite peculiar, sign of the reversal from full literacy. A new balance of writers-readers has been forming not by the deficit of readers but by the explosion of authors. But readership is declining, too, at least in quality (the decline in the length of reading.) All these statistical factors have contributed to the emergence of digital orality.

Digital orality

The term "digital orality" was introduced by Robert Logan in 2007 as "tertiary orality" to augment Ong's concept of secondary orality. At the time, Logan saw tertiary or digital orality as "the orality of emails, blog posts, listservs, instant messages (IM) and SMS, which are mediated paradoxically by written text transmitted by the Internet."[1]

Social media have validated this insight by creating a new form of language that serves digital conversation: digital speech. Digital speech possesses the characteristics of both oral and written communication. Similar to oral speech, it enables the instantaneous exchange of replies; akin to writing, it leaves a record behind and can be transmitted across

[1] Robert Logan first introduced the term "tertiary or digital orality" in the 2007 article "The Emergence of Artistic Expression and Secondary Perception" and then developed it in: Logan, Robert. (2010). *Understanding New Media: Extending Marshall McLuhan*. New York: Peter Lang. (Second edition: 2016.)

time and space. These features imply that people's spontaneous and mostly emotive efforts to establish their social statuses in conversation are no longer evanescent. The interactions of millions of people are accumulated, disseminated, and displayed for everyone else to react to.

This new type of conversation has its benefits. It allows socialization at an unprecedented pace and scale. But the ease of exchanging digital speech has shifted the focus of communication from reflections to reflexes, from substance to attitude. Social media demand that everyone relate to others, to their ideas, to their troubles and achievements, to their very existence. The Viral Editor of the blogosphere has evolved into the Viral Inquisitor of social media.[1]

Digital orality tends to *de-literalize* written (typed) communication. The instant exchange of replies dissolves the syntax of written text. Written text was innately monological, and therefore its unfolding relied on its own structure. Oral communication is dialogical. Dialogue allows utterances to be replies – to structurally and thematically rely on the previous utterances of other interlocutors. The replies sustain and "unfold" each other, reducing the need for syntactic and thema-rhematic efforts.

This dialogical property of mutual structuring has been transferred to digital orality, thus "reducing" its syntax. However, the replies of digital orality are, at the same time, relatively autonomous and self-focused, as their authors do not share physical space and type their replies in isolation. Besides, such conversation often has more than two interlocutors, and the exchange becomes chaotic. The oral thema-rhematic reliance of replies on preceding utterances is often broken, and the written syntax does not apply either. All this makes digital conversation a weird hybrid in which interlocutors often simply do not "hear" each other. Their dialogue is not coherent; it is fragmented, causing emotional frustration, which is so typical for digital conversations.

Moreover, since digital speech is recorded, it is not just a mere exchange; it is an exchange displayed to others who can judge and contribute. Therefore, it is an exchange aimed to affect others. The agonistic mentality of orality flourishes in digital orality and amplifies frustration and polarization even more.

---

[1] Mir, Andrey. (2023, Spring). "The Viral Inquisitor. Social media have unleashed a culture of instant judging." *City Journal*. I augmented the concept of the Viral Editor with the notion of the Viral Inquisitor after Martin Gurri made such a suggestion at a seminar.

If electronic orality (Ong's secondary orality) still valued the virtues of written speech and inclined towards the vocabulary and syntactic norms of writing, digital orality tends to revert back to the primary orality of the preliterate mind. In their syntax and vocabulary, electronic orality is more literate, whereas digital orality is more oral.

Digital orality is heading even further back – to pre-speech communication, communication that was not mediated by words: digital orality tends to *de-speech* communication. Verbomotor features of primary orality, such as gestures, facial expressions, tone of voice, and others, have found their digital forms: likes, smileys, emoticons, and emojis. Interjections, the most primitive units of speech that directly express emotions, are paralleled in digital reality by abbreviations like LOL, OMG, and so on. Digital orality also employs reels, gifs, and memes, which are somewhat similar to formulaic oral expressions but can be totally deprived of verbal components.

By affording the utmost rapid gain of status, digital orality serves the highest need in Maslow's hierarchy – the need for self-actualization. Digital orality creates an affordance for physically and socially unlimited requests for affirmation. It even automatizes affirmative responses by letting people react by pressing "like" and other buttons for emotional reactions. In return, or as a price, digital orality trains the brain to experience tiny and repetitive hormonal gratification for minuscule efforts of participation or even for simple presence. This incites digital addiction and the inability to engage in long efforts or control the time of media consumption, thus adding to frustration and anxiety.[1]

Digital orality – the digitized lay orality of the masses – is a phenomenon that requires further exploration, as it has become the operating system of billions. But this is not yet the final observable operating system shaped by media evolution.

Digital sensorium

As soon as we humans transfer all our activities onto the digital, humankind itself is going to resettle there. Not metaphorically but literally, by uploading consciousness on the net to merge with AI.

---

1 Mir, Andrey. (2022, Winter). "The medium is the menace. Ubiquitous digital media offer potent rewards—but at the price of eroding our sensory and social capacities." *City Journal.*

The technical details of this transition may be left to specialists. The best human minds have been working on it and will surely find how to connect the green wire with the red one. Generative AI has already created the augmented workforce – a new division of labour between machines and humans that accelerates labour productivity, including productivity in the area of IT innovations. Due to this acceleration and according to the principle of the exponential growth of knowledge, the most crucial knowledge needed for the transition will be acquired by AI in the last seconds before the Singularity. It will not be reported in the news or reflected upon by the public simply due to the lack of time (actually, due to the end of time).

So, we can stop worrying about the technical feasibility of this transition – it will occur when the time comes. Instead, we should focus on its cultural patterns that are already observable. The logic of media evolution as well as the Jaspersian "goal of history" leads there and will eventually deliver us there. The technological imperative of media evolution will have caught up with the Jaspersian Axial imperative, as they are basically different readings of the same process.

I cannot tell yet whether it will be a single person who achieves the transhumanistic transition and merger with AI through a cognitive interface or it will be a networked AI that represents and appropriates the entire human legacy after awakening. However, some contours and tendencies of our final merger with our media and the environment induced by them can already be observed.

Neuroplasticity and synesthesia allow the brain to adjust the equilibrium of the senses to any (survivable) environment. If some sensory faculties are impaired, others can compensate for orientation in the environment to a certain extent. In the same vein, if some senses are more important or "better" triggered, they amplify their role in orientation. Neuroplasticity means that senses are versatile, and the equilibrium of the senses could be – must be – adjusted to the environment.

Given that the environment is available to us through our interfaces – our media – the equilibrium of senses in a highly mediated environment adjusts, actually, to media. Using our naturally given set of basic senses and the capacity of neuroplasticity, media define this or that state of the sensorium for an individual and, through individuals' cognitive adjustments, shape society.

Since the entirety of human activities is going to move into the digital environment, it is possible to assume that new senses can be induced that will be specific to the orientation in the digital space. We are now dealing with two types of digital technologies. Some reproduce physical reality (VR, AR, immersive media, videogames, etc.), while others reproduce social reality (social media, recommendation-based networked services such as Airbnb, Uber, and other first attempts at social scoring). The former digitally relocate the body, while the latter relocate the mind. Both will converge in a human-machine interface – in a medium that digitally connects the body but relocates the mind.

At the same time, body-centered digital technologies are a clumsy concession to the past, confirming McLuhan's concept of the rearview mirror: "We march backwards into the future."[1] The concept of being without a body still sounds unusual, but it is already clear that there is no need for a body where we are resettling. Humankind already spends a tremendous number of man-hours without the body.

Mimicking the body as a familiar vessel of impersonation, a physical avatar, is necessary in the digital world only at a transitional stage. But when digital technologies fully unfold their own nature, they will stop pretending to enhance the nature of previous media and will complete the long transition of humans from pure biology to pure "sociality." Since cognition needs to be digitally oriented, the old sensory-cognitive links will be torn, the body will be "amputated", and new, digital senses will emerge.

McLuhan mentioned that electronic media give humans an angelic and god-like ability of omnipresence in the form of a "disembodied spirit" or "the angelic discarnate man of the electric age who is always in the presence of all the other men in the world."[2] This mutual presence – a new, digital form of both environmental immersion and collective involvement – is cemented and fueled by constant requests for affirmation. These requests for affirmation are generally requests for time. We want the time of each other, while platforms want our time; both intents are served and amplified by platforms' algorithms.

[1] McLuhan, Marshall, and Fiore, Quentin. (1967). *The Medium Is the Massage: An Inventory of Effects*, p. 74-75.

[2] McLuhan, Marshall. (1971, November 14). Interview with Father Patrick Peyton on TV show *Family Theatre*.

This new environment is space-ignorant and time-biased, representing the tectonic shift of the sensorium towards time. The colonization of digital space is essentially the utilization of time. Humans evolve, along with their media, from the conquest of space to the request for time. The shift from space bias to time bias commenced in the beginning of history with the emergence of writing: if prehistoric beings and animals sought safety in space, historic beings started seeking salvation in time. Digital media are making time the ultimate value in the colonization of living space, which is digital space now.

Examples of changing the sensorium are all around, with spatial orientation debilitating and temporal senses sharpening. Biohackers augment the senses with devices to enhance digital-environmental involvement. After several hours of playing a 3D-shooter with flying mode, a user easily dismisses the sense of gravity, as it is not required in the digital space.[1] The distance to an object in physical space is replaced with the distance to others in the digital space – and so we develop the sense of digital-social proximity. Is there somebody around my digital presence, or are my digital surroundings empty? For a digital being, the sense of an empty or full stomach will be replaced by the sense of an empty or full bank account or rather a social score account. The sense of fullness-emptiness mimics physical properties but, in the digital, is social and time-biased.

Before long, humans will either donate their agency to AI through a cognitive interface or AI will acquire self-awareness through self-awakening (as humans once did), and the Singularity will occur. Given that AI is now being trained to provide us with various replicas of us and

[1] Miroshnichenko, Andrey. (2016). "Extrapolating on McLuhan...," p. 179.

gradually learning to replace us, the ultimate user of the ultimate medium may become AI itself; in fact, AI has to become the self-user.

Since media are extensions of humans, media evolution exploded humankind into the world. The final stage of this explosion, the Singularity, will also be the last reversal – it will implode the world into humankind, when humankind, its new medium, and its environment become one.

Conclusion: What was the Axial Age anyway?

For Karl Jaspers, the historical significance of the Axial Age lies in: 1) the awakening of humans as humankind, and 2) the revelation of intellectual, moral, and spiritual universals that continue to define our lives and lead humankind to unity. "The Axial Period founded universal history and, spiritually, drew all men into itself," writes Jaspers.[1]

The processes that constituted the Axial Age can also be described in terms of media evolution. All the fundamental breakthroughs of the Axial Age are media effects of the transition from orality to literacy.

Jaspers suggests that history commenced with agrarian civilizations and their central administrations and writings. They created the conditions that, with an additional or external catalyst (Jaspers considers the equestrian invasion as a catalyst), culminated in the Axial Age. The transition from orality to literacy has the same pattern: it began with the bureaucratic writing of agrarian civilizations and culminated in a state of mind capable of producing and comprehending Buddha, Confucius, and Plato.

There are some discrepancies between the pace and location of literacy's development in the ancient world and the ways Jaspers defines the location and timing of his Axial Age, but those discrepancies we are going to tolerate. Much more important is the large pattern of the intellectual and spiritual – truly Axial – shift from orality to literacy. Its culmination in Greece, on the one hand, represents the most condensed transition from orality to literacy in its utmost abstract form, the alphabet, and, on the other hand, perfectly aligns with the timing and essence of the Axial Age, as described by Jaspers.

However, China and likely India reached their Axial revelations without the alphabet. Their Axial breakthroughs were not as evidently tied to the development of writing as in the Hebrew or Greek cultures; or these connections have not yet been detected, given that literacy studies are

[1] Jaspers, Karl. (2021 [1949]). *The Origin and Goal of History*, p. 27.

mostly focused on the alphabet. However, the cognitive and social patterns of the transition from orality to literacy, in its Axial culmination, were evidently present in China and India, too, as they experienced the transformative effect of writing during the same period that was identified by Jaspers as the Axial Age.

Most importantly, the media approach to the Axial Age – the interpretation of the Axial events as the transition from orality to literacy – allows us to extend the Axial events to other locations and cultures, thus overcoming Jaspersian geo-historical "exclusivity." The Axial contributions of the Chinese, Indians, Hebrews, and Greeks were undoubtedly crucial. However, other cultures that underwent a similar – cumulated and culminating – shift from orality to literacy contributed to the formation and dissemination of the Axial message, too.

After all, this hypothesis is not about framing the past; it is about identifying patterns that led from the past to the present and are now shaping the future.

Just as linguistics can reconstruct unknown changes in languages and predict forthcoming changes based on the understanding of certain patterns and regularities, media ecology can trace the patterns of media effects both in the past and future. If the Axial Age characterized the global shift from orality to literacy, a new Digital Axis can be defined as the reversal of literacy and retrieval of orality. The Digital Axis replays the Jaspersian Axial Age in reverse. McLuhan recognized this reversal, observing the effects of electronic media:

> The transformation to visual space from acoustic space occurred in ancient Greece. What took several thousand years to complete has taken us several decades to reverse: the West now bathes in the emotions of postliteracy.[1]

It is not a symmetric reversal: instead of primary orality, digital orality emerges as we settle into the digital environment. We are living through this Digital Axis and are approximately in the middle of it. All the disruptions we identify as the consequences of political or cultural turmoil are, in fact, media effects. The near future will be defined by the struggle between literacy and orality. The struggle has been revived and intensified

---

[1] McLuhan, Marshall, and McLuhan, Eric. (1988). *Laws of Media*, p. 4.

by digital media, which have taken the side of orality. Understanding the features of orality and literacy will help us to deal with the collateral damage we are going to suffer as a result of this media struggle.

Orality vs. Literacy

Environmental immersion	Environmental detachment
Acoustic space: spherical and simultaneous perception	Visual space: linear and sequential perception
Equilibrium of senses: audile-tactile integrity	Isolated vision as a cognitive faculty
Holism and synthesis	Fragmentation and analysis
Syntagmatic connections	Paradigmatic selections
Relation-oriented	Object-oriented
Verbomotor, extralinguistic speech-behaviour	Speech as the actualization of language
Rhythm	Melody
Dialogue	Monologue
Collective immersion	Individualism
Personal exposure	Private space
Bragging	Modesty
Authenticity	Hypocrisy
Agonistic mentality	Tolerance
Mocking	Irony
Customs	Codified law
Situational/analog thinking	Abstract thinking
Presentism	Historism
Answering	Questioning
Wisdom	Thinking
Magic	Rationality
Mythology	Religion, ideology
Negotiated truth	Absolute truth

Figure 30.

Bibliography

Ahmed, Sara. (2004). "Affective Economies." *Social Text*, 79 (Volume 22, Number 2), Summer 2004, pp. 117-139.

Anthony, David W. (2007). *The Horse, the Wheel, and Language: How Bronze-Age Riders from the Eurasian Steppes Shaped the Modern World.* Princeton University Press.

Anton, Corey. (2023). "Reading good books, further defended." *Exploration in Media Ecology*, Volume 22 Number 1, 2023, pp. 119-125.

Arendt, Hannah. (1970). *Men in Dark Times*. NY: Harcourt, Brace & World, Inc.

Beccaria, Cesare. (1995). *On Crimes and Punishments, and Other Writings*. Cambridge: Cambridge University Press.

Cali, Dennis D. (2017). *Mapping Media Ecology: Introduction to the Field*, Peter Lang Inc.

Carey, James W. (1969). "Harold Adams Innis and Marshall McLuhan." In: *McLuhan Pro & Con*. Raymond Rosenthal, editor. Baltimore: Pelican Books.

Chrystall, Andrew. (2015). "After the Global Village." *The Canadian Journal of Media Studies*, 2011, 9 (1).

Culkin, John. (1967). "Each culture develops its own sense ratio to meet the demands of its environment." In *McLuhan: Hot and cool.* Gerald Stearn, editor. Pp. 49–57. NY: New American Library.

Eisenstein, Elizabeth L. (1979). *The Printing Press as an Agent of Change. Communications and cultural transformations in early-modern Europe*. Cambridge University Press.

Gelb, Ignace. (1963 [1952]). *A study of writing*. The University of Chicago Press

Gibson, James J. (1986 [1979]). *The Ecological Approach to Visual Perception*. Hillsdale, NJ, London: Lawrence Erlbaum Associates.

Goody, Jack, and Watt, Ian. (1963). "The Consequences of Literacy." *Comparative Studies in Society and History*, Vol. 5, No. 3 (April 1963), pp. 304-345.

Granata, Paolo. (2021). *Introduction to Media Ecology*. First Italian edition: *Ecologia dei Media*, FrancoAngeli, 2015.

Gurri, Martin. (2018). *The Revolt of The Public and the Crisis of Authority in the New Millennium*. The 2nd edition. Stripe Press.

Hall, Stuart. (1980). "Encoding/decoding." In: *Media and Cultural Studies: Key Works*. (2012 [1980]). The 2nd Edition. Meenakshi Gigi Durham and Douglas M. Kellner, editors. John Wiley & Sons, Ltd. Pp. 137-144.

Havelock, Eric A. (1963). *Preface to Plato*. Harvard University Press.

Havelock, Eric A. (1978). "The Alphabetization of Homer." In: *Communication Arts In The Ancient World*. Eric A. Havelock and Jackson P. Hershbell, editors. NY: Hastings House – Publishers.

Havelock, Eric A. (1979). "The Ancient Art of Oral Poetry." *Philosophy and Rhetoric*, Vol. 12, No. 3, Summer 1979, pp. 187-202.

Havelock, Eric A. (1986). *The Muse Learns to Write. Reflections on Orality and Literacy from Antiquity to the Present*. New Haven and London: Yale University Press.

Illich, Ivan, and Sanders, Barry. (1978). *ABC: The Alphabetization of the Popular Mind*. New York: Vintage Books.

Innis, Harold. (1950). *Empire and Communications*. Oxford: Clarendon Press.

Innis, Harold. (2008 [1951]). *Bias of Communication*. Toronto: University of Toronto Press.

Jarvis, Jeff. (2023). *The Gutenberg Parenthesis: The Age of Print and Its Lessons for the Age of the Internet*. Bloomsbury Publishing.

Jaspers, Karl. (2021 [1949]). *The Origin and Goal of History*. Translated by Michael Bullock. NY: Routledge Classics

Jenkins, Henry. (2006). *Convergence culture. Where old and new media collide*. New York University Press.

Korzybski, Alfred. (2022 [1921]). *Manhood of Humanity*. Good Press.

Kukarkin, Alexandr (1985 [1978]). *Bourgeois Mass Culture: Theories. Ideas. Types. Examples*. Moscow: Politizdat. // Кукаркин, Александр Викторович. (1985 [1978]). *Буржуазная массовая культура: Теории. Идеи. Разновидности. Образцы*. Москва: Политиздат.

Kurzweil, Ray. (2005). *The Singularity Is Near: When Humans Transcend Biology*. Penguin Publishing Group.

Lakoff, George, and Johnson, Mark. (1980). *Metaphors We Live By*. The University of Chicago Press.

Lenin, Vladimir. (1909). *Materialism and Empirio-Criticism*.

Lenin, Vladimir. (1920, December 22). "Report on the work of the Council of People's Commissars." in V. I. Lenin, *Collected Works* (Moscow: Progress Publishers, 1964), Vol. XXXI, pp. 513-518.

Levinson, Paul. (1999). *Digital McLuhan: A guide to the information millennium*. NY: Routledge.

Levinson, Paul. (2017). *Human Replay: A Theory of the Evolution of Media*. Connected Education, Inc.

Lippmann, Walter. (1998 [1922]). *Public Opinion*. NJ: Transaction Publishers.

Logan, Robert K. (2004 [1986]). *The Alphabet Effect: A Media Ecology Understanding of the Making of Western Civilization*. The 2nd edition. NJ: Hampton Press.

Logan, Robert K. (2010). *Understanding New Media: Extending Marshall McLuhan*. NY: Peter Lang. (The 2nd edition: 2016.)

Logan, Robert K. (2013). *McLuhan Misunderstood: Setting the Record Straight*. The Key Publishing House Inc.

Logan, Robert K. (2017). "The Alphabet Effect re-visited, McLuhan reversals and complexity theory." *Philosophies*, 2(1), 2.

Logan, Robert K. (2020) "'The alphabet, of course': How I met Marshall McLuhan." *The New Explorations Blog*.

Luria, Alexander. (1976). *Cognitive Development: Its Cultural and Social Foundations*. Harvard University Press.

Luria, Alexander. (1979). *Language and Cognition*. //Лурия, Александр. (1979). *Язык и Сознание*. Издательство МГУ.

Marx, Karl. (1847). *The Poverty of Philosophy*.

Marx, Karl. (1859). *A Contribution to the Critique of Political Economy*.

McLuhan, Eric, and Zingrone, Frank, editors. (2005). *Essential McLuhan*. Routledge.

McLuhan, Marshall, and Fiore, Quentin. (1967). *The Medium Is the Massage: An Inventory of Effects*. NY: Random House.

McLuhan, Marshall, and Fiore, Quentin. (1968). *War & Peace in the*

Global Village. Gingko Press.

McLuhan, Marshall, and Logan, Robert K. (1977). "Alphabet, mother of invention". *Et Cetera*, December 1977, pp. 373-383.

McLuhan, Marshall, and McLuhan, Eric. (1988). *Laws of Media: The New Science*. University of Toronto Press

McLuhan, Marshall. (1959). "Myth and Mass Media." *Daedalus*, Spring, 1959, Vol. 88, No. 2, pp. 339–348.

McLuhan, Marshall. (1962). "8 mm in context: the modern media and externalized senses", Dinner Address to Conference on 8 mm Sound Film and Education, Teachers College, Columbia University, 8 November 1961. *The Proceedings of the Conference*, edited by Louis Forsdale.

McLuhan, Marshall. (1962). *The Gutenberg Galaxy. The Making of Typographic Man*. University of Toronto Press.

McLuhan, Marshall. (1969). *The Interior Landscape: The Literary Criticism of Marshall McLuhan 1943–1962*. Eugene McNamara, editor. NY: McGraw-Hill

McLuhan, Marshall. (1969, March). "The Playboy Interview." *Playboy Magazine*, pp. 53-74, 158.

McLuhan, Marshall. (1970 [1969]). *Counterblast*. London: Rapp & Whiting Limited.

McLuhan, Marshall. (1970). *Culture is Our Business*. NY: McGraw-Hill.

McLuhan, Marshall. (1971 [1970]). *From Cliché to Archetype*. Pocketbook edition, NY: Pocket Books.

McLuhan, Marshall. (1971). "Interview with Marshall McLuhan by Father Patrick Peyton." *Television Show "Family Theatre"*, November 14, 1971.

McLuhan, Marshall. (1974). "At the moment of Sputnik the planet became a global theater in which there are no spectators but only actors." *Journal of Communication*, March 1974, Volume 24, Issue 1, pp. 48-58.

McLuhan, Marshall. (1987). *Letters of Marshall McLuhan*. Matie Molinaro, Corinne McLuhan, William Toye, editors. Toronto: Oxford University Press.

McLuhan, Marshall. (1994 [1964]). *Understanding Media. The extensions of man*. MIT Press.

McLuhan, Marshall. (1997 [1967]). "The Hot and Cool Interview" to Gerald Stearn. In: *Media Research: Technology, Art, Communication:*

Essays / Marshall McLuhan. Michel A. Moos, editor. Amsterdam: G+B Arts, 1997. Pp. 45–78.

McLuhan, Marshall. (2003). "Living at the Speed of Light" (1974). In: *Understanding me: Lectures and interviews*. Stephanie McLuhan and David Staines, editors. Toronto: McClelland & Stewart. Pp. 225–243.

Meyrowitz, Joshua. (2010). "Media evolution and cultural change". In: *Handbook of cultural sociology*. John R. Hall, Laura Grindstaff, and Ming-Cheng M. Lo, editors. NY: Routledge. Pp. 52-63.

Mir, Andrey. (2020). *Postjournalism and the death of newspapers. The media after Trump: manufacturing anger and polarization.*

Mir, Andrey. (2022). "Media-ecological engineering of the Soviets." *Explorations in Media Ecology*, Volume 21, Issue 2-3, October 2022, pp. 143–155.

Miroshnichenko, Andrey. (2014). *Human as media. The emancipation of authorship.*

Miroshnichenko, Andrey. (2016). "Extrapolating on McLuhan: how media environments of the given, the represented, and the induced shape and reshape our sensorium." *Philosophies*, 2016, 1(3), pp. 170-189.

Miroshnichenko, Andrey. (2021). "Media and responsibility for their effects: instrumental vs. environmental views". *Laws*, 10, no. 2, p. 48.

Narasimhan, Vagheesh M., et al. (2019). "The formation of human populations in South and Central Asia." *Science*, September 6, 2019, Vol 365, Issue 6457.

Nazaretyan, Akop (2017). "Mega-history and the twenty-first century Singularity puzzle." *Social Evolution & History*, Volume 16, Number 1, March 2017.

Nazaretyan, Akop. (2005 [2001]). *Psychology of Spontaneous Mass Behavior*. Crowd, *rumors, political and advertising campaigns*. Moscow: Academia. // Назаретян, Акоп. (2005 [2001]). Психология стихийного массового поведения. Толпа, слухи, политические и рекламные капании. 2-е издание. Москва: Академия.

Norman, Donald A. (1988). *The Psychology of Everyday Things*. NY: Basic Books.

Norman, Donald A. (1999). "Affordances, Conventions, and Design." *Interactions*, 6 (3), pp. 38-41.

Ong, Walter J. (1967). *The Presence of the Word: Some Prolegomena for Cultural and Religious History*. Yale University Press.

Ong, Walter J. (1975). "The writer's audience is always a fiction." *PMLA*, Vol. 90, No. 1 (January 1975), pp. 9-21.

Ong, Walter J. (1977). *Interfaces of the Word: Studies in the Evolution of Consciousness and Culture*. Cornell University Press.

Ong, Walter J. (1980). "Literacy and orality in our times." *Journal of Communication*, 03/1980, Volume 30, Issue 1, pp. 197-204

Ong, Walter J. (1986). "Writing is a technology that restructures thought." In: *The Written Word. Literacy in Transition*. Gerd Bauman, editor. Oxford: Clarendon Press. Pp. 23-50.

Ong, Walter J. (2002 [1982]). *Orality and Literacy. The Technologizing of the Word*. London and New York: Routledge.

Ortega y Gasset, Jose. (1930). *The Revolt of the Masses*.

Parikka, Jussi. (2012). *What is media archaeology?* Cambridge: Polity.

Pariser, Eli. (2011). *The Filter Bubble: How the New Personalized Web Is Changing What We Read and How We Think*. Penguin Publishing Group.

Park, Robert E. (1923). "The natural history of the newspaper." *The American Journal of Sociology*. Volume XXIX, November 1923, Number 3, pp. 273-289.

Peters, John Durham. (2017). "'You mean my whole fallacy is wrong': On Technological Determinism." *Representations*, Fall 2017, No. 140, Special Issue: *Fallacies* (Fall 2017), pp. 10-26.

Peterson, Valerie V. (2017). "Plato's Allegory of the Cave: literacy and 'the good'." *Review of Communication*, 17:4, pp. 273-287.

Petrov, Mikhail. (1995 [1966]). *Pirates of the Aegean and Individuality*. // Петров М. К. (1966). «Пираты Эгейского моря и личность» в: *Искусство и наука. Пираты Эгейского моря и личность*. М: РОССПЭН, 1995.

Plekhanov, Georgi. (1895). *The Development of the Monist View of History*.

Postman, Neil. (1970). "The reformed English curriculum." In: *High School 1980: The Shape of the Future in American Secondary Education*. Alvin C. Eurich. editor. NY: Pittman. Pp. 160-168.

Postman, Neil. (1992). *Technopoly: The Surrender of Culture to*

Technology. NY: Knopf Doubleday Publishing Group.

Postman, Neil. (2000 [1999]). *Building a Bridge to the 18th Century. How the Past Can Improve Our Future*. NY: Vintage Book

Postman, Neil. (2006 [1985]). *Amusing Ourselves to Death: Public Discourse in the Age of Show Business*. Penguin Publishing Group.

Pruska-Oldenhof, Izabella, and Logan, Robert K. (2017). "The spiral structure of Marshall McLuhan's thinking." *Philosophies*, 2 (4). p. 9.

Rushkoff, Douglas. (2019). *Team Human*. W. W. Norton & Company.

Schmandt-Besserat, Denise. (1997). *How Writing Came About*. Austin, Texas: University of Texas Press.

Schmandt-Besserat, Denise. (2013). "Tokens and writing: the cognitive development." In: *Symbols at 'Ain Ghazal. Excavation Reports 3*. Denise Schmandt-Besserat, editor. Bilbiotheca neolithica Asiae meridionalis et occidentalis & Monograph of the Faculty of Archaeology and Anthropology, Yarmouk University, Ex Oriente, Berlin.

Schmandt-Besserat, Denise. (2014). "The Evolution of Writing" In: *International Encyclopedia of Social and Behavioral Sciences*. James Wright, editor. Elsevier.

Scolari, Carlos A. (2013). "Media evolution: Emergence, dominance, survival, and extinction in the media ecology". *International Journal of Communication*, 7 (2013), pp. 1418–1441

Scolari, Carlos A. (2022). "Evolution of the media: map of a discipline under construction. A review". *Profesional de la información*, v. 31, n. 2, e310217.

Strate, Lance. (2008). "Studying media as media: McLuhan and the media ecology approach." *MediaTropes, eJournal* Vol. I (2008), pp. 127–142.

Strate, Lance. (2017). *Media Ecology: An Approach to Understanding the Human Condition* ("Understanding Media Ecology" Series, Book 1). NY: Peter Lang.

Trautmann, Martin, et al. (2023). "First bioanthropological evidence for Yamnaya horsemanship." *Science Advances*, Vol 9, Issue 9.

Turkle, Sherry. (2012). *Alone together*. Basic Books.

Vygotsky, Lev. (1934). *Thinking and Speech*. // Выготский, Лев. (1934). *Мышление и речь*. Москва, Ленинград: Государственное социально-экономическое издательство.

Williams, Raymond. (1975 [1974]). *Television: Technology and Cultural Form*. NY: Schocken.

Williams, Raymond. (2005 [1964]). “A structure of insights.” In: *Marshall McLuhan. Critical evaluations in cultural theory*. Cary Cenosko, editor. Routledge. Volume 1. Pp. 3-6.

***

Other books by Andrey Mir (available on Amazon)

Human as Media. The Emancipation of Authorship. (2014).

"With its concept of the 'viral editor' (now transformed, in our harsher decade, into 'viral inquisitor'), 'Human as Media' remains mandatory reading for anyone wishing to understand the disruptions of the digital."

– Martin Gurri, author of "The Revolt of the Public."

Postjournalism and the Death of Newspapers. The Media after Trump: Manufacturing Anger and Polarization. (2020).

"As Mir argues, this change in the economic structure of the news media has quietly transformed journalism from a theoretically neutral means of “manufacturing consent” into a political cause that people are rallied into supporting, usually by inciting them to some form of outrage."

– Murtaza Hussain, “The Intercept”.

Made in United States
Cleveland, OH
05 November 2026

47673392R00181